The Editor

PAUL E. SIGMUND is Professor of Politics at Princeton University. He is the author of many books, among them *Nicholas of Cusa and Medieval Political Thought*, *Natural Law in Political Thought*, *The United States and Democracy in Chile*, and *Liberation Theology at the Crossroads*. He is the translator and editor of the Norton Critical Edition of *St. Thomas Aquinas on Politics and Ethics*.

NORTON CRITICAL EDITIONS IN THE
HISTORY OF IDEAS

AQUINAS • St. Thomas Aquinas on Politics and Ethics
translated and edited by Paul. E Sigmund

DARWIN • Darwin
selected and edited by Philip Appleman (Third Edition)

ERASMUS • The Praise of Folly and Other Writings
translated and edited by Robert M. Adams

HERODOTUS • The Histories
translated by Walter Blanco, edited by Walter Blanco and Jennifer Tolbert Roberts

HOBBES • Leviathan
edited by Richard E. Flathman and David Johnston

LOCKE • The Selected Political Writings of John Locke
edited by Paul E. Sigmund

MACHIAVELLI • The Prince
translated and edited by Robert M. Adams (Second Edition)

MALTHUS • An Essay on the Principle of Population
edited by Philip Appleman (Second Edition)

MARX • The Communist Manifesto
edited by Frederic L. Bender

MILL • Mill
edited by Alan Ryan

MORE • Utopia
translated and edited by Robert M. Adams (Second Edition)

NEWMAN • Apologia pro Vita Sua
edited by David J. DeLaura (Second Edition)

NEWTON • Newton
selected and edited by I. Bernard Cohen and Richard S. Westfall

ROUSSEAU • Rousseau's Political Writings
translated by Julia Conaway Bondanella, edited by Alan Ritter

ST. PAUL • The Writings of St. Paul
edited by Wayne A. Meeks

THOREAU • Walden and Resistance to Civil Government
edited by William Rossi (Second Edition)

THUCYDIDES • The Peloponnesian War
translated by Walter Blanco, edited by Walter Blanco and Jennifer Tolbert Roberts

WATSON • The Double Helix: A Personal Account of the Discovery of
the Structure of DNA
edited by Gunther S. Stent

WOLLSTONECRAFT • A Vindication of the Rights of Woman
edited by Carol H. Poston (Second Edition)

For a complete list of Norton Critical Editions, visit
www.wwnorton.com/college/English/nce_home.htm

A NORTON CRITICAL EDITION

THE SELECTED POLITICAL WRITINGS OF JOHN LOCKE

TEXTS
BACKGROUND SELECTIONS
SOURCES
INTERPRETATIONS

Edited by

PAUL E. SIGMUND

PRINCETON UNIVERSITY

W. W. NORTON & COMPANY

New York • London

W. W. Norton & Company has been independent since its founding in 1923, when William Warder Norton and Mary D. Herter Norton first published lectures delivered at the People's Institute, the adult education division of New York City's Cooper Union. The Nortons soon expanded their program beyond the Institute, publishing books by celebrated academics from America and abroad. By mid-century, the two major pillars of Norton's publishing program—trade books and college texts—were firmly established. In the 1950s, the Norton family transferred control of the company to its employees, and today—with a staff of four hundred and a comparable number of trade, college, and professional titles published each year—W. W. Norton & Company stands as the largest and oldest publishing house owned wholly by its employees.

Manufacturing by the Maple-Vail Book Group.
Composition by PennSet, Inc.
Book design by Antonina Krass.
Production manager: Benjamin Reynolds.

Library of Congress Cataloging-in-Publication Data
Locke, John, 1632–1704.
 [Selections. 2004]
 The selected political writings of John Locke: authoritative texts,
contexts, sources, interpretations / edited by Paul E. Sigmund.
  p. cm.— (A Norton critical edition)
 Includes bibliographical references.

ISBN 0–393–96451–5 (pbk.)

 1. Political science—Early works to 1800.   I. Sigmund, Paul E.
II. Title.   III. Series.

JC153.L793 2004
320.51'2—dc22

                                                2004058330

W. W. Norton & Company, Inc., 500 Fifth Avenue, New York, N.Y. 10110
www.wwnorton.com

W. W. Norton & Company Ltd., Castle House,
75/76 Wells Street, London W1T 3QT

      1   2   3   4   5   6   7   8   9   0

Contents

Acknowledgments

For their help in preparing this edition, I wish to thank Alex Tuckness, John Holzworth, Ilya Shapiro, Joseph Prud'homme, and Muhammad Rumi Oodally. I have also benefited from the advice of Mark Goldie, John Dunn, John and Philip Milton, Victor Nuovo, John Rogers, Jerome Schneewind, John Yolton, and George Kateb. I am especially indebted to my graduate and undergraduate students at Harvard and Princeton who have deepened my understanding and increased my appreciation of a great political philosopher.

Introduction

John Locke is one of the most important theorists in the history of political thought. His writings inspired and helped justify the American Revolution; the basic assumptions of his thought underlie many of the fundamental political ideas of American liberal constitutional democracy; and his arguments in favor of human rights, religious and economic freedom, political equality, government by consent, and the right of revolution are widely accepted—in theory, if not always in practice—around the world.

This has not always been the case, nor is it true everywhere today. At the time Locke wrote, his principles were accepted in theory by a few and in practice by none. Divine right monarchy was the norm, and democracy based on majority rule, nonexistent. Religious uniformity was enforced with coercive sanctions, and arguments for toleration were rare. Mercantilist state policies and government monopolies limited trade and commerce. Society functioned on the basis of "great chain of being" hierarchies and deference to one's betters. Groups had rights, based in tradition, law, or religion; but the idea of individual rights was only beginning to develop. Armed conflict and rebellions were frequent, but revolution—in the sense of a fundamental restructuring of society—was advocated only by extreme groups such as millenarian religious sects.

Today Locke's principles are more generally accepted, but they are not uncontested. On the right, the claims of order, tradition, national security, and the need for social or religious cohesion or economic growth are often cited to justify departures from the Lockean ideals of freedom and democracy. On the left, the demands of social justice are seen by some as requiring the sacrifice of political and/or economic freedoms. Postmodern, structuralist, and antifoundationalist critics deny the possibility of a philosophical defense of freedom and democracy on the basis of universal values. Locke's ideas are viewed as historically and culturally conditioned or as an ideological justification for Western domination.

Even within the Lockean framework there is a continuing argument over the meaning and application of his ideas. The values for which he argued are not always consistent with one another. What is the relation of political equality and economic freedom, of government by consent and the right of revolution, of majority rule and minority rights, of freedom of religion and freedom from religion? Those debates have often focused on the acceptance, rejection, or interpretation of the thought of John Locke, the founding father of modern liberalism.

The continuing, even increasing, importance of Locke and the controversies about his ideas are the reasons for this collection of his political and related writings, the sources on which he drew, and the conflicting interpretations of his thought. The debate about Locke has intensified during the fifty years in which I have taught his political thought in ways that reflect both the continuing philosophical disagreements about his ideas and our considerably enlarged knowledge of his thinking because of newly published sources that were not available to earlier commentators. In the same period, the ideals of equality, political democracy, and human rights that he espoused have led to the lessening of racial, religious, gender, and national barriers in ways that would have been inconceivable to him.

This collection is published with two goals in mind. The first is to enable students to benefit from the vast scholarly output on Locke to achieve a more accurate understanding of the meaning of what he wrote, in terms both of his original intention and of later interpretations of his work. The second goal is to stimulate thought and debate about the implications of the principles he defended for the contemporary world.

The literature on Locke, most of it published during the last fifty years, is enormous. The Princeton University library lists more than 950 books written by or about him, 171 of them since 1990. It is a rich literature, which examines not only his political thinking but also his ideas on religion, economics, ethics, epistemology, and more recently race and gender. Relevant excerpts from and commentaries on his writings on these related subjects are included in this book. Locke wrote in a time of transition, from tradition to modernity, from religious conformity to religious pluralism, from feudal aristocracy to bourgeois democracy, from group domination to individualism, and from social norms based on ascription to those based on achievement. He believed that his ideas were founded on the political inheritance of the classical and Christian tradition in which he was educated, but he combined and applied them in a different way—with significant implications for the modern world.

John Locke was born in 1632 in Wrington, near Bristol in the west of England. He was ten years old when the struggle between the Stuart monarchy and the Puritan-dominated parliament led to the outbreak of the English Civil War (1642–48). He was sixteen when Charles I was executed and a commonwealth was established under Oliver Cromwell. Locke's father was an attorney, small landowner, and friend of Alexander Popham, a wealthy magistrate. The elder Locke fought along with Popham in the early years of the Civil War; and in 1647, after the Puritan-dominated Long Parliament took control of the most important of the English public (i.e., private) schools, Westminster School, in London, Popham nominated John Locke, then fifteen, to a place at the school. There he received an intensive education in the classics and was exposed to a different set of religious and political views from his earlier Calvinism. The headmaster of Westminster was strongly pro-royalist and kept the boys in school for public prayers in January 1649, as Charles I was beheaded outside the nearby palace of Whitehall (Cranston 1957:20).

In 1652 Locke was chosen as one of six Westminster recipients of scholarships to Christ Church at Oxford. There he studied classics, logic, rhetoric, and geometry, receiving his B.A. in 1656 and his M.A. in 1658. An Oxford education was still in many ways medieval. The lectures and disputations were in Latin, students arose at 5 A.M., and daily chapel was compulsory. Aristotle and Cicero dominated the curriculum (Bill 1988:195 ff.), and Locke found the required scholastic disputations unsatisfying, spending much of his undergraduate years reading romances (Bourne 1876:I:54), although attendance at lectures was required. While Locke was still an undergraduate, an Oxford and Westminster friend introduced him to the study of medicine, which became a lifelong interest.

After receiving his master's degree, Locke received a studentship (fellowship) at Christ College and was appointed a tutor in classics, lecturer in Greek, and in 1663 censor in moral philosophy. During this period he seems to have given lectures and conducted disputations on the subject of natural law, and his essays on the subject— unpublished until the 1950s (Locke 1954)—reflect both his acquaintance with the classical tradition and the beginnings of the empiricism that was to characterize his later *Essay Concerning Human Understanding*. His notebooks on his readings (which still survive) demonstrate that he read more books on medicine and science than on any other subject. He became acquainted with Robert Boyle, who is sometimes regarded as the father of modern chemistry, and he carried out chemical experiments on his own. In this same period he wrote English and Latin tracts in support of the "absolute and arbitrary power" of the magistrate to regulate "things indifferent" in the area of religion, a view that sharply differs from those expressed in his later political writings (Locke

1967). Maurice Cranston (1957:62), his biographer, also detects the influence of Hobbes in Locke's description of the unpleasantness of life without government and the need to surrender "primitive liberty" to the magistrate.

In 1665 he left Oxford to participate in an English diplomatic mission to the elector of Brandenburg in Cleves (Kleve), in northwest Germany, where he was impressed with the mutual good relations and toleration for one another's religion among Calvinists, Lutherans, and Catholics. When he returned to Oxford in 1666 he decided against becoming a clergyman, the career of most holders of studentships (fellowships), and he continued to pursue his medical studies. His petition to be granted a doctorate in medicine without attending lectures was denied, although he later received the degree of bachelor of medicine.

In connection with his medical interests, he met and favorably impressed Anthony Ashley Cooper, Lord Ashley, later the first Earl of Shaftesbury and founder of the Whig Party. In the following year Ashley invited him to join his London household, and Locke became his part-time physician, secretary, and speech writer. In 1667 under Ashley's influence, and in sharp contrast to his earlier writings, he wrote an essay on religious toleration, described by one writer as "a founding document of liberalism" (Locke 1993:38), that anticipated much of the argument of his later *Letter Concerning Toleration* (1685). It argued for toleration because the magistrate's duty was "the preservation and peace of men in society," and "hath nothing to do with the good of men's souls and concernments in another life." Like the later *Letter Concerning Toleration,* it denied toleration to Catholics on political grounds, because their loyalty was to Rome. In 1668 Locke also wrote a draft of a treatise opposing the legal regulation of the interest rate, a later version of which he published in 1692. In the following year, as secretary to the lord proprietors of the colony of Carolina, he supervised the preparation of a draft constitution for the colony. He continued to be interested in Carolina, and the colony provided many of the American examples that he cited in the *Second Treatise* (Armitage 2004). The constitution differed, however, from his later political writings in its support for a hereditary aristocracy as well as African—but not Indian—slavery.

In 1671 Locke and a group of friends began to discuss "the issue of human understanding" of "the principles of morality and religion," and Locke wrote two preliminary drafts of what was to become the *Essay Concerning Human Understanding,* published at the end of 1689. When Ashley became Lord Chancellor and Earl of Shaftesbury in 1672, Locke was appointed secretary for presentations of income-producing positions ("livings") in the Anglican church. The following year he became secretary of the Council on Trade and Plantations, which brought him into further contact with the English colonies, where he had already invested some of the income from his inheritance from his father, including investments in the slave trade (see James Farr, p. 374 herein). In 1675 he returned to Oxford and received a medical studentship and the degree of bachelor of medicine.

He did not remain in Oxford but left for France in November 1675, where he spent the next three and a half years. His journals indicate that he met leading Huguenots, the outlawing of whose religion in 1685 led him to write the *Letter Concerning Toleration* (Lough 1953). During his time in France, his mentor, the earl of Shaftesbury, was imprisoned for a time in the Tower of London for, among other reasons, advocating annual elections of Parliament. By the time Locke returned, Shaftesbury had become the chief prosecutor against the supposed participants in a "Popish Plot" to kill King Charles II and to place his Catholic brother, the duke of York and future James II, on the throne. In February 1680 Locke purchased a copy of the recently published political writings of Sir Robert Filmer. In November 1680 the House of Commons passed the Exclusion Bill, blocking the Catholic duke of York from succeeding to the throne. The House of Lords rejected the bill, and the king, hoping to find a less hostile atmosphere outside of London, called a meeting of parliament in Oxford in March 1681. When it became clear that Commons would insist on the exclusion of James, the king dissolved the Parliament with no indication that he would convene it again. In July Shaftesbury was arrested and charged with high treason, but a pro-Whig jury acquitted him in November. In the summer of 1682 he and other Whigs began to plan a rebellion to prevent James, the duke of York, from succeeding to the throne. In November when the revolt failed to materialize, Shaftesbury fled to Holland, where he died in January 1683.

This was the period, we now know, when the *Two Treatises of Government*, published in 1689, were written. References, subsequently corrected, in the 1689 edition to "King James" rather than James I, indicating composition before the accession to the throne of James II in 1685; the fact that Locke mentions in the preface the loss of "the papers that should have filled up the middle, and were more than all the rest"; and other evidence from a collection of Locke's papers that Oxford acquired in the mid-twentieth century (Locke 1988:45 ff.) have forced a revision of the earlier view that the *Two Treatises* were written by Locke after the Glorious Revolution of 1688, that replaced James II with William, prince of Orange, and Mary, James's Protestant daughter.

There is consensus among Locke scholars that the first draft of the *First Treatise* was written in 1680, after Locke bought the *Patriarcha* and other writings of Filmer that had been published in connection with the contemporary debate about the relation of the king to Parliament. There is less agreement about the exact date of composition of the *Second Treatise;* but most of the conflicting accounts, using among other evidence his recorded purchases of books used in the *Second Treatise,* place it in 1681 and 1682, and all agree that some updating took place at the time of publication (Milton 1995:380). The earlier date of composition makes Locke's theory more radical, in terms of the context in which it is written, than if it had appeared as an ex post facto defense of the 1688 Glorious Revolution (see the section "Locke as Revolutionary?" p. 353 herein).

The *First Treatise* is a refutation of Filmer's patriarchalism—that is, his defense of the divine right of kings as based on the descent of their right to rule from God's original grant of authority to Adam. It contains important theoretical discussions, but it is much less known and read than the *Second Treatise* because much of it is devoted to the exegesis of the meaning of the passages from the first book of Genesis cited by Filmer. It was relatively easy for Locke to refute Filmer's interpretations of his principal biblical texts. He answers Filmer's argument that the first book of Genesis subjects "every living thing that moveth upon the earth" (v. 28) to Adam by demonstrating that the passage refers to animals rather than to men. The text and context of the passage cited by Filmer in which Eve is made subject to Adam after the Fall (Genesis 2:16) clearly indicate, Locke argues, that this was God's punishment of Eve after the Fall for her disobedience and not a general grant of political authority over all mankind. Filmer's third reference to the divine commandment to "Honor thy father" is answered by quoting the rest of the sentence: "and thy mother" (Exodus 20:12; Deuteronomy 5:16).

Yet the *First Treatise* goes well beyond biblical hermeneutics. Locke argues against divine right by an appeal to natural freedom and consent, describing absolute government as a form of slavery. To deny that the king has absolute property rights, he makes an important argument on the duty of charity, which gives a starving man title to enough of the surplus goods of others to enable him to preserve himself (*First Treatise* 42). Our duty to God to preserve his creation becomes the basis of a defense of property rights and of the inheritance rights of children. In this connection, Locke also criticizes primogeniture as a violation of the rights of the other offspring to inherit enough for their "comfortable preservation" (ibid. 87) The section on Eve's subjection to Adam includes a broader discussion of conjugal authority that both admits there is a "foundation in nature" for male dominance and that "condition or contract" may alter that relationship (ibid. 47). There are also discussions that are similar to passages in the *Essays on the Law of Nature* and the *Essay concerning Human Understanding,* on the way reason and the senses can give us knowledge of the natural law as well as on the degradation that history demonstrates is the result of departure from reason, "our only star and compass" (ibid. 58, 86).

The *Second Treatise* does not argue from biblical texts as the *First Treatise* does, although biblical examples are cited, principally from the Old Testament. Except for a few references, it also does not argue from the history or constitution of England, which were central to most of the contemporary debate. It is a philosophical treatise that attempts to develop a systematic theory of legitimacy, obligation, limited government, political equality, and natural rights, including the right to revolution. It begins with individuals in the state of nature, a condition of life without government or organized political life. In that state, Locke argues all "men" (*Second Treatise* 95, but see 96 "individuals") are free, equal, and rational. Their reason tells them that, as God's "workmanship," he wishes them to preserve themselves and "the rest of mankind" (*Second Treatise* 6). Because of the duty of self-preservation humans cannot surrender their lives and liberty, either by enslavement (except through criminal actions that forfeit their humanity) or by subjecting themselves to an absolute monarch. They have voluntarily contracted with each other to form families and to bring up children to whom they owe nurture and education. They provide for their preservation through a system of private property, which is created by mixing their labor with the goods of the earth that God has intended for that purpose. Only then does humankind perceive the need to establish law and government because, although the state of nature is initially a state of peace being made up of men who can know their moral obligations to each other, it is marred by conflicts. These conflicts are the result of disagreements over the application of the natural law, which arise because of the lack of a written law and a common judge on its implementation and because of the actions of "degenerate men" who violate the natural law. Because of these "inconveniences," individuals in the state of nature surrender their right to enforce the natural law and agree to act by majority rule to establish governments that will defend their rights to life, liberty, and property through a system of common laws and judges. The laws should be adopted by legislatures that represent those who choose them and enforced by an executive that is, at least in part; separate from the legislature and that has wide discretion in the conduct of foreign affairs ("the federative power"). If the government violates the purposes for which it was established, the people (i.e., the majority), or even—since "every man is judge for himself" (ibid. 241)—"any single man" (ibid., 168), can "appeal to heaven" through resort to revolution. This will happen, however, only after "a long train" of abuses (ibid., 225), and the individual will be successful only if he persuades the majority that the violation of his rights will threaten theirs (ibid., 208).

What is new about Locke's theory is its emphasis on the grant and possible withdrawal of *individual* consent, even though it is diluted by admitting the possibility of tacit consent and by allowing a majority, to which he has consented, or its representatives to act for the individual. Beginning with individual consent, Locke makes a systematic argument for the rule of law, responsible and limited government, and individual rights in a way that makes the *Second Treatise* the classic expression of liberal constitutionalism, which has as its foundational principles individual judgment and political equality.

The association of the *Second Treatise* with advocacy of armed revolution meant that Locke was in some personal danger at a time when those who opposed the king were being imprisoned or executed. What he had written became all the more dangerous in 1683 when the Rye House Plot to murder the king and his brother was discovered and Algernon Sidney (later revered as a martyr by the American revolutionaries), who had also written a work opposing Filmer and supporting resistance to the king, was arrested, tried, and executed. Although he was not directly implicated in the plotting, Locke knew many of the plotters and government spies were reporting on him. In early September 1683, after arranging for the safekeeping of his papers, Locke went into exile in Holland.

During his exile years (1683–89) he continued to work on the *Essay Concerning Human Understanding* and wrote his famous *Letter Concerning Toleration*. He was spied on by agents of the English monarchy; at one point he adopted a pseudonym; and he wrote a friend about a work he had entrusted to his keeping, *De Morbo Gallico* (On the French Disease), which has been interpreted by some scholars as a reference to his treatises against monarchical absolutism. *The Letter Concerning Toleration* was written in Latin for a European audience, in response to King Louis XIV's October 1685 revocation of the Edict of Nantes, which had granted religious toleration to the Huguenots. Locke's letter argued that religious belief should not be subject to government coercion because faith, especially the Christian faith, is a matter of free rather than coerced acceptance ("A church, I take to be, a voluntary society of men, joining themselves together . . . for the public worshipping of God") and because it exceeds the competence of the magistrate and the purposes of government, which are "life, liberty, health, and indolency [freedom from pain] of body." It denied religious toleration to advocates of "moral rules which . . . manifestly undermine the foundations of society" as well as to Catholics and atheists, the former because of their subjection to a foreign power, and the latter because they could not be trusted to keep their oaths since they lacked fear of God's punishment after death. The *Letter* was influenced by theological discussions with dissident Calvinists in Holland (Remonstrants) with whom Locke developed close friendships in exile. It was published in England without attribution in 1689 and immediately translated into English by William Popple, an adherent of Socinianism, which because it denied the Trinity was beginning to be called Unitarianism. Popple took some liberties with Locke's Latin text and introduced the work by calling for "absolute [religious] liberty," which was not what Locke advocated in the *Letter*.

The *Letter Concerning Toleration* and the *Two Treatises of Government* were published anonymously after Locke's return from Holland with Princess—soon to be Queen—Mary in February 1689. Locke may not have wished to acknowledge authorship of the *Letter Concerning Toleration* (indeed, in his will he denied involvement in the preparation of the translation, although in fact he did see it before it was published [Ashcraft 1986:498–99]). The 1689 Toleration Act extended religious freedom only to Protestant Trinitarian Christians, so that his reticence may have been related to the fact that Popple was the author of *A Rationalist Catechism* and was associated with Unitarianism (Robbins 1967). The subversive character of the *Two Treatises* at the time they were originally written may also explain Locke's reluctance to be named as their author. He seems to have made a few changes in the *Second Treatise* (to chapters 1, 9, and 15 and substantial revisions and updating of chapter 19) before its publication, and he also added a preface that argued that the title of "our great restorer, our present King William" was based on "the consent of the people" (Locke 1988).

At the end of the year, with a date of 1690, he also published, under his own name, the *Essay Concerning Human Understanding*, a work that made his reputation as a philosopher. The *Essay*'s denial of innate ideas, the criticisms that it made of traditional philosophic categories, and its association of morality with pleasure and pain led to attacks on it by religious conservatives. In response Locke added to later editions the explanation that the divine law, discussed in the first edition, should be understood to include both revelation and the law of reason. He also referred in his correspondence (Cranston 1957:134) to his insistence in the *Essay* (1.3.13) that, while he denied innate ideas, he continued to believe in the law of nature as "something that we being ignorant of may attain the knowledge of, by the use and due application of our natural faculties." Both the *Essay* and the earlier *Essays on the Law of Nature* make it clear that he always believed that human beings are capable of arriving at certainty about basic moral truths on the basis of sense-experience and rational analysis.

Immediately after his return Locke was offered the post of British ambassador to the Elector of Brandenburg. He declined for reasons of health and because as "the soberest man" in England he could not match the "warm drinking" of the Germans (Cranston 1957:312). In 1690, to avoid the polluted air of London that aggravated his asthma, he moved to an estate belonging to the husband of a longtime friend, Lady Masham. In December 1691, with a date of 1692, he published his essay opposing the legal regulation of the interest rate. In 1692 he was urged by a friend to write a treatise on morality that would show, as he had claimed several times in the *Essay Concerning Human Understanding*, that morality was as demonstrable as mathematics. He responded that he was considering it, but "while I thought I saw that morality might be demonstratively made out, yet whether I am able to make it out is another question. . . . I shall not decline the first leisure I get to employ some thoughts that way" (Locke, 1976–1989: IV:524, no. 1538). Some critics (Bluhm et al. 1980; Coby 1987) have argued that Locke said this because he realized there was a contradiction between the supposed hedonism of the *Essay* and his earlier commitment to natural law. However, already in the *Essays on the Law of Nature* Locke described how we leave the natural law from sense-experience (p. 175) while insisting that "utility is not the basis of the law or the ground of obligation, but the cousequence of obedience to it (p. 184). When the same friend pressed him once more on the subject in 1696, Locke replied that he was gathering some materials for such a work but that, in any case, "the Gospel contains such a perfect body of Ethicks, that reason may be excused from that enquiry" (Locke 1976–1989: VI:595, no. 2059). In the *Second Vindication* and in *The Conduct of Understanding*, both written in the late 1690s, Locke continued to assert the possibility, indeed the duty, of studying the natural law, along with the truths of revelation (Marshall 1994:441–47).

In 1693 Locke published *Some Thoughts on Education,* based on letters that he (a bachelor) had written from Holland to an English friend concerning the education of children. Locke recommended developing self-control, restraint of desire ("the true foundation of ability and happiness" is "to resist the importunity of pleasure and pain for the sake of what reason tells him is fit to be done"; no. 45), and regularity of habits (including bowel movements) in the child. He advised the study of French and Latin, but not Greek, emphasizing conversational and practical approaches rather than rote memorization and rules of grammar. Rather than logic and rhetoric, he recommended geography, astronomy, anatomy, history, and the principles of English law as well as ethics, based principally on the Bible but also on works by Cicero, Pufendorf, and Grotius (see sources herein for selections by Pufendorf, p. 251, and Grotius, p. 233; on the influence of Cicero on Locke, see Sigmund 1997).

In 1695, Locke published, again anonymously, *The Reasonableness of Christianity*. It argued for a minimal Christian creed of repentance for sin and belief in Jesus as the Messiah, whose resurrection gives the promise of immortality. *The Reasonableness* maintained that the Bible provided the best source of morality ("the law of nature knowable by reason") for those who did not have the time or ability to study and learn its precepts. Some have taken Locke's doubts about human capacities to know natural law to be in tension with his belief in majority rule. However, his pessimism about whether one can know the natural law "all entire as law" was also expressed in the early *Essays on the Law of Nature* (see herein Essays III, p. 175, and V, p. 177) and thus does not contradict the possibility that basic principles of equality, liberty, and property can be sufficiently known to establish society and government.

The Reasonableness provoked further attacks, because of both its denial of the inherited guilt of original sin as a consequence of Adam's Fall and its lack of a clear statement that belief in the Trinity is a central doctrine of Christianity. In lengthy replies Locke denied that he was a "Socinian" (i.e, Unitarian), declaring that his works contained "not one word of Socinianism." His comments on the opening passages of the Gospel of John as well as other similar passages demonstrate a certain evasiveness about the divinity of Christ, although he believed that Jesus had a special relationship to God from all eternity (Locke 1987: I:38, 58). At the very least he did not think that the Trinity was part of the minimal doctrinal commitment required for all Christians (Marshall 1996, 2000). Nevertheless he was a devout Christian who believed that the Bible was God's revelation and that Jesus was the Messiah, although the purpose of His coming was not to atone for the sin of Adam but to show us the way to eternal life.

In 1696 Locke was appointed to the newly established Board of Trade and Plantations. This was a well-paid position, but it meant that he had to spend considerable time in London. The board dealt with such topics as piracy; the development of the colonies, including those in America; and issues of unemployment and poverty. In 1697 Locke submitted to the board a proposal for reform of the government of Virginia that reflected the thinking of the *Second Treatise* in its proposals for judicial independence and the powers of the legislature (Ashcraft 1969b) He also submitted a proposal (never adopted) on government policy toward the poor. It called for Draconian regulation of begging and poor relief, making sure that the able-bodied poor were compelled to work and requiring that the children of the poor be placed in work-schools at the age of three, fed bread provided by the parish along with (in winter) "water-gruel," and "taught spinning or knitting" (see Locke 1993: 446–61). Locke's biographer, Maurice Cranston, calls the proposal "an appalling document" but balances its ferocity with a quotation from Lady Masham attesting to the fact that "he was naturally compassionate and exceedingly charitable to those in want" while adding that "his charity was directed to encourage working, labourious, industrious people, and not to relieve idle beggars to whom he never gave anything. . . . People who had been industrious, but through age and infirmity passed labour, he was very bountiful to" (Cranston 1957:426). He also notes that Locke's will provided for a simple burial for himself, with the money saved going to the poor of the parish (ibid.: 480).

Also in 1697 Locke began work on *The Conduct of Understanding*, published posthumously, in which he recommended the study of theology as "one science . . . incomparably above the rest . . . that noble study which is every man's duty and everyone that can be called a rational creature is capable of" (Locke 1996: no. 23). In his last years Locke composed a paraphrase of, and notes on, the Epistles of St. Paul in which he seems to have interpreted Paul's assertion that "the wages of sin is death" as indicating that those who died unrepentant would be annihilated at the Last Judgment rather than subjected to eternal torment (Locke 1987: I:53) Shortly before his death he received the Sacrament from the local minister, after which he said, "I am in perfect charity with all men and in sincere communion with the whole church of Christ, by whatever names Christ's followers call themselves" (Bourne 1876: II:557). He died on October 28, 1704, while the Psalms were being read to him by Lady Masham. In his will he bequeathed copies of his books to the Bodleian Library at Oxford (admitting in a codicil, that he had written *The Two Treatises* and *The Letter Concerning Toleration*). He left his manuscripts and half his library of five thousand books to his young cousin Peter King; this later became the Lovelace Collection, acquired by Oxford in the mid-twentieth century. His Latin epitaph speaks of his contentment with his "modest lot" (the translation by his nineteenth-century biographer of *mediocritate*) and his devotion to truth. He cites the Gospel as an example of morality and his grave as proof of the certainty of death (ibid. II: 560–61).

The *Essay Concerning Human Understanding* was widely known, both in England and on the Continent, and the *Letter Concerning*

Toleration was the subject of debate in England, although the Toleration Act of 1689 did not go as far as it recommended since the act retained religious tests for public office and extended toleration only to Protestants who believed in the Trinity. The *Two Treatises* were less well known; but the *Second Treatise* was cited, and arguments drawn from it were used in defending the Glorious Revolution of 1688 and the settlement that followed. More often, however, the defenders of the 1689 settlement cited the "ancient constitution" of England and the historical role of Parliament in consenting to legislation and taxation (absent from Locke) rather than the more philosophical arguments used by Locke. As the six-volume collection of early writings on Locke, edited by Mark Goldie (1999), demonstrates, Locke was sometimes interpreted in a more radical direction ("If all men are born free, how is it that all women are born slaves?"; Mary Astell, "Some Reflections Upon Marriage," 1706, cited in Goldie 1999:II:116), and his theories of natural freedom and equality were attacked by Tory conservatives such as Bolingbroke. His argument for the social contract and his defense of property were widely known, both through reprints of his works and through the many editions of the English translation of Samuel Pufendorf's *On the Law of Nature and Nations,* with commentaries by Jean Barbeyrac, who used Locke to correct what he felt were inadequacies of Pufendorf (Hutchinson 1991:chap. 2). Leading Enlightenment figures referred to Locke's work, principally the *Essay Concerning Human Understanding*; and Voltaire's library included, besides English and French editions of the *Essay,* two editions of the *Reasonableness of Christianity* in French translation as well as a translation of the *Two Treatises of Government* (ibid.: 206).

Locke's theories were sometimes used by antiroyalist republican theorists who also drew on the history of the Roman republic to argue for constitutional government and revolution. An example of such literature that was particularly influential in the American colonies was Thomas Gordon and John Trenchard, *Cato's Letters* (1720–23), which combined arguments based on the Roman republic, for civic virtue and against the corruption of the English monarchy with appeals to natural rights and original freedom in the state of nature (Goldie 1999:II:229 ff.; full text in Trenchard and Gordon 1995). Twentieth-century scholars have attempted to oppose the republican tradition to that of Locke; but as discussed below, there is now persuasive documentary evidence that the colonists were *both* republicans and Lockeans (see Dworetz p. 388 herein).

Although some scholars (Dunn 1969b; Wills 1976) have tried to downplay their influence, Locke's political ideas were widely diffused in the American colonies, both directly and through the use of his theories in Sunday sermons (Lutz 1988; Huyler 1994). In

1764 James Otis argued against British taxation of the colonies by appealing to the principle of "no taxation without representation," which was drawn from Locke, and he condemned British participation in the slave trade, arguing that "all men, white or black" were "by the law of nature freeborn" (Goldie 1999:III) James Madison read Locke's *Two Treatises* at Princeton and heard President John Witherspoon repeat his arguments in his lectures on moral philosophy (Thompson 1976; Muñoz 2002).

Thomas Jefferson drew heavily on Locke in composing the Declaration of Independence, basing the colonists' right of revolution on the violation of their natural rights. There were minor differences. Jefferson claimed that those rights were self-evident, while Locke made an argument for them from reason and our common creation by God. The Jeffersonian triad of life, liberty, and the pursuit of happiness differed from that of Locke, but Locke's formulation—life, liberty, and property—reappeared in the Fifth and Fourteenth Amendments to the U.S. Constitution. In 1779 Jefferson also paraphrased and made verbatim use of Locke's *Letter Concerning Toleration* in his argument for a bill establishing religious freedom in Virginia. (His notes and comments on the *Letter* have been published in volume I of the Jefferson Papers. For a direct comparison of Locke's *Letter* and Jefferson's notes and argument for the bill, see Sandler 1960.)

Lockean contractualism fared less well on the European continent. In 1762, Rousseau's *Du Contrat Social* attacked the theories of Grotius and Hobbes rather than Locke but developed a version of the social contract involving the surrender of all rights to "the general will," which was radically different from that of Locke. The French Declaration of the Rights of Man and the Citizen (1789) was an uneasy combination of Rousseau and Locke. Article 1 states that "men are born free and equal" and article 14 requires that taxation be based on consent, either personally or through representatives; but article 3 derives all authority from the nation and article 6 declares that "law is the expression of the general will." Conservatives rejected the Revolution, whereas radicals felt it had not gone far enough and began to move in the direction of what later became socialism. The maintenance of monarchical absolutism and established religion meant that liberalism on the European continent met with greater resistance and took more radical forms, only occasionally invoking Locke, who was cited more often in favor of property rights than of revolution (Goldie 1999:VI).

Meanwhile in England, Locke's theories of the social contract and natural rights were the object of powerful assaults by David Hume, Jeremy Bentham, and Edmund Burke. In *The Treatise of Human Nature* (1739) Hume attacked natural law theories as based on a confusion between statements of fact and statements of value, arguing that it is logically impossible to derive an "ought" from an "is." Hume also criticized attempts to base government on contracts, since the obligation to keep contracts, like that of promise keeping in general, is based on the needs of society rather than any preexisting moral standard. He repeated these arguments in his essay "Of the Original Contract" (1748) in a way that made it clear that they were directed at Locke's argument for the popular origin of political authority.

Where Locke had referred to pleasure and pain as indicators of good and evil, Jeremy Bentham (1748–1832) argued that utility based on a hedonistic calculus was, and should be, the basis of morality and legislation. He described the appeal to natural rights in the French *Declaration of Rights* as "nonsense" and to natural and imprescriptible rights as "nonsense on stilts." The theory of the social contract, he said was "a fiction, or in other words, a falsehood" ("The Declaration of Rights," in *Anarchical Fallacies*).

English conservatives have looked to Edmund Burke as one of their major political theorists, despite the fact that he belonged to a faction of the Whig party, the ancestor of the Liberals. Burke accepted the 1688 revolution, not because it defended abstract rights but because he thought that it was carried out in defense of the ancient constitution and the principles of the Magna Carta, In Burke's *Reflections on the Revolution in France* (1791) he criticized "arithmetical" (i.e., political) equality and declared that "government is not made in virtue of natural rights. . . . Government is a contrivance of human wisdom to provide for human needs." "Society is indeed a contract," he wrote, but it is not a "partnership in things subservient to a gross animal interest. Each contract of each particular state is but a clause in the great primeval contract of eternal society." Tradition, religion, and social institutions were necessary for stability, and reforms should be carried out gradually rather than in pursuit of abstract theories.

In the nineteenth century Benthan's utilitarianism was further developed by John Stuart Mill and others. Despite the fact that a modernized edition of Locke's works, published in 1823, was available, utilitarianism rather than natural rights and the social contract became the predominant philosophy of English liberalism.

Locke's theories lived on, however, alive and well in the United States. In the 1830s Alexis de Tocqueville, in his book *Democracy in America,* identified equality as the distinguishing feature of American culture. School children absorbed Locke's teachings as they memorized the opening sentences of the Declaration of Independence. His theory of property was also cited, inaccurately, as a defense of unlimited property rights. However much discrimination against women, immigrants, and nonwhites departed in practice from his theory of political equality, Locke's belief in equal rights was widely shared; and only in the South (e.g., the writings of John C. Calhoun) were attempts made to develop a political theory that challenged it.

In the twentieth century Carl L. Becker's (1922) *The Declaration of Independence* (1922) identified Locke's political theory as the principal inspiration both of the Declaration and of American political thought in general. On the left an occasional scholar might be critical of Locke's dominance, usually by identifying him as the classic defender of property (e.g., Parrington 1930). On the right Willmoore Kendall's (1941) *John Locke and the Doctrine of Majority Rule* warned, incorrectly, that Locke's theory required the surrender of individual rights to an omnipotent majority. The widely used political theory text by George Sabine (1961:540); *A History of Political Theory*, praised Locke as the most important writer in "propagating the ideals of liberal but not violent reform," since he was unaware of the circumstances of the composition of the *Two Treatises*. The classic argument for the Lockean consensus was Lewis Hartz (1955), *The Liberal Tradition in America*, which attributed the near-universality of "Lockeian" liberalism and the weakness of socialism in America to the absence of European feudal inequalities.

The more recent intense scholarly interest in and debate about Locke's political theory—what one participant has called "the Locke industry"—which has produced hundreds of books relating to his work since 1950, can be linked to the rise of intellectual movements on the right and the left that saw liberalism as exemplified by Locke as the enemy. In the 1950s and early 1960s, two scholars in particular, Leo Strauss on the right and C. B. Macpherson on the left, wrote critical, and flawed, interpretations of his political theory that were both widely accepted and vigorously attacked. In 1953 Strauss, a charismatic German émigré professor at the University of Chicago, published *Natural Right and History*, an interpretation of the Western political thought that categorized its principal representatives as advocates either of "natural right," a belief, typified by Plato's political thought, in transcendent universal values accessible to only the few, or of "natural rights," represented by Hobbes, based on the individual pursuit of security and pleasure. Challenging the conventional view that Locke wrote against Hobbes and drawing on his own earlier book *Persecution and the Art of Writing* (1952), Strauss argued that Locke, like many past writers who feared persecution, had concealed his true beliefs and, like his predecessor Hobbes, was committed to a hedonistic individualism ("the joyless quest for joy") that would ultimately lead to the nihilism of Nietzsche and modern totalitarianism. His methodology was attacked by John Yolton (see p. 281 herein) and many others both for sloppy scholarship and for the subjective nature of interpretations based on secret writing. However, articles and books using Strauss's methodology and categories of analysis continued to be written by his students and by students of his students.

Strauss's interpretation of Locke as a closet Hobbesian requires us to ignore the documented, and clearly acknowledged, influence on his thinking of the German natural law theorist Samuel von Pufendorf (p. 251 herein), who used the state of nature (as Hobbes did) as an analytical tool but recognized (as Locke did) both the competitive and the cooperative elements in human nature, criticizing, (as Locke also did [*Second Treatise* 19]), Hobbes's view of the state of nature. The Straussians also dismissed Locke's frequent quotations from the Anglican natural law theorist Richard Hooker as an attempt to give a cover of legitimacy to his secret Hobbesian views. It is true, as the example of Algernon Sidney demonstrates, that the justification of revolution in the early 1680s could put one's life in danger, but there is overwhelming evidence in Locke's writings, journals, notebooks, and correspondence that there are many differences from Hobbes, the most significant of which is Locke's belief in a divinely ordained law of nature that commands the preservation of oneself and *all mankind* (*Second Treatise* 6, 8.135), which is in contrast with Hobbes's emphasis on individual self-preservation and the war of all against all.

Strauss's case was challenged in 1954, when Locke's early *Essays on the Law of Nature* were translated and published. While the essays argued that we derive our understanding of natural law from reflection on sense experience, a view Locke shares with St. Thomas Aquinas (whom he quotes in Essay I, probably borrowing the quotation from Hooker), they described a theologically based natural law theory that rejected Hobbesian self-interest as the basis of moral obligation (see Essay VIII, p. 179 herein). In 1958 Strauss wrote a review of the *Essays* that argued, unpersuasively, that Locke's rejection in Essay V of Hooker's argument for natural law from universal consensus demonstrated an important discontinuity between them. Strauss also pointed out supposed contradictions in Locke's *Essays* that "cannot have escaped his notice," including statements on natural law that "he had come to see were wholly wrong" (1958:403).

In the 1970s and 1980s the literature associated with the bicentennial of the American revolution produced a major division among Strauss's followers concerning the evaluation of Locke's influence on American political thought. The "West Coast Straussians," represented principally by Harry Jaffa and Martin Diamond at the Clarement Colleges, maintained that the principles of equal- ity and natural rights contained in the Declaration of Indepen- dence and derived from the "exoteric" Locke (i.e., as understood by the Founding Fathers rather than as decoded by Strauss) were based on the classical and Christian tradition. The "East Coast Straussians," including Walter Berns and Thomas Pangle, on the other hand, argued that Locke's influence on America has been to foster self-interest and materialism and to undermine the moral and religious principles on which the country was founded. (See, for example, Jaffa [1984] and the 1985 exchange between Pangle and Jaffa concerning the relation of the Declaration of Indepen- dence to "Hobbesian-Lockian hedonism" [*The National Review*, November 29, 1985].)

In 1988 Pangle's *The Spirit of Modern Republicanism* mounted a full-scale attack on Locke and his influence on the Founders. Pan- gle (1988:276) declared that his purpose was to "unearth the full— and for many, and perhaps all, of the Founders—the still partly- hidden implications" of Locke's theories. He argued that in the *Es- say Concerning Human Understanding* Locke subtly teaches that "there exists no moral law" (p. 176), and that moral rules are sim- ply ways to maximize happiness, defined as the pursuit of pleasure and the avoidance of pain (p. 186). Pangle accused Locke of "a fundamental lack of piety and reverence" (p. 214) but maintained that America's "biblical faith" and "classical republican theory" were still resistant to the "secularizing" effects of Locke's "teaching on the prosaic rights of the individual" (p. 277).

Pangle was the most influential member of a neo-Straussian school that emerged in the 1980s and 1990s that focused on Locke's covert opposition to Christianity rather than his relation to Hobbes (see Bluhm et al. 1980; Coby 1987; Forde 2001; Horwitz et al. in Locke, 1990; Josephson 2002; Myers 1998; Rabieh 1991; Rahe 1994; Zinaich 2000; Zuckert 1994, 2002). Michael Zuckert (1994:207), for example, argued that the *Essays on the Law of Na- ture* "reveal to the attentive reader" that Locke did not believe *any* of the arguments he presented in defense of natural law. In two major books he used selective quotations from the *Essay Concern- ing Human Understanding* to demonstrate that Locke believed that the afterlife cannot be proved by reason and that, since for Locke reason is the judge of revelation the eternal rewards and punish- ments essential to his moral theory are undermined, a flaw that re- veals that he did not actually believe in the moral theories he was describing (Zuckert 1994:210, 272, 2002:32). Zuckert cites as proof, as did Pangle (1988), Locke's assertion that the resurrection *of the body* ("that the dead shall rise and live again"; *Essay* IV.18.7), not the immortality of the soul, cannot be proved by reason. As a recent neo-Straussian work demonstrates (Josephson 2002:19–21) Locke occasionally wrote of the need for care and caution in speaking and writing, but these arguments would make him a major prevaricator throughout his life.

The support for the Strauss interpretation was linked to the emergence of a conservative movement in American politics. The connection that he drew between liberalism and totalitarianism, skepticism and relativism, appealed to religious and moral conservatives like Russell Kirk (1953), whose *Conservative Mind* argued for Burke rather than Locke as the model for American politics Strauss's students at the University of Chicago idolized him, and the Straussian school of political theory became a major influence in American political theory and educated some of the leaders of the later neo-conservative movement. (After the 2003 overthrow of Saddam Hussein in Iraq, articles in the *New York Times* and *Wall Street Journal* argued that Strauss's elitist and antidemocratic ideas were an important influence on the thinking of the neo-conservative advocates of U.S. intervention.)

There are tensions, but not contradictions between Locke's discussion of natural law in the *Essays on the Law of Nature*, the *Essay Concerning Human Understanding*, the *Second Treatise on Civil Government*, and *The Reasonableness of Christianity*. The *Essays on the Law of Nature* argue for natural law in quasi-scholastic fashion but recognize there are great moral differences among various peoples historically and geographically; in the *Essay Concerning Human Understanding* there are repeated references to pleasure and pain as the way in which we know morality; in the *Second Treatise* it is assumed that all people are capable of perceiving, at a minimum, fundamental human equality before God and their duty to preserve his workmanship; and in the *Reasonableness* Locke's doubts about the capacity of most human beings to know the natural law "all entire" by reason lead him to argue that Christ came to teach us how to live a moral life. But these are differences in emphasis rather than differences in kind. Locke is aware of the historical, personal, and cultural impediments to knowing the natural law, Yet in none of his works does he depart from his belief that the God of biblical revelation has also revealed himself to human reason by creating a rational universe that is governed by natural law, the basic principles of which can be known by men. As he says in the *Essay Concerning Human Understanding*, "God has furnished men with the faculties sufficient to direct them in the way that they should take, if they will but employ them in that way when their ordinary vocations allow them the leisure" (IV.20.3). As in Aquinas and Hooker, revelation supplements reason but does not contradict it.

In a series of articles in the 1950s and in *The Political Theory of Possessive Individualism* (1962) C. B. Macpherson of the University of Toronto attacked the *Second Treatise* from the left, interpreting it as the ideological justification for emerging capitalism. Locke's theory, he argued, justified the removal of traditional moral limits on property accumulation and contained a contradictory understanding of human nature that both assumed natural equality in justifying government by consent and natural inequality in identifying property holding with rationality and political rights. Thus, while all are presumed to have consented to government, usually tacitly, only property holders give express consent and only they actually participate in government by electing representatives, thus avoiding a potential conflict between majority rule and the property rights of the minority. He also cited a hitherto-unnoticed passage about the right to "the turfs my servant has cut" (*Second Treatise* 28) to argue that Locke was a defender of wage labor.

Macpherson's interpretation struck a responsive chord, in his case among 1960s radicals who took it up as part of their rejection of modern liberal capitalism. In response, scholars such as Alan Ryan (see p. 299 herein) pointed out that Locke's statement that the social contract was made to defend property explicitly included life and liberty, as well as "estate" and that express and tacit consent were given in different ways from those described by Macpherson. Somewhat later, James Tully (1980) in *A Discourse on Property* found another passage, this time in the *First Treatise* (no. 42), that placed an important limit on the supposed absolute right of private property. From the divinely ordained obligation of preservation of oneself and all mankind, Locke derived a duty of charity imposed on property holders to distribute their surplus property to those in need, since "charity gives every man a title to so much out of another's surplusage as will keep him from extreme want when he has no means to subsist otherwise" (on the origins of the subsistence rights in medieval scholasticism, see Swanson 1997). Tully (p. 325 herein) also revived the argument, made earlier by Kendall, that by consenting to majority rule the individual surrendered to the community his judgment as to the interpretation of his rights—in effect giving it complete freedom to dispose of his property.

Critics of Tully (see Waldron p. 330 herein), while acknowledging that Locke believed in the obligation of charity as a limit on property rights, pointed out that the purpose of the social contract was to protect individual rights and that there would be little protection if it required that one abandon one's rights to the will of the majority—and, even worse, to the will of the legislature to which the majority had consented. In addition, directly following the statement about giving up one's right to execute the natural law, Locke argues that the legislature is limited to the public good and must conform to "the law of nature, i.e. to the will of God" (no. 135), and later he recognizes the right of resistance by "any single man" (no. 168).

Neal Wood (1986) was critical of both Macpherson and Tully, noting in *John Locke and Agrarian Capitalism* that Locke's arguments on private property were intended to defend neither commercial capitalism nor community limits on property but to encourage the development of agricultural production and to defend the enclosure of communal property.

Two more recent interpreters of the subsistence right have argued that a thoroughgoing application of the subsistence right would imply redistribution to the poor of all inherited property that was not necessary for the support of one's heirs (Sreenivasan 1995) as well as a worldwide program to give gainful employment to everyone who needs it (Kramer 1997). (They both admit that Locke himself would have been horrified by such proposals.) However, the first part of Locke's sentence in the *First Treatise* about the subsistence right specifically states that "justice gives every man a title to the product of his honest industry and the fair acquisitions of his ancestors descended to him," a passage that was the textual basis for Robert Nozick's (1974) identification as Lockean his argument against all government redistribution programs. (It was probably also the reason that Steven Forbes, one of the Republican presidential candidates in 2000, declared that Locke was his favorite political philosopher.)

So, is Locke an individualist or a collectivist, a free enterprise conservative or a socialist? Ruth Grant (p. 339 herein), criticizing Charles Taylor's claim that Locke espouses extreme ("atomistic") individualism, points out that, Locke's purpose in beginning with original freedom and equality is to argue for individual consent and the protection of rights, and not to deny the social and moral obligations or the natural law which apply before and after consent to the social contract. There is disagreement about how that consent is given (see Simmons's criticism of Hanna Pitkin on p. 344 herein), but it clearly implies limits on an absolute right of private property, at the very least taxation by consent for common purposes. (What those purposes are or should be is the subject of continuing public policy debate.)

The view that Locke's political theory is excessively individualistic, and property oriented underlies the next development in interpretations of his thought. Beginning with Bermard Bailyn's (1967)

The Ideological Origins of the American Revolution, a number of works, notably Gordon Wood's (1969) influential *The Creation of the American Republic,* argued for an alternative (and presumably superior) tradition in eighteenth-century America, republicanism or civic humanism. John Dunn (1969b), who had just written a major study of Locke's political thought also published an article that concluded from an examination of colonial libraries that Locke's influence on colonial America was mainly through the *Essay Concerning Human Understanding* rather than the *Second Treatise.* John Pocock's (1975) *The Machiavellian Moment* traced the republican tradition from Machiavelli's *Discourses* to the Founding Fathers. Writing at the time of the bicentennial of the Declaration of Independence, Garry Wills (1978) even denied that Jefferson knew Locke's work, arguing that he was influenced by the more socially oriented thinkers of the eighteenth-century Scottish Enlightenment, a claim that was quickly demolished by Jefferson scholars (e.g., Hamowy 1979).

The Lockean (selfish) liberalism versus civic republican (altruistic) humanism debate was wrongheaded from the start since it was based on interpretations of his thought, such as those of Strauss and Macpherson, that argued that by beginning with the individual in the state of nature Locke denied the social obligations contained in the natural law. The research in the sources that the liberalism—republicanism debate provoked finally concluded that the colonists were *both* Lockeans and republicans and that they did not see any contradiction between the right to private property and the recognition of, usually religiously based, social duties (Huyler 1995).

A similar misrepresentation of liberalism characterized the criticisms of liberalism made by its "communitarian" critics in the 1980s. Beginning with *Liberalism and the Limits of Justice* by Michael Sandel (1982), the communitarians accused liberals of basing their political theory on an unrealistic conception of man as, in Sandel's words, an "unencumbered self" free of all associations, traditions, and religious, and moral assumptions, Although aimed principally at the twentieth-century liberal thinker John Rawls (1971), the criticism was also seen as applicable to Locke's conception of man in the state of nature. In both cases, it ignored the fact that the contractualist starting point of liberal political thought was not a denial of the social nature of human beings but a method of explaining the nature and limits of political obligation.

The communitarian criticism, was often voiced by political conservatives, but around the same time another ideologically influenced debate developed on Locke's thought. It focused on the degree to which Locke could be described as a radical. Before Laslett made his argument about an earlier date of composition, it was assumed that Locke had written the *Two Treatises* after 1688 so that, despite their revolutionary rhetoric, they served a basically conservative purpose, the justification after the fact of the Glorious Revolution. Once Laslett's argument that the *Treatises* were written at the time of the Exclusion Crisis of 1680–83, the campaign of the Whigs to exclude the Catholic duke of York from succeeding to the throne, they appeared to be more radical in their purpose. In a path-breaking article and a later book Richard Ashcraft (p. 354 herein; 1986) argued that Locke was part of a group of Whigs associated with the Earl of Shaftesbury, who first attempted to use Parliament to block James's succession and then, when Charles II dissolved the Oxford Parliament with no intention of reconvening it, turned to plotting revolution. The *First Treatise* was written, Ashcraft argued, in 1680 to respond to the challenge of Filmer's works, which had been published in 1679 as part of the royalist anti-Whig propaganda war. The *Second Treatise*, he claimed, was one of several works written for Shaftesbury after the dissolution of the Oxford Parliament in March 1681 and drew on earlier theories of consent, such as those of the Levellers, to justify resistance by the people, especially the merchants and craftsmen of London.

Ashcraft's evidence, particularly the interpretations of apparently straightforward letters regarding seeds and plants as coded communications relating to the plot, has been subjected to withering criticisms by British scholars (Wootton in Locke 1993:83–94; Milton 2000). In addition, it is doubtful that a lengthy philosophical work like the *Second Treatise* would have been useful in a propaganda campaign. Locke knew many of the plotters, but he was a cautious and careful person, whose theoretical radicalism was combined with conservatism in practice, and he was careful to keep clear of any direct involvement. His political theory also had conservative implications since it justified economic inequality and a property qualification for voting (*Second Treatise* 37, 158) and he believed that the English system of government by the king in Parliament had received the consent of the English people. Yet his arguments that their consent was based on original political equality and could be withdrawn in case of abuse radically challenged the basic assumptions of his time. As in the case of the individualism—collectivism debate, he cannot be identified with one side or the other.

A similar ambivalence is present in Locke's writings on the issues of race and of equal rights for women. In the 1980s and 1990s, once again influenced by contemporary political debate, scholars began to evaluate Locke's position on both these subjects. Locke in the *Second Treatise* justified slavery only in the case of the vanquished soldiers on the wrong side of an unjust war, and even then he argued their wives and children should not be enslaved and must be left by the conqueror with the means of subsistence (see Farr on p. 373 herein). Yet Locke was a successful investor in the slave trade and must have known that the conduct of the slave traders did not follow those norms. He helped draw up a constitution for the Carolinas that provided for Negro—but not Indian— slavery, and he continued to be involved with the colony (see Armitage 2004; see also Farr on p. 378 herein for evidence that Locke was not a racist). Particularly in the discussion of property in chapter 5 of the *Second Treatise*, Locke drew many examples from the New World and viewed it as undeveloped land ("empty places") that was available for colonization. His theories basing the property right on development through labor could be, and were, used to justify the occupation by the colonists of the lands that were not being developed by the hunter-gatherer American Indians (see Arneil 1996).

When the feminists looked at Locke they found an opponent of patriarchalism who argued for independent property rights of wives, a contractualist view of marriage, and the possibility of divorce after the children have grown. Yet Locke's references in the *Second Treatise* to the husband having the final say because he is "the abler and stronger" and his assertion in the *First Treatise* that male superiority over "the weaker sex" has "a foundation in nature" incurred their ire (see Butler on p. 379 herein; see also Kateman 1985 and a defense of Locke in Simmons 2001). Once again there is something for everyone.

Locke's *Letter Concerning Toleration* has received fewer criticisms. Its argument that government should be concerned with civil matters, and not with men's souls, is part of the American creed. Students are surprised, however, to find that Locke excludes Catholics and atheists from toleration. Yet as recently as the 1960 presidential election, the possibly divided loyalties of Catholics were an issue in American politics, and the Supreme Court has only gradually extended the protections of the First Amendment to agnostics and atheists.

There have been other criticisms. In 1980 Robert Kraynak, a scholar of the Straussian school, criticized the *Letter* for giving priority to the claims of public order over those of conscience, allowing, in his view, the magistrate to place any limitation on religious freedom that can be justified on secular grounds. However, his argument ignored Locke's entire system of institutional, legal, and moral checks on such abuses as well as his specific reference to religious oppression as a justification of revolution (*Second Treatise* 209). Later in the decade Jeremy Waldron (1993) pointed out the weaknesses of Locke's argument for the ineffectiveness of religious persecution, since as a matter of fact government coercion can affect belief. However David Wootton (p. 369 herein) replied that Locke had more fundamental and persuasive arguments for toleration, the example of Christ, the rights of conscience, and the lack of religious expertise of the magistrate whose responsibility is for civil order and the protection of rights, not the determination of the true road to salvation.

The discussion of Locke's views on toleration was related to an increasingly important literature on Locke's religious beliefs. In 1969 John Dunn's book on Locke had emphasized the importance of Locke's Calvinist upbringing, and in an article that he later retracted, Dunn (1990) asserted that Locke's religious views are so central to his theories as to make them irrelevant in an age that does not share his religious beliefs. In an article published in the same year, Ashcraft (1969a) also drew attention to the importance of religion to Locke. He and others (e.g., Eisenach 1992) also noted Locke's anticlericalism and hatred of "priestcraft" as a continuing theme in his writings.

As early as 1917 and 1925 articles in the *Catholic Historical Review* had made a somewhat dubious argument linking Catholic theories of popular sovereignty, as expressed in Cardinal Robert Bellarmine's attack on James I's theory of the divine right of kings, with Jefferson and Madison by way of Filmer's attack on Bellarmine in the *Patriarcha* and Locke's references to him in no. 6 of the *First Treatise* (Hunt 1917; Rager 1925). A polemical Protestant attack on the Bellarmine–Jefferson link (Schiff 1927) pointed out some significant differences between Bellarmine and Locke/Jefferson, notably their opposing views on religious toleration. Again scholarly debates were linked to contemporary political controversies, in this case the relation of Catholicism and American democracy.

Shortly before the presidential election of John F. Kennedy, a leading Jesuit intellectual, John Courtney Murray (1960: Chap. 13), took a different approach. He argued that Thomistic natural law theory provided a better basis for human rights, just law, and true freedom than Locke's theory of a "law of nature," which begins with the individual in the state of nature. Murray (1960:302–308) said that Locke's view of man as "an omnipotent sociological nomad" leads to an "atomistic social outlook" that can only balance the "absolute lordship" of the individual with (quoting Locke, *Second Treatise* 95) "the greater force" of the majority in which is embodied "the power of the whole." For Murray (1960:302–303), "the logic of Locke's theory" led to "Rousseau's omnipotent democracy . . . and the consequent subjection of all forms of community life to total state control." The Murray view of Locke had certain resemblances to that of Strauss (although for Strauss, the contrast was with Plato rather than Aquinas) in identifying Lockean liberalism with atomistic individualism leading to nihilism and totalitarianism. It was thus not difficult to explain the support for the Straussian view in a number of Catholic universities in succeeding years.

Protestants were also divided in their attitudes toward Locke. The more liberal churches viewed the Locke of *The Reasonableness of Christianity* as one of their own. Calvinists noted the influence on Locke of the sixteenth-century Huguenot tract the *Vindiciae contra Tyrannos* (1579) and the writings of the leader of the Scottish Reformation George Buchanan. Predictably, more conservative evangelicals took a more critical stance, like the neo-Straussians viewing Locke as a subverter of Christianity, although on religious rather than philosophical grounds.

John Colman's (1983) *John Locke's Moral Theory* was the first of many books and articles that drew on newly published materials and manuscript sources to examine the relation of Locke's religious views to his political and ethical thought. Criticizing those who argued that there were contradictions between Locke's belief in God's will as the source of obligation, in an objective law of nature known by reason, and in the idea of pleasure and pain as the motives for good conduct, Colman (1983:6–7) traced the development of Locke's moral thought throughout his life to demonstrate that Locke had a "consistent theological ethic" that is based on "the way that God has created human nature" and "human needs and interests which are universal and permanent.

A few years later, W. M. Spellman's (1938) *John Locke and the Problem of Depravity* examined the relationship of Locke's rejection of original sin to his views on human nature. Spellman rejected the common view that Locke believed in the perfectibility of man, given the right environment and education (see Spellman p. 363 herein). He argued that, while Locke did not believe in original sin in the sense of inherited guilt of all mankind because of the sin of Adam, he was fully aware of the human inclination to evil as a result of the Fall, and in *The Reasonableness of Christianity* Locke cited it as one of the reasons for the coming of Christ.

The most comprehensive treatment of Locke's religious views was John Marshall's (1994) *John Locke: Resistance, Religion, and Responsibility*. Drawing on many unpublished writings of Locke and details of his life and friendships, he identified Locke as a deeply committed Christian who was neither a Calvinist nor a Deist (he rejected both positions at the beginning of *The Reasonableness of Christianity*) nor a latitudinarian ("Broad Church") Anglican (since he did not believe in the divinity of Christ, the atonement, or in inherited original sin). He had Socinian (Unitarian) friends, his library contained many of their books, and he shared much (but not all) of their theology. Yet he lived and died as a member of the

Church of England. God for Locke was rational ("reasonable") and wished men to be "industrious and rational" (*Second Treatise* 34), but he had also sent Jesus Christ, his Son, to save the world from sin, not by his death but by his preaching and resurrection.

Two years later Kirstie McClure (1996) published the study *Judging Rights,* which argued for a more communitarian interpretation of Locke's politics based on his assumption of a divinely created ordered cosmos that resolved the supposed inconsistencies and confusions of his theory. (A similar argument for the importance of Locke's theism in unifying his thought was made in Tuckness [1999].)

In 1997 Victor Nuovo published a reprint of *The Reasonableness of Christianity* along with Locke's 1696 and 1697 replies to his critics as well as a separate volume of contemporary responses to it In 1999 the definitive Clarendon edition of *The Reasonableness* was published. (Locke 1999). In 2002 Nuovo included it along with a number of Locke's shorter writings on religion. (Locke 2002) The interest in Locke's religious views was continued with the publication in the same year of *God, Locke, and Equality* by Jeremy Waldron (2002), who argues that Locke's theory of equality is founded on the capacity of all human beings to recognize their moral obligations to God and therefore to each other. Waldron denies that there is a fundamental contradiction between the epistemology of the *Essay* and the belief in natural law in the *Second Treatise,* as had been argued by the followers of Strauss and, more influentially, by Peter Laslett in the introduction to his widely used text (Locke 1988:82–83). Waldron seems to share Locke's belief expressed in the *Letter on Toleration* that "[t]he taking away of God, though but even in thought, dissolves all." He is critical of "thinner" nonreligious conceptions of the moral basis of human equality developed by such contemporary liberal theorists as John Rawls, Waldron (p. 318 herein) argues that an atheist "has no basis in his philosophy" for a belief that human beings are morally equal and that religiously based arguments like Locke's are so important and so persuasive that they should not be excluded from the public forum, as secular liberals wish to do.

The issue that Waldron raises is an important one. Conservative critics of liberalism are ideologically motivated in describing Locke as a materialist, egoist defender of absolute property rights because they see liberalism as devoid of moral content beyond a philosophy of "live and let live." This is why they are so eager to associate Locke with the Hobbesian view of government as chiefly concerned with controlling inevitable conflicts among self-interested competitive individuals. Yet Locke and most liberal theorists—at least until the late twentieth century—believed that there must be a broader shared moral foundation for liberalism. The question that Waldron raises is whether, to survive, that foundation must be religious.

Thanks to the vast scholarship on Locke over the last half century and to the availability of so many original sources, we probably know more about Locke's thinking than about the thought of any other great political philosopher. A review of the literature demonstrates that there is such a thing as progress in understanding of the classic texts of the history of political thought. In the last fifty years we have learned that Locke was not a covert Hobbesian or an apologist for unrestrained accumulation of property. The arguments that he was a hedonist, materialist, atomistic individualist, collectivist, deist, secularist, advocate of majority tyranny, and naive believer in human perfectibility have been refuted. His views on women and on race have been seen as more nuanced than at first appears; distinctions have been made between his original intentions and later interpretations that invoke his name; and many of the disagreements of the past have given way to a new scholarly consensus because of access to new sources. We have a greater understanding of the continuities and discontinuities with the past represented in his thought, viewing him neither as the central figure in the quasi-Hegelian march of liberalism through history nor as the subverter of the Western tradition. More recently Locke scholarship has made us aware that Locke's religiously based belief in the possibility of understanding, by the use of reason, God's intentions for human moral conduct, individually and politically, provides a unity to his political thought, which modern secular commentators had seen as full of contradictions.

These advances in scholarship have not always been incorporated into contemporary discussions. George Lodge (1976) of the Harvard Business School has called for a "new American ideology" to replace the untrammeled capitalism of the "Lockean paradigm," and Mary Ann Glendon (1991:71) of Harvard Law School describes Lockean man as a "lone rights-bearer" to the detriment of social responsibility. More recently, in a well-received intellectual history of the modern world, Jacques Barzun (2000:362–63) of Columbia University could still note that the *Second Treatise* was written to justify the 1688 Glorious Revolution and that Locke's political theory merely summarized "well-ripened ideas" and, despite his "pro forma" references to God, was "completely secular."

The three examples illustrate the tendency to reduce the complexity of Locke's political thought to a few simple but inaccurate stereotypes about his role as herald of modernity. To be sure Locke was an innovator in political theory. His arguments for private property and the market system, the priority of individual rights, and the exclusion of government from the determination of religious truth marked a break with past theory and practice. However, the texts and commentaries collected here demonstrate that there were also important continuities with earlier thought and significant moral and social limitations on his individualism.

Locke's political theory has also been invoked in discussion of foreign policy, contrasting the Lockean view of international relations, shared by Presidents Carter and Clinton, as an area where it is possible to develop the rule of law by mutual consent, with the Hobbesian view, adopted by the administration of George W. Bush, which holds that international relations are inevitably characterized by conflict and opposing interests. As this example indicates, the questions that Locke addresses are still with us today, and his answers have a continuing relevance. The relation of religion and politics, political equality and individual freedom, democracy and property (now called "politics and markets"), the justification of human rights, and the appropriate limits on government power have not ceased to be central issues of politics. More fundamentally his argument for universal values, which he calls natural law, and his belief in the possibility that human reason, especially if reinforced by faith, can perceive a basic moral order in the universe continue to offer Americans, and an increasingly globalized world, an explanation and justification of liberal constitutional democracy.

It is in the hope that one can arrive at a more thorough and accurate understanding of a great political theorist that this book has been written. It is dedicated to the participants in my 1992 junior seminar at Princeton on Locke's political thought, in which the outline of this book was first developed—several of whom are now fellow academics.

Paul E. Sigmund
Princeton University

The Selected Political Writings of
JOHN LOCKE

TWO

TREATISES

OF

GOVERNMENT.

IN THE FORMER,

THE FALSE PRINCIPLES AND FOUNDATION OF SIR ROBERT FIL-
MER, AND HIS FOLLOWERS, ARE DETECTED AND OVER-
THROWN:

THE LATTER,

IS AN ESSAY CONCERNING THE TRUE ORIGINAL, EXTENT, AND
END, OF CIVIL GOVERNMENT.

From *The Works of John Locke*, vol. V, Aalen: Scientia Verlag, 1963 (reprint of 1823 London edition) with corrections by the editor.

From The Preface

Reader,

Thou hast here the beginning and end of a discourse concerning government; what fate has otherwise disposed of the papers that should have filled up the middle, and were more than all the rest, it is not worthwhile to tell thee. Those which remain, I hope are sufficient to establish the throne of our great restorer, our present King William; to make good his title in the consent of the people, which being the only one of all lawful governments he has more fully and clearly than any prince in Christendom; and to justify to the world the people of England, whose love of their just and natural rights with their resolution to preserve them, saved the nation when it was on the brink of slavery and ruin. * * * I should not have writ[ten] against Sir Robert [Filmer][1], or taken the pains to show his mistakes, inconsistencies, and want of (what he so much boasts and pretends to build on) Scripture-proofs, were there not men amongst us who, by crying up his books and espousing his doctrine, save me from the reproach of writing against a dead adversary. * * *

From The First Treatise of Government

Book I

CHAPTER I.

1. Slavery is so vile and miserable an estate of man, and so directly opposite to the generous temper of our nation that it is hardly to be conceived that an Englishman, much less a gentleman should plead for it. And truly, I should have taken Sir Robert Filmer's *Patriarcha* as any other treatise which would persuade all men that they are slaves, and ought to be so, for such another exercise of wit * * * had not the gravity of the title and epistle, the picture in the front of the book, and the applause that followed it, required me to believe that the author and publisher were both in earnest.

* * *

---

1. Sir Robert Filmer (1588–1623), author of *Patriarcha* (p. 263 herein) and a number of other works defending the divine right of Kings, which based royal authority on inheritance from a divine grant to Adam. Although written as much as fifty years earlier, his works were published in 1679–80 and were widely cited by supporters of royal authority. All notes are the editor's unless otherwise specified.

3. In this last age a generation of men has sprung up amongst us, who would flatter princes with an opinion that they have a divine right to absolute power, let the laws by which they are constituted and are to govern, and the conditions under which they enter upon their authority, be what they will; and their engagements to observe them never so well ratified, by solemn oaths and promises. To make way for this doctrine, they have denied mankind a right to natural freedom; whereby they have not only, as much as in them lies, exposed all subjects to the utmost misery of tyranny and oppression, but have also unsettled the titles, and shaken the thrones of princes; (for they too, by these men's system, except only one, are all born slaves, and by divine right are subjects to Adam's right heir;) as if they had designed to make war upon all government, and subvert the very foundations of human society, to serve their present turn.

* * *

FROM CHAPTER 4. OF ADAM'S TITLE TO SOVEREIGNTY BY DONATION
GEN. 1:28

23. But let us see the argument. The words of the text are these: "And God blessed them, and God said unto them, be fruitful and multiply, and replenish the earth, and subdue it, and have dominion over the fish of the sea, and over the fowl of the air, and over every living thing that moves upon the earth," Gen. 1:28. From whence our author concludes, that "Adam having here dominion given him over all creatures, was thereby the monarch of the whole world."[2]

33. * * * "Be fruitful and multiply, and replenish the earth", says God in this blessing. * * * How much absolute monarchy helps to fulfill this great and primary blessing of God Almighty which contains in it the improvement too of arts and sciences, and the conveniences of life, may be seen in those large and rich countries which are happy under the Turkish government, where are not now to be found one third, nay in many, if not most, of them are not to be found one thirtieth, perhaps I might say not one hundredth of the people that were formerly, as will easily appear to anyone who will compare the accounts we have of it at this time with ancient history. * * *

40.8 * * * [W]e have examined our author's argument for Adam's "monarchy," founded on the blessing pronounced, Gen. 1:28. Wherein I think it is impossible for any sober reader to find any

2. A quotation from Filmer's *Observations on Aristotle's Politics* (see Filmer, *Patriarcha and Other Writings*, ed. Johann P. Sommerville [Cambridge: Cambridge University Press, 1991], 236).

other but the setting of mankind above the other kinds of creatures in this habitable earth of ours. It is nothing but the giving to man, the whole species of man, as the chief inhabitant, who is the image of his maker, the dominion over the other creatures. This lies so obvious in the plain words, that anyone but our author would have thought it necessary to have shown how these words, that seemed to say the quite contrary, gave Adam monarchical absolute power over other men, or the sole property in all the creatures; and methinks in a business of this moment, and that whereon he builds all that follows, he should have done something more than barely cite words which apparently make against him; for I confess I cannot see any thing in them tending to Adam's monarchy or private dominion, but quite the contrary. And I the less deplore the dullness of my apprehension herein, since I find the apostle [Paul] seems to have as little notion of any such private dominion of Adam as I, when he says, "God gives us all things richly to enjoy" [1 Timothy 6] which he could not do, if it were all given away already to monarch Adam, and the monarchs his heirs and successors. To conclude, this text is so far from proving Adam sole proprietor, that, on the contrary, it is a confirmation of the original community of all things amongst the sons of men, which appearing from this donation of God as well as other places of scripture, the sovereignty of Adam, built upon his private dominion, must fall, not having any foundation to support it.

41. But yet, if after all, any one will needs have it so, that by this donation of God Adam was made sole proprietor of the whole earth, what will this be to his sovereignty, and how will it appear that propriety in land gives a man power over the life of another, or how will the possession even of the whole earth give anyone a sovereign arbitrary authority over the persons of men? The most specious thing to be said is that he that is proprietor of the whole world may deny all the rest of mankind food, and so at his pleasure starve them if they will not acknowledge his sovereignty and obey his will. If this were true, it would be a good argument to prove that there never was any such property, that God never gave any such private dominion; since it is more reasonable to think that God, who bid mankind increase and multiply, should rather himself give them all a right to make use of the food and raiment and other conveniences of life, the materials whereof he had so plentifully provided for them, than to make them depend upon the will of a man for their subsistence, who should have power to destroy them all when he pleased, and who, being no better than other men, was in succession likelier, by want and the dependence of a scanty fortune, to tie them to hard service than by liberal allowance of the conveniences of life promote the great design of God, "increase and

multiply"; he that doubts this, let him look into the absolute monarchies of the world, and see what becomes of the conveniences of life, and the multitudes of people.

42. But we know God hath not left one man so to the mercy of another, that he may starve him if he please: God the Lord and Father of all, has given no one of his children such a property in his peculiar portion of the things of this world, but that he has given his needy brother a right to the surplusage of his goods; so that it cannot justly be denied him, when his pressing wants call for it. And therefore no man could ever have a just power over the life of another by right of property in land or possessions; since it would always be a sin in any man of estate, to let his brother perish for want of affording him relief out of his plenty. As justice gives every man a title to the product of his honest industry, and the fair acquisitions of his ancestors descended to him; so charity gives every man a title to so much out of another's plenty, as will keep him from extreme want, where he has no means to subsist otherwise: and a man can no more justly make use of another's necessity to force him to become his vassal by withholding that relief God requires him to afford to the wants of his brother, than he that has more strength can seize upon a weaker, master him to his obedience, and with a dagger at his throat, offer his death or slavery.

* * *

FROM CHAPTER 5 OF ADAM'S TITLE TO SOVEREIGNTY BY THE
SUBJECTION OF EVE

44. The next place of Scripture we find our author builds his monarchy of Adam on, is Gen. 3:16. "And thy desire shall be to thy husband, and he shall rule over thee." "Here we have", says he, "the original grant of government," from whence he concludes, in the following part of the page[3] that "the supreme power is settled in the fatherhood, and limited to one kind of government, that is to monarchy." For let his premises be what they will, this is always the conclusion; let "rule" in any text be but once named, and presently "absolute monarchy" is by divine right established. If anyone will but carefully read our author's own reasoning from these words * * *, and consider among other things the line and posterity of Adam as he there brings them in, he will find some difficulty to make sense of what he says. But we will allow this at present to his peculiar way of writing, and consider the force of the text in hand. The words are the curse of God upon the woman, for having been

---

3. Here Locke gives the page number of the 1679 edition of Filmer's works, which did not include the *Patriarcha*. The reference is to Filmer's *The Anarchy of Limited or Mixed Monarchy* (see Filmer, *Patriarcha and Other Writings*, 138).

the first and forwardest in the disobedience, and if we will consider
the occasion of what God says here to our first parents, that he was
denouncing judgment and declaring his wrath against them both,
for their disobedience, we cannot suppose that this was the time
wherein God was granting Adam prerogatives and privileges, invest-
ing him with dignity and authority, elevating him to dominion and
monarchy. For though as a helper in the temptation, * * * Eve was
laid below him, and so he had accidentally a superiority over her for
her greater punishment, yet he too had his share in the fall, as well
as the sin, and was laid lower, as may be seen in the following
verses, and it would be hard to imagine, that God, in the same
breath, should make him universal monarch over all mankind, and
a day labourer for his life, turn him out of Paradise "to till the
ground" (verse 23), and at the same time advance him to a throne,
and all the privileges and ease of absolute power.

* * *

47. Further, it is to be noted, that these words here of Gen. 3:16,
which our author calls "the original grant of government," were not
spoken to Adam, neither indeed was there any grant in them made
to Adam, but a punishment laid upon Eve: and if we will take them
as they were directed in particular to her, or in her, as their representative to all other women, they will at most concern the female
sex only, and import no more but that subjection they should ordinarily be in to their husbands: but there is here no more law to
oblige a woman to such a subjection, if the circumstances either of
her condition or contract with her husband should exempt her
from it, than there is that she should bring forth her children in
sorrow and pain, if there could be found a remedy for it, which is
also a part of the same curse upon her: for the whole verse runs
thus: "Unto the woman he said, I will greatly multiply thy sorrow
and thy conception; in sorrow thou shalt bring forth children, and
thy desire shall be to thy husband, and he shall rule over thee." It
would, I think, have been a hard matter for anybody but our author
to have found out a grant of monarchical government to Adam in
these words, which were neither spoken to, nor of, him. Neither
will any one, I suppose, by these words, think the weaker sex, as by
a law so subjected to the curse contained in them, that it is their
duty not to endeavour to avoid it. And will any one say that Eve, or
any other woman, sinned, if she were brought to bed without those
multiplied pains God threatens her here with? Or that either of our
Queens Mary or Elizabeth, had they married any of their subjects,
had been by this text put into a political subjection to him; Or that
he should thereby have had monarchical rule over her? God, in this
text, gives not, that I see, any authority to Adam over Eve, or to
men over their wives, but only foretells what should be the woman's

lot; how by his providence he would order it so, that she should be subject to her husband, as we see that generally the laws of mankind and customs of nations have ordered it so; and there is, I grant, a foundation in nature for it.

*   *   *

48. * * * But if these words here spoke to Eve must needs be understood as a law to bind her and all other women to subjection, it can be no other subjection than what every wife owes her husband, and then if this be "the original grant of government and the foundation of monarchical power", there will be as many monarchs as there are husbands. If, therefore, these words give any power to Adam, it can be only a conjugal power, not political; the power that every husband hath to order the things of private concernment in his family, as proprietor of the goods and land there, and to have his will take place before that of his wife in all things of their common concernment; but not a political power of life and death over her, much less over anybody else.

*   *   *

FROM CHAPTER 6. OF ADAM'S TITLE TO SOVEREIGNTY BY FATHERHOOD

*   *   *

56. They who allege the practice of mankind for exposing or selling their children as proof of their power over them are with Sir Robert happy arguers, and cannot but recommend their opinion by founding it on the most shameful action and most unnatural murder human nature is capable of.

*   *   *

58. Thus far can the busy mind of man carry him to a brutality below the level of beasts when he quits his reason, which places him almost equal of angels. Nor can it be otherwise in creatures whose thoughts are more than the sands and wider than the ocean, where fancy and passion must needs run him into strange courses, if reason, which is his only star and compass, be not that he steers by. The imagination is always restless and suggests variety of thoughts, and the will, reason being laid aside, is ready for every extravagant project, and in this state he that goes farthest out of his way is thought fittest to lead and is sure of most followers; and when fashion hath once established what folly or craft began, custom makes sacred and it will be called impudence or madness to contradict or question it. He that will impartially survey the nations of the world will find so much of their governments, religions, and manners brought in and continued by these means that he will have but little reverence for the practices which are in use and credit among men.

*   *   *

59. Be it then as Sir Robert says, that "anciently it was usual for men to sell and castrate their children."[4] Let it be that they exposed them; add too, if you please, for this is still greater power, that they begat them for their tables to fat[ten] and eat them; if this proves a right to do so, we may by the same argument justify adultery, incest, and sodomy, for there are examples of these too, both ancient and modern, sins which, I suppose, have their principal aggravation from this, that they cross the main intention of nature which willeth the increase of mankind, and the continuation of the species in the highest perfection, and the distinction of families with the security of the marriage bed as necessary thereto.

*   *   *

66. "The law that enjoins obedience to kings, is delivered," says our author, "in the terms, 'Honour thy father', as if all power were originally in the father, and that law is also delivered, say I, in the terms, "Honour thy mother," as if all power were originally in the mother. I appeal whether the argument be not as good on one side as the other, "father and mother" being joined all along in the Old and New Testament wherever honour or obedience is enjoined children. Again our author tells us, that "this command, 'Honour thy father', gives the right to govern, and makes the form of government monarchical."[5] To which I answer, that if by "Honour thy father" be meant obedience to the political power of the magistrate, it concerns not any duty we owe to our natural fathers, who are subjects; because they, by our author's doctrine, are divested of all that power, it being placed wholly in the prince, and so being equally subjects and slaves with their children, can have no right by that title, to any such honour or obedience, as contains in it political subjection: if "Honour thy father and mother" signifies the duty we owe our natural parents, as by our Savior's interpretation, Matthew 15:4, and all the other mentioned places, it is plain it does; then it cannot concern political obedience, but a duty that is owing to persons who have no title to sovereignty, nor any political authority, as magistrates over subjects. For the person of a private father, and a title to obedience, due to the supreme magistrate, are things inconsistent; and therefore this command, which must necessarily comprehend the persons of natural fathers, must mean a duty we owe them distinct from our obedience to the magistrate, and from which the most absolute power of princes cannot absolve us. What this duty is, we shall in its due place examine.

*   *   *

4. Filmer's *Observations on Aristotle's Politics*, 282.
5. Paraphrase of the sentence following the one quoted above from *The Anarchy of Limited or Mixed Monarchy*.

FROM CHAPTER 9. OF MONARCHY BY INHERITANCE FROM ADAM

* * *

86. But not to follow our author too far out of the way, the plain of the case is this: God having made man, and planted in him, as in all other animals, a strong desire of self-preservation, and furnished the world with things fit for food and raiment, and other necessaries of life, subservient to his design, that man should live and abide for some time upon the face of the earth, and not that so curious and wonderful a piece of workmanship, by its own negligence, or want of necessaries, should perish again, presently after a few moments continuance; God, I say, having made man and the world thus, spoke to him, (that is) directed him by his senses and reason, as he did the inferior animals by their sense and instinct, which he had placed in them to that purpose, to the use of those things which were serviceable for his subsistence, and given him as the means of his preservation. And therefore I doubt not, but before these words were pronounced, Gen. 1:28–29, (if they must be understood literally to have been spoken) and without any such verbal donation, man had a right to an use of the creatures by the will and grant of God. For the desire, strong desire, of preserving his life and being having been planted in him as a principle of action by God himself, reason, "which was the voice of God in him," could not but teach him and assure him, that pursuing that natural inclination[6] he had to preserve his being, he followed the will of his maker, and therefore had a right to make use of those creatures which by his reason or senses he could discover would be serviceable thereunto. And thus man's property in the creatures was founded upon the right he had to make use of those things that were necessary or useful to his being.

87. This being the reason and foundation of Adam's property, gave the same title, on the same ground, to all his children, not only after his death, but in his lifetime: So that here was no privilege of his heir above his other children which could exclude them from an equal right to the use of the inferior creatures for the comfortable preservation of their beings, which is all the property man hath in them: and so Adam's sovereignty built on property, or, as our author calls it, private dominion, comes to nothing. Every man had a right to the creatures, by the same title Adam had, viz. by the right every one had to take care of, and provide for their subsistence. And thus men had a right in common, Adam's children in

---

6. On the derivation of the provisions of the natural law, including self-preservation, from natural inclinations, see St. Thomas Aquinas's *Summa Theologiae*, I–II, qu. 94.a.2. On the law of reason, see Richard Hooker's *The Laws of Ecclesiastical Polity*, I.9 (p. 223 herein). On property as a divinely intended means to the preservation of all mankind, see Locke, *Second Treatise*, 25–26 (p. 28 herein).

common with him. But if anyone had begun, and made himself a property in any particular thing, (which how he, or anyone else could do, shall be shown in another place) that thing, that possession, if he disposed not otherwise of it by his positive grant, descended naturally to his children, and they had a right to succeed to it, and possess it.

88. It might reasonably be asked here, how come children by this right of possessing, before any other, the properties of their parents upon their decease? For it being personally the parents', when they die, without actually transferring their right to another, why does it not return again to the common stock of mankind? It will perhaps be answered that common consent hath disposed of it to their children. Common practice, we see, indeed does so dispose of it, but we cannot say that it is the common consent of mankind;[7] for that hath never been asked, nor actually given: and if common tacit consent hath established it, it would make but a positive, and not a natural right of children to inherit the goods of their parents. But where the practice is universal, it is reasonable to think the cause is natural. The ground, then, I think to be this. The first and strongest desire God planted in men, and wrought into the very principles of their nature, being that of self-preservation, that is the foundation of a right to the creatures for the particular support and use of each individual person himself. But next to this, God planted in men a strong desire also of propagating their kind, and continuing themselves in their posterity, and this gives children a title to share in the property of their parents, and right to inherit their possessions. Men are not proprietors of what they have merely for themselves, their children have a title to part of it, and have their kind of right joined with their parents', in the possession: which comes to be wholly theirs, when death having put an end to their parents' use of it, hath taken them from their possessions, and this we call inheritance: men being by a like obligation bound to preserve what they have begotten as to preserve themselves, their issue come to have a right in the goods they are possessed of. That children have such a right, is plain from the laws of God, and that men are convinced that children have such a right is evident from the law of the land, both which laws require parents to provide for their children.

89. For children being, by the course of nature, born weak, and unable to provide for themselves, they have by the appointment of God himself, who hath thus ordered the course of nature, a right to be nourished and maintained by their parents, nay a right not only

---

7. This is a criticism of Pufendorf. See *On the Law of Nature and of Nations*, IV.4.4, 6 (p. 256 herein).

to a bare subsistence but to the conveniences and comforts of life, as far as the conditions of their parents can afford it. Hence it comes, that when their parents leave the world, and so the care due to their children ceases, the effects of it are to extend as far as possibly they can, and the provisions they have made in their lifetime are understood to be intended, as nature requires they should, for their children, whom, after themselves, they are bound to provide for, though the dying parents, by express words, declare nothing about them, nature appoints the descent of their property to their children, who thus come to have a title, and natural right of inheritance to their father's goods, which the rest of mankind cannot pretend to.

* * *

91. I have been the larger, in showing upon what ground children have a right to succeed to the possession of their fathers' properties, not only because by it it will appear that if Adam had a property (a titular insignificant, useless property; for it could be no better, for he was bound to nourish and maintain his children and posterity out of it) in the whole earth and its product, yet all his children coming to have by the law of nature and right of inheritance a joint title and a right of property in it after his death, it could convey no right of sovereignty to any one of his posterity over the rest: since everyone having a right of inheritance to his portion, they might enjoy their inheritance, or any part of it, in common, or share it, or some parts of it, by division, as it best liked them. But no one could pretend to the whole inheritance, or any sovereignty supposed to accompany it, since a right of inheritance gave every one of the rest, as well as any one, a title to share in the goods of his father. Not only upon this account, I say, have I been so particular in examining the reason of children's inheriting the property of their fathers, but also because it will give us farther light in the inheritance of rule and power, which in countries where their particular municipal laws give the whole possession of land entirely to the first-born, and descent of power has gone so to men by this custom, some have been apt to be deceived into an opinion that there was a natural or divine right of primogeniture to both estate and power; and that the inheritance of both rule over men and property in things sprang from the same original, and were to descend by the same rules.

92. Property, whose original is from the right a man has to use any of the inferior creatures for the subsistence and comfort of his life, is for the benefit and sole advantage of the proprietor, so that he may even destroy the thing that he has property in by his use of it, where need requires; but government, being for the preservation of every man's right and property, by preserving him from the vio-

lence or injury of others, is for the good of the governed. For the magistrate's sword being for a terror to evil doers,[8] and by that terror to enforce men to observe the positive laws of the society, made conformable to the laws of nature for the public good, i.e. the good of every particular member of that society, as far as by common rules it can be provided for, the sword is not given the magistrate for his own good alone.

93. Children, therefore, as has been showed, by the dependence they have on their parents for subsistence, have a right of inheritance to their father's property, as that which belongs to them for their proper good and behoof,[9] and therefore are fitly termed goods, wherein the firstborn has not a sole or peculiar right by any law of God and nature, the younger children having an equal title with him founded on that right they all have to maintenance, support, and comfort from their parents, and on nothing else. But government being for the benefit of the governed, and not the sole advantage of the governors (but only for theirs with the rest, as they make a part of that politic body, each of whose parts and members are taken care of, and directed in its peculiar functions for the good of the whole by the laws of the society), cannot be inherited by the same title that children have to the goods of their father. The right a son has to be maintained and provided with the necessaries and conveniences of life out of his father's stock, gives him a right to succeed to his father's property for his own good, but this can give him no right to succeed also to the rule which his father had over other men. All that a child has right to claim from his father is nourishment and education, and the things nature furnishes for the support of life; but he has no right to demand rule or dominion from him. He can subsist and receive from him the portion of good things, and advantages of education, naturally due to him without empire and dominion. That (if his father hath any) was vested in him for the good and behoof of others, and therefore the son cannot claim or inherit it by a title, which is founded wholly on his own private good and advantage.

94. We must know how the first ruler, from whom anyone claims, came by his authority, upon what ground any one has empire, what his title is to it, before we can know who has a right to succeed him in it, and inherit it from him. If the agreement and consent of men first gave a sceptre into anyone's hand, or put a crown on his head, that also must direct its descent and conveyance. For the same authority that made the first a lawful ruler, must make the second too, and so give right of succession. In this case inheritance or primo-

8. See Romans 13:3.
9. Benefit.

geniture, can in itself have no right, no pretence to it, any farther than that consent which established the form of the government hath so settled the succession. And thus we see the succession of crowns in several countries places it on different heads, and he comes by right of succession to be a prince in one place, who would be a subject in another.

*   *   *

FROM CHAPTER II. WHO HEIR?

106. The great question which in all ages has disturbed mankind and brought on them the greatest part of those mischiefs which have ruined cities, depopulated countries, and disordered the peace of the world, has been, not whether there be power in the world, nor whence it came, but who should have it. The settling of this point being of no smaller moment than the security of princes and the peace and welfare of their kingdoms, a reformer of politics, I would think, should lay this sure and be very clear in it. For if this remains disputable, all the rest will be to little purpose, and the skill used in dressing up power with all the splendor and temptation absoluteness can add to it, without showing who has a right to have it will serve only to give a greater edge to man's natural ambition which of itself is too keen. What can this do but set men on the more eagerly to scramble, and so lay a sure and lasting foundation of endless contention and disorder instead of that peace and tranquility which is the business of government and the end of human society?

*   *   *

The Second Treatise of Government.
An Essay Concerning The True Original, Extent, and End of Civil Government

Chapter I.

§ 1. It having been shown in the foregoing discourse, 1. That Adam had not, either by natural right of fatherhood, or by positive donation from God, any such authority over his children, or dominion over the world, as is pretended:

2. That if he had, his heirs yet had no right to it:

3. That if his heirs had, there being no law of nature nor positive law of God that determines which is the right heir in all cases that may arise, the right of succession, and consequently of bearing rule, could not have been certainly determined:

4. That if even that had been determined, yet the knowledge of which is the eldest line of Adam's posterity being so long since utterly lost, that in the races of mankind and families of the world there remains not to one above another the least pretence to be the eldest house, and to have the right of inheritance:

All these premises having, as I think, been clearly made out, it is impossible that the rulers now on earth should make any benefit, or derive any the least shadow of authority from that, which is held to be the fountain of all power, Adam's private dominion and paternal jurisdiction; so that he that will not give just occasion to think that all government in the world is the product only of force and violence, and that men live together by no other rules but that of beasts, where the strongest carries it, and so lay a foundation for perpetual disorder and mischief, tumult, sedition, and rebellion, (things that the followers of that hypothesis so loudly cry out against) must of necessity find out another rise of government, another original of political power, and another way of designing and knowing the persons that have it, than what Sir Robert Filmer[1] hath taught us.

§ 2. To this purpose, I think it may not be amiss to set down what I take to be political power; that the power of a magistrate over a subject may be distinguished from that of a father over his children, a master over his servants, a husband over his wife, and a lord over his slave. All which distinct powers happening sometimes together in the same man, if he be considered under these different relations, it may help us to distinguish these powers one from another, and show the difference betwixt a ruler of a commonwealth, a father of a family, and a captain of a galley.

---

1. Locke devotes the *First Treatise* to refuting Filmer but rarely refers to him in the *Second Treatise*. All notes are the editor's unless otherwise specified.

§ 3. Political power, then, I take to be a right of making laws with penalties of death, and consequently all less penalties, for the regulating and preserving of property, and of employing the force of the community, in the execution of such laws, and in the defence of the commonwealth from foreign injury; and all this only for the public good.

Chapter II.

OF THE STATE OF NATURE.

§ 4. To understand political power right, and derive it from its original, we must consider what state all men are naturally in, and that is, a state of perfect freedom to order their actions and dispose of their possessions and person, as they think fit, within the bounds of the law of nature; without asking leave, or depending upon the will of any other man.

A state also of equality, wherein all the power and jurisdiction is reciprocal, no one having more than another; there being nothing more evident than that creatures of the same species and rank, promiscuously born to all the same advantages of nature, and the use of the same faculties, should also be equal one amongst another without subordination or subjection; unless the Lord and Master of them all should, by any manifest declaration of his will, set one above another, and confer on him, by an evident and clear appointment, an undoubted right to dominion and sovereignty.

§ 5. This equality of men by nature the judicious Hooker[2] looks upon as so evident in itself, and beyond all question, that he makes it the foundation of that obligation to mutual love amongst men, on which he builds the duties they owe one another, and from whence he derives the great maxims of justice and charity. His words are,

"The like natural inducement hath brought men to know that it is no less their duty to love others than themselves; for seeing those things which are equal must needs all have one measure; if I cannot but wish to receive good, even as much at every man's hands as any man can wish unto his own soul, how should I look to have any part of my desire herein satisfied, unless myself be careful to satisfy the like desire, which is undoubtedly in other men, being of one and the same nature? To have anything offered them repugnant to this desire must needs in all respects grieve them as much as me; so that, if I do harm, I must look to suffer, there being no reason

---

2. Richard Hooker (1554–1600), Anglican theologian who wrote *On the Laws of Ecclesiastical Polity* (see p. 222 herein), a defense of Anglicanism that draws on the Aristotelian—Thomistic tradition in discussions of natural law and community consent. It is quoted frequently in the *Second Treatise*.

that others should show greater measure of love to me than they
have by me showed unto them: my desire therefore to be loved of
my equals in nature, as much as possibly may be, imposeth upon
me a natural duty of bearing to them-ward fully the like affection:
from which relation of equality between ourselves and them that
are as ourselves, what several rules and canons natural reason hath
drawn, for direction of life, no man is ignorant."[3]

§ 6. But though this be a state of liberty, yet it is not a state of licence: though man in that state have an uncontrollable liberty to
dispose of his person or possessions, yet he has not liberty to destroy himself, or so much as any creature in his possession, but
where some nobler use than its bare preservation calls for it. The
state of nature has a law of nature to govern it, which obliges everyone: and reason, which is that law, teaches all mankind, who will
but consult it, that being all equal and independent, no one ought
to harm another in his life, health, liberty, or possessions: for men
being all the workmanship of one omnipotent and infinitely wise
Maker;[4] all the servants of one sovereign Master, sent into the
world by his order, and about his business; they are his property,
whose workmanship they are, made to last during his, not one another's pleasure: and being furnished with like faculties, sharing all
in one community of nature, there cannot be supposed any such
subordination among us that may authorize us to destroy another,
as if we were made for one another's uses, as the inferior ranks of
creatures are for ours. Everyone, as he is bound to preserve himself, and not to quit his station wilfully, so by the like reason, when
his own preservation comes not in competition, ought he, as much
as he can, to preserve the rest of mankind, and may not, unless it
be to do justice to an offender, take away or impair the life, or what
tends to the preservation of life, the liberty, health, limb, or goods
of another.

§ 7. And that all men may be restrained from invading others'
rights, and from doing hurt to one another, and the law of nature
be observed, which willeth the peace and preservation of all
mankind, the execution of the law of nature is, in that state, put
into every man's hands, whereby everyone has a right to punish the
transgressors of that law to such a degree as many hinder its violation: for the law of nature would, as all other laws that concern
men in this world, be in vain, if there were nobody that in the state
of nature had a power to execute that law, and thereby preserve the

3. Hooker's *Ecclesiastical Polity*, I.8.7.
4. Locke's arguments for equality and the right (duty) of self-preservation are based on
common creation by God. On the relation of Locke's theism to his theory, see A. John
Simmons (p. 286 herein), John Dunn (p. 366 herein), and Jeremy Waldron (p. 313
herein).

innocent, and restrain offenders. And if anyone in the state of nature may punish another for any evil he has done, everyone may do
so: for in that state of perfect equality, where naturally there is no
superiority or jurisdiction of one over another, what any may do in
prosecution of that law everyone must needs have a right to do.

§ 8. And thus, in the state of nature, one man comes by a power
over another; but yet no absolute or arbitrary power to use a criminal, when he has got him in his hands, according to the passionate
heats or boundless extravagancy of his own will; but only to retribute to him, so far as calm reason and conscience dictate, what is
proportionate to his transgression; which is so much as may serve
for reparation and restraint: for these two are the only reasons why
one man may lawfully do harm to another, which is that we call
punishment. In transgressing the law of nature, the offender declares himself to live by another rule than that of reason and common equity, which is that measure God has set to the actions of
men for their mutual security; and so he becomes dangerous to
mankind, the tie, which is to secure them from injury and violence,
being slighted and broken by him: which being a trespass against
the whole species, and the peace and safety of it, provided for by
the law of nature; every man upon this score, by the right he hath
to preserve mankind in general, may restrain, or, where it is necessary, destroy things noxious to them, and so may bring such evil on
any one, who hath transgressed that law, as may make him repent
the doing of it, and thereby deter him, and by his example others,
from doing the like mischief. And in this case, and upon this
ground, every man hath a right to punish the offender, and be executioner of the law of nature.

§ 9. I doubt not but this will seem a very strange doctrine to
some men: but, before they condemn it, I desire them to resolve me
by what right any prince or state can put to death or punish an
alien for any crime he commits in their country. It is certain their
laws, by virtue of any sanction they receive from the promulgated
will of the legislative, reach not a stranger: they speak not to him,
nor, if they did, is he bound to hearken to them. The legislative authority, by which they are in force over the subjects of that commonwealth, hath no power over him. Those who have the supreme
power of making laws in England, France, or Holland, are to an Indian but like the rest of the world, men without authority: and
therefore, if by the law of nature every man hath not a power to
punish offences against it, as he soberly judges the case to require,
I see not how the magistrates of any community can punish an
alien of another country; since, in reference to him, they can have
no more power than what every man naturally may have over another.

§ 10. Besides the crime which consists in violating the law, and varying from the right rule of reason, whereby a man so far becomes degenerate, and declares himself to quit the principles of human nature, and to be a noxious creature, there is commonly injury done to some person or other, and some other man receives damage by his transgression: in which case he who hath received any damage, has, besides the right of punishment common to him with other men, a particular right to seek reparation from him that has done it: and any other person, who finds it just, may also join with him that is injured, and assist him in recovering from the offender so much as may make satisfaction for the harm he has suffered.

§ 11. From these two distinct rights, the one of punishing the crime for restraint, and preventing the like offence, which right of punishing is in everybody; the other of taking reparation, which belongs only to the injured party; comes it to pass that the magistrate, who by being magistrate hath the common right of punishing put into his hands, can often, where the public good demands not the execution of the law, remit the punishment of criminal offences by his own authority, but yet cannot remit the satisfaction due to any private man for the damage he has received. That he who has suffered the damage has a right to demand in his own name, and he alone can remit: the damnified person has this power of appropriating to himself the goods or service of the offender, by right of self-preservation, as every man has a power to punish the crime, to prevent its being committed again, "by the right he has of preserving all mankind," and doing all reasonable things he can in order to that end: and thus it is that every man, in the state of nature, has a power to kill a murderer, both to deter others from doing the like injury, which no reparation can compensate, by the example of the punishment that attends it from every body; and also to secure men from the attempts of a criminal, who having renounced reason, the common rule and measure God hath given to mankind, hath, by the unjust violence and slaughter he hath committed upon one, declared war against all mankind; and therefore may be destroyed as a lion or a tiger, one of those wild savage beasts with whom men can have no society nor security: and upon this is grounded that great law of nature, "Whoso sheddeth man's blood, by man shall his blood be shed."[5] And Cain was so fully convinced that everyone had a right to destroy such a criminal, that, after the murder of his brother, he cries out, "Every one that findeth me shall slay me;" so plain was it writ in the hearts of mankind.[6]

5. Genesis 9:6.
6. Genesis 4:14.

§ 12. By the same reason may a man in the state of nature punish the lesser breaches of that law. It will perhaps be demanded,
with death? I answer, each transgression may be punished to that
degree, and with so much severity, as will suffice to make it an ill
bargain to the offender, give him cause to repent, and terrify others
from doing the like. Every offence, that can be committed in the
state of nature, may in the state of nature be also punished equally,
and as far forth, as it may in a commonwealth: for though it would
be beside my present purpose to enter here into the particulars of
the law of nature, or its measures of punishment, yet it is certain
there is such a law, and that too as intelligible and plain to a rational creature, and a studier of that law,[7] as the positive laws of
commonwealths; nay, possibly plainer, as much as reason is easier
to be understood than the fancies and intricate contrivances of
men, following contrary and hidden interests put into words; for so
truly are a great part of the municipal laws of countries, which are
only so far right, as they are founded on the law of nature, by which
they are to be regulated and interpreted.

§ 13. To this strange doctrine, viz. That "in the state of nature
everyone has the executive power" of the law of nature, I doubt not
but it will be objected, that it is unreasonable for men to be judges
in their own cases, that self-love will make men partial to themselves and their friends: and, on the other side, that ill-nature, passion, and revenge will carry them too far in punishing others; and
hence nothing but confusion and disorder will follow: and that
therefore God hath certainly appointed government to restrain the
partiality and violence of men. I easily grant, that civil government
is the proper remedy for the inconveniencies of the state of nature,
which must certainly be great, where men may be judges in their
own case; since it is easy to be imagined, that he who was so unjust
as to do his brother an injury, will scarce be so just as to condemn
himself for it: but I shall desire those who make this objection to
remember, that absolute monarchs are but men; and if government
is to be the remedy of those evils, which necessarily follow from
men's being judges in their own cases, and the state of nature is
therefore not to be endured; I desire to know what kind of government that is, and how much better it is than the state of nature,
where one man, commanding a multitude, has the liberty to be
judge in his own case, and may do to all his subjects whatever he
pleases, without the least liberty to anyone to question or control
those who execute his pleasure and whatsoever he doth, whether
led by reason, mistake, or passion, must be submitted to? Much

---

7. Cf. Locke's later discussion of the accessibility of natural law in *The Reasonableness of
   Christianity* (p. 214 herein).

better it is in the state of nature, wherein men are not bound to submit to the unjust will of another: and if he that judges, judges amiss in his own, or any other case, he is answerable for it to the rest of mankind.

§ 14. It is often asked, as a mighty objection, "where are or ever were there any men in such a state of nature?" To which it may suffice as an answer at present, that since all princes and rulers of independent governments, all through the world, are in a state of nature, it is plain the world never was, nor ever will be, without numbers of men in that state. I have named all governors of independent communities, whether they are, or are not, in league with others: for it is not every compact that puts an end to the state of nature between men, but only this one of agreeing together mutually to enter into one community, and make one body politic; other promises and compacts men may make one with another, and yet still be in the state of nature. The promises and bargains for truck, &c. between the two men in the desert island, mentioned by Garcilasso de la Vega, in his history of Peru;[8] or between a Swiss and an Indian, in the woods of America; are binding to them, though they are perfectly in a state of nature, in reference to one another: for truth and keeping of faith belongs to men as men, and not as members of society.

§ 15. To those that say, there were never any men in the state of nature, I will not only oppose the authority of the judicious Hooker, Eccl. Pol. lib.i. sect. 10, where he says, "The laws which have been hitherto mentioned," *i.e.* the laws of nature, "do bind men absolutely, even as they are men, although they have never any settled fellowship, never any solemn agreement amongst themselves what to do, or not to do: but forasmuch as we are not by ourselves sufficient to furnish ourselves with competent store of things, needful for such a life as our nature doth desire, a life fit for the dignity of man; therefore to supply those defects and imperfections which are in us, as living singly and solely by ourselves, we are naturally induced to seek communion and fellowship with others. This was the cause of men's uniting themselves at first in politic societies." But I moreover affirm, that all men are naturally in that state, and remain so, till by their own consents they make themselves members of some politic society; and I doubt not in the sequel of this discourse to make it very clear.

---

8. *Commentarios Reales*, 1.1.8. Locke used the French translation, *Histoire des Incas*. For a modern translation see de la Vega, *Royal Commentaries of the Incas*, trans. Harold V. Livermore (Austin: University of Texas Press, 1966).

Chapter III.

OF THE STATE OF WAR.

§ 16. THE state of war is a state of enmity and destruction: and therefore declaring by word or action, not a passionate and hasty, but a sedate, settled design upon another man's life, puts him in a state of war with him against whom he has declared such an intention, and so has exposed his life to the other's power to be taken away by him, or anyone that joins with him in his defence, and espouses his quarrel; it being reasonable and just, I should have a right to destroy that which threatens me with destruction: for, by the fundamental law of nature, man being to be preserved as much as possible, when all cannot be preserved, the safety of the innocent is to be preferred: and one may destroy a man who makes war upon him, or has discovered an enmity to his being, for the same reason that he may kill a wolf or a lion; because such men are not under the ties of the common law of reason, have no other rule but that of force and violence, and so may be treated as beasts of prey, those dangerous and noxious creatures, that will be sure to destroy him whenever he falls into their power.

§ 17. And hence it is, that he who attempts to get another man into his absolute power, does thereby put himself into a state of war with him; it being to be understood as a declaration of a design upon his life: for I have reason to conclude, that he who would get me into his power without my consent, would use me as he pleased when he got me there, and destroy me too when he had a fancy to it; for nobody can desire to have me in his absolute power, unless it be to compel me by force to that which is against the right of my freedom, *i.e.* make me a slave. To be free from such force is the only security of my preservation; and reason bids me look on him as an enemy to my preservation, who would take away that freedom which is the fence to it; so that he who makes an attempt to enslave me, thereby puts himself into a state of war with me. He that, in the state of nature, would take away the freedom that belongs to anyone in that state, must necessarily be supposed to have a design to take away everything else, that freedom being the foundation of all the rest; as he that, in the state of society, would take away the freedom belonging to those of that society or commonwealth, must be supposed to design to take away from them everything else, and so be looked on as in a state of war.

§ 18. This makes it lawful for a man to kill a thief, who has not in the least hurt him, nor declared any design upon his life, any farther than, by the use of force, so to get him in his power, as to take away his money, or what he pleases, from him; because using force, where he has no right, to get me into his power, let his pretence be what it will, I have no reason to suppose, that he, who would take away my liberty, would not, when he had me in his power, take away every thing else. And therefore it is lawful for me to treat him as one who has put himself into a state of war with me, *i. e.* kill him if I can; for to that hazard does he justly expose himself, whoever introduces a state of war, and is aggressor in it.

§ 19. And here we have the plain difference between the state of nature and the state of war; which, however some men have confounded, are as far distant as a state of peace, good-will, mutual assistance and preservation, and a state of enmity, malice, violence, and mutual destruction, are one from another. Men living together according to reason, without a common superior on earth, with authority to judge between them, is properly the state of nature. But force, or a declared design of force, upon the person of another, where there is no common superior on earth to appeal to for relief, is the state of war: and it is the want of such an appeal gives a man the right of war even against an aggressor, though he be in society, and a fellow-subject. Thus a thief, whom I cannot harm, but by appeal to the law, for having stolen all that I am worth, I may kill, when he sets on me to rob me but of my horse or coat; because the law, which was made for my preservation, where it cannot interpose to secure my life from present force, which, if lost, is capable of no reparation, permits me my own defence, and the right of war, a liberty to kill the aggressor, because the aggressor allows not time to appeal to our common judge, nor the decision of the law, for remedy in a case where the mischief may be irreparable. Want of a common judge with authority puts all men in a state of nature: force without right, upon a man's person, makes a state of war, both where there is, and is not, a common judge.

§ 20. But when the actual force is over, the state of war ceases between those that are in society, and are equally on both sides subjected to the fair determination of the law; because then there lies open the remedy of appeal for the past injury, and to prevent future harm: but where no such appeal is, as in the state of nature, for want of positive laws, and judges with authority to appeal to, the state of war once begun, continues with a right to the innocent party to destroy the other whenever he can, until the aggressor offers peace, and desires reconciliation on such terms as may repair any wrongs he has already done, and secure the innocent for the future; nay, where an appeal to the law, and constituted judges, lies open, but the remedy is denied by a manifest perverting of justice, and a barefaced wresting of the laws to protect or indemnify the violence or injuries of some men, or party of men; there it is hard to imagine anything but a state of war: for wherever violence is used, and injury done, though by hands appointed to administer justice, it is still violence and injury, however coloured with the name, pretences, or forms of law, the end whereof being to protect and redress the innocent, by an unbiassed application of it, to all who are under it; wherever that is not *bona fide* done, war is made upon the sufferers, who having no appeal on earth to right them, they are left to the only remedy in such cases, an appeal to Heaven.[9]

§ 21. To avoid this state of war (wherein there is no appeal but to Heaven, and wherein every the least difference is apt to end, where there is no authority to decide between the contenders) is one great reason of men's putting themselves into society, and quitting the state of nature: for where there is an authority, a power on earth, from which relief can be had by appeal, there the continuance of the state of war is excluded, and the controversy is decided by that power. Had there been any such court, any superior jurisdiction on earth, to determine the right between Jephthah and the Ammonites, they had never come to a state of war: but we see he was forced to appeal to Heaven: "The Lord the Judge (says he) be judge this day, between the children of Israel and the children of Ammon," Judg. xi. 27; and then prosecuting, and relying on his appeal, he leads out his army to battle: and therefore in such controversies, where the question is put, who shall be judge? it cannot be meant, who shall decide the controversy; everyone knows what Jephthah here tells us, that "the Lord the Judge" shall judge. Where there is no judge on earth, the appeal lies to God in heaven. That question then cannot mean, who shall judge whether another hath put himself in a state of war with me, and whether I may, as Jephthah did, appeal to Heaven in it. Of that I myself can only be judge in my own conscience, as I will answer it, at the great day, to the supreme Judge of all men.

Chapter IV.

OF SLAVERY.

§ 22. THE natural liberty of man is to be free from any superior power on earth, and not to be under the will or legislative authority of man, but to have only the law of nature for his rule. The liberty of man, in society, is to be under no other legislative power, but that established, by consent, in the commonwealth; nor under the dominion of any will, or restraint of any law, but what that legislative shall enact, according to the trust put in it. Freedom, then, is not what sir Robert Filmer tells us, "a liberty for everyone to do

---

9. I.e., the resort to arms.

what he lists, to live as he pleases, and not to be tied by any laws:"[1] but freedom of men under government is, to have a standing rule to live by, common to everyone of that society, and made by the legislative power erected in it; a liberty to follow my own will in all things, where the rule prescribes not; and not to be subject to the inconstant, uncertain, unknown, arbitrary will of another man: as freedom of nature is, to be under no other restraint but the law of nature.

§ 23. This freedom from absolute, arbitrary power, is so necessary to, and closely joined with, a man's preservation, that he cannot part with it, but by what forfeits his preservation and life together: for a man, not having the power of his own life, cannot, by compact, or his own consent, enslave himself to any one, nor put himself under the absolute, arbitrary power of another, to take away his life when he pleases. Nobody can give more power than he has himself; and he that cannot take away his own life, cannot give another power over it. Indeed, having by his fault forfeited his own life, by some act that deserves death; he, to whom he has forfeited it, may (when he has him in his power) delay to take it, and make use of him to his own service, and he does him no injury by it: for, whenever he finds the hardship of his slavery outweigh the value of his life, it is in his power, by resisting the will of his master, to draw on himself the death he desires.

§ 24. This is the perfect condition of slavery, which is nothing else but the state of war continued, between a lawful conqueror and a captive: for, if once compact enter between them, and make an agreement for a limited power on the one side, and obedience on the other, the state of war and slavery ceases, as long as the compact endures: for, as has been said, no man can, by agreement, pass over to another that which he hath not in himself, a power over his own life.

I confess, we find among the Jews, as well as other nations, that men did sell themselves; but, it is plain, this was only to drudgery, not to slavery: for, it is evident, the person sold was not under an absolute, arbitrary, despotical power: for the master could not have power to kill him, at any time, whom, at a certain time, he was obliged to let go free out of his service; and the master of such a servant was so far from having an arbitrary power over his life, that he could not, at pleasure, so much as maim him, but the loss of an eye, or tooth, set him free. Exod. xxi.

---

1. Filmer's *Observations on Aristotle* in *Patriarcha and Other Writings*, ed. Johann P. Sommerville (Cambridge: Cambridge University Press, 1991), 275.

Chapter V.

OF PROPERTY.

§ 25. WHETHER we consider natural reason, which tells us, that men, being once born, have a right to their preservation, and consequently to meat and drink, and such other things as nature affords for their subsistence; or revelation, which gives us an account of those grants God made of the world to Adam, and to Noah, and his sons; it is very clear, that God, as King David says, Psal. cxv. 16, "has given the earth to the children of men;" given it to mankind in common. But this being supposed, it seems to some a very great difficulty how anyone should ever come to have a property in any thing: I will not content myself to answer, that if it be difficult to make out property, upon a supposition that God gave the world to Adam and his posterity in common, it is impossible that any man, but one universal monarch, should have any property, upon an supposition that God gave the world to Adam, and his heirs in succession, exclusive of all the rest of his posterity. But I shall endeavour to show how men might come to have a property in several parts of that which God gave to mankind in common, and that without any express compact of all the commoners.

§ 26. God, who hath given the world to men in common, hath also given them reason to make use of it to the best advantage of life and convenience. The earth, and all that is therein, is given to men for the support and comfort of their being. And though all the fruits it naturally produces, and beasts it feeds, belong to mankind in common, as they are produced by the spontaneous hand of nature; and nobody has originally a private dominion, exclusive of the rest of mankind, in any of them, as they are thus in their natural state: yet being given for the use of men, there must of necessity be a means to appropriate them some way or other before they can be of any use, or at all beneficial to any particular man. The fruit, or venison, which nourishes the wild Indian, who knows no enclosure, and is still a tenant in common, must be his, and so his, *i. e.* a part of him, that another can no longer have any right to it, before it can do him any good for the support of his life.

§ 27. Though the earth, and all inferior creatures, be common to all men, yet every man has a property in his own person: this nobody has any right to but himself. The labour of his body, and the work of his hands, we may say, are properly his. Whatsoever then he removes out of the state that nature hath provided, and left it in, he hath mixed his labour with, and joined to it something that is his own, and thereby makes it his property. It being by him removed from the common state nature hath placed it in, it hath by this labour something annexed to it that excludes the common right of other men. For this labour being the unquestionable property of the labourer, no man but he can have a right to what that is once joined to, at least where there is enough, and as good, left in common for others.

§ 28. He that is nourished by the acorns he picked up under an oak, or the apples he gathered from the trees in the wood, has certainly appropriated them to himself. Nobody can deny but the nourishment is his. I ask then, when did they begin to be his? when he digested? or when he ate? or when he boiled? or when he brought them home? or when he picked them up? and it is plain, if the first gathering made them not his, nothing else could. That labour put a distinction between them and common: that added something to them more than nature, the common mother of all, had done; and so they became his private right. And will anyone say, he had no right to those acorns or apples he thus appropriated, because he had not the consent of all mankind to make them his? was it a robbery thus to assume to himself what belonged to all in common? If such a consent as that was necessary, man had starved, notwithstanding the plenty God had given him. We see in commons, which remain so by compact, that it is the taking any part of what is common, and removing it out of the state nature leaves it in, which begins the property; without which the common is of no use. And the taking of this or that part does not depend on the express consent of all the commoners. Thus the grass my horse has bit; the turfs my servant has cut; and the ore I have digged in any place, where I have a right to them in common with others; become my property, without the assignation or consent of any body. The labour that was mine, removing them out of that common state they were in, hath fixed my property in them.

§ 29. By making an explicit consent of every commoner necessary to any one's appropriating to himself any part of what is given in common, children or servants could not cut the meat, which their father or master had provided for them in common, without assigning to every one his peculiar part. Though the water running in the fountain be everyone's, yet who can doubt but that in the pitcher is his only who drew it out? His labour hath taken it out of the hands of nature, where it was common, and belonged equally to all her children, and hath thereby appropriated it to himself.

§ 30. Thus this law of reason makes the deer that Indian's who hath killed it; it is allowed to be his goods who hath bestowed his labour upon it, though before it was the common right of everyone. And amongst those who are counted the civilized part of mankind, who have made and multiplied positive laws to determine property, this original law of nature, for the beginning of property, in what was before common, still takes place; and by virtue thereof, what fish any one catches in the ocean, that great and still remaining common of mankind; or what ambergris[2] any one takes up here, is by the labour that removes it out of that common state nature left it in made his property who takes that pains about it. And even amongst us, the hare that any one is hunting is thought his who pursues her during the chase: for being a beast that is still looked upon as common, and no man's private possession; whoever has employed so much labour about any of that kind, as to find and pursue her, has thereby removed her from the state of nature, wherein she was common, and hath begun a property.

§ 31. It will perhaps be objected to this, that if gathering the acorns, or other fruits of the earth, &c. makes a right to them, then anyone may engross as much as he will. To which I answer, Not so. The same law of nature, that does by this means give us property, does also bound that property too. "God has given us all things richly," 1 Tim. vi. 17, is the voice of reason confirmed by inspiration. But how far has he given it us? To enjoy. As much as anyone can make use of to any advantage of life before it spoils, so much he may by his labour fix a property in: whatever is beyond this, is more than his share, and belongs to others. Nothing was made by God for man to spoil or destroy. And thus, considering the plenty of natural provisions there was a long time in the world, and the few spenders; and to how small a part of that provision the industry of one man could extend itself, and engross it to the prejudice of others; especially keeping within the bounds, set by reason, of what might serve for his use; there could be then little room for quarrels or contentions about property so established.

§ 32. But the chief matter of property being now not the fruits of the earth, and the beasts that subsist on it, but the earth itself; as that which takes in, and carries with it all the rest; I think it is plain, that property in that too is acquired as the former. As much land as a man tills, plants, improves, cultivates, and can use the product of, so much is his property. He by his labour does, as it were, enclose it from the common. Nor will it invalidate his right, to say every body else has an equal title to it, and therefore he cannot appropriate, he cannot enclose, without the consent of all his fellow-commoners, all mankind. God, when he gave the world in common to all mankind, commanded man also to labour, and the penury of his condition required it of him. God and his reason commanded him to subdue the earth, *i. e.* improve it for the benefit of life, and therein lay out something upon it that was his own, his labour. He that, in obedience to this command of God, sub-

2. Wax-like substance found in tropical seas and used in perfumery.

dued, tilled, and sowed any part of it, thereby annexed to it something that was his property, which another had no title to, nor could without injury take from him.

§ 33. Nor was this appropriation of any parcel of land, by improving it, any prejudice to any other man, since there was still enough, and as good left; and more than the yet unprovided could use. So that, in effect, there was never the less left for others because of his enclosure for himself: for he that leaves as much as another can make use of, does as good as take nothing at all. Nobody could think himself injured by the drinking of another man, though he took a good draught, who had a whole river of the same water left him to quench his thirst; and the case of land and water, where there is enough of both, is perfectly the same.

§ 34. God gave the world to men in common; but since he gave it them for their benefit, and the greatest conveniencies of life they were capable to draw from it, it cannot be supposed he meant it should always remain common and uncultivated. He gave it to the use of the industrious and rational (and labour was to be his title to it), not to the fancy or covetousness of the quarrelsome and contentious. He that had as good left for his improvement as was already taken up, needed not complain, ought not to meddle with what was already improved by another's labour: if he did, it is plain he desired the benefit of another's pains, which he had no right to, and not the ground which God had given him in common with others to labour on, and whereof there was as good left as that already possessed, and more than he knew what to do with, or his industry could reach to.

§ 35. It is true, in land that is common in England, or any other country, where there is plenty of people under government, who have money and commerce, no one can enclose or appropriate any part without the consent of all his fellow-commoners; because this is left common by compact, *i.e.* by the law of the land, which is not to be violated. And though it be common, in respect of some men, it is not so to all mankind, but is the joint property of this county, or this parish. Besides, the remainder, after such enclosure, would not be as good to the rest of the commoners as the whole was when they could all make use of the whole; whereas in the beginning and first peopling of the great common of the world it was quite otherwise. The law man was under was rather for appropriating. God commanded, and his wants forced him to labour. That was his property which could not be taken from him wherever he had fixed it. And hence subduing or cultivating the earth, and having dominion, we see are joined together. The one gave title to the other. So that God, by commanding to subdue, gave authority so far to appropriate: and the condition of human life, which requires labour

and materials to work on, necessarily introduces private possessions.

§ 36. The measure of property nature has well set by the extent
of men's labour and the conveniences of life: no man's labour could
subdue, or appropriate all; nor could his enjoyment consume more
than a small part; so that it was impossible for any man, this way, to
intrench upon the right of another, or acquire to himself a property,
to the prejudice of his neighbour, who would still have room for as
good and as large a possession (after the other had taken out his) as
before it was appropriated. This measure did confine every man's
possession to a very moderate proportion, and such as he might appropriate to himself, without injury to any body, in the first ages of
the world, when men were more in danger to be lost, by wandering
from their company, in the then vast wilderness of the earth, than
to be straitened for want of room to plant in. And the same measure may be allowed still without prejudice to any body, as full as
the world seems: for supposing a man, or family, in the state they
were at first peopling of the world by the children of Adam, or
Noah; let him plant in some inland, vacant places of America, we
shall find that the possessions he could make himself, upon the
measures we have given, would not be very large, nor, even to this
day, prejudice the rest of mankind, or give them reason to complain, or think themselves injured by this man's encroachment;
though the race of men have now spread themselves to all the corners of the world, and do infinitely exceed the small number
[which] was at the beginning. Nay, the extent of ground is of so little value, without labour, that I have heard it affirmed, that in
Spain itself a man may be permitted to plough, sow, and reap, without being disturbed, upon land he has no other title to, but only his
making use of it. But, on the contrary, the inhabitants think themselves beholden to him, who, by his industry on neglected, and consequently waste land, has increased the stock of corn, which they
wanted. But be this as it will, which I lay no stress on; this I dare
boldly affirm, that the same rule of propriety, viz. that every man
should have as much as he could make use of, would hold still in
the world, without straitening anybody; since there is land enough
in the world to suffice double the inhabitants, had not the invention of money, and the tacit agreement of men to put a value on it,
introduced (by consent) larger possessions, and a right to them;
which, how it has done, I shall by and by show more at large.

§ 37. This is certain, that in the beginning, before the desire of
having more than men needed had altered the intrinsic value of
things, which depends only on their usefulness to the life of man;
or had agreed, that a little piece of yellow metal, which would keep
without wasting or decay, should be worth a great piece of flesh, or

a whole heap of corn; though men had a right to appropriate, by
their labour, each one to himself, as much of the things of nature
as he could use: yet this could not be much, nor to the prejudice of
others, where the same plenty was still left to those who would use
the same industry. To which let me add, that he who appropriates
land to himself by his labour, does not lessen, but increase the
common stock of mankind: for the provisions serving to the support
of human life, produced by one acre of enclosed and cultivated
land, are (to speak much within compass) ten times more than
those which are yielded by an acre of land of an equal richness lying waste in common. And therefore he that encloses land, and has
a greater plenty of the conveniences of life from ten acres, than he
could have from an hundred left to nature, may truly be said to give
ninety acres to mankind: for his labour now supplies him with provisions out of ten acres, which were by the product of an hundred
lying in common. I have here rated the improved land very low, in
making its product but as ten to one, when it is much nearer an
hundred to one: for I ask, whether in the wild woods and uncultivated waste of America, left to nature, without any improvement,
tillage, or husbandry, a thousand acres yield the needy and
wretched inhabitants as many conveniencies of life as ten acres
equally fertile land do in Devonshire, where they are well cultivated.

Before the appropriation of land, he who gathered as much of
the wild fruit, killed, caught, or tamed, as many of the beasts, as he
could; he that so employed his pains about any of the spontaneous
products of nature, as any way to alter them from the state which
nature put them in, by placing any of his labour on them, did
thereby acquire a propriety in them: but if they perished, in his possession, without their due use; if the fruits rotted, or the venison
putrefied, before he could spend it; he offended against the common law of nature, and was liable to be punished; he invaded his
neighbour's share, for he had no right, farther than his use called
for any of them, and they might serve to afford him conveniencies
of life.

§ 38. The same measures governed the possession of land too:
whatsoever he tilled and reaped, laid up and made use of, before it
spoiled, that was his peculiar right; whatsoever he enclosed, and
could feed, and make use of, the cattle and product was also his.
But if either the grass of his enclosure rotted on the ground, or the
fruit of his planting perished without gathering and laying up; this
part of the earth, notwithstanding his enclosure, was still to be
looked on as waste, and might be the possession of any other. Thus,
at the beginning, Cain might take as much ground as he could till,
and make it his own land, and yet leave enough to Abel's sheep to

feed on; a few acres would serve for both their possessions. But as families increased, and industry enlarged their stocks, their possessions enlarged with the need of them; but yet it was commonly without any fixed property in the ground they made use of, till they incorporated, settled themselves together, and built cities; and then, by consent, they came in time to set out the bounds of their distinct territories, and agree on limits between them and their neighbours; and by laws within themselves settled the properties of those of the same society: for we see that in that part of the world which was first inhabited, and therefore like to be best peopled, even as low down as Abraham's time, they wandered with their flocks, and their herds, which was their substance, freely up and down; and this Abraham did, in a country where he was a stranger. Whence it is plain, that at least a great part of the land lay in common; that the inhabitants valued it not, nor claimed property in any more than they made use of. But when there was not room enough in the same place for their herds to feed together, they by consent, as Abraham and Lot did, Gen. xiii. 5, separated and enlarged their pasture, where it best liked them. And for the same reason Esau went from his father, and his brother, and planted in Mount Seir, Gen. xxxvi. 6.

§ 39. And thus, without supposing any private dominion and property in Adam, over all the world, exclusive of all other men, which can no way be proved, nor anyone's property be made out from it; but supposing the world given, as it was, to the children of men in common, we see how labour could make men distinct titles to several parcels of it, for their private uses; wherein there could be no doubt of right, no room for quarrel.

§ 40. Nor is it so strange, as perhaps before consideration it may appear, that the property of labour should be able to overbalance the community of land: for it is labour indeed that put the difference of value on everything; and let any one consider what the difference is between an acre of land planted with tobacco or sugar, sown with wheat or barley, and an acre of the same land lying in common, without any husbandry upon it, and he will find, that the improvement of labour makes the far greater part of the value. I think it will be but a very modest computation to say, that of the products of the earth useful to the life of man, nine-tenths are the effects of labour: nay, if we will rightly estimate things as they come to our use, and cast up the several expenses about them, what in them is purely owing to nature, and what to labour, we shall find, that in most of them ninety-nine hundredths are wholly to be put on the account of labour.

§ 41. There cannot be a clearer demonstration of anything, than several nations of the Americans are of this, who are rich in land,

and poor in all the comforts of life; whom nature having furnished as liberally as any other people with the materials of plenty, *i.e.* a fruitful soil, apt to produce in abundance what might serve for food, raiment, and delight; yet, for want of improving it by labour, have not one-hundredth part of the conveniencies we enjoy: and a king of a large and fruitful territory there feeds, lodges, and is clad worse than a day-labourer in England.

§ 42. To make this a little clearer, let us but trace some of the ordinary provisions of life, through their several progresses, before they come to our use, and see how much of their value they receive from human industry. Bread, wine, and cloth, are things of daily use, and great plenty; yet notwithstanding, acorns, water, and leaves, or skins, must be our bread, drink, and clothing, did not labour furnish us with these more useful commodities: for whatever bread is more worth than acorns, wine than water, and cloth or silk than leaves, skins, or moss, that is wholly owing to labour and industry; the one of these being the food and raiment which unassisted nature furnishes us with; the other, provisions which our industry and pains prepare for us; which, how much they exceed the other in value, when anyone hath computed, he will then see how much labour makes the far greatest part of the value of things we enjoy in this world: and the ground which produces the materials is scarce to be reckoned in as any, or, at most, but a very small part of it; so little, that even amongst us, land that is left wholly to nature, that hath no improvement of pasturage, tillage, or planting, is called, as indeed it is, waste; and we shall find the benefit of it amount to little more than nothing.

This shows how much numbers of men are to be preferred to largeness of dominions; and that the increase of hands, and the right of employing of them, is the great art of government: and that prince, who shall be so wise and godlike, as by established laws of liberty to secure protection and encouragement to the honest industry of mankind, against the oppression of power and narrowness of party, will quickly be too hard for his neighbours: but this by the by. To return to the argument in hand.

§ 43. An acre of land, that bears here twenty bushels of wheat, and another in America, which, with the same husbandry, would do the like, are, without doubt, of the same natural intrinsic value: but yet the benefit mankind receives from the one in a year is worth 5£. [pounds] and from the other possibly not worth a penny, if all the profit an Indian received from it were to be valued, and sold here; at least, I may truly say, not one thousandth. It is labour, then, which puts the greatest part of the value upon land, without which it would scarcely be worth anything: it is to that we owe the greatest part of all its useful products; for all that the straw, bran, bread, of that acre of wheat, is more worth than the product of an acre of as good land, which lies waste, is all the effect of labour: for it is not barely the ploughman's pains, the reaper's and thresher's toil, and the baker's sweat [that] is to be counted into the bread we eat; the labour of those who broke the oxen, who digged and wrought the iron and stones, who felled and framed the timber employed about the plough, mill, oven, or any other utensils, which are a vast number, requisite to this corn, from its being seed to be sown to its being made bread, must all be charged on the account of labour, and received as an effect of that: nature and the earth furnished only the almost worthless materials, as in themselves. It would be a strange catalogue of things, that industry provided and made use of, about every loaf of bread, before it came to our use, if we could trace them; iron, wood, leather, bark, timber, stone, bricks, coals, lime, cloth, dyeing, drugs, pitch, tar, masts, ropes, and all the materials made use of in the ship, that brought any of the commodities used by any of the workmen, to any part of the work: all which it would be almost impossible, at least too long, to reckon up.

§ 44. From all which it is evident, that though the things of nature are given in common, yet man, by being master of himself, and proprietor of his own person, and the actions or labour of it, had still in himself the great foundation of property; and that which made up the greater part of what he applied to the support or comfort of his being, when invention and arts had improved the conveniencies of life, was perfectly his own, and did not belong in common to others.

§ 45. Thus labour, in the beginning, gave a right of property wherever anyone was pleased to employ it upon what was common, which remained a long while the far greater part, and is yet more than mankind makes use of. Men, at first, for the most part, contented themselves with what unassisted nature offered to their necessities: and though afterwards, in some parts of the world, (where the increase of people and stock, with the use of money, had made land scarce, and so of some value) the several communities settled the bounds of their distinct territories, and by laws within themselves regulated the properties of the private men of their society, and so, by compact and agreement, settled the property which labour and industry began: and the leagues that have been made between several states and kingdoms, either expressly or tacitly disowning all claim and right to the land in the others' possession, have, by common consent, given up their pretences to their natural common right, which originally they had to those countries, and so have, by positive agreement, settled a property amongst themselves, in distinct parts and parcels of the earth; yet there are still great tracts of ground to be found, which (the inhabitants thereof not having joined with the rest of mankind in the consent of the use of their common money) lie waste, and are more than the people who dwell on it do or can make use of, and so still lie in common; though this can scarce happen amongst that part of mankind that have consented to the use of money.

§ 46. The greatest part of things really useful to the life of man, and such as the necessity of subsisting made the first commoners of the world look after, as it doth the Americans now, are generally things of short duration; such as, if they are not consumed by use, will decay and perish of themselves: gold, silver, and diamonds, are things that fancy or agreement hath put the value on, more than real use, and the necessary support of life. Now of those good things which nature hath provided in common, everyone had a right (as hath been said) to as much as he could use, and property in all that he could effect with his labour; all that his industry could extend to, to alter from the state nature had put it in, was his. He that gathered a hundred bushels of acorns or apples, had thereby a property in them; they were his goods as soon as gathered. He was only to look that he used them before they spoiled, else he took more than his share, and robbed others. And indeed it was a foolish thing, as well as dishonest, to hoard up more than he could make use of. If he gave away a part to anybody else, so that it perished not uselessly in his possession, these he also made use of. And if he also bartered away plums, that would have rotted in a week, for nuts that would last good for his eating a whole year, he did no injury; he wasted not the common stock; destroyed no part of the portion of the goods that belonged to others, so long as nothing perished uselessly in his hands. Again, if he would give his nuts for a piece of metal, pleased with its colour; or exchange his sheep for shells, or wool for a sparkling pebble or a diamond, and keep those by him all his life, he invaded not the right of others; he might heap as much of these durable things as he pleased; the exceeding of the bounds of his just property not lying in the largeness of his possession, but the perishing of any thing uselessly in it.

§ 47. And thus came in the use of money, some lasting thing that men might keep without spoiling, and that by mutual consent men would take in exchange for the truly useful, but perishable supports of life.

§ 48. And as different degrees of industry were apt to give men possessions in different proportions, so this invention of money gave them the opportunity to continue and enlarge them: for supposing an island, separate from all possible commerce with the rest of the world, wherein there were but an hundred families, but there were sheep, horses, and cows, with other useful animals, wholesome fruits, and land enough for corn for a hundred thousand

times as many, but nothing in the island, either because of its com-
monness, or perishableness, fit to supply the place of money; what
reason could anyone have there to enlarge his possessions beyond
the use of his family and a plentiful supply to its consumption, either in what their own industry produced, or they could barter for
like perishable, useful commodities with others? Where there is not
something, both lasting and scarce, and so valuable, to be hoarded
up, there men will not be apt to enlarge their possessions of land,
were it ever so rich, ever so free for them to take: for I ask, what
would a man value ten thousand, or an hundred thousand acres of
excellent land, ready cultivated, and well stocked too with cattle, in
the middle of the inland parts of America, where he had no hopes
of commerce with other parts of the world, to draw money to him
by the sale of the product? It would not be worth the enclosing, and
we should see him give up again to the wild common of nature,
whatever was more than would supply the conveniencies of life to
be had there for him and his family.

§ 49. Thus in the beginning all the world was America, and more
so than that is now; for no such thing as money was any where
known. Find out something that hath the use and value of money
amongst his neighbours, you shall see the same man will begin
presently to enlarge his possessions.

§ 50. But since gold and silver, being little useful to the life of
man in proportion to food, raiment, and carriage, has its value only
from the consent of men, whereof labour yet makes, in great part,
the measure; it is plain, that men have agreed to a disproportionate
and unequal possession of the earth; they having, by a tacit and voluntary consent, found out a way how a man may fairly possess
more land than he himself can use the product of, by receiving, in
exchange for the overplus, gold and silver, which may be hoarded
up without injury to anyone; these metals not spoiling or decaying
in the hands of the possessor. This partage of things in an inequality of private possessions, men have made practicable out of the
bounds of society, and without compact; only by putting a value on
gold and silver, and tacitly agreeing in the use of money: for in governments, the laws regulate the right of property, and the possession of land is determined by positive constitutions.

§ 51. And thus, I think, it is very easy to conceive, how labour
could at first begin a title of property in the common things of nature, and how the spending it upon our uses bounded it. So that
there could then be no reason of quarrelling about title, nor any
doubt about the largeness of possession it gave. Right and conveniency went together; for as a man had a right to all he could employ his labour upon, so he had no temptation to labour for more

than he could make use of. This left no room for controversy about
the title, nor for encroachment on the right of others; what portion
a man carved to himself was easily seen: and it was useless, as well
as dishonest, to carve himself too much, or take more than he
needed.

Chapter VI.

OF PATERNAL POWER.

§ 52. It may perhaps be censured as an impertinent criticism, in
a discourse of this nature, to find fault with words and names that
have obtained in the world: and yet possibly it may not be amiss to
offer new ones when the old are apt to lead men into mistakes, as
this of paternal power probably has done; which seems so to place
the power of parents over their children wholly in the father, as if
the mother had no share in it: whereas, if we consult reason or revelation, we shall find she hath an equal title.[3] This may give one
reason to ask, whether this might not be more properly called
parental power for whatever obligation nature and the right of generation lays on children, it must certainly bind them equally to both
concurrent causes of it. And accordingly we see the positive law of
God everywhere joins them together, without distinction, when it
commands the obedience of children: "Honour thy father and thy
mother," Exod. xx. 12. "Whosoever curseth his father or his mother," Lev. xx. 9. "Ye shall fear every man his mother and his father,"
Lev. xix. 5. "Children, obey your parents," &c. Eph. vi. 1, is the style
of the Old and New Testament.

§ 53. Had but this one thing been well considered, without looking any deeper into the matter, it might perhaps have kept men
from running into those gross mistakes they have made, about this
power of parents; which, however it might, without any great
harshness, bear the name of absolute dominion, and regal authority, when under the title of paternal power it seemed appropriated
to the father, would yet have sounded but oddly, and in the very
name shown the absurdity, if this supposed absolute power over
children had been called parental; and thereby have discovered,
that it belonged to the mother too: for it will but very ill serve the
turn of those men who contend so much for the absolute power
and authority of the fatherhood, as they call it, that the mother
should have any share in it; and it would have but ill supported the
monarchy they contend for, when by the very name it appeared that

3. On Locke's ambiguous view of equality of the sexes, see Melissa Butler (p. 379 herein).

that fundamental authority, from whence they would derive their government of a single person only, was not placed in one, but two persons jointly. But to let this of names pass.

§ 54. Though I have said above, chap. ii. that all men by nature are equal, I cannot be supposed to understand all sorts of equality: age or virtue may give men a just precedency: excellency of parts and merit may place others above the common level: birth may subject some, and alliance or benefits others, to pay an observance to those whom nature, gratitude, or other respects, may have made it due: and yet all this consists with the equality which all men are in, in respect of jurisdiction or dominion one over another; which was the equality I there spoke of, as proper to the business in hand, being that equal right that every man hath to his natural freedom, without being subjected to the will or authority of any other man.

§ 55. Children, I confess, are not born in this state of equality, though they are born to it. Their parents have a sort of rule and jurisdiction over them when they come into the world, and for some time after; but it is but a temporary one. The bonds of this subjection are like the swaddling-clothes they are wrapt up in, and supported by, in the weakness of their infancy: age and reason, as they grow up, loosen them, till at length they drop quite off, and leave a man at his own free disposal.

§ 56. Adam was created a perfect man, his body and mind in full possession of their strength and reason, and so was capable from the first instant of his being to provide for his own support and preservation, and govern his actions according to the dictates of the law of reason which God had implanted in him. From him the world is peopled with his descendants, who are all born infants, weak and helpless, without knowledge or understanding: but to supply the defects of this imperfect state, till the improvement of growth and age hath removed them, Adam and Eve, and after them all parents were, by the law of nature, under an obligation to preserve, nourish, and educate the children they had begotten; not as their own workmanship, but the workmanship of their own maker, the Almighty, to whom they were to be accountable for them.

§ 57. The law that was to govern Adam was the same that was to govern all his posterity, the law of reason. But his offspring having another way of entrance into the world, different from him, by a natural birth, that produced them ignorant and without the use of reason, they were not presently under that law; for nobody can be under a law which is not promulgated to him; and this law being promulgated or made known by reason only, he that is not come to the use of his reason cannot be said to be under this law; and Adam's children, being not presently as soon as born under this law of reason, were not presently free: for law, in its true notion, is not so much the limitation, as the direction of a free and intelligent agent to his proper interest, and prescribes no farther than is for the general good of those under that law: could they be happier without it, the law, as an useless thing, would of itself vanish; and that ill deserves the name of confinement which hedges us in only from bogs and precipices. So that, however it may be mistaken, the end of law is not to abolish or restrain, but to preserve and enlarge freedom: for in all the states of created beings capable of laws, "where there is no law, there is no freedom;" for liberty is to be free from restraint and violence from others; which cannot be where there is not law: but freedom is not, as we are told, a liberty for every man to do what he lists: (for who could be free, when every other man's humour might domineer over him?) but a liberty to dispose and order as he lists his person, actions, possessions, and his whole property, within the allowance of those laws under which he is, and therein not to be subject to the arbitrary will of another, but freely follow his own.

§ 58. The power, then, that parents have over their children arises from that duty which is incumbent on them, to take care of their offspring during the imperfect state of childhood. To inform the mind, and govern the actions of their yet ignorant nonage, till reason shall take its place, and ease them of that trouble, is what the children want, and the parents are bound to: for God having given man an understanding to direct his actions, has allowed him a freedom of will, and liberty of acting, as properly belonging thereunto, within the bounds of that law he is under. But whilst he is in an estate wherein he has not understanding of his own to direct his will, he is not to have any will of his own to follow: he that understands for him, must will for him too; he must prescribe to his will, and regulate his actions; but when he comes to the estate that made his father a freeman, the son is a freeman too.

§ 59. This holds in all the laws a man is under, whether natural or civil. Is a man under the law of nature? What made him free of that law? What gave him a free disposing of his property, according to his own will, within the compass of that law? I answer, a state of maturity, wherein he might be supposed capable to know that law, that so he might keep his actions within the bounds of it. When he has acquired that state, he is presumed to know how far that law is to be his guide, and how far he may make use of his freedom, and so comes to have it; till then, somebody else must guide him, who is presumed to know how far the law allows a liberty. If such a state of reason, such an age of discretion made him free, the same shall make his son free too. Is a man under the law of England? What made him free of that law that is, to have the liberty to dispose of his actions and possessions according to his own will, within the permission of that law? A capacity of knowing that law, which is supposed by that law at the age of one-and-twenty years, and in some cases sooner. If this made the father free, it shall make the son free too. Till then we see the law allows the son to have no will, but he is to be guided by the will of his father or guardian, who is to understand for him. And if the father die, and fail to substitute a deputy in his trust; if he hath not provided a tutor to govern his son during his minority, during his want of understanding, the law takes care to do it; some other must govern him, and be a will to him, till he hath attained to a state of freedom, and his understanding be fit to take the government of his will. But after that, the father and son are equally free as much as tutor and pupil after nonage; equally subjects of the same law together, without any dominion left in the father over the life, liberty, or estate of his son, whether they be only in the state and under the law of nature, or under the positive laws of an established government.

§ 60. But if, through defects that may happen out of the ordinary course of nature, any one comes not to such a degree of reason wherein he might be supposed capable of knowing the law, and so living within the rules of it, he is never capable of being a free man, he is never let loose to the disposure of his own will, (because he knows no bounds to it, has not understanding, its proper guide) but is continued under the tuition and government of others, all the time his own understanding is incapable of that charge. And so lunatics and idiots are never set free from the government of their parents. "Children, who are not as yet come unto those years whereat they may have; and innocents which are excluded by a natural defect from ever having; thirdly, madmen, which for the present cannot possibly have the use of right reason to guide themselves, have for their guide the reason that guideth other men which are tutors over them, to seek and procure their good for them," says Hooker, Eccl. Pol. lib.i. sect. 7. All which seems no more than that duty which God and nature has laid on man, as well as other creatures, to preserve their offspring till they can be able to shift for themselves, and will scarce amount to an instance or proof of parents' regal authority.

§ 61. Thus we are born free, as we are born rational; not that we have actually the exercise of either: age, that brings one, brings with it the other too. And thus we see how natural freedom and subjection to parents may consist together, and are both founded on the same principle. A child is free by his father's title, by his father's understanding, which is to govern him till he hath it of his own. The freedom of a man at years of discretion, and the subjection of a child to his parents, whilst yet short of that age, are so consistent, and so distinguishable, that the most blinded contenders for monarchy, by right of fatherhood, cannot miss this difference; the most obstinate cannot but allow their consistency: for were their doctrine all true, were the right heir of Adam now known, and by that title settled a monarch in his throne, invested with all the absolute unlimited power Sir Robert Filmer talks of; if he should die as soon as his heir were born, must not the child, notwithstanding he were ever so free, ever so much sovereign, be in subjection to his mother and nurse, to tutors and governors, till age and education brought him reason and ability to govern himself and others? The necessities of his life, the health of his body, and the information of his mind, would require him to be directed by the will of others, and not his own; and yet will anyone think that this restraint and subjection were inconsistent with, or spoiled him of that liberty or sovereignty he had a right to, or gave away his empire to those who had the government of his nonage? This government over him only prepared him the better and sooner for it. If anybody should ask me, when my son is of age to be free I shall answer, just when his monarch is of age to govern. "But at what time," says the judicious Hooker, Eccl. Pol. lib. i. sect. 6, "a man may be said to have attained so far forth the use of reason, as sufficeth to make him capable of those laws whereby he is then bound to guide his actions: this is a great deal more easy for sense to discern than for any one by skill and learning to determine."

§ 62. Commonwealths themselves take notice of, and allow, that there is a time when men are to begin to act like freemen, and therefore till that time require not oaths of fealty or allegiance, or other public owning of, or submission to, the government of their countries.

§ 63. The freedom then of man, and liberty of acting according to his own will, is grounded on his having reason, which is able to instruct him in that law he is to govern himself by, and make him know how far he is left to the freedom of his own will. To turn him loose to an unrestrained liberty, before he has reason to guide him, is not the allowing him the privilege of his nature to be free; but to thrust him out amongst brutes, and abandon him to a state as wretched, and as much beneath that of a man, as theirs. This is that which puts the authority into the parents' hands to govern the minority of their children. God hath made it their business to employ this care on their offspring, and hath placed in them suitable inclinations of tenderness and concern to temper this power, to apply it, as his wisdom designed it, to the children's good, as long as they should need to be under it.

§ 64. But what reason can hence advance this care of the parents due to their offspring into an absolute arbitrary dominion of the father, whose power reaches no farther than, by such a discipline as he finds most effectual, to give such strength and health to their bodies, such vigour and rectitude to their minds, as may best fit his children to be most useful to themselves and others; and, if it be necessary to his condition, to make them work, when they are able, for their own subsistence. But in this power the mother too has her share with the father.

§ 65. Nay, this power so little belongs to the father by any peculiar right of nature, but only as he is guardian of his children, that when he quits his care of them, he loses his power over them, which goes along with their nourishment and education, to which it is inseparably annexed; and it belongs as much to the foster-father of an exposed child, as to the natural father of another. So little power does the bare act of begetting give a man over his issue, if all his care ends there, and this be all the title he hath to the name and authority of a father. And what will become of this paternal power in that part of the world where one woman hath more than one husband at a time or in those parts of America, where, when the husband and wife part, which happens frequently, the children are all left to the mother, follow her, and are wholly under her care and provision? If the father die whilst the children are young, do they not naturally every where owe the same obedience to their mother, during their minority, as to their father were he alive? And will anyone say, that the mother hath a legislative power over her children? That she can make standing rules, which shall be of perpetual obligation, by which they ought to regulate all the concerns of their property, and bound their liberty all the course of their lives? Or can she enforce the observation of them with capital punishments? For this is the proper power of the magistrate, of which the father hath not so much as the shadow. His command over his children is but temporary, and reaches not their life or property: it is but a help to the weakness and imperfection of their nonage, a discipline necessary to their education: and though a father may dispose of his own possessions as he pleases, when his children are out of danger of perishing for want, yet his power extends not to the lives or goods, which either their own industry or another's bounty has made theirs; nor to their liberty neither, when they are once arrived to the enfranchisement of the years of discretion. The father's empire then ceases, and can from thenceforwards no more dispose of the liberty of his son than that of any other man: and it must be far from an absolute or perpetual jurisdiction, from which a man may withdraw himself, having licence from divine authority to "leave father and mother, and cleave to his wife."[4]

§ 66. But though there be a time when a child comes to be as

4. Genesis 2:24; Matthew 19:5.

free from subjection to the will and command of his father, as the father himself is free from subjection to the will of anybody else, and they are each under no other restraint but that which is common to them both, whether it be the law of nature, or municipal law of their country; yet this freedom exempts not a son from that honour which he ought, by the law of God and nature, to pay his parents. God having made the parents instruments in his great design of continuing the race of mankind, and the occasions of life to their children; as he hath laid on them an obligation to nourish, preserve, and bring up their offspring; so he has laid on the children a perpetual obligation of honouring their parents, which containing in it an inward esteem and reverence to be shown by all outward expressions, ties up the child from any thing that may ever injure or affront, disturb or endanger, the happiness or life of those from whom he received his; and engages him in all actions of defence, relief, assistance, and comfort of those by whose means he entered into being, and has been made capable of any enjoyments of life: from this obligation no state, no freedom, can absolve children. But this is very far from giving parents a power of command over their children, or authority to make laws and dispose as they please of their lives and liberties. It is one thing to owe honour, respect, gratitude, and assistance; another to require an absolute obedience and submission. The honour due to parents, a monarch in his throne owes his mother; and yet this lessens not his authority, nor subjects him to her government.

§ 67. The subjection of a minor, places in the father a temporary government, which terminates with the minority of the child: and the honour due from a child, places in the parents perpetual right to respect, reverence, support, and compliance too, more or less, as the father's care, cost, and kindness in his education, have been more or less. This ends not with minority, but holds in all parts and conditions of a man's life. The want of distinguishing these two powers, viz. that which the father hath in the right of tuition, during minority, and the right of honour all his life, may perhaps have caused a great part of the mistakes about this matter: for, to speak properly of them, the first of these is rather the privilege of children, and duty of parents, than any prerogative of paternal power. The nourishment and education of their children is a charge so incumbent on parents for their children's good, that nothing can absolve them from taking care of it: and though the power of commanding and chastising them go along with it, yet God hath woven into the principles of human nature such a tenderness for their offspring, that there is little fear that parents should use their power with too much rigour; the excess is seldom on the severe side, the strong bias of nature drawing the other way. And therefore

God Almighty, when he would express his gentle dealing with the Israelites, he tells them, that though he chastened them, "he chastened them as a man chastens his son," Deut. viii. 5. *i.e.* with tenderness and affection, and kept them under no severer discipline than what was absolutely best for them, and had been less kindness to have slackened. This is that power to which children are commanded obedience, that the pains and care of their parents may not be increased, or ill rewarded.

§ 68. On the other side, honour and support, all that which gratitude requires to return for the benefits received by and from them, is the indispensable duty of the child, and the proper privilege of the parents. This is intended for the parents' advantage, as the other is for the child's; though education, the parents' duty, seems to have most power, because the ignorance and infirmities of childhood stand in need of restraint and correction; which is a visible exercise of rule, and a kind of dominion. And that duty which is comprehended in the word honour requires less obedience, though the obligation be stronger on grown than younger children: for who can think the command, "Children obey your parents," requires in a man that has children of his own the same submission to his father, as it does in his yet young children to him; and that by this precept he were bound to obey all his father's commands, if, out of a conceit of authority, he should have the indiscretion to treat him still as a boy?

§ 69. The first part then of paternal power, or rather duty, which is education, belongs so to the father, that it terminates at a certain season; when the business of education is over, it ceases of itself, and is also alienable before: for a man may put the tuition of his son in other hands; and he that has made his son an apprentice to another, has discharged him, during that time, of a great part of his obedience both to himself and to his mother. But all the duty of honour, the other part, remains nevertheless entire to them; nothing can cancel that: it is so inseparable from them both, that the father's authority cannot dispossess the mother of this right, nor can any man discharge his son from honouring her that bore him. But both these are very far from a power to make laws, and enforcing them with penalties that may reach estate, liberty, limbs, and life. The power of commanding ends with nonage; and though after that, honour and respect, support and defence, and whatsoever gratitude can oblige a man to, for the highest benefits he is naturally capable of, be always due from a son to his parents; yet all this puts no sceptre into the father's hand, no sovereign power of commanding. He has no dominion over his son's property, or actions; nor any right that his will should prescribe to his son's in all things; however it may become his son in many things, not very inconvenient to him and his family, to pay a deference to it.

§ 70. A man may owe honour and respect to an ancient or wise man; defence to his child or friend; relief and support to the distressed; and gratitude to a benefactor, to such a degree, that all he has, all he can do, cannot sufficiently pay it: but all these give no authority, no right to anyone, of making laws over him from whom they are owing. And it is plain, all this is due not only to the bare title of father; not only because, as has been said, it is owing to the mother too, but because these obligations to parents, and the degrees of what is required of children, may be varied by the different care and kindness, trouble and expense, which are often employed upon one child more than another.

§ 71. This shows the reason how it comes to pass, that parents in societies, where they themselves are subjects, retain a power over their children, and have as much right to their subjection as those who are in the state of nature. Which could not possibly be, if all political power were only paternal, and that in truth they were one and the same thing: for then, all paternal power being in the prince, the subject could naturally have none of it. But these two powers, political and paternal, are so perfectly distinct and separate, are built upon so different foundations, and given to so different ends, that every subject, that is a father, has as much a paternal power over his children as the prince has over his: and every prince, that has parents, owes them as much filial duty and obedience as the meanest of his subjects do to theirs; and can therefore contain not any part or degree of that kind of dominion which a prince or magistrate has over his subjects.

§ 72. Though the obligation on the parents to bring up their children, and the obligation on children to honour their parents, contain all the power on the one hand, and submission on the other, which are proper to this relation, yet there is another power ordinary in the father, whereby he has a tie on the obedience of his children; which though it be common to him with other men, yet the occasions of showing it almost constantly happening to fathers in their private families, and the instances of it elsewhere being rare, and less taken notice of, it passes in the world for a part of paternal jurisdiction. And this is the power men generally have to bestow their estates on those who please them best; the possession of the father being the expectation and inheritance of the children, ordinarily in certain proportions, according to the law and custom of each country; yet it is commonly in the father's power to bestow it with a more sparing or liberal hand, according as the behaviour of this or that child hath comported with his will and humour.

§ 73. This is no small tie on the obedience of children: and there being always annexed to the enjoyment of land a submission to the government of the country, of which that land is a part; it has been commonly supposed, that a father could oblige his posterity to that government, of which he himself was a subject, and that his compact held them; whereas, it being only a necessary condition annexed to the land, and the inheritance of an estate which is under that government, reaches only those who will take it on that condition, and so is no natural tie or engagement, but a voluntary submission: for every man's children being by nature as free as himself, or any of his ancestors ever were, may, whilst they are in that freedom, choose what society they will join themselves to, what commonwealth they will put themselves under. But if they will enjoy the inheritance of their ancestors, they must take it on the same terms their ancestors had it, and submit to all the conditions annexed to such a possession. By this power indeed fathers oblige their children to obedience to themselves, even when they are past minority, and most commonly too subject them to this or that political power: but neither of these by any peculiar right of fatherhood, but by the reward they have in their hands to enforce and recompense such a compliance; and is no more power than what a Frenchman has over an Englishman, who, by the hopes of an estate he will leave him, will certainly have a strong tie on his obedience: and if, when it is left him, he will enjoy it, he must certainly take it upon the conditions annexed to the possession of land in that country where it lies, whether it be France or England.

§ 74. To conclude then, though the father's power of commanding extends no farther than the minority of his children, and to a degree only fit for the discipline and government of that age; and though that honour and respect, and all that which the Latins called piety, which they indispensably owe to their parents all their lifetimes, and in all estates, with all that support and defence which is due to them, gives the father no power of governing, *i.e.* making laws and enacting penalties on his children; though by all this he has no dominion over the property or actions of his son: yet it is obvious to conceive how easy it was, in the first ages of the world, and in places still, where the thinness of people gives families leave to separate into unpossessed quarters, and they have room to remove or plant themselves in yet vacant habitations, for the father of the family to become the prince[5] of it; he had been a ruler from the beginning of the infancy of his children: and since without some government it would be hard for them to live together, it was likeliest it should, by the express or tacit consent of

5. It is no improbable opinion, therefore, which the arch-philosopher [Aristotle] was of, "That the chief person in every household was always, as it were, a king: so when numbers of households joined themselves in civil societies together, kings were the first kind of governors amongst them, which is also, as it seemeth, the reason why the name of fathers continued still in them, who, of fathers, were made rulers; as also the ancient custom of governors to do as Melchizedeck, and being kings, to exercise the office of

the children when they were grown up, be in the father, where it seemed without any change barely to continue; when indeed nothing more was required to it than the permitting the father to exercise alone, in his family, that executive power of the law of nature, which every free man naturally hath, and by that permission resigning up to him a monarchical power, whilst they remained in it. But that this was not by any paternal right, but only by the consent of his children, is evident from hence, that nobody doubts, but if a stranger, whom chance or business had brought to his family, had there killed any of his children, or committed any other fact, he might condemn and put him to death, or otherwise punish him, as well as any of his children: which it was impossible he should do by virtue of any paternal authority over one who was not his child, but by virtue of that executive power of the law of nature, which, as a man, he had a right to: and he alone could punish him in his family, where the respect of his children had laid by the exercise of such a power, to give way to the dignity and authority they were willing should remain in him, above the rest of his family.

§ 75. Thus it was easy, and almost natural for children, by a tacit, and scarce avoidable consent, to make way for the father's authority and government. They had been accustomed in their childhood to follow his direction, and to refer their little differences to him; and when they were men, who fitter to rule them? Their little properties, and less covetousness, seldom afforded greater controversies; and when any should arise, where could they have a fitter umpire than he, by whose care they had every one been sustained and brought up, and who had a tenderness for them all? It is no wonder that they made no distinction betwixt minority and full age; nor looked after one-and-twenty, or any other age that might make them the free disposers of themselves and fortunes, when they could have no desire to be out of their pupilage: the government they had been under during it, continued still to be more their protection than restraint: and they could nowhere find a greater security to their peace, liberties, and fortunes, than in the rule of a father.

§ 76. Thus the natural fathers of families by an insensible change became the politic monarchs of them too: and as they chanced to live long, and leave able and worthy heirs, for several successions, or otherwise; so they laid the foundations of hereditary, or elective kingdoms, under several constitutions and man-

---

priests, which fathers did at the first, grew perhaps by the same occasion. Howbeit, this is not the only kind of regiment that has been received in the world. The inconveniencies of one kind have caused sundry others to be devised; so that, in a word, all public regiment, of what kind soever, seemeth evidently to have risen from the deliberate advice, consultation, and composition between men, judging it convenient and behoveful; there being no impossibility in nature considered by itself, but that man might have lived without any public regiment." *Hooker's* Eccl. P. lib. i. sect. 10 [Locke's note].

ners, according as chance, contrivance, or occasions happened to mould them. But if princes have their titles in the father's right, and it be a sufficient proof of the natural right of fathers to political authority, because they commonly were those in whose hands we find, *de facto*, the exercise of government: I say, if this argument be good, it will as strongly prove, that all princes, nay princes only, ought to be priests, since it is as certain, that in the beginning, "the father of the family was priest, as that he was ruler in his own household."

Chapter VII.

OF POLITICAL OR CIVIL SOCIETY.

§ 77. GOD having made man such a creature, that in his own judgment it was not good for him to be alone, put him under strong obligations of necessity, convenience, and inclination, to drive him into society, as well as fitted him with understanding and language to continue and enjoy it.[6] The first society was between man and wife, which gave beginning to that between parents and children; to which, in time, that between master and servant came to be added: and though all these might, and commonly did meet together, and make up but one family, wherein the master or mistress of it had some sort of rule proper to a family; each of these, or all together, came short of political society, as we shall see, if we consider the different ends, ties, and bounds of each of these.

§ 78. Conjugal society is made by a voluntary compact between man and woman; and though it consist chiefly in such a communion and right in one another's bodies as is necessary to its chief end, procreation; yet it draws with it mutual support and assistance, and a communion of interests too, as necessary not only to unite their care and affection, but also necessary to their common offspring, who have a right to be nourished and maintained by them, till they are able to provide for themselves.

§ 79. For the end of conjunction between male and female being not barely procreation, but the continuation of the species; this conjunction betwixt male and female ought to last, even after procreation, so long as is necessary to the nourishment and support of the young ones, who are to be sustained by those that got them, till they are able to shift and provide for themselves. This rule, which the infinite wise Maker hath set to the works of his hands, we find the inferior creatures steadily obey. In those viviparous animals which feed on grass, the conjunction between male and female lasts no

6. For a debate about whether or not Locke had an "atomistic" asocial view of human nature, see Charles Taylor (p. 334 herein) and Ruth Grant (p. 339 herein).

longer than the very act of copulation; because the teat of the dam being sufficient to nourish the young, till it be able to feed on grass, the male only begets, but concerns not himself for the female or young, to whose sustenance he can contribute nothing. But in beasts of prey the conjunction lasts longer: because the dam not being able well to subsist herself, and nourish her numerous offspring by her own prey alone, a more laborious, as well as more dangerous way of living, than by feeding on grass; the assistance of the male is necessary to the maintenance of their common family, which cannot subsist till they are able to prey for themselves, but by the joint care of male and female. The same is to be observed in all birds, (except some domestic ones, where plenty of food excuses the cock from feeding, and taking care of the young brood) whose young needing food in the nest, the cock and hen continue mates, till the young are able to use their wing, and provide for themselves.

§ 80. And herein I think lies the chief, if not the only reason, why the male and female in mankind are tied to a longer conjunction than other creatures, viz. because the female is capable of conceiving, and *de facto* is commonly with child again, and brings forth too a new birth, long before the former is out of a dependency for support on his parents' help, and able to shift for himself, and has all the assistance that is due to him from his parents: whereby the father, who is bound to take care for those he hath begot, is under an obligation to continue in conjugal society with the same woman longer than other creatures, whose young being able to subsist of themselves before the time of procreation returns again, the conjugal bond dissolves of itself, and they are at liberty, till Hymen[7] at his usual anniversary season summons them again to choose new mates. Wherein one cannot but admire the wisdom of the great Creator, who having given to man foresight, and an ability to lay up for the future, as well as to supply the present necessity, hath made it necessary, that society of man and wife should be more lasting than of male and female amongst other creatures; that so their industry might be encouraged, and their interest better united, to make provision and lay up goods for their common issue, which uncertain mixture, or easy and frequent solutions of conjugal society, would mightily disturb.

§ 81. But though these are ties upon mankind, which make the conjugal bonds more firm and lasting in man than the other species of animals; yet it would give one reason to inquire, why this compact, where procreation and education are secured, and inheritance taken care for, may not be made determinable, either by consent, or at a certain time, or upon certain conditions, as well as

7. God of marriage.

any other voluntary compacts, there being no necessity in the nature of the thing, nor to the ends of it, that it should always be for life; I mean, to such as are under no restraint of any positive law, which ordains all such contracts to be perpetual.

§ 82. But the husband and wife, though they have but one common concern, yet having different understandings, will unavoidably sometimes have different wills too; it therefore being necessary that the last determination, *i.e.* the rule, should be placed somewhere; it naturally falls to the man's share, as the abler and the stronger. But this reaching but to the things of their common interest and property, leaves the wife in the full and free possession of what by contract is her peculiar right, and gives the husband no more power over her life than she has over his; the power of the husband being so far from that of an absolute monarch, that the wife has in many cases a liberty to separate from him, where natural right or their contract allows it; whether that contract be made by themselves in the state of nature, or by the customs or laws of the country they live in; and the children upon such separation fall to the father's or mother's lot, as such contract does determine.

§ 83. For all the ends of marriage being to be obtained under politic government, as well as in the state of nature, the civil magistrate doth not abridge the right or power of either naturally necessary to those ends, viz. procreation and mutual support and assistance whilst they are together; but only decides any controversy that may arise between man and wife about them. If it were otherwise, and that absolute sovereignty and power of life and death naturally belonged to the husband, and were necessary to the society between man and wife, there could be no matrimony in any of those countries where the husband is allowed no such absolute authority. But the ends of matrimony requiring no such power in the husband, the condition of conjugal society put it not in him, it being not at all necessary to that state. Conjugal society could subsist and attain its ends without it; nay, community of goods, and the power over them, mutual assistance and maintenance, and other things belonging to conjugal society, might be varied and regulated by that contract which unites man and wife in that society, as far as may consist with procreation and the bringing up of children till they could shift for themselves; nothing being necessary to any society, that is not necessary to the ends for which it is made.

§ 84. The society betwixt parents and children, and the distinct rights and powers belonging respectively to them, I have treated of so largely, in the foregoing chapter, that I shall not here need to say any thing of it. And I think it is plain, that it is far different from a politic society.

§ 85. Master and servant are names as old as history, but given to those of far different condition; for a freeman makes himself a servant to another, by selling him, for a certain time, the service he undertakes to do, in exchange for wages he is to receive: and though this commonly puts him into the family of his master, and under the ordinary discipline thereof: yet it gives the master but a temporary power over him, and no greater than what is contained in the contract between them. But there is another sort of servants, which by a peculiar name we call slaves, who being captives taken in a just war, are by the right of nature subjected to the absolute dominion and arbitrary power of their masters. These men having, as I say, forfeited their lives, and with it their liberties, and lost their estates; and being in the state of slavery, not capable of any property; cannot in that state be considered as any part of civil society; the chief end whereof is the preservation of property.

§ 86. Let us therefore consider a master of a family with all these subordinate relations of wife, children, servants, and slaves, united under the domestic rule of a family; which, what resemblance soever it may have in its order, offices, and number too, with a little commonwealth, yet is very far from it, both in its constitution, power, and end: or if it must be thought a monarchy, and the pater-familias[8] the absolute monarch in it, absolute monarchy will have but a very shattered and short power, when it is plain, by what has been said before, that the master of the family has a very distinct and differently limited power, both as to time and extent, over those several persons that are in it: for excepting the slave (and the family is as much a family, and his power as pater-familias as great, whether there be any slaves in his family or no), he has no legislative power of life and death over any of them, and none too but what a mistress of a family may have as well as he. And he certainly can have no absolute power over the whole family, who has but a very limited one over every individual in it. But how a family, or any other society of men, differ from that which is properly political society, we shall best see by considering wherein political society itself consists.

§ 87. Man being born, as has been proved, with a title to perfect freedom, and uncontrolled enjoyment of all the rights and privileges of the law of nature, equally with any other man, or number of men in the world, hath by nature a power, not only to preserve his property, that is, his life, liberty, and estate, against the injuries and attempts of other men; but to judge of and punish the breaches of that law in others, as he is persuaded the offence deserves, even with death itself, in crimes where the heinousness of the fact, in his opinion, requires it. But because no political society can be, nor

8. The father of the family.

subsist, without having in itself the power to preserve the property, and, in order thereunto, punish the offences of all those of that society; there, and there only is political society, where everyone of the members hath quitted this natural power, resigned it up into the hands of the community in all cases that exclude him not from appealing for protection to the law established by it. And thus all private judgment of every particular member being excluded,[9] the community comes to be umpire, by settled standing rules, indifferent, and the same to all parties; and by men having authority from the community, for the execution of those rules, decides all the differences that may happen between any members of that society concerning any matter of right; and punishes those offences which any member hath committed against the society, with such penalties as the law has established: whereby it is easy to discern who are, and who are not, in political society together. Those who are united into one body, and have a common established law and judicature to appeal to, with authority to decide controversies between them, and punish offenders, are in civil society one with another: but those who have no such common appeal, I mean on earth, are still in the state of nature, each being, where there is no other, judge for himself, and executioner: which is, as I have before showed it, the perfect state of nature.

§ 88. And thus the commonwealth comes by a power to set down what punishment shall belong to the several transgressions which they think worthy of it, committed amongst the members of that society, (which is the power of making laws) as well as it has the power to punish any injury done unto any of its members, by anyone that is not of it, (which is the power of war and peace:) and all this for the preservation of the property of all the members of that society, as far as is possible. But though every man who has entered into civil society, and is become a member of any commonwealth, has thereby quitted his power to punish offences against the law of nature, in prosecution of his own private judgment; yet with the judgment of offences, which he has given up to the legislative in all cases, where he can appeal to the magistrate, he has given a right to the commonwealth to employ his force, for the execution of the judgments of the commonwealth, whenever he shall be called to it; which indeed are his own judgments, they being made by himself, or his representative. And herein we have the original of the legislative and executive power of civil society, which is to judge by standing laws, how far offences are to be punished, when committed within the commonwealth; and also to determine, by occa-

---

9. This passage is the basis of the argument that Locke is an advocate of the tyranny of the majority made by Willmoore Kendall (1940).

sional judgments founded on the present circumstances of the fact, how far injuries from without are to be vindicated; and in both these to employ all the force of all the members, when there shall be need.

§ 89. Whenever therefore any number of men are so united into one society, as to quit every one his executive power of the law of nature, and to resign it to the public, there and there only is a political or civil society. And this is done, wherever any number of men, in the state of nature, enter into society to make one people, one body politic, under one supreme government; or else when any one joins himself to, and incorporates with any government already made: for hereby he authorizes the society, or, which is all one, the legislative thereof, to make laws for him, as the public good of the society shall require; to the execution whereof, his own assistance (as to his own degrees) is due. And this puts men out of a state of nature into that of a commonwealth, by setting up a judge on earth, with authority to determine all the controversies, and redress the injuries that may happen to any member of the commonwealth; which judge is the legislative, or magistrate appointed by it. And wherever there are any number of men, however associated, that have no such decisive power to appeal to, there they are still in the state of nature.

§ 90. Hence it is evident, that absolute monarchy, which by some men is counted the only government in the world, is indeed inconsistent with civil society, and so can be no form of civil government at all: for the end of civil society being to avoid and remedy those inconveniencies of the state of nature which necessarily follow from every man being judge in his own case, by setting up a known authority, to which everyone of that society may appeal upon any injury received, or controversy that may arise, and which every one of the society[1] ought to obey; wherever any persons are, who have not such an authority to appeal to, for the decision of any difference between them, there those persons are still in the state of nature; and so is every absolute prince, in respect of those who are under his dominion.

§ 91. For he being supposed to have all, both legislative and executive power in himself alone, there is no judge to be found, no appeal lies open to any one, who may fairly, and indifferently, and with authority decide, and from whose decision relief and redress may be expected of any injury or inconveniency, that may be suf-

---

1. "The public power of all society is above every soul contained in the same society; and the principal use of that power is, to give laws unto all that are under it, which laws in such cases we must obey, unless there be reason showed which may necessarily inforce, that the law of reason, or of God, doth enjoin the contrary."—Hooker. Eccl. Pol. l. i. sect. 16 [Locke's note].

fered from the prince, or by his order: so that such a man, however entitled, czar, or grand seignior, or how you please, is as much in the state of nature, with all under his dominion, as he is with the rest of mankind: for wherever any two men are, who have no standing rule, and common judge to appeal to on earth, for the determination of controversies of right betwixt them, there they are still in the state of nature,[2] and under all the inconveniencies of it, with only this woful difference to the subject, or rather slave of an absolute prince: that whereas in the ordinary state of nature he has a liberty to judge of his right, and, according to the best of his power, to maintain it; now, whenever his property is invaded by the will and order of his monarch, he has not only no appeal, as those in society ought to have, but, as if he were degraded from the common state of rational creatures, is denied a liberty to judge of, or to defend his right: and so is exposed to all the misery and inconveniencies, that a man can fear from one, who being in the unrestrained state of nature, is yet corrupted with flattery, and armed with power.

§ 92. For he that thinks absolute power purifies men's blood, and corrects the baseness of human nature, need read but the history of this, or any other age, to be convinced of the contrary. He that would have been insolent and injurious in the woods of America, would not probably be much better on a throne; where perhaps learning and religion shall be found out to justify all that he shall do to his subjects, and the sword presently silence all those that dare question it: for what the protection of absolute monarchy is, what kind of fathers of their countries it makes princes to be, and to what a degree of happiness and security it carries civil society, where this sort of government is grown to perfection; he that will look into the late Relation of Ceylon may easily see.[3]

§ 93. In absolute monarchies indeed, as well as other governments of the world, the subjects have an appeal to the law, and judges to decide any controversies, and restrain any violence that

---

2. "To take away all such mutual grievances, injuries, and wrongs," *i.e.* such as attend men in the state of nature, "there was no way but only by growing into composition and agreement amongst themselves by ordaining some kind of government public, and by yielding themselves subject thereunto, that unto whom they granted authority to rule and govern, by them the peace, tranquillity, and happy state of the rest might be procured. Men always knew that where force and injury was offered, they might be defenders of themselves; they knew that however men may seek their own commodity, yet if this were done with injury unto others, it was not to be suffered, but by all men, and all good means, to be withstood. Finally, they knew that no man might in reason take upon him to determine his own right, and according to his own determination proceed in maintenance thereof, inasmuch as every man is towards himself, and them whom he greatly affects, partial; and therefore that strifes and troubles would be endless, except they gave their common consent, all to be ordered by some, whom they should agree upon, without which consent there would be no reason that one man should take upon him to be lord or judge over another." *Hooker* Eccl. Pol. l. i. sect. 10 [Locke's note].

3. Robert Knox's *An Historical Relation of the Island of Ceylon* (1680).

may happen betwixt the subjects themselves, one amongst another. This everyone thinks necessary, and believes he deserves to be thought a declared enemy to society and mankind who should go about to take it away. But whether this be from a true love of mankind and society, and such a charity as we all owe one to another, there is reason to doubt: for this is no more than what every man, who loves his own power, profit, or greatness, may and naturally must do, keep those animals from hurting or destroying one another, who labour and drudge only for his pleasure and advantage; and so are taken care of, not out of any love the master has for them, but love of himself, and the profit they bring him: for if it be asked, what security, what fence is there, in such a state, against the violence and oppression of this absolute ruler the very question can scarce be borne. They are ready to tell you, that it deserves death only to ask after safety. Betwixt subject and subject, they will grant, there must be measures, laws, and judges, for their mutual peace and security: but as for the ruler, he ought to be absolute, and is above all such circumstances; because he has power to do more hurt and wrong, it is right when he does it. To ask how you may be guarded from harm, or injury, on that side where the strongest hand is to do it, is presently the voice of faction and rebellion: as if when men quitting the state of nature entered into society, they agreed that all of them but one should be under the restraint of laws, but that he should still retain all the liberty of the state of nature, increased with power, and made licentious by impunity. This is to think, that men are so foolish, that they take care to avoid what mischiefs may be done them by pole-cats, or foxes; but are content, nay think it safety, to be devoured by lions.

§ 94. But whatever flatterers may talk to amuse people's understandings, it hinders not men from feeling; and when they perceive that any man, in what station soever, is out of the bounds of the civil society which they are of, and that they have no appeal on earth against any harm they may receive from him, they are apt to think themselves in the state of nature in respect of him whom they find to be so; and to take care, as soon as they can, to have that safety and security in civil society for which it was instituted, and for which only they entered into it. And therefore, though perhaps at first (as shall be showed more at large hereafter in the following part of this discourse), some one good and excellent man having got a pre-eminency amongst the rest, had this deference paid to his goodness and virtue, as to a kind of natural authority, that the chief rule, with arbitration of their differences, by a tacit consent devolved into his hands, without any other caution but the assurance they had of his uprightness and wisdom; yet when time, giving authority, and (as some men would persuade us) sacredness to customs, which the negligent and unforeseeing innocence of the first ages began, had brought in successors of another stamp; the people finding their properties not secure under the government as then it was (whereas government has no other end but the preservation of property[4]), could never be safe nor at rest, nor think themselves in civil society, till the legislature was placed in collective bodies of men, call them senate, parliament, or what you please. By which means every single person became subject, equally with other the meanest men, to those laws which he himself, as part of the legislative, had established; nor could any one, by his own authority, avoid the force of the law when once made; nor by any pretence of superiority plead exemption, thereby to license his own, or the miscarriages of any of his dependents.[5] "No man in civil society can be exempted from the laws of it:" for if any man may do what he thinks fit, and there be no appeal on earth, for redress or security against any harm he shall do; I ask, whether he be not perfectly still in the state of nature, and so can be no part or member of that civil society; unless any one will say the state of nature and civil society are one and the same thing, which I have never yet found anyone so great a patron of anarchy as to affirm.

Chapter VIII.

OF THE BEGINNING OF POLITICAL SOCIETIES.

§ 95. MEN being, as has been said, by nature all free, equal, and independent, no one can be put out of this estate, and subjected to the political power of another, without his own consent. The only way whereby any one divests himself of his natural liberty, and puts on the bonds of civil society, is by agreeing with other men to join and unite into a community, for their comfortable, safe, and peaceable living one amongst another, in a secure enjoyment of their properties, and a greater security against any that are not of it. This any number of men may do, because it injures not the freedom of the rest; they are left as they were in the liberty of the state of nature. When any number of men have so consented to make one community or government, they are thereby presently incorporated,

---

4. "At the first, when some certain kind of regiment was once appointed, it may be that nothing was then farther thought upon for the manner of governing, but all permitted unto their wisdom and discretion, which were to rule, till by experience they found this for all parts very inconvenient, so as the thing which they had devised for a remedy did indeed but increase the sore which it should have cured. They saw that to live by one man's will became the cause of all men's misery. This constrained them to come into laws, wherein all men might see their duty beforehand, and know the penalties of transgressing them." *Hooker'* Eccl. Pol. l. i. sect. 10 [Locke's note].
5. "Civil law, being the act of the whole body politic, doth therefore overrule each several part of the same body." *Hooker's* Eccl. Pol. l. i. sect. 10 [Locke's note].

and make one body politic, wherein the majority have a right to act and conclude the rest.

§ 96. For when any number of men have, by the consent of every individual, made a community, they have thereby made that community one body, with a power to act as one body, which is only by the will and determination of the majority; for that which acts any community being only the consent of the individuals of it, and it being necessary to that which is one body to move one way; it is necessary the body should move that way whither the greater force carries it,[6] which is the consent of the majority: or else it is impossible it should act or continue one body, one community, which the consent of every individual that united into it agreed that it should; and so every one is bound by that consent to be concluded by the majority. And therefore we see that in assemblies, empowered to act by positive laws, where no number is set by that positive law which empowers them, the act of the majority passes for the act of the whole, and of course determines; as having, by the law of nature and reason, the power of the whole.

§ 97. And thus every man, by consenting with others to make one body politic under one government, puts himself under an obligation to every one of that society to submit to the determination of the majority, and to be concluded by it; or else this original compact, whereby he with others incorporate into one society, would signify nothing, and be no compact, if he be left free, and under no other ties than he was in before in the state of nature. For what appearance would there be of any compact what new engagement, if he were no farther tied by any decrees of the society than he himself thought fit, and did actually consent to? This would be still as great a liberty as he himself had before his compact, or any one else in the state of nature hath, who may submit himself and consent to any acts of it if he thinks fit.

§ 98. For if the consent of the majority shall not, in reason, be received as the act of the whole, and conclude every individual, nothing but the consent of every individual can make any thing to be the act of the whole: but such a consent is next to impossible ever to be had, if we consider the infirmities of health, and avocations of business, which in a number, though much less than that of a commonwealth, will necessarily keep many away from the public assembly. To which if we add the variety of opinions, and contrariety of inter-

6. Locke's argument has been criticized as based on a crude physicalism. However, if force is seen as moral rather than physical, it is more persuasive, since a majority of morally equal individuals would have more moral weight than the minority. In contrast to Locke, earlier references to "the major part" (e.g., canon law discussions of voting in the church: "the greater and sounder part" and Marsilius's *The Defender of Peace* "the weightier part as to quality and quantity") generally did not adhere to a strict numerical conception. See Paul E. Sigmund (p. 306 herein).

ests which unavoidably happen in all collections of men, the coming into society upon such terms would be only like Cato's coming into the theatre, only to go out again.[7] Such a constitution as this would make the mighty leviathan[8] of a shorter duration than the feeblest creatures, and not let it outlast the day it was born in: which cannot be supposed, till we can think that rational creatures should desire and constitute societies only to be dissolved: for where the majority cannot conclude the rest, there they cannot act as one body, and consequently will be immediately dissolved again.

§ 99. Whosoever therefore out of a state of nature unite into a community, must be understood to give up all the power necessary to the ends for which they unite into society, to the majority of the community, unless they expressly agreed in any number greater than the majority. And this is done by barely agreeing to unite into one political society, which is all the compact that is, or needs be, between the individuals that enter into, or make up a commonwealth. And thus that which begins and actually constitutes any political society, is nothing but the consent of any number of freemen capable of a majority, to unite and incorporate into such a society. And this is that, and that only, which did or could give beginning to any lawful government in the world.

§ 100. To this I find two objections made.

First, That there are no instances to be found in story, of a company of men independent and equal one amongst another, that met together, and in this way began and set up a government.

Secondly, It is impossible of right, that men should do so, because all men being born under government, they are to submit to that, and are not at liberty to begin a new one.

§ 101. To the first there is this to answer, that it is not at all to be wondered, that history gives us but a very little account of men that lived together in the state of nature. The inconveniencies of that condition, and the love and want of society, no sooner brought any number of them together, but they presently united and incorporated, if they designed to continue together. And if we may not suppose men ever to have been in the state of nature, because we hear not much of them in such a state, we may as well suppose the armies of Salmanasser or Xerxes[9] were never children, because we

---

7. This incident occurs in the preface to Martial's *Epigrams*, Cato (95–46) was the defender of the Roman republic against Julius Caesar.
8. Originally a large sea animal, mentioned in the Old Testament, but also the title of Hobbes's major work of political theory (published in 1651). Locke denied having read it and described it as "justly decried"; but he seems to have been familiar with its contents. Except for a criticism of Hobbes's equation of the state of nature with the state of war (*Second Treatise* 19), Locke's target in this treatise is Filmer and the leviathan is mentioned here as a general reference to government.
9. King of Persia (5th century B.C.E.). Salmanassar (9th century), Assyrian ruler.

hear little of them till they were men, and embodied in armies. Government is everywhere antecedent to records, and letters seldom come in amongst a people till a long continuation of civil society has, by other more necessary arts, provided for their safety, ease, and plenty: and then they begin to look after the history of their founders, and search into their original, when they have outlived the memory of it: for it is with commonwealths as with particular persons, they are commonly ignorant of their own births and infancies: and if they know any thing of their original, they are beholden for it to the accidental records that others have kept of it. And those that we have of the beginning of any polities in the world, excepting that of the Jews, where God himself immediately interposed, and which favours not at all paternal dominion, are all either plain instances of such a beginning as I have mentioned, or at least have manifest footsteps of it.

§ 102. He must show a strange inclination to deny evident matter of fact, when it agrees not with his hypothesis, who will not allow, that the beginnings of Rome and Venice were by the uniting together of several men free and independent one of another, amongst whom there was no natural superiority or subjection. And if Josephus Acosta's word may be taken, he tells us, that in many parts of America there was no government at all. "There are great and apparent conjectures," says he, "that these men (speaking of those of Peru) for a long time had neither kings nor commonwealths, but lived in troops, as they do this day in Florida, the Cheriquanas, those of Brasil, and many other nations, which have no certain kings, but as occasion is offered, in peace or war, they choose their captains as they please," [Bk.i, c. 25].[1] If it be said that every man there was born subject to his father, or the head of his family; that the subjection due from a child to a father took not away his freedom of uniting into what political society he thought fit, has been already proved. But be that as it will, these men, it is evident, were actually free; and whatever superiority some politicians now would place in any of them, they themselves claimed it not, but by consent were all equal, till by the same consent they set rulers over themselves. So that their politic societies all began from a voluntary union, and the mutual agreement of men freely acting in the choice of their governors and forms of government.

§ 103. And I hope those who went away from Sparta with Palantus, mentioned by Justin, [Bk. iii, c. 4],[2] will be allowed to have been

---

1. Joseph Acosta's *The National and Moral History of the Indies*, trans. Edward Grimstone (London, 1604; rpnt. 1880). Locke read Acosta in 1681 while he was writing the *Two Treatises*. His use, and misuse, of Acosta's account is discussed in Barbara Arnneil, *John Locke and America* (Oxford, 1996), 33–36.
2. Roman historian (2nd or 3rd century), who wrote a summary (epitome) of Trogus Pompeius's *Philippic History* (1st century). Palantus was the leader of the Spartans, who

freemen, independent one of another, and to have set up a government over themselves, by their own consent. Thus I have given several examples out of history, of people free and in the state of nature, that being met together incorporated and began a commonwealth. And if the want of such instances be an argument to prove that governments were not, nor could not be so begun, I suppose the contenders for paternal empire were better let it alone than urge it against natural liberty: for if they can give so many instances out of history, of governments begun upon paternal right, I think (though at best an argument from what has been, to what should of right be, has no great force) one might, without any great danger, yield them the cause. But if I might advise them in the case, they would do well not to search too much into the original of governments, as they have begun *de facto*; lest they should find, at the foundation of most of them, something very little favourable to the design they promote, and such a power as they contend for.

§ 104. But to conclude, reason being plain on our side, that men are naturally free, and the examples of history showing, that the governments of the world, that were begun in peace, had their beginning laid on that foundation, and were made by the consent of the people; there can be little room for doubt, either where the right is, or what has been the opinion or practice of mankind about the first erecting of governments.

§ 105. I will not deny that if we look back as far as history will direct us, towards the original of commonwealths, we shall generally find them under the government and administration of one man. And I am also apt to believe, that where a family was numerous enough to subsist by itself, and continued entire together, without mixing with others, as it often happens, where there is much land and few people, the government commonly began in the father: for the father having, by the law of nature, the same power with every man else to punish, as he thought fit, any offences against that law, might thereby punish his transgressing children, even when they were men, and out of their pupilage; and they were very likely to submit to his punishment, and all join with him against the offender in their turns, giving him thereby power to execute his sentence against any transgression, and so in effect make him the law-maker and governor over all that remained in conjunction with his family. He was fittest to be trusted; paternal affection secured their property and interest under his care; and the custom of obeying him in their childhood, made it easier to submit to him rather

---

founded the city of Tarentum (now Taranto) in the 8th century B.C.E. For a modern translation of the work to which Locke is referring, see Justin's *Epitome of the Philippic History of Pompeius Trogus*, introduction and notes by R. Develin (Atlanta: Scholars Press, 1994), book 3.4,8–11, pp. 48–49.

than to any other. If, therefore, they must have one to rule them, as government is hardly to be avoided amongst men that live together, who so likely to be the man as he that was their common father, unless negligence, cruelty, or any other defect of mind or body made him unfit for it? But when either the father died, and left his next heir, for want of age, wisdom, courage, or any other qualities, less fit for rule, or where several families met and consented to continue together, there, it is not to be doubted, but they used their natural freedom to set up him whom they judged the ablest, and most likely to rule well over them. Conformable hereunto, we find the people of America, who, living out of the reach of the conquering swords and spreading domination of the two great empires of Peru and Mexico, enjoyed their own natural freedom, though, *cæteris paribus*,[3] they commonly prefer the heir of their deceased king; yet if they find him any way weak or incapable, they pass him by, and set up the stoutest and bravest man for their ruler.

§ 106. Thus, though looking back as far as records give us any account of peopling the world, and the history of nations, we commonly find the government to be in one hand; yet it destroys not that which I affirm, viz. that the beginning of politic society depends upon the consent of the individuals, to join into, and make one society; who, when they are thus incorporated, might set up what form of government they thought fit. But this having given occasion to men to mistake, and think that by nature government was monarchical, and belonged to the father, it may not be amiss here to consider, why people in the beginning generally pitched upon this form: which though perhaps the father's preeminency might, in the first institution of some commonwealth, give a rise to, and place in the beginning the power in one hand; yet it is plain that the reason that continued the form of government in a single person, was not any regard or respect to paternal authority; since all petty monarchies, that is, almost all monarchies, near their original, have been commonly, at least upon occasion, elective.

§ 107. First then, in the beginning of things, the father's government of the childhood of those sprung from him, having accustomed them to the rule of one man, and taught them that where it was exercised with care and skill, with affection and love to those under it, it was sufficient to procure and preserve to men all the political happiness they sought for in society; it was no wonder that they should pitch upon, and naturally run into that form of government, which from their infancy they had been all accustomed to; and which, by experience, they had found both easy and safe. To which, if we add, that monarchy being simple, and most obvious to

---

3. Other things being equal.

men, whom neither experience had instructed in forms of government, nor the ambition or insolence of empire had taught to beware of the encroachments of prerogative, or the inconveniencies of absolute power, which monarchy in succession was apt to lay claim to, and bring upon them; it was not at all strange that they should not much trouble themselves to think of methods of restraining any exorbitancies of those to whom they had given the authority over them, and of balancing the power of government, by placing several parts of it in different hands. They had neither felt the oppression of tyrannical dominion, nor did the fashion of the age, nor their possessions, or way of living (which afforded little matter for covetousness or ambition), give them any reason to apprehend or provide against it; and therefore it is no wonder they put themselves into such a frame of government, as was not only, as I said, most obvious and simple, but also best suited to their present state and condition, which stood more in need of defence against foreign invasions and injuries, than of multiplicity of laws. The equality of a simple poor way of living, confining their desires within the narrow bounds of each man's small property, made few controversies, and so no need of many laws to decide them, and there wanted not of justice where there were but few trespasses, and few offenders. Since then those who liked one another so well as to join into society, cannot but be supposed to have some acquaintance and friendship together, and some trust one in another; they could not but have greater apprehensions of others than of one another: and therefore their first care and thought cannot but be supposed to be, how to secure themselves against foreign force. It was natural for them to put themselves under a frame of government which might best serve to that end, and choose the wisest and bravest man to conduct them in their wars, and lead them out against their enemies, and in this chiefly be their ruler.

§ 108. Thus we see that the kings of the Indians in America, which is still a pattern of the first ages in Asia and Europe, whilst the inhabitants were too few for the country, and want of people and money gave men no temptation to enlarge their possessions of land, or contest for wider extent of ground, are little more than generals of their armies; and though they command absolutely in war, yet at home and in time of peace they exercise very little dominion, and have but a very moderate sovereignty; the resolutions of peace and war being ordinarily either in the people, or in a council. Though the war itself, which admits not of plurality of governors, naturally devolves the command into the king's sole authority.

§ 109. And thus, in Israel itself, the chief business of their judges and first kings, seems to have been to be captains in war, and leaders of their armies; which (besides what is signified by "going out and in before the people,"[4] which was to march forth to war, and home again at the heads of their forces) appears plainly in the story of Jephthah. The Ammonites making war upon Israel, the Gilea-dites in fear sent to Jephthah, a bastard of their family whom they had cast off, and article with him, if he will assist them against the Ammonites, to make him their ruler; which they do in these words, "And the people made him head and captain over them," Judg. xi. 11. which was, as it seems, all one as to be judge. "And he judged Israel," Judg. xii. 7, that is, was their captain-general, "six years." So when Jotham upbraids the Shechemites with the obligation they had to Gideon, who had been their judge and ruler, he tells them, "He fought for you, and adventured his life far, and delivered you out of the hands of Midian," Judg. ix. 17. Nothing is mentioned of him but what he did as a general: and indeed that is all is found in his history, or in any of the rest of the judges. And Abimelech par-ticularly is called king, though at most he was but their general. And when, being weary of the ill conduct of Samuel's sons, the children of Israel desired a king, "like all the nations, to judge them, and to go out before them, and to fight their battles," 1 Sam. viii. 20, God, granting their desire, says to Samuel, "I will send thee a man, and thou shalt anoint him to be captain over my people Israel, that he may save my people out of the hands of the Philistines," ix. 16. As if the only business of a king had been to lead out their armies, and fight in their defence; and accordingly Samuel, at his inauguration, pouring a vial of oil upon him, de-clares to Saul, that "the Lord had anointed him to be captain over his inheritance," x. 1. And therefore those who, after Saul's being solemnly chosen and saluted king by the tribes of Mispeh, were un-willing to have him their king, made no other objection but this, "How shall this man save us?" v. 27; as if they should have said, this man is unfit to be our king, not having skill and conduct enough in war to be able to defend us. And when God resolved to transfer the government to David, it is in these words, "But now thy kingdom shall not continue: the Lord hath sought him a man after his own heart, and the Lord hath commanded him to be captain over his people," xiii. 14. As if the whole kingly authority were nothing else but to be their general: and therefore the tribes who had stuck to Saul's family, and opposed David's reign, when they came to He-bron with terms of submission to him, they tell him, amongst other arguments they had to submit to him as to their king, that he was in effect their king in Saul's time, and therefore they had no reason but to receive him as their king now. "Also (say they) in time past, when Saul was king over us, thou wast he that leddest out and

4. Numbers 27:17.

broughtest in Israel, and the Lord said unto thee, Thou shalt feed my people Israel, and thou shalt be a captain over Israel."[5]

§ 110. Thus, whether a family by degrees grew up into a commonwealth, and the fatherly authority being continued on to the elder son, every one in his turn growing up under it, tacitly submitted to it; and the easiness and equality of it not offending anyone, everyone acquiesced, till time seemed to have confirmed it, and settled a right of succession by prescription: or whether several families, or the descendants of several families, whom chance, neighbourhood, or business brought together, uniting into society: the need of a general, whose conduct might defend them against their enemies in war, and the great confidence the innocence and sincerity of that poor but virtuous age, (such as are almost all those which begin governments, that ever come to last in the world) gave men of one another, made the first beginners of commonwealths generally put the rule into one man's hand, without any other express limitation or restraint, but what the nature of the thing and the end of government required: whichever of those it was that at first put the rule into the hands of a single person, certain it is that nobody was intrusted with it but for the public good and safety, and to those ends, in the infancies of commonwealths, those who had it, commonly used it. And unless they had done so, young societies could not have subsisted; without such nursing fathers, tender and careful of the public weal, all governments would have sunk under the weakness and infirmities of their infancy, and the prince and the people had soon perished together.

§ 111. But though the golden age (before vain ambition, and *amor sceleratus habendi*,[6] evil concupiscence, had corrupted men's minds into a mistake of true power and honour) had more virtue, and consequently better governors, as well as less vicious subjects: and there was then no stretching prerogative on the one side, to oppress the people; nor consequently on the other, any dispute about privilege, to lessen or restrain the power of the magistrate; and so no contest betwixt rulers any people about governors or government: yet, when ambition and luxury in future ages[7] would retain and increase the power, without doing the business for which it was given; and, aided by flattery, taught princes to have distinct and

---

5. 2 Samuel 5:2.
6. Criminal love of possessions.
7. "At first, when some certain kind of regiment was once approved, it may be nothing was then farther thought upon for the manner of governing, but all permitted unto their wisdom and discretion which were to rule, till by experience they found this for all parts very inconvenient, so as the thing which they had devised for a remedy, did indeed but increase the sore which it should have cured. They saw, that to live by one man's will, became the cause of all men's misery. This constrained them to come unto laws wherein all men might see their duty beforehand, and know the penalties of transgressing them." Hooker's Eccl. Pol. l. i. sect. 10 [Locke's note].

separate interests from their people; men found it necessary to examine more carefully the original and rights of government, and to
find out ways to restrain the exorbitancies, and prevent the abuses
of that power, which they having intrusted in another's hands only
for their own good, they found was made use of to hurt them.

§ 112. Thus we may see how probable it is, that people that were
naturally free, and by their own consent either submitted to the
government of their father, or united together out of different families to make a government, should generally put the rule into one
man's hands, and choose to be under the conduct of a single person, without so much as by express conditions limiting or regulating his power, which they thought safe enough in his honesty and
prudence: though they never dreamed of monarchy being *jure di-
vino*,[8] which we never heard of among mankind, till it was revealed
to us by the divinity of this last age; nor ever allowed paternal
power to have a right to dominion, or to be the foundation of all
government. And thus much may suffice to show, that, as far as we
have any light from history, we have reason to conclude, that all
peaceful beginnings of government have been laid in the consent of
the people. I say peaceful, because I shall have occasion in another
place to speak of conquest, which some esteem a way of beginning
of governments.

The other objection I find urged against the beginning of politics,
in the way I have mentioned, is this, viz.

§ 113. That all men being born under government, some or
other, it is impossible any of them should ever be free, and at liberty to unite together, and begin a new one, or ever be able to erect
a lawful government.

If this argument be good, I ask, how came so many lawful
monarchies into the world? For if anybody, upon this supposition,
can show me any one man in any age of the world free to begin a
lawful monarchy, I will be bound to show him ten other free men at
liberty at the same time to unite and begin a new government under a regal, or any other form; it being demonstration, that if any
one, born under the dominion of another, may be so free as to have
a right to command others in a new and distinct empire, every one
that is born under the dominion of another may be so free too, and
may become a ruler, or subject of a distinct separate government.
And so by this their own principle, either all men, however born,
are free, or else there is but one lawful prince, one lawful government in the world. And then they have nothing to do, but barely to
show us which that is; which when they have done, I doubt not but
all mankind will easily agree to pay obedience to him.

8. By divine right.

§ 114. Though it be a sufficient answer to their objection, to show that it involves them in the same difficulties that it doth those they use it against; yet I shall endeavour to discover the weakness of this argument a little farther.

All men, say they, are born under government, and therefore they cannot be at liberty to begin a new one. Everyone is born a subject to his father, or his prince, and is therefore under the perpetual tie of subjection and allegiance. It is plain mankind never owned nor considered any such natural subjection that they were born in, to one or to the other, that tied them, without their own consents, to a subjection to them and their heirs.

§ 115. For there are no examples so frequent in history, both sacred and profane, as those of men withdrawing themselves, and their obedience, from the jurisdiction they were born under, and the family or community they were bred up in, and setting up new governments in other places; from whence sprang all that number of petty commonwealths in the beginning of ages, and which always multiplied as long as there was room enough, till the stronger, or more fortunate, swallowed the weaker; and those great ones again breaking to pieces, dissolved into lesser dominions. All which are so many testimonies against paternal sovereignty, and plainly prove that it was not the natural right of the father descending to his heirs, that made governments in the beginning, since it was impossible, upon that ground, there should have been so many little kingdoms; all must have been but only one universal monarchy, if men had not been at liberty to separate themselves from their families and the government, be it what it will, that was set up in it, and go and make distinct commonwealths and other governments, as they thought fit.

§ 116. This has been the practice of the world from its first beginning to this day; nor is it now any more hinderance to the freedom of mankind, that they are born under constituted and ancient polities, that have established laws and set forms of government, than if they were born in the woods, amongst the unconfined inhabitants that run loose in them: for those who would persuade us, that by being born under any government, we are naturally subjects to it, and have no more any title or pretence to the freedom of the state of nature; have no other reason (bating[9] that of paternal power, which we have already answered) to produce for it, but only because our fathers or progenitors passed away their natural liberty, and thereby bound up themselves and their posterity to a perpetual subjection to the government which they themselves submitted to. It is true, that whatever engagement or promises any one has made for himself, he is under the obligation of them, but cannot, by any

9. Excepting.

compact whatsoever, bind his children or posterity: for his son, when a man, being altogether as free as the father, any act of the father can no more give away the liberty of the son, than it can of anybody else: he may indeed annex such conditions to the land he enjoyed as a subject of any commonwealth, as may oblige his son to be of that community, if he will enjoy those possessions which were his father's; because that estate being his father's property; he may dispose or settle it as he pleases.

§ 117. And this has generally given the occasion to mistake in this matter; because commonwealths not permitting any part of their dominions to be dismembered, nor to be enjoyed by any but those of their community, the son cannot ordinarily enjoy the possessions of his father, but under the same terms his father did, by becoming a member of the society; whereby he puts himself presently under the government he finds there established, as much as any other subject of that commonwealth. And thus "the consent of freemen, born under government, which only makes them members of it," being given separately in their turns, as each comes to be of age, and not in a multitude together; people take no notice of it, and thinking it not done at all, or not necessary, conclude they are naturally subjects as they are men.

§ 118. But it is plain governments themselves understand it otherwise; they claim no power over the son, because of that they had over the father; nor look on children as being their subjects, by their fathers being so. If a subject of England have a child by an English woman in France, whose subject is he? Not the king of England's; for he must have leave to be admitted to the privileges of it: nor the king of France's; for how then has his father a liberty to bring him away, and breed him as he pleases? And who ever was judged as a traitor or deserter, if he left or warred against a country, for being barely born in it of parents that were aliens there? It is plain then, by the practice of governments themselves, as well as by the law of right reason, that a child is born a subject of no country or government. He is under his father's tuition and authority till he comes to age of discretion; and then he is a freeman, at liberty what government he will put himself under, what body politic he will unite himself to: for if an Englishman's son, born in France, be at liberty, and may do so, it is evident there is no tie upon him by his father's being a subject of this kingdom; nor is he bound up by any compact of his ancestors. And why then hath not his son, by the same reason, the same liberty, though he be born any where else? Since the power that a father hath naturally over his children is the same, wherever they be born, and the ties of natural obligations are not bounded by the positive limits of kingdoms and commonwealths.

§ 119. Every man being, as has been showed, naturally free, and nothing being able to put him into subjection to any earthly power, but only his own consent; it is to be considered, what shall be understood to be a sufficient declaration of a man's consent, to make him subject to the laws of any government. There is a common distinction of an express and a tacit consent, which will concern our present case. Nobody doubts but an express consent of any man entering into any society, makes him a perfect member of that society, a subject of that government. The difficulty is, what ought to be looked upon as a tacit consent, and how far it binds, *i.e.* how far anyone shall be looked on to have consented, and thereby submitted to any government, where he has made no expressions of it at all. And to this I say, that every man, that hath any possessions, or enjoyment of any part of the dominions of any government, doth thereby give his tacit consent, and is as far forth obliged to obedience to the laws of that government, during such enjoyment, as anyone under it; whether this his possession be of land, to him and his heirs for ever, or a lodging only for a week; or whether it be barely travelling freely on the highway; and, in effect, it reaches as far as the very being of any one within the territories of that government.

§ 120. To understand this the better, it is fit to consider, that every man, when he at first incorporates himself into any commonwealth, he, by his uniting himself thereunto, annexes also, and submits to the community those possessions which he has, or shall acquire, that do not already belong to any other government: for it would be a direct contradiction for any one to enter into society with others for the securing and regulating of property, and yet to suppose his land, whose property is to be regulated by the laws of the society, should be exempt from the jurisdiction of that government, to which he himself, the proprietor of the land, is a subject. By the same act therefore, whereby any one unites his person, which was before free, to any commonwealth, by the same he unites his possessions, which were before free, to it also: and they become, both of them, person and possession, subject to the government and dominion of that commonwealth, as long as it hath a being. Whoever, therefore, from thenceforth, by inheritance, purchase, permission, or otherways, enjoys any part of the land so annexed to, and under the government of that commonwealth, must take it with the condition it is under; that is, of submitting to the government of the commonwealth, under whose jurisdiction it is, as far forth as any subject of it.

§ 121. But since the government has a direct jurisdiction only over the land, and reaches the possessor of it (before he has actually incorporated himself in the society) only as he dwells upon, and enjoys that; the obligation anyone is under, by virtue of such enjoyment, to submit to the government, begins and ends with the enjoyment: so that whenever the owner, who has given nothing but such a tacit consent to the government, will, by donation, sale, or otherwise, quit the said possession, he is at liberty to go and incorporate himself into any other commonwealth; or to agree with others to begin a new one, in *vacuis locis*,[1] in any part of the world they can find free and unpossessed: whereas he that has once, by actual agreement, and any express declaration, given his consent to be of any commonwealth, is perpetually and indispensably obliged to be, and remain unalterably a subject to it, and can never be again in the liberty of the state of nature; unless, by any calamity, the government he was under comes to be dissolved, or else by some public act cuts him off from being any longer a member of it.

§ 122. But submitting to the laws of any country, living quietly, and enjoying privileges and protection under them, makes not a man a member of that society: this is only a local protection and homage due to and from all those, who, not being in a state of war, come within the territories belonging to any government, to all parts whereof the force of its laws extends. But this no more makes a man a member of that society, a perpetual subject of that commonwealth, than it would make a man a subject to another, in whose family he found it convenient to abide for some time; though, whilst he continued in it, he were obliged to comply with the laws, and submit to the government he found there. And thus we see, that foreigners, by living all their lives under another government, and enjoying the privileges and protection of it, though they are bound, even in conscience, to submit to its administration, as far forth as any denison;[2] yet do not thereby come to be subjects or members of that commonwealth. Nothing can make any man so, but his actually entering into it by positive engagement, and express promise and compact. This is that which I think concerning the beginning of political societies, and that consent which makes any one a member of any commonwealth.

Chapter IX.

OF THE ENDS OF POLITICAL SOCIETY AND GOVERNMENT.

§ 123. IF man in the state of nature be so free as has been said; if he be absolute lord of his own person and possessions, equal to the greatest, and subject to nobody, why will he part with his freedom, why will he give up this empire, and subject himself to the dominion and control of any other power? To which it is obvious to

1. Empty places.
2. Inhabitant.

answer, that though in the state of nature he hath such a right, yet the enjoyment of it is very uncertain, and constantly exposed to the invasion of others; for all being kings as much as he, every man his equal, and the greater part no strict observers of equity and justice, the enjoyment of the property he has in this state is very unsafe, very insecure. This makes him willing to quit a condition, which, however free, is full of fears and continual dangers: and it is not without reason that he seeks out, and is willing to join in society with others, who are already united, or have a mind to unite, for the mutual preservation of their lives, liberties, and estates, which I call by the general name property.

§ 124. The great and chief end, therefore, of men's uniting into commonwealths, and putting themselves under government, is the preservation of their property. To which in the state of nature there are many things wanting.

First, There wants an established, settled, known law, received and allowed by common consent to be the standard of right and wrong, and the common measure to decide all controversies between them: for though the law of nature be plain and intelligible to all rational creatures; yet men being biassed by their interest, as well as ignorant for want of studying it, are not apt to allow of it as a law binding to them in the application of it to their particular cases.

§ 125. Secondly, In the state of nature there wants a known and indifferent judge, with authority to determine all differences according to the established law: for everyone in that state being both judge and executioner of the law of nature, men being partial to themselves, passion and revenge is very apt to carry them too far, and with too much heat, in their own cases; as well as negligence and unconcernedness, to make them too remiss in other men's.

§ 126. Thirdly, In the state of nature there often wants power to back and support the sentence when right, and to give it due execution. They who by any injustice offend, will seldom fail, where they are able, by force to make good their injustice; such resistance many times makes the punishment dangerous, and frequently destructive to those who attempt it.

§ 127. Thus mankind, notwithstanding all the privileges of the state of nature, being but in an ill condition, while they remain in it, are quickly driven into society. Hence it comes to pass, that we seldom find any number of men live any time together in this state. The inconveniencies that they are therein exposed to, by the irregular and uncertain exercise of the power every man has of punishing the transgressions of others, make them take sanctuary under the established laws of government, and therein seek the preservation of their property. It is this makes them so willingly give up every one his single power of punishing, to be exercised by such alone as shall be appointed to it amongst them; and by such rules as the community, or those authorized by them to that purpose, shall agree on. And in this we have the original right of both the legislative and executive power, as well as of the governments and societies themselves.

§ 128. For in the state of nature, to omit the liberty he has of innocent delights, a man has two powers.

The first is to do whatsoever he thinks fit for the preservation of himself and others within the permission of the law of nature: by which law, common to them all, he and all the rest of mankind are one community, make up one society, distinct from all other creatures. And, were it not for the corruption and viciousness of degenerate men, there would be no need of any other; no necessity that men should separate from this great and natural community, and by positive agreements combine into smaller and divided associations.

The other power a man has in the state of nature, is the power to punish the crimes committed against that law. Both these he gives up when he joins in a private, if I may so call it, or particular politic society, and incorporates into any commonwealth, separate from the rest of mankind.

§ 129. The first power, viz. of doing whatsoever he thought fit for the preservation of himself and the rest of mankind, he gives up to be regulated by laws made by the society, so far forth as the preservation of himself and the rest of that society shall require; which laws of the society in many things confine the liberty he had by the law of nature.

§ 130. Secondly, The power of punishing he wholly gives up, and engages his natural force (which he might before employ in the execution of the law of nature, by his own single authority, as he thought fit), to assist the executive power of the society, as the law thereof shall require: for being now in a new state, wherein he is to enjoy many conveniencies, from the labour, assistance, and society of others in the same community, as well as protection from its whole strength; he is to part also with as much of his natural liberty, in providing for himself, as the good, prosperity, and safety of the society shall require; which is not only necessary, but just, since the other members of the society do the like.

§ 131. But though men, when they enter into society, give up the equality, liberty, and executive power they had in the state of nature, into the hands of the society, to be so far disposed of by the legislative as the good of the society shall require; yet it being only with an intention in everyone the better to preserve himself, his liberty and property (for no rational creature can be supposed to change his condition with an intention to be worse); the power of the society, or legislative constituted by them, can never be sup-

posed to extend farther than the common good; but is obliged to secure everyone's property, by providing against those three defects
above-mentioned, that made the state of nature so unsafe and uneasy. And so whoever has the legislative or supreme power of any
commonwealth, is bound to govern by established standing laws,
promulgated and known to the people, and not by extemporary decrees; by indifferent and upright judges, who are to decide controversies by those laws; and to employ the force of the community at
home, only in the execution of such laws; or abroad to prevent or
redress foreign injuries, and secure the community from inroads
and invasion. And all this to be directed to no other end but the
peace, safety, and public good of the people.

Chapter X.

OF THE FORMS OF A COMMONWEALTH.

§132. THE majority having, as has been showed, upon men's first
uniting into society, the whole power of the community naturally in
them, may employ all that power in making laws for the community
from time to time, and executing those laws by officers of their own
appointing; and then the form of the government is a perfect
democracy: or else may put the power of making laws into the
hands of a few select men, and their heirs or successors; and then
it is an oligarchy: or else into the hands of one man, and then it is
a monarchy: if to him and his heirs, it is an hereditary monarchy: if
to him only for life, but upon his death the power only of nominat-
ing a successor to return to them, an elective monarchy. And so
accordingly of these the community may make compounded and
mixed forms of government, as they think good. And if the legislative power be at first given by the majority to one or more persons
only for their lives, or any limited time, and then the supreme
power to revert to them again; when it is so reverted, the community may dispose of it again anew into what hands they please, and
so constitute a new form of government: for the form of government depending upon the placing the supreme power, which is the
legislative (it being impossible to conceive that an inferior power
should prescribe to a superior, or any but the supreme make laws),
according as the power of making laws is placed, such is the form
of the commonwealth.

§ 133. By commonwealth, I must be understood all along to
mean, not a democracy, or any form of government, but any independent community, which the Latines[3] signified by the word *civi-*

3. Romans.

tas; to which the word which best answers in our language is commonwealth, and most properly expresses such a society of men, which community or city in English does not: for there may be subordinate communities in government; and city amongst us has a quite different notion from commonwealth: and therefore, to avoid ambiguity, I crave leave to use the word commonwealth in that sense, in which I find it used by King James the First;[4] and I take it to be its genuine signification; which if any body dislike, I consent with him to change it for a better.

Chapter XI.

OF THE EXTENT OF THE LEGISLATIVE POWER.

§ 134. The great end of men's entering into society being the enjoyment of their properties in peace and safety, and the great instrument and means of that being the laws established in that society; the first and fundamental positive law of all commonwealths is the establishing of the legislative power; as the first and fundamental natural law, which is to govern even the legislative itself, is the preservation of the society, and (as far as will consist with the public good) of every person in it. This legislative is not only the supreme power of the commonwealth, but sacred and unalterable in the hands where the community have once placed it; nor can any edict of anybody else, in what form soever conceived, or by what power soever backed, have the force and obligation of a law, which has not its sanction from that legislative which the public has chosen and appointed: for without this the law could not have that which is absolutely necessary to its being a law,[5] the consent of the society; over whom nobody can have a power to make laws, but by their own consent, and by authority received from them. And therefore all the obedience, which by the most solemn ties anyone can be obliged to pay, ultimately terminates in this supreme power, and

---

4. The first edition of the *Two Treatises* has "King James himself," referring to James I, an indication that it was written before the accession to the throne of James II in 1685. Here and in paragraph 200 Locke added "the First" in later editions.
5. "The lawful power of making laws to command whole politic societies of men, belonging so properly unto the same entire societies, that for any prince or potentate of what kind soever upon earth, to exercise the same of himself, and not by express commission immediately and personally received from God, or else by authority derived at the first from their consent, upon whose persons they impose laws, it is no better than mere tyranny. Laws they are not, therefore, which public approbation hath not made so." *Hooker's* Eccl. Pol. l. i. sect. 10. "Of this point therefore we are to note, that sith men naturally have no full and perfect power to command whole politic multitudes of men, therefore utterly without our consent, we could in such sort be at no man's commandment living. And to be commanded we do consent, when that society, whereof we be a part, hath at any time before consented, without revoking the same by the like universal agreement."
   "Laws therefore human, of what kind soever, are available by consent." *Ibid.* [Locke's note].

is directed by those laws which it enacts: nor can any oaths to any foreign power whatsoever, or any domestic subordinate power, discharge any member of the society from his obedience to the legislative, acting pursuant to their trust; nor oblige him to any obedience contrary to the laws so enacted, or farther than they do allow; it being ridiculous to imagine one can be tied ultimately to obey any power in the society which is not supreme.

§ 135. Though the legislative, whether placed in one or more, whether it be always in being, or only by intervals, though it be the supreme power in every commonwealth; yet,

First, It is not, nor can possibly be absolutely arbitrary over the lives and fortunes of the people: for it being but the joint power of every member of the society given up to that person or assembly which is legislator; it can be no more than those persons had in a state of nature before they entered into society, and gave up to the community: for nobody can transfer to another more power than he has in himself; and nobody has an absolute arbitrary power over himself, or over any other, to destroy his own life, or take away the life or property of another. A man, as has been proved, cannot subject himself to the arbitrary power of another; and having in the state of nature no arbitrary power over the life, liberty, or possession of another, but only so much as the law of nature gave him for the preservation of himself and the rest of mankind; this is all he doth, or can give up to the commonwealth, and by it to the legislative power, so that the legislative can have no more than this. Their power, in the utmost bounds of it, is limited to the public good of the society. It is a power that hath no other end but preservation, and therefore can never[6] have a right to destroy, enslave, or designedly to impoverish the subjects. The obligations of the law of nature cease not in society, but only in many cases are drawn closer, and have by human laws known penalties annexed to them, to enforce their observation. Thus the law of nature stands as an eternal rule to all men, legislators as well as others. The rules that they make for other men's actions must, as well as their own and other men's actions be conformable to the law of nature, *i.e.* to the

6. "Two foundations there are which bear up public societies; the one a natural inclination, whereby all men desire sociable life and fellowship; the other an order, expressly or secretly agreed upon, touching the manner of their union in living together: the latter is that which we call the law of a commonweal, the very soul of a politic body, the parts whereof are by law animated, held together, and set on work in such actions as the common good requireth: Laws politic, ordained for external order and regiment amongst men, are never framed as they should be, unless presuming the will of man to be inwardly obstinate, rebellious, and averse from all obedience to the sacred laws of his nature; in a word, unless presuming man to be, in regard of his depraved mind, little better than a wild beast, they do accordingly provide, notwithstanding, so to frame his outward actions, that they be no hindrance unto the common good, for which societies are instituted. Unless they do this, they are not perfect." *Hooker*'s Eccl. Pol. l. i. sect. 10 [Locke's note].

will of God, of which that is a declaration; and the fundamental law of nature being the preservation of mankind, no human sanction can be good or valid against it.

§ 136. Secondly,[7] The legislative or supreme authority cannot assume to itself a power to rule by extemporary, arbitrary decrees; but is bound to dispense justice, and to decide the rights of the subject, by promulgated, standing laws, and known authorized judges. For the law of nature being unwritten, and so nowhere to be found, but in the minds of men, they who, through passion, or interest, shall miscite, or misapply it, cannot so easily be convinced of their mistake, where there is no established judge: and so it serves not, as it ought, to determine the rights, and fence the properties of those that live under it; especially where everyone is judge, interpreter, and executioner of it too, and that in his own case: and he that has right on his side, having ordinarily but his own single strength, hath not force enough to defend himself from injuries, or to punish delinquents. To avoid these inconveniencies, which disorder men's properties in the state of nature, men unite into societies, that they may have the united strength of the whole society to secure and defend their properties, and may have standing rules to bound it, by which every one may know what is his. To this end it is that men give up all their natural power to the society which they enter into, and the community put the legislative power into such hands as they think fit; with this trust, that they shall be governed by declared laws, or else their peace, quiet, and property will still be at the same uncertainty as it was in the state of nature.

§ 137. Absolute arbitrary power, or governing without settled standing laws, can neither of them consist with the ends of society and government, which men would not quit the freedom of the state of nature for, and tie themselves up under, were it not to preserve their lives, liberties, and fortunes, and by stated rules of right and property to secure their peace and quiet. It cannot be supposed that they should intend, had they a power so to do, to give to any one, or more, an absolute arbitrary power over their persons and estates, and put a force into the magistrate's hand to execute his unlimited will arbitrarily upon them. This were to put themselves into a worse condition than the state of nature, wherein they had a liberty to defend their right against the injuries of others, and were upon equal terms of force to maintain it, whether invaded by a sin-

---

7. "Human laws are measures in respect of men whose actions they must direct, howbeit such measures they are as have also their higher rules to be measured by, which rules are two, the law of God, and the law of nature; so that laws human must be made according to the general laws of nature, and without contradiction to any positive law of scripture, otherwise they are ill made." *Hooker*'s Eccl. Pol. l. iii. sect. 9.

"To constrain men to any thing inconvenient doth seem unreasonable." *Ibid.* l, i. sect. 10 [Locke's note].

gle man, or many in combination. Whereas by supposing they have given up themselves to the absolute arbitrary power and will of a legislator, they have disarmed themselves, and armed him, to make a prey of them when he pleases; he being in a much worse condition, who is exposed to the arbitrary power of one man, who has the command of 100,000, than he that is exposed to the arbitrary power of 100,000 single men; nobody being secure that his will, who has such a command, is better than that of other men, though his force be 100,000 times stronger. And therefore, whatever form the commonwealth is under, the ruling power ought to govern by declared and received laws, and not by extemporary dictates and undetermined resolutions; for then mankind will be in a far worse condition than in the state of nature, if they shall have armed one or a few men with the joint power of a multitude, to force them to obey at pleasure the exorbitant and unlimited degrees of their sudden thoughts, or unrestrained, and till that moment unknown wills, without having any measures set down which may guide and justify their actions: for all the power the government has being only for the good of the society, as it ought not to be arbitrary and at pleasure, so it ought to be exercised by established and promulgated laws; that both the people may know their duty, and be safe and secure within the limits of the law; and the rulers too kept within their bounds, and not be tempted, by the power they have in their hands, to employ it to such purposes, and by such measures, as they would not have known, and own not willingly.

§ 138. Thirdly, The supreme power cannot take from any man part of his property without his own consent: for the preservation of property being the end of government, and that for which men enter into society, it necessarily supposes and requires, that the people should have property, without which they must be supposed to lose that, by entering into society, which was the end for which they entered into it; too gross an absurdity for any man to own. Men therefore in society having property, they have such right to the goods, which by the law of the community are theirs, that nobody hath a right to take their substance or any part of it from them, without their own consent: without this they have no property at all; for I have truly no property in that, which another can by right take from me, when he pleases, against my consent. Hence it is a mistake to think, that the supreme or legislative power of any commonwealth can do what it will, and dispose of the estates of the subject arbitrarily, or take any part of them at pleasure. This is not much to be feared in governments where the legislative consists, wholly or in part, in assemblies which are variable, whose members, upon the dissolution of the assembly, are subjects under the common laws of their country, equally with the rest. But in govern-

ments where the legislative is in one lasting assembly always in being, or in one man, as in absolute monarchies, there is danger still
that they will think themselves to have a distinct interest from the
rest of the community; and so will be apt to increase their own
riches and power, by taking what they think fit from the people: for
a man's property is not at all secure, though there be good and eq-
uitable laws to set the bounds of it between him and his fellow-
subjects, if he who commands those subjects have power to take
from any private man what part he pleases of his property, and use
and dispose of it as he thinks good.

§ 139. But government, into whatsoever hands it is put, being, as
I have before showed, entrusted with this condition, and for this
end, that men might have and secure their properties; the prince,
or senate, however it may have power to make laws for the regulating of property between the subjects one amongst another, yet can
never have a power to take to themselves the whole or any part of
the subject's property without their own consent: for this would be
in effect to leave them no property at all. And to let us see, that
even absolute power, where it is necessary, is not arbitrary by being
absolute, but is still limited by that reason, and confined to those
ends, which required it in some cases to be absolute, we need look
no farther than the common practice of martial discipline: for the
preservation of the army, and in it of the whole commonwealth, requires an absolute obedience to the command of every superior officer, and it is justly death to disobey or dispute the most dangerous
or unreasonable of them; but yet we see, that neither the serjeant,
that could command a soldier to march up to the mouth of a can-
non, or stand in a breach, where he is almost sure to perish, can
command that soldier to give him one penny of his money; nor the
general, that can condemn him to death for deserting his post, or
for not obeying the most desperate orders, can yet, with all his
absolute power of life and death, dispose of one farthing of that soldier's estate, or seize one jot of his goods; whom yet he can command any thing, and hang for the least disobedience; because such
a blind obedience is necessary to that end for which the com-
mander has his power, viz. the preservation of the rest; but the disposing of his goods has nothing to do with it.

§ 140. It is true, governments cannot be supported without great
charge, and it is fit every one who enjoys his share of the protection, should pay out of his estate his proportion for the maintenance of it. But still it must be with his own consent, *i.e.* the
consent of the majority, giving it either by themselves, or their representatives chosen by them: for if any one shall claim a power to
lay and levy taxes on the people by his own authority, and without
such consent of the people, he thereby invades the fundamental

law of property, and subverts the end of government: for what property have I in that which another may by right take, when he pleases, to himself?

§ 141. Fourthly, The legislative cannot transfer the power of making laws to any other hands: for it being but a delegated power from the people, they who have it cannot pass it over to others. The people alone can appoint the form of the commonwealth, which is by constituting the legislative, and appointing in whose hands that shall be. And when the people have said, we will submit to rules, and be governed by laws made by such men, and in such forms, nobody else can say other men shall make laws for them; nor can the people be bound by any laws but such as are enacted by those whom they have chosen, and authorized to make laws for them. The power of the legislative being derived from the people by a positive voluntary grant and institution, can be no other than what that positive grant conveyed, which being only to make laws, and not to make legislators, the legislative can have no power to transfer their authority of making laws and place it in other hands.

§ 142. These are the bounds which the trust that is put in them by the society, and the law of God and nature, have set to the legislative power of every commonwealth, in all forms of government.

First, They are to govern by promulgated established laws, not to be varied in particular cases, but to have one rule for rich and poor, for the favourite at court, and the countryman at plough.

Secondly, These laws also ought to be designed for no other end ultimately, but the good of the people.

Thirdly, They must not raise taxes on the property of the people, without the consent of the people, given by themselves or their deputies. And this properly concerns only such governments where the legislative is always in being, or at least where the people have not reserved any part of the legislative to deputies, to be from time to time chosen by themselves.

Fourthly, The legislative neither must nor can transfer the power of making laws to any body else, or place it any where, but where the people have.

Chapter XII.

OF THE LEGISLATIVE, EXECUTIVE,
AND FEDERATIVE POWER OF THE COMMONWEALTH.

§ 143. THE legislative power is that, which has a right to direct how the force of the commonwealth shall be employed for preserving the community and the members of it. But because those laws which are constantly to be executed, and whose force is always to continue, may be made in a little time, therefore there is no need that the legislative should be always in being, not having always business to do. And because it may be too great a temptation to human frailty, apt to grasp at power, for the same persons who have the power of making laws, to have also in their hands the power to execute them; whereby they may exempt themselves from obedience to the laws they make, and suit the law, both in its making and execution, to their own private advantage, and thereby come to have a distinct interest from the rest of the community, contrary to the end of society and government: therefore in well ordered commonwealths, where the good of the whole is so considered, as it ought, the legislative power is put into the hands of divers persons, who, duly assembled, have by themselves, or jointly with others,[8] a power to make laws; which when they have done, being separated again, they are themselves subject to the laws they have made; which is a new and near tie upon them, to take care that they make them for the public good.

§ 144. But because the laws, that are at once, and in a short time made, have a constant and lasting force, and need a perpetual execution, or an attendance thereunto; therefore it is necessary there should be a power always in being, which should see to the execution of the laws that are made, and remain in force. And thus the legislative and executive power come often to be separated.

§ 145. There is another power in every commonwealth, which one may call natural, because it is that which answers to the power every man naturally had before he entered into society: for though in a commonwealth, the members of it are distinct persons still in reference to one another, and as such are governed by the laws of the society; yet in reference to the rest of mankind, they make one body, which is, as every member of it before was, still in the state of nature with the rest of mankind. Hence it is, that the controversies that happen between any man of the society with those that are out of it, are managed by the public; and an injury done to a member of their body engages the whole in the reparation of it. So that, under this consideration, the whole community is one body in the state of nature, in respect of all other states or persons out of its community.

§ 146. This therefore contains the power of war and peace, leagues and alliances, and all the transactions with all persons and communities without the commonwealth; and may be called federative, if any one pleases. So the thing be understood, I am indifferent as to the name.

8. A reference to the English government in which legislation is adopted by the king (or queen) in Parliament.

§ 147. These two powers, executive and federative, though they be really distinct in themselves, yet one comprehending the execution of the municipal laws of the society within itself, upon all that are parts of it; the other the management of the security and interest of the public without, with all those that it may receive benefit or damage from; yet they are always almost united. And though this federative power in the well or ill management of it be of great moment to the commonwealth, yet it is much less capable to be directed by antecedent, standing, positive laws, than the executive; and so must necessarily be left to the prudence and wisdom of those whose hands it is in, to be managed for the public good: for the laws that concern subjects one amongst another, being to direct their actions, may well enough precede them. But what is to be done in reference to foreigners, depending much upon their actions, and the variation of designs, and interests, must be left in great part to the prudence of those who have this power committed to them, to be managed by the best of their skill, for the advantage of the commonwealth.

§ 148. Though, as I said, the executive and federative power of every community be really distinct in themselves, yet they are hardly to be separated, and placed at the same time in the hands of distinct persons: for both of them requiring the force of the society for their exercise, it is almost impracticable to place the force of the commonwealth in distinct, and not subordinate hands; or that the executive and federative power should be placed in persons that might act separately, whereby the force of the public would be under different commands; which would be apt some time or other to cause disorder and ruin.

Chapter XIII.

OF THE SUBORDINATION OF THE POWERS OF THE COMMONWEALTH.

§ 149. THOUGH in a constituted commonwealth, standing upon its own basis, and acting according to its own nature, that is, acting for the preservation of the community, there can be but one supreme power, which is the legislative, to which all the rest are and must be subordinate; yet the legislative being only a fiduciary power to act for certain ends, there remains still in the people a supreme power to remove or alter the legislative, when they find the legislative act contrary to the trust reposed in them: for all power given with trust for the attaining an end, being limited by that end: whenever that end is manifestly neglected or opposed, the trust must necessarily be forfeited, and the power devolve into the hands of those that gave it, who may place it anew where they shall think best for their safety and security. And thus the community perpetually retains a supreme power of saving themselves from the attempts and designs of any body, even of their legislators, whenever they shall be so foolish, or so wicked, as to lay and carry on designs against the liberties and properties of the subject: for no man, or society of men, having a power to deliver up their preservation, or consequently the means of it, to the absolute will and arbitrary dominion of another; whenever any one shall go about to bring them into such a slavish condition, they will always have a right to preserve what they have not a power to part with; and to rid themselves of those who invade this fundamental, sacred, and unalterable law of self-preservation, for which they entered into society. And thus the community may be said in this respect to be always the supreme power, but not as considered under any form of government, because this power of the people can never take place till the government be dissolved.

§ 150. In all cases, whilst the government subsists, the legislative is the supreme power: for what can give laws to another, must needs be superior to him; and since the legislative is no otherwise legislative of the society, but by the right it has to make laws for all the parts, and for every member of the society, prescribing rules to their actions, and giving power of execution, where they are transgressed; the legislative must needs be the supreme, and all other powers, in any members or parts of the society, derived from and subordinate to it.

§ 151. In some commonwealths, where the legislative is not always in being, and the executive is vested in a single person, who has also a share in the legislative; there that single person in a very tolerable sense may also be called supreme; not that he has in himself all the supreme power, which is that of law-making; but because he has in him the supreme execution, from whom all inferior magistrates derive all their several subordinate powers, or at least the greatest part of them: having also no legislative superior to him, there being no law to be made without his consent, which cannot be expected should ever subject him to the other part of the legislative, he is properly enough in this sense supreme. But yet it is to be observed, that though oaths of allegiance and fealty are taken to him, it is not to him as supreme legislator, but as supreme executor of the law, made by a joint power of him with others: allegiance being nothing but an obedience according to law, which when he violates, he has no right to obedience, nor can claim it otherwise than as the public person invested with the power of the law; and so is to be considered as the image, phantom, or representative of the commonwealth, acted by the will of the society, declared in its laws; and thus he has no will, no power, but that of the law. But when he quits this representation, this public will, and acts by his own private will, he degrades himself, and is but a single private person without power, and without will, that has no right to obedience; the members owing no obedience but to the public will of the society.

§ 152. The executive power, placed any where but in a person that has also a share in the legislative, is visibly subordinate and accountable to it, and may be at pleasure changed and displaced; so that it is not the supreme executive power that is exempt from subordination: but the supreme executive power vested in one, who having a share in the legislative, has no distinct superior legislative to be subordinate and accountable to, farther than he himself shall join and consent; so that he is no more subordinate than he himself shall think fit, which one may certainly conclude will be but very little. Of other ministerial and subordinate powers in a commonwealth we need not speak, they being so multiplied with infinite variety, in the different customs and constitutions of distinct commonwealths, that it is impossible to give a particular account of them all. Only thus much, which is necessary to our present purpose, we may take notice of concerning them, that they have no manner of authority, any of them, beyond what is by positive grant and commission delegated to them, and are all of them accountable to some other power in the commonwealth.

§ 153. It is not necessary, no, nor so much as convenient, that the legislative should be always in being; but absolutely necessary that the executive power should; because there is not always need of new laws to be made, but always need of execution of the laws that are made. When the legislative hath put the execution of the laws they make into other hands, they have a power still to resume it out of those hands, when they find cause, and to punish for any maladministration against the laws. The same holds also in regard of the federative power, that and the executive being both ministerial and subordinate to the legislative, which, as has been showed, in a constituted commonwealth is the supreme. The legislative also in this case being supposed to consist of several persons, (for if it be a single person, it cannot but be always in being, and so will, as supreme, naturally have the supreme executive power, together with the legislative) may assemble, and exercise their legislature, at the times that either their original constitution, or their own adjournment, appoints, or when they please; if neither of these hath appointed any time, or there be no other way prescribed to convoke them: for the supreme power being placed in them by the people, it is always in them, and they may exercise it when they please, unless by their original constitution they are limited to certain seasons, or by an act of their supreme power they have adjourned to a certain time; and when that time comes, they have a right to assemble and act again.

§ 154. If the legislative, or any part of it, be made up of representatives chosen for that time by the people, which afterwards return into the ordinary state of subjects, and have no share in the legislature but upon a new choice, this power of choosing must also be exercised by the people, either at certain appointed seasons, or else when they are summoned to it; and in this latter case the power of convoking the legislative is ordinarily placed in the executive, and has one of these two limitations in respect of time: that either the original constitution requires their assembling and acting at certain intervals, and then the executive power does nothing but ministerially issue directions for their electing and assembling according to due forms; or else it is left to his prudence to call them by new elections, when the occasions or exigencies of the public require the amendment of old, or making of new laws, or the redress or prevention of any inconveniences, that lie on, or threaten the people.

§ 155. It may be demanded here, What if the executive power, being possessed of the force of the commonwealth, shall make use of that force to hinder the meeting and acting of the legislative, when the original constitution or the public exigencies require it? I say, using force upon the people without authority, and contrary to the trust put in him that does so, is a state of war with the people, who have a right to reinstate their legislative in the exercise of their power: for having erected a legislative, with an intent they should exercise the power of making laws, either at certain set times, or when there is need of it; when they are hindered by any force from what is so necessary to the society, and wherein the safety and preservation of the people consists, the people have a right to remove it by force. In all states and conditions, the true remedy of force without authority is to oppose force to it. The use of force without authority always puts him that uses it into a state of war, as the aggressor, and renders him liable to be treated accordingly.

§ 156. The power of assembling and dismissing the legislative, placed in the executive, gives not the executive a superiority over it, but is a fiduciary trust placed in him for the safety of the people, in a case where the uncertainty and variableness of human affairs could not bear a steady fixed rule: for it not being possible that the first framers of the government should, by any foresight, be so much masters of future events as to be able to prefix so just periods of return and duration to the assemblies of the legislative, in all times to come, that might exactly answer all the exigencies of the commonwealth; the best remedy could be found for this defect was to trust this to the prudence of one who was always to be present, and whose business it was to watch over the public good. Constant frequent meetings of the legislative, and long continuations of their assemblies, without necessary occasion, could not but be burdensome to the people, and must necessarily in time produce more dangerous inconveniencies, and yet the quick turn of affairs might be sometimes such as to need their present help; any delay of their convening might endanger the public; and sometimes too their business might be so great, that the limited time of their sitting might be too short for their work, and rob the public of that benefit which could be had only from their mature deliberation. What then could be done in this case to prevent the community from being exposed some time or other to eminent hazard, on one side or the other, by fixed intervals and periods, set to the meeting and acting of the legislative; but to intrust it to the prudence of some, who being present, and acquainted with the state of public affairs, might make use of this prerogative for the public good? And where else could this be so well placed as in his hands, who was intrusted with the execution of the laws for the same end? Thus supposing the regulation of times for the assembling and sitting of the legislative not settled by the original constitution, it naturally fell into the hands of the executive, not as an arbitrary power depending on his good pleasure, but with this trust always to have it exercised only for the public weal, as the occurrences of times and change of affairs might require. Whether settled periods of their convening, or a liberty left to the prince for convoking the legislative, or perhaps a mixture of both, hath the least inconvenience attending it, it is not my business here to inquire; but only to show, that though the executive power may have the prerogative of convoking and dissolving such conventions of the legislative, yet it is not thereby superior to it.

§ 157. Things of this world are in so constant a flux, that nothing remains long in the same state. Thus people, riches, trade, power, change their stations, flourishing mighty cities come to ruin, and prove in time neglected desolate corners, whilst other unfrequented places grow into populous countries, filled with wealth and inhabitants. But things not always changing equally, and private interest often keeping up customs and privileges, when the reasons of them are ceased; it often comes to pass, that in governments, where part of the legislative consists of representatives chosen by the people, that in tract of time this representation becomes very unequal and disproportionate to the reasons it was at first established upon. To what gross absurdities the following of custom, when reason has left it, may lead, we may be satisfied, when we see the bare name of a town, of which there remains not so much as the ruins, where scarce so much housing as a sheepcote, or more inhabitants than a shepherd is to be found, sends as many representatives to the grand assembly of law-makers as a whole county, numerous in people, and powerful in riches. This strangers stand amazed at, and every one must confess needs a remedy; though most think it hard to find one; because the constitution of the legislative being the original and supreme act of the society, antecedent to all positive laws in it, and depending wholly on the people, no inferior power can alter it. And therefore the people, when the legislative is once constituted, having, in such a government as we have been speaking of, no power to act as long as the government stands; this inconvenience is thought incapable of a remedy.

§ 158. *Salus populi suprema lex*,[9] is certainly so just and fundamental a rule, that he, who sincerely follows it, cannot dangerously err. If therefore the executive, who has the power of convoking the legislative, observing rather the true proportion than fashion of representation, regulates not by old custom, but true reason, the number of members in all places that have a right to be distinctly represented, which no part of the people, however incorporated, can pretend to, but in proportion to the assistance which it affords to the public;[1] it cannot be judged to have set up a new legislative, but to have restored the old and true one, and to have rectified the disorders which succession of time had insensibly, as well as inevitably introduced; for it being the interest as well as intention of the people, to have a fair and equal representative; whoever brings it nearest to that, is an undoubted friend to, and establisher of the government, and cannot miss the consent and approbation of the community: prerogative being nothing but a power in the hands of the prince, to provide for the public good, in such cases, which depending upon unforeseen and uncertain occurrences, certain and unalterable laws could not safely direct; whatsoever shall be done manifestly for the good of the people, and the establishing the government upon its true foundations, is, and always will be, just prerogative. The power of erecting new corporations, and therewith new representatives, carries with it a supposition that in time the measures of representation might vary, and those places have a just right to be represented which before had none; and by the same reason, those cease to have a right, and be too inconsiderable for such a privilege, which before had it. It is not a change from the present state, which perhaps corruption or decay has introduced, that makes an inroad upon the government; but the tendency of it

---

9. The safety of the people is the highest law.
1. Locke's theory of legitimacy is based on political equality, but here he seems to allow for a property qualification, such as the contemporary English requirement of a "forty-shilling freehold" for voting, while proposing a reform that does away with unrepresentative "rotten boroughs."

to injure or oppress the people, and to set up one part or party, with a distinction from, and an unequal subjection of the rest. Whatsoever cannot but be acknowledged to be of advantage to the society, and people in general, upon just and lasting measures, will always, when done, justify itself; and whenever the people shall choose their representatives upon just and undeniably equal measures, suitable to the original frame of the government, it cannot be doubted to be the will and act of the society, whoever permitted or caused them so to do.

Chapter XIV.

OF PREROGATIVE.

§ 159. WHERE the legislative and executive power are in distinct hands, (as they are in all moderated monarchies and well-framed governments) there the good of the society requires, that several things should be left to the discretion of him that has the executive power: for the legislators not being able to foresee, and provide by laws, for all that may be useful to the community, the executor of the laws having the power in his hands, has by the common law of nature a right to make use of it for the good of the society, in many cases, where the municipal law has given no direction, till the legislative can conveniently be assembled to provide for it. Many things there are, which the law can by no means provide for; and those must necessarily be left to the discretion of him that has the executive power in his hands, to be ordered by him as the public good and advantage shall require: nay, it is fit that the laws themselves should in some cases give way to the executive power, or rather to this fundamental law of nature and government, viz. that, as much as may be, all the members of the society are to be preserved: for since many accidents may happen, wherein a strict and rigid observation of the laws may do harm; (as not to pull down an innocent man's house to stop the fire, when the next to it is burning) and a man may come sometimes within the reach of the law, which makes no distinction of persons, by an action that may deserve reward and pardon; it is fit the ruler should have a power, in many cases, to mitigate the severity of the law, and pardon some offenders: for the end of government being the preservation of all, as much as may be, even the guilty are to be spared, where it can prove no prejudice to the innocent.

§ 160. This power to act according to discretion for the public good, without the prescription of the law, and sometimes even against it, is that which is called prerogative: for since in some gov-

ernments the law-making power is not always in being, and is usually too numerous, and so too slow for the despatch requisite to execution; and because also it is impossible to foresee, and so by laws
to provide for all accidents and necessities that may concern the
public, or to make such laws as will do no harm, if they are executed with an inflexible rigour on all occasions, and upon all persons that may come in their way; therefore there is a latitude left to
the executive power, to do many things of choice which the laws do
not prescribe.

§ 161. This power, whilst employed for the benefit of the community, and suitably to the trust and ends of the government, is undoubted prerogative, and never is questioned; for the people are
very seldom or never scrupulous or nice in the point; they are far
from examining prerogative, whilst it is in any tolerable degree
employed for the use it was meant; that is, for the good of the people, and not manifestly against it: but if there comes to be a question between the executive power and the people, about a thing
claimed as a prerogative, the tendency of the exercise of such prerogative to the good or hurt of the people will easily decide that
question.

§ 162. It is easy to conceive, that in the infancy of governments,
when commonwealths differed little from families in number of
people, they differed from them too but little in number of laws:
and the governors being as the fathers of them, watching over them
for their good, the government was almost all prerogative. A few established laws served the turn, and the discretion and care of the
ruler supplied the rest. But when mistake or flattery prevailed with
weak princes to make use of this power for private ends of their
own, and not for the public good, the people were fain by express
laws to get prerogative determined in those points wherein they
found disadvantage from it: and thus declared limitations of prerogative were by the people found necessary in cases which they
and their ancestors had left, in the utmost latitude, to the wisdom
of those princes who made no other but a right use of it; that is, for
the good of their people.

§ 163. And therefore they have a very wrong notion of government, who say, that the people have encroached upon the prerogative, when they have got any part of it to be defined by positive
laws: for in so doing they have not pulled from the prince any thing
that of right belonged to him, but only declare, that that power
which they indefinitely left in his or his ancestors' hands, to be exercised for their good, was not a thing which they intended him
when he used it otherwise: for the end of government being the
good of the community, whatsoever alterations are made in it, tend-

ing to that end, cannot be an encroachment upon any body, since nobody in government can have a right tending to any other end: and those only are encroachments which prejudice or hinder the public good. Those who say otherwise, speak as if the prince had a distinct and separate interest from the good of the community, and was not made for it; the root and source from which spring almost all those evils and disorders which happen in kingly governments. And indeed, if that be so, the people under his government are not a society of rational creatures, entered into a community for their mutual good; they are not such as have set rulers over themselves, to guard and promote that good; but are to be looked on as an herd of inferior creatures under the dominion of a master, who keeps them and works them for his own pleasure or profit. If men were so void of reason, and brutish, as to enter into society upon such terms, prerogative might indeed be, what some men would have it, an arbitrary power to do things hurtful to the people.

§ 164. But since a rational creature cannot be supposed, when free, to put himself into subjection to another, for his own harm; (though, where he finds a good and wise ruler, he may not perhaps think it either necessary or useful to set precise bounds to his power in all things) prerogative can be nothing but the people's permitting their rulers to do several things, of their own free choice, where the law was silent, and sometimes too against the direct letter of the law, for the public good; and their acquiescing in it when so done: for as a good prince, who is mindful of the trust put into his hands, and careful of the good of his people, cannot have too much prerogative, that is, power to do good; so a weak and ill prince, who would claim that power which his predecessors exercised without the direction of the law, as a prerogative belonging to him by right of his office, which he may exercise at his pleasure, to make or promote an interest distinct from that of the public; gives the people an occasion to claim their right, and limit that power, which, whilst it was exercised for their good, they were content should be tacitly allowed.

§ 165. And therefore he that will look into the history of England, will find, that prerogative was always largest in the hands of our wisest and best princes; because the people, observing the whole tendency of their actions to be the public good, contested not what was done without law to that end: or, if any human frailty or mistake (for princes are but men, made as others) appeared in some small declinations from that end; yet it was visible, the main of their conduct tended to nothing but the care of the public. The people, therefore, finding reason to be satisfied with these princes, whenever they acted without, or contrary to the letter of the law, acqui-

esced in what they did, and, without the least complaint, let them
enlarge their prerogative as they pleased; judging rightly, that they
did nothing herein to the prejudice of their laws, since they acted
conformably to the foundation and end of all laws, the public good.

§ 166. Such God-like princes, indeed, had some title to arbitrary
power by that argument, that would prove absolute monarchy the
best government, as that which God himself governs the universe
by; because such kings partook of his wisdom and goodness. Upon
this is founded that saying, That the reigns of good princes have
been always most dangerous to the liberties of their people: for
when their successors, managing the government with different
thoughts, would draw the actions of those good rulers into precedent, and make them the standard of their prerogative, as if what
had been done only for the good of the people was a right in them
to do for the harm of the people, if they so pleased; it has often occasioned contest, and sometimes public disorders, before the people could recover their original right, and get that to be declared
not to be prerogative, which truly was never so: since it is impossible that any body in the society should ever have a right to do the
people harm; though it be very possible and reasonable that the
people should not go about to set any bounds to the prerogative of
those kings or rulers, who themselves transgressed not the bounds
of the public good; for prerogative is nothing but the power of doing public good without a rule.

§ 167. The power of calling parliaments in England, as to precise
time, place, and duration, is certainly a prerogative of the king, but
still with this trust, that it shall be made use of for the good of the nation, as the exigencies of the times, and variety of occasions shall require: for it being impossible to foresee which should always be the
fittest place for them to assemble in, and what the best season, the
choice of these was left with the executive power, as might be most
subservient to the public good, and best suit the ends of parliaments.

§ 168. The old question will be asked in this matter of prerogative, But who shall be judge when this power is made a right use
of? I answer: between an executive power in being, with such a
prerogative, and a legislative that depends upon his will for their
convening, there can be no judge on earth; as there can be none
between the legislative and the people, should either the executive
or the legislative, when they have got the power in their hands, design or go about to enslave or destroy them. The people have no
other remedy in this, as in all other cases where they have no judge
on earth, but to appeal to heaven: for the rulers, in such attempts,
exercising a power the people never put into their hands (who can
never be supposed to consent that any body should rule over them

for their harm), do that which they have not a right to do. And where the body of the people, or any single man,[2] is deprived of their right, or under the exercise of a power without right, and have no appeal on earth, then they have a liberty to appeal to heaven, whenever they judge the cause of sufficient moment. And therefore, though the people cannot be judge, so as to have, by the constitution of that society, any superior power to determine and give effective sentence in the case; yet they have, by a law antecedent and paramount to all positive laws of men, reserved that ultimate determination to themselves which belongs to all mankind, where there lies no appeal on earth, viz. to judge whether they have just cause to make their appeal to heaven. And this judgment they cannot part with, it being out of a man's power so to submit himself to another, as to give him a liberty to destroy him; God and nature never allowing a man so to abandon himself, as to neglect his own preservation: and since he cannot take away his own life, neither can he give another power to take it. Nor let any one think this lays a perpetual foundation for disorder; for this operates not till the inconveniency is so great that the majority feel it, and are weary of it, and find a necessity to have it amended. But this the executive power, or wise princes, never need come in the danger of: and it is the thing, of all others, they have most need to avoid, as of all others the most perilous.

Chapter XV.

OF PATERNAL, POLITICAL, AND DESPOTICAL POWER, CONSIDERED TOGETHER.

§ 169. THOUGH I have had occasion to speak of these separately before, yet the great mistakes of late about government having, as I suppose, arisen from confounding these distinct powers one with another, it may not, perhaps, be amiss to consider them here together.

§ 170. First, then, paternal or parental power is nothing but that which parents have over their children, to govern them for the children's good, till they come to the use of reason, or a state of knowledge, wherein they may be supposed capable to understand that rule, whether it be the law of nature, or the municipal law of their country, they are to govern themselves by: capable, I say, to know it, as well as several others, who live as freemen under that law. The af-

---

2. Despite his earlier assertions of the rights of the majority, Locke here allows an individual ("any single man") whose rights have been violated to resort to armed rebellion. Later in the paragraph he links it to the duty of self-preservation and the prohibition of suicide.

fection and tenderness which God hath planted in the breast of parents towards their children, makes it evident, that this is not intended to be a severe arbitrary government, but only for the help, instruction, and preservation of their offspring. But happen it as it will, there is, as I have proved, no reason why it should be thought to extend to life and death, at any time, over their children, more than over any body else; neither can there be any pretence why this parental power should keep the child, when grown to a man, in subjection to the will of his parents, any farther than having received life and education from his parents, obliges him to respect, honour, gratitude, assistance, and support, all his life, to both father and mother. And thus, it is true, the paternal is a natural government, but not at all extending itself to the ends and jurisdictions of that which is political. The power of the father doth not reach at all to the property of the child, which is only in his own disposing.

§ 171. Secondly, political power is that power which every man having in the state of nature, has given up into the hands of the society, and therein to the governors, whom the society hath set over itself, with this express or tacit trust, that it shall be employed for their good, and the preservation of their property: now this power, which every man has in the state of nature, and which he parts with to the society in all such cases where the society can secure him, is to use such means for the preserving of his own property as he thinks good, and nature allows him; and to punish the breach of the law of nature in others, so as (according to the best of his reason) may most conduce to the preservation of himself and the rest of mankind. So that the end and measure of this power, when in every man's hands in the state of nature, being the preservation of all of his society, that is, all mankind in general, it can have no other end or measure, when in the hands of the magistrate, but to preserve the members of that society in their lives, liberties, and possessions; and so cannot be an absolute arbitrary power over their lives and fortunes, which are as much as possible to be preserved; but a power to make laws, and annex such penalties to them, as may tend to the preservation of the whole, by cutting off those parts, and those only, which are so corrupt that they threaten the sound and healthy, without which no severity is lawful. And this power has its original only from compact and agreement, and the mutual consent of those who make up the community.

§ 172. Thirdly, despotical power is an absolute, arbitrary power one man has over another, to take away his life whenever he pleases. This is a power, which neither nature gives, for it has made no such distinction between one man and another, nor compact can convey; for man not having such an arbitrary power over his own life, cannot give another man such a power over it; but it is the effect only of forfeiture, which the aggressor makes of his own life, when he puts himself into the state of war with another: for having quitted reason, which God hath given to be the rule betwixt man and man, and the common bond whereby human kind is united into one fellowship and society, and having renounced the way of peace which that teaches, and made use of the force of war, to compass his unjust ends upon another, where he has no right; and so revolting from his own kind to that of beasts, by making force, which is theirs, to be his rule of right; he renders himself liable to be destroyed by the injured person, and the rest of mankind, that will join with him in the execution of justice, as any other wild beast, or noxious brute, with whom mankind can have neither society nor security.[3] And thus captives, taken in a just and lawful war, and such only, are subject to a despotical power; which, as it arises not from compact, so neither is it capable of any, but is the state of war continued: for what compact can be made with a man that is not master of his own life? what condition can he perform? and if he be once allowed to be master of his own life, the despotical arbitrary power of his master ceases. He that is master of himself, and his own life, has a right too to the means of preserving it; so that, as soon as compact enters, slavery ceases, and he so far quits his absolute power, and puts an end to the state of war, who enters into conditions with his captive.

§ 173. Nature gives the first of these, viz. paternal power, to parents for the benefit of their children during their minority, to supply their want of ability and understanding how to manage their property. (By property I must be understood here, as in other places, to mean that property which men have in their persons as well as goods.) Voluntary agreement gives the second, viz. political power to governors for the benefit of their subjects, to secure them in the possession and use of their properties. And forfeiture gives the third despotical power to lords, for their own benefit, over those who are stripped of all property.

§ 174. He that shall consider the distinct rise and extent, and the different ends of these several powers, will plainly see, that paternal power comes as far short of that of the magistrate, as despotical exceeds it; and that absolute dominion, however placed, is so far from being one kind of civil society, that it is as inconsistent with it, as slavery is with property. Paternal power is only where minority makes the child incapable to manage his property; political, where men have property in their own disposal; and despotical, over such as have no property at all.

---

3. Another copy, corrected by Mr. Locke, has it thus, "Noxious brute that is destructive to their being."

Chapter XVI.

OF CONQUEST.

§ 175. Though governments can originally have no other rise than that before-mentioned, nor politics be founded on any thing but the consent of the people; yet such have been the disorders ambition has filled the world with, that in the noise of war, which makes so great a part of the history of mankind, this consent is little taken notice of: and therefore many have mistaken the force of arms for the consent of the people, and reckon conquest as one of the originals of government. But conquest is as far from setting up any government, as demolishing a house is from building a new one in the place. Indeed, it often makes way for a new frame of a commonwealth, by destroying the former; but, without the consent of the people, can never erect a new one.

§ 176. That the aggressor, who puts himself into the state of war with another, and unjustly invades another man's right, can, by such an unjust war, never come to have a right over the conquered, will be easily agreed by all men, who will not think that robbers and pirates have a right of empire over whomsoever they have force enough to master, or that men are bound by promises which unlawful force extorts from them. Should a robber break into my house, and with a dagger at my throat make me seal deeds to convey my estate to him, would this give him any title? Just such a title, by his sword, has an unjust conqueror, who forces me into submission. The injury and the crime are equal, whether committed by the wearer of the crown or some petty villain. The title of the offender, and the number of his followers, make no difference in the offence, unless it be to aggravate it. The only difference is, great robbers punish little ones, to keep them in their obedience; but the great ones are rewarded with laurels and triumphs, because they are too big for the weak hands of justice in this world, and have the power in their own possession which should punish offenders. What is my remedy against a robber, that so broke into my house? Appeal to the law for justice. But perhaps justice is denied, or I am crippled and cannot stir, robbed and have not the means to do it. If God has taken away all means of seeking remedy, there is nothing left but patience. But my son, when able, may seek the relief of the law, which I am denied: he or his son may renew his appeal, till he recover his right. But the conquered, or their children, have no court, no arbitrator on earth to appeal to. Then they may appeal, as Jephthah did, to heaven, and repeat their appeal till they have recovered the native right of their ancestors, which was, to have such a legislative over them as the majority should approve, and freely acquiesce in. If it be objected, this would cause endless trouble; I answer, no more than justice does, where she lies open to all that appeal to her. He that troubles his neighbour without a cause, is punished for it by the justice of the court he appeals to; and he that appeals to heaven must be sure he has right on his side, and a right too that is worth the trouble and cost of the appeal, as he will answer at a tribunal that cannot be deceived, and will be sure to retribute to every one according to the mischiefs he hath created to his fellow-subjects; that is, any part of mankind: from whence it is plain, that he that conquers in an unjust war, can thereby have no title to the subjection and obedience of the conquered.

§ 177. But supposing victory favours the right side, let us consider a conqueror in a lawful war, and see what power he gets, and over whom.

First, It is plain he gets no power by his conquest over those that conquered with him. They that fought on his side cannot suffer by the conquest, but must at least be as much freemen as they were before. And most commonly they serve upon terms, and on conditions to share with their leader, and enjoy a part of the spoil, and other advantages that attended the conquering sword; or at least have a part of the subdued country bestowed upon them. And the conquering people are not, I hope, to be slaves by conquest, and wear their laurels only to show they are sacrifices to their leader's triumph. They that found absolute monarchy upon the title of the sword, make their heroes, who are the founders of such monarchies, arrant Draw-can-sirs,[4] and forget they had any officers and soldiers that fought on their side in the battles they won, or assisted them in the subduing, or shared in possessing, the countries they mastered. We are told by some, that the English monarchy is founded in the Norman conquest, and that our princes have thereby a title to absolute dominion: which if it were true (as by the history it appears otherwise), and that William had a right to make war on this island, yet his dominion by conquest could reach no farther than to the Saxons and Britons, that were then inhabitants of this country. The Normans that came with him, and helped to conquer, and all descended from them, are freemen, and no subjects by conquest, let that give what dominion it will. And if I, or any body else, shall claim freedom, as derived from them, it will be very hard to prove the contrary; and it is plain the law, that has made no distinction between the one and the other, intends not there should be any difference in their freedom or privileges.

4. Indiscriminate killers. From *The Rehearsal*, a popular play composed in 1663–64 (see Locke, 1988, 387).

§ 178. But supposing, which seldom happens, that the conquerors and conquered never incorporate into one people, under the same laws and freedom; let us see next what power a lawful conqueror has over the subdued: and that I say is purely despotical. He has an absolute power over the lives of those who by an unjust war have forfeited them; but not over the lives or fortunes of those who engaged not in the war, nor over the possessions even of those who were actually engaged in it.

§ 179. Secondly, I say then the conqueror gets no power but only over those who have actually assisted, concurred, or consented to that unjust force that is used against him: for the people having given to their governors no power to do an unjust thing, such as is to make an unjust war (for they never had such a power in themselves) they ought not to be charged as guilty of the violence and injustice that is committed in an unjust war, any farther than they actually abet it, no more than they are to be thought guilty of any violence or oppression their governors should use upon the people themselves, or any part of their fellow-subjects, they having empowered them no more to the one than to the other. Conquerors, it is true, seldom trouble themselves to make the distinction, but they willingly permit the confusion of war to sweep all together: but yet this alters not the right; for the conqueror's power over the lives of the conquered being only because they have used force to do, or maintain an injustice, he can have that power only over those who have concurred in that force; all the rest are innocent; and he has no more title over the people of that country, who have done him no injury, and so have made no forfeiture of their lives, than he has over any other, who, without any injuries or provocations, have lived upon fair terms with him.

§ 180. Thirdly, The power a conqueror gets over those he overcomes in a just war, is perfectly despotical: he has an absolute power over the lives of those, who, by putting themselves in a state of war, have forfeited them; but he has not thereby a right and title to their possessions. This I doubt not but at first sight will seem a strange doctrine, it being so quite contrary to the practice of the world; there being nothing more familiar in speaking of the dominion of countries, than to say such an one conquered it; as if conquest, without any more ado, conveyed a right of possession. But when we consider, that the practice of the strong and powerful, how universal soever it may be, is seldom the rule of right, however it be one part of the subjection of the conquered, not to argue against the conditions cut out to them by the conquering sword.

§ 181. Though in all war there be usually a complication of force and damage, and the aggressor seldom fails to harm the estate, when he uses force against the persons of those he makes war upon; yet it is the use of force only that puts a man into the state of war: for whether by force he begins the injury, or else having quietly, and by fraud, done the injury, he refuses to make reparation, and by force maintains it (which is the same thing, as at first to have done it by force), it is the unjust use of force that makes the war: for he that breaks open my house, and violently turns me out of doors; or, having peaceably got in, by force keeps me out, does in effect the same thing; supposing we are in such a state that we have no common judge on earth whom I may appeal to, and to whom we are both obliged to submit; for of such I am now speaking. It is the unjust use of force then, that puts a man into the state of war with another; and thereby he that is guilty of it makes a forfeiture of his life: for quitting reason, which is the rule given between man and man, and using force, the way of beasts, he becomes liable to be destroyed by him he uses force against, as any savage ravenous beast, that is dangerous to his being.

§ 182. But because the miscarriages of the father are no faults of the children, and they may be rational and peaceable, notwithstanding the brutishness and injustice of the father; the father, by his miscarriages and violence, can forfeit but his own life, but involves not his children in his guilt or destruction. His goods, which nature, that willeth the preservation of all mankind as much as is possible, hath made to belong to the children to keep them from perishing, do still continue to belong to his children; for supposing them not to have joined in the war, either through infancy, absence, or choice, they have done nothing to forfeit them: nor has the conqueror any right to take them away, by the bare title of having subdued him that by force attempted his destruction; though perhaps he may have some right to them, to repair the damages he has sustained by the war, and the defence of his own right; which how far it reaches to the possessions of the conquered, we shall see by and by. So that he that by conquest has a right over a man's person to destroy him if he pleases, has not thereby a right over his estate to possess and enjoy it; for it is the brutal force the aggressor has used that gives his adversary a right to take away his life, and destroy him, if he pleases, as a noxious creature; but it is damage sustained that alone gives him title to another man's goods: for though I may kill a thief that sets on me in the highway, yet I may not (which seems less) take away his money and let him go: this would be robbery on my side. His force, and the state of war he put himself in, made him forfeit his life, but gave me no title to his goods. The right then of conquest extends only to the lives of those who joined in the war, not to their estates, but only in order to make reparation for the damages received, and the charges of the war; and that too with reservation of the right of the innocent wife and children.

§ 183. Let the conqueror have as much justice on his side as could be supposed, he has no right to seize more than the vanquished could forfeit: his life is at the victor's mercy; and his service and goods he may appropriate to make himself reparation; but he cannot take the goods of his wife and children: they too had a title to the goods he enjoyed, and their shares in the estate he possessed: for example, I in the state of nature (and all commonwealths are in the state of nature one with another) have injured another man, and refusing to give satisfaction, it comes to a state of war, wherein my defending by force what I had gotten unjustly makes me the aggressor. I am conquered: my life, it is true, as forfeit, is at mercy, but not my wife's and children's. They made not the war, nor assisted in it. I could not forfeit their lives; they were not mine to forfeit. My wife had a share in my estate; that neither could I forfeit. And my children also, being born of me, had a right to be maintained out of my labour or substance. Here then is the case: the conqueror has a title to reparation for damages received, and the children have a title to their father's estate for their subsistence: for as to the wife's share, whether her own labour, or compact, gave her a title to it, it is plain her husband could not forfeit what was hers. What must be done in the case? I answer; the fundamental law of nature being, that all, as much as may be, should be preserved, it follows, that if there be not enough fully to satisfy both, viz. for the conqueror's losses, and children's maintenance, he that hath, and to spare, must remit something of his full satisfaction, and give way to the pressing and preferable title of those who are in danger to perish without it.

§ 184. But supposing the charge and damages of the war are to be made up to the conqueror, to the utmost farthing; and that the children of the vanquished, spoiled of all their father's goods, are to be left to starve and perish; yet the satisfying of what shall, on this score, be due to the conqueror, will scarce give him a title to any country he shall conquer: for the damages of war can scarce amount to the value of any considerable tract of land, in any part of the world, where all the land is possessed, and none lies waste. And if I have not taken away the conqueror's land, which, being vanquished, it is impossible I should; scarce any other spoil I have done him can amount to the value of mine, supposing it equally cultivated, and of an extent any way coming near what I had overrun of his. The destruction of a year's product or two (for it seldom reaches four or five) is the utmost spoil that usually can be done: for as to money, and such riches and treasure taken away, these are none of nature's goods, they have but a fantastical imaginary value: nature has put no such upon them: they are of no more account by her standard, than the wampompeke[5] of the Americans to an European prince, or the silver money of Europe would have been formerly to an American. And five years product is not worth the perpetual inheritance of land, where all is possessed, and none remains waste, to be taken up by him that is disseized:[6] which will be easily granted, if one do but take away the imaginary value of money, the disproportion being more than between five and five hundred; though, at the same time, half a year's product is more worth than the inheritance, where there being more land than the inhabitants possess and make use of, any one has liberty to make use of the waste: but there conquerors take little care to possess themselves of the lands of the vanquished. No damage, therefore, that men in the state of nature (as all princes and governments are in reference to one another) suffer from one another, can give a conqueror power to dispossess the posterity of the vanquished, and turn them out of their inheritance, which ought to be the possession of them and their descendants to all generations. The conqueror indeed will be apt to think himself master: and it is the very condition of the subdued not to be able to dispute their right. But if that be all, it gives no other title than what bare force gives to the stronger over the weaker: and, by this reason, he that is strongest will have a right to whatever he pleases to seize on.

§ 185. Over those then that joined with him in the war, and over those of the subdued country that opposed him not, and the posterity even of those that did, the conqueror, even in a just war, hath, by his conquest, no right of dominion: they are free from any subjection to him, and if their former government be dissolved, they are at liberty to begin and erect another to themselves.

§ 186. The conqueror, it is true, usually, by the force he has over them, compels them, with a sword at their breasts, to stoop to his conditions, and submit to such a government as he pleases to afford them; but the inquiry is, what right he has to do so? If it be said, they submit by their own consent, then this allows their own consent to be necessary to give the conqueror a title to rule over them. It remains only to be considered, whether promises extorted by force, without right, can be thought consent, and how far they bind. To which I shall say, they bind not at all; because whatsoever another gets from me by force, I still retain the right of, and he is obliged presently to restore. He that forces my horse from me, ought presently to restore him, and I have still a right to retake

5. Wampum.
6. Dispossessed.

him. By the same reason, he that forced a promise from me, ought presently to restore it, *i.e.* quit me of the obligation of it; or I may resume it myself, *i.e.* choose whether I will perform it: for the law of nature laying an obligation on me only by the rules she prescribes, cannot oblige me by the violation of her rules: such is the extorting any thing from me by force. Nor does it at all alter the case to say, "I gave my promise," no more than it excuses the force, and passes the right, when I put my hand in my pocket and deliver my purse myself to a thief, who demands it with a pistol at my breast.

§ 187. From all which it follows, that the government of a conqueror, imposed by force on the subdued, against whom he had no right of war, or who joined not in the war against him, where he had right, has no obligation upon them.

§ 188. But let us suppose that all the men of that community, being all members of the same body politic, may be taken to have joined in that unjust war wherein they are subdued, and so their lives are at the mercy of the conqueror.

§ 189. I say, this concerns not their children who are in their minority: for since a father hath not, in himself, a power over the life or liberty of his child, no act of his can possibly forfeit it. So that the children, whatever may have happened to the fathers, are freemen, and the absolute power of the conqueror reaches no farther than the persons of the men that were subdued by him, and dies with them: and should he govern them as slaves, subjected to his absolute arbitrary power, he has no such right or dominion over their children. He can have no power over them but by their own consent, whatever he may drive them to say or do; and he has no lawful authority, whilst force, and not choice, compels them to submission.

§ 190. Every man is born with a double right: first, a right of freedom to his person, which no other man has a power over, but the free disposal of it lies in himself. Secondly, a right, before any other man, to inherit with his brethren his father's goods.

§ 191. By the first of these, a man is naturally free from subjection to any government, though he be born in a place under its jurisdiction; but if he disclaim the lawful government of the country he was born in, he must also quit the right that belonged to him by the laws of it, and the possessions there descending to him from his ancestors, if it were a government made by their consent.

§ 192. By the second, the inhabitants of any country, who are descended, and derive a title to their estates from those who are subdued, and had a government forced upon them against their free consents, retain a right to the possession of their ancestors, though they consent not freely to the government, whose hard conditions were by force imposed on the possessors of that country: for, the first conqueror never having had a title to the land of that country, the people who are the descendants of, or claim under those who were forced to submit to the yoke of a government by constraint, have always a right to shake it off, and free themselves from the usurpation or tyranny which the sword hath brought in upon them, till their rulers put them under such a frame of government as they willingly and of choice consent to. Who doubts but the Grecian Christians, descendants of the ancient possessors of that country, may justly cast off the Turkish yoke, which they have so long groaned under, whenever they have an opportunity to do it? For no government can have a right to obedience from a people who have not freely consented to it; which they can never be supposed to do, till either they are put in a full state of liberty to choose their government and governors, or at least till they have such standing laws, to which they have by themselves or their representatives given their free consent; and also till they are allowed their due property, which is so to be proprietors of what they have, that nobody can take away any part of it without their own consent, without which, men under any government are not in the state of freemen, but are direct slaves under the force of war.

§ 193. But granting that the conqueror in a just war has a right to the estates, as well as power over the persons of the conquered; which, it is plain, he hath not: nothing of absolute power will follow from hence, in the continuance of the government; because the descendants of these being all freemen, if he grants them estates and possessions to inhabit his country, (without which it would be worth nothing) whatsoever he grants them, they have, so far as it is granted, property in. The nature whereof is, that without a man's own consent, it cannot be taken from him.

§ 194. Their persons are free by a native right, and their properties, be they more or less, are their own, and at their own disposal, and not at his; or else it is no property. Supposing the conqueror gives to one man a thousand acres, to him and his heirs for ever; to another he lets a thousand acres for his life, under the rent of 50£. or 500£. per ann.: has not the one of these a right to his thousand acres for ever, and the other during his life, paying the said rent and hath not the tenant for life a property in all that he gets over and above his rent, by his labour and industry during the said term, supposing it to be double the rent Can any one say, the king, or conqueror, after his grant, may by his power of conqueror take away all, or part of the land from the heirs of one, or from the other during his life, he paying the rent? or can he take away from either the goods or money they have got upon the said land, at his pleasure? If he can, then all free and voluntary contracts cease, and are void in the world; there needs nothing to dissolve them at any time, but power enough; and all the grants and promises of men in power are but mockery and collusion: for can there be any thing more ridiculous than to say, I give you and yours this for ever, and that in the surest and most solemn way of conveyance can be devised; and yet it is to be understood, that I have right, if I please, to take it away from you again to-morrow?

§ 195. I will not dispute now, whether princes are exempt from the laws of their country; but this I am sure, they owe subjection to the laws of God and nature. Nobody, no power, can exempt them from the obligations of that eternal law. Those are so great, and so strong, in the case of promises, that omnipotency itself can be tied by them. Grants, promises, and oaths, are bonds that hold the Almighty: whatever some flatterers say to princes of the world, who all together, with all their people joined to them, are in comparison of the great God, but as a drop of the bucket, or a dust on the balance, inconsiderable, nothing.

§ 196. The short of the case in conquest is this: the conqueror, if he have a just cause, has a despotical right over the persons of all that actually aided, and concurred in the war against him, and a right to make up his damage and cost out of their labour and estates, so he injure not the right of any other. Over the rest of the people, if there were any that consented not to the war, and over the children of the captives themselves, or the possessions of either, he has no power; and so can have, by virtue of conquest, no lawful title himself to dominion over them, or derive it to his posterity; but is an aggressor, if he attempts upon their properties, and thereby puts himself in a state of war against them: and has no better a right of principality, he, nor any of his successors, than Hingar, or Hubba, the Danes, had here in England; or Spartacus,[7] had he conquered Italy, would have had; which is to have their yoke cast off, as soon as God shall give those under their subjection courage and opportunity to do it. Thus, notwithstanding whatever title the kings of Assyria had over Judah, by the sword, God assisted Hezekiah to throw off the dominion of that conquering empire. "And the Lord was with Hezekiah, and he prospered; wherefore he went forth, and he rebelled against the king of Assyria; and served him not," 2 Kings, xviii. 7. Whence it is plain, that shaking off a power, which force, and not right, hath set over any one, though it hath the name of rebellion, yet is no offence before God, but is that which he allows and countenances, though even promises and covenants, when obtained by force, have intervened: for it is very

---

7. Gladiator (1st century), who led a revolt against Rome. Ingware and Ubba (Hingar and Hubba), 9th-century invaders of England.

probable, to any one that reads the story of Ahaz and Hezekiah attentively, that the Assyrians subdued Ahaz, and deposed him, and made Hezekiah king in his father's lifetime; and that Hezekiah by agreement had done him homage, and paid him tribute all this time.

Chapter XVII.

OF USURPATION.

§ 197. As conquest may be called a foreign usurpation, so usurpation is a kind of domestic conquest; with this difference, that an usurper can never have right on his side, it being no usurpation but where one is got into the possession of what another has right to. This, so far as it is usurpation, is a change only of persons, but not of the forms and rules of the government: for if the usurper extend his power beyond what of right belonged to the lawful princes or governors of the commonwealth, it is tyranny added to usurpation.

§ 198. In all lawful governments, the designation of the persons, who are to bear rule, is as natural and necessary a part as the form of the government itself; and is that which had its establishment originally from the people. Hence all commonwealths, with the form of government established, have rules also of appointing those who are to have any share in the public authority, and settled methods of conveying the right to them: for the anarchy is much alike to have no form of government at all, or to agree that it shall be monarchical, but to appoint no way to know or design the person that shall have the power, and be the monarch. Whoever gets into the exercise of any part of the power, by other ways than what the laws of the community have prescribed, hath no right to be obeyed, though the form of the commonwealth be still preserved; since he is not the person the laws have appointed, and consequently not the person the people have consented to. Nor can such an usurper, or any deriving from him, ever have a title, till the people are both at liberty to consent, and have actually consented to allow, and confirm in him the power he hath till then usurped.

Chapter XVIII.

OF TYRANNY.

§ 199. As usurpation is the exercise of power, which another hath a right to, so tyranny is the exercise of power beyond right, which nobody can have a right to. And this is making use of the power any one has in his hands, not for the good of those who are under it, but for his own private, separate advantage. When the governor, however entitled, makes not the law, but his will, the rule; and his commands and actions are not directed to the preservation of the properties of his people, but the satisfaction of his own ambition, revenge, covetousness, or any other irregular passion.

§ 200. If one can doubt this to be truth or reason, because it comes from the obscure hand of a subject, I hope the authority of a king will make it pass with him. King James the First,[8] in his speech to the parliament, 1603, tells them thus: "I will ever prefer the weal of the public, and of the whole commonwealth, in making of good laws and constitutions, to any particular and private ends of mine; thinking ever the wealth and weal of the commonwealth to be my greatest weal and worldly felicity; a point wherein a lawful king doth directly differ from a tyrant: for I do acknowledge, that the special and greatest point of difference that is between a rightful king and an usurping tyrant is this, that whereas the proud and ambitious tyrant doth think his kingdom and people are only ordained for satisfaction of his desires and unreasonable appetites, the righteous and just king doth, by the contrary, acknowledge himself to be ordained for the procuring of the wealth and property of his people." And again, in his speech to the parliament, 1609, he hath these words: "The king binds himself by a double oath to the observation of the fundamental laws of his kingdom; tacitly, as by being a king, and so bound to protect as well the people, as the laws of his kingdom; and expressly, by his oath at his coronation; so as every just king, in a settled kingdom, is bound to observe that paction made to his people by his laws, in framing his government agreeable thereunto, according to that paction which God made with Noah after the deluge: Hereafter, seed-time and harvest, and cold and heat, and summer and winter, and day and night, shall not cease while the earth remaineth. And therefore a king governing in a settled kingdom, leaves to be a king, and degenerates into a tyrant, as soon as he leaves off to rule according to his laws." And a little after, "Therefore all kings that are not tyrants, or perjured, will be glad to

---

8. Added by Locke to the third edition (1698), again indicating that this section was written before the accession of James II to the throne in 1685.

bound themselves within the limits of their laws; and they that persuade them the contrary, are vipers, and pests both against them and the commonwealth." Thus that learned king, who well understood the notions of things, makes the difference betwixt a king and a tyrant to consist only in this, that one makes the laws the bounds of his power, and the good of the public the end of his government; the other makes all give way to his own will and appetite.

§ 201. It is a mistake to think this fault is proper only to monarchies; other forms of government are liable to it, as well as that: for wherever the power, that is put in any hands for the government of the people, and the preservation of their properties, is applied to other ends, and made use of to impoverish, harass, or subdue them to the arbitrary and irregular commands of those that have it; there it presently becomes tyranny, whether those that thus use it are one or many. Thus we read of the thirty tyrants at Athens, as well as one at Syracuse; and the intolerable dominion of the decemviri[9] at Rome was nothing better.

§ 202. Wherever law ends, tyranny begins, if the law be transgressed to another's harm; and whosoever in authority exceeds the power given him by the law, and makes use of the force he has under his command, to compass that upon the subject which the law allows not, ceases in that to be a magistrate; and, acting without authority, may be opposed as any other man who by force invades the right of another. This is acknowledged in subordinate magistrates. He that hath authority to seize my person in the street, may be opposed as a thief and a robber if he endeavours to break into my house to execute a writ, notwithstanding that I know he has such a warrant, and such a legal authority as will impower him to arrest me abroad. And why this should not hold in the highest, as well as in the most inferior magistrate, I would gladly be informed. Is it reasonable that the eldest brother, because he has the greatest part of his father's estate, should thereby have a right to take away any of his younger brother's portions or that a rich man, who possessed a whole country, should from thence have a right to seize, when he pleased, the cottage and garden of his poor neighbour? The being rightfully possessed of great power and riches, exceedingly beyond the greatest part of the sons of Adam, is so far from being an excuse, much less a reason, for rapine and oppression, which the endamaging another without authority is, that it is a great aggravation of it: for the exceeding the bounds of authority is no more a right in a great, than in a petty officer; no more justifiable in a king than a constable; but is so much the worse in him, in

---

9. Ten patrician rulers of Rome, forced out in 449 B.C.E. The thirty tyrants ruled Athens in 404–403 B.C.E. Syracuse, in Sicily, was ruled by the tyrant Hiero in the 3rd century B.C.E.

that he has more trust put in him, has already a much greater share than the rest of his brethren, and is supposed, from the advantages of his education, employment, and counsellors, to be more knowing in the measures of right and wrong.

§ 203. May the commands then of a prince be opposed? may he be resisted as often as any one shall find himself aggrieved, and but imagine he has not right done him? This will unhinge and overturn all all polities, and, instead of government and order, leave nothing but anarchy and confusion.

§ 204. To this I answer, that force is to be opposed to nothing but to unjust and unlawful force; whoever makes any opposition in any other case, draws on himself a just condemnation both from God and man; and so no such danger or confusion will follow, as is often suggested: for,

§ 205. First, As, in some countries, the person of the prince by the law is sacred; and so, whatever he commands or does, his person is still free from all question or violence, not liable to force, or any judicial censure or condemnation. But yet opposition may be made to the illegal acts of any inferiour officer, or other commissioned by him; unless he will, by actually putting himself into a state of war with his people, dissolve the government, and leave them to that defence which belongs to every one in the state of nature: for of such things who can tell what the end will be? And a neighbour kingdom [England] has showed the world an odd example. In all other cases the sacredness of the person exempts him from all inconveniencies, whereby he is secure, whilst the government stands, from all violence and harm whatsoever; than which there cannot be a wiser constitution; for the harm he can do in his own person not being likely to happen often, nor to extend itself far; nor being able by his single strength to subvert the laws, nor oppress the body of the people; should any prince have so much weakness and ill-nature as to be willing to do it, the inconveniency of some particular mischiefs that may happen sometimes, when a heady prince comes to the throne, are well recompensed by the peace of the public, and security of the government, in the person of the chief magistrate, thus set out of the reach of danger: it being safer for the body that some few private men should be sometimes in danger to suffer, than that the head of the republic should be easily, and upon slight occasions, exposed.

§ 206. Secondly, But this privilege belonging only to the king's person, hinders not, but they may be questioned, opposed, and resisted, who use unjust force, though they pretend a commission from him, which the law authorizes not; as is plain in the case of him that has the king's writ to arrest a man, which is a full commission from the king; and yet he that has it cannot break open a man's house to do it, nor execute this command of the king upon certain days, nor in certain places, though this commission have no such exception in it; but they are the limitations of the law, which if any one transgress, the king's commission excuses him not: for the king's authority being giving him only by the law, he cannot impower any one to act against the law, or justify him, by his commission, in so doing; the commission or command of any magistrate, where he has no authority, being as void and insignificant, as that of any private man; the difference between the one and the other being that the magistrate has some authority so far, and to such ends, and the private man has none at all: for it is not the commission, but the authority, that gives the right of acting; and against the laws there can be no authority. But notwithstanding such resistance, the king's person and authority are still both secured, and so no danger to governor or government.

§ 207. Thirdly, supposing a government wherein the person of the chief magistrate is not thus sacred; yet this doctrine of the lawfulness of resisting all unlawful exercises of his power, will not upon every slight occasion endanger him, or embroil the government: for where the injured party may be relieved, and his damages repaired by appeal to the law, there can be no pretence for force, which is only to be used where a man is intercepted from appealing to the law: for nothing is to be accounted hostile force, but where it leaves not the remedy of such an appeal: and it is such force alone, that puts him that uses it into a state of war, and makes it lawful to resist him. A man with a sword in his hand, demands my purse in the highway, when perhaps I have not twelve-pence in my pocket: this man I may lawfully kill. To another I deliver 100£, to hold only whilst I alight, which he refuses to restore me, when I am got up again, but draws his sword to defend the possession of it by force, if I endeavour to retake it. The mischief this man does me is an hundred, or possibly a thousand times more than the other perhaps intended me (whom I killed before he really did me any); and yet I might lawfully kill the one, and cannot so much as hurt the other lawfully. The reason whereof is plain; because the one using force, which threatened my life, I could not have time to appeal to the law to secure it; and when it was gone, it was too late to appeal. The law could not restore life to my dead carcass, the loss was irreparable: which to prevent, the law of nature gave me a right to destroy him, who had put himself into a state of war with me, and threatened my destruction. But in the other case, my life not being in danger, I may have the benefit of appealing to the law, and have reparation for my 100£ that way.

§ 208. Fourthly, But if the unlawful acts done by the magistrate be maintained (by the power he has got), and the remedy which is

due by law be by the same power obstructed, yet the right of resisting, even in such manifest acts of tyranny, will not suddenly, or
on slight occasions, disturb the government: for if it reach no farther than some private mens' cases, though they have a right to
defend themselves, and to recover by force what by unlawful force
is taken from them; yet the right to do so will not easily engage
them in a contest, wherein they are sure to perish; it being as impossible for one, or a few oppressed men to disturb the government, where the body of the people do not think themselves
concerned in it, as for a raving madman, or heady malcontent, to
overturn a well-settled state; the people being as little apt to follow
the one as the other.

§ 209. But if either these illegal acts have extended to the majority of the people, or if the mischief and oppression has lighted only
on some few, but in such cases, as the precedent and consequences
seem to threaten all; and they are persuaded in their consciences,
that their laws, and with them their estates, liberties, and lives are
in danger, and perhaps their religion too;[1] how they will be hindered from resisting illegal force, used against them, I cannot tell.
This is an inconvenience, I confess, that attends all governments
whatsoever, when the governors have brought it to this pass, to be
generally suspected of their people; the most dangerous state which
they can possibly put themselves in; wherein they are less to be
pitied, because it is so easy to be avoided; it being as impossible for
a governor, if he really means the good of his people, and the
preservation of them, and their laws together, not to make them see
and feel it, as it is for the father of a family not to let his children
see he loves and takes care of them.

§ 210. But if all the world shall observe pretences of one kind,
and actions of another; arts used to elude the law, and the trust of
prerogative (which is an arbitrary power in some things left in the
prince's hand to do good, not harm to the people) employed contrary to the end for which it was given: if the people shall find the
ministers and subordinate magistrates chosen suitable to such
ends, and favoured, or laid by, proportionably as they promote or
oppose them: if they see several experiments made of arbitrary
power, and that religion underhand favoured (though publicly proclaimed against), which is readiest to introduce it; and the opera-
tors in it supported, as much as may be; and when that cannot be
done, yet approved still, and liked the better: if a long train of actions show the councils all tending that way, how can a man any
more hinder himself from being persuaded in his own mind which

---

1. A reflection of the fears of Locke and the Whigs in the early 1680's that the future
James II would impose his own Roman Catholic religion on England.

way things are going; or from casting about how to save himself, than he could from believing the captain of the ship he was in, was carrying him, and the rest of the company, to Algiers,[2] when he found him always steering that course, though cross winds, leaks in his ship, and want of men and provisions did often force him to turn his course another way for some time, which he steadily returned to again, as soon as the wind, weather, and other circumstances would let him.

Chapter XIX.

OF THE DISSOLUTION OF GOVERNMENT.

§ 211. HE that will with any clearness speak of the dissolution of government, ought in the first place to distinguish between the dissolution of the society and the dissolution of the government. That which makes the community, and brings men out of the loose state of nature into one politic society, is the agreement which every one has with the rest to incorporate, and act as one body, and so be one distinct commonwealth. The usual, and almost only way whereby this union is dissolved, is the inroad of foreign force making a conquest upon them: for in that case (not being able to maintain and support themselves as one entire and independent body), the union belonging to that body which consisted therein, must necessarily cease, and so every one return to the state he was in before, with a liberty to shift for himself, and provide for his own safety, as he thinks fit, in some other society. Whenever the society is dissolved, it is certain the government of that society cannot remain. Thus conquerors' swords often cut up governments by the roots, and mangle societies to pieces, separating the subdued or scattered multitude from the protection of, and dependence on, that society which ought to have preserved them from violence. The world is too well instructed in, and too forward to allow of, this way of dissolving of governments, to need any more to be said of it; and there wants not much argument to prove, that where the society is dissolved, the government cannot remain; that being as impossible, as for the frame of a house to subsist when the materials of it are scattered and dissipated by a whirlwind, or jumbled into a confused heap by an earthquake.

§ 212. Besides this overturning from without, governments are dissolved from within.

First, When the legislative is altered. Civil society being a state of peace, amongst those who are of it from whom the state of war is excluded by the umpirage, which they have provided in their leg-

2. North African Muslim slave market.

islative, for the ending all differences that may arise amongst any of them; it is in their legislative, that the members of a commonwealth are united, and combined together into one coherent living body. This is the soul that gives form, life, and unity to the commonwealth: from hence the several members have their mutual influence, sympathy, and connexion: and therefore, when the legislative is broken or dissolved, dissolution and death follows: for, the essence and union of the society consisting in having one will, the legislative, when once established by the majority, has the declaring, and as it were keeping of that will. The constitution of the legislative is the first and fundamental act of society, whereby provision is made for the continuation of their union, under the direction of persons, and bonds of laws, made by persons authorized thereunto, by the consent and appointment of the people; without which no one man, or number of men, amongst them, can have authority of making laws that shall be binding to the rest. When any one, or more, shall take upon them to make laws, whom the people have not appointed so to do, they make laws without authority, which the people are not therefore bound to obey; by which means they come again to be out of subjection, and may constitute to themselves a new legislative, as they think best, being in full liberty to resist the force of those, who without authority would impose any thing upon them. Every one is at the disposure of his own will, when those who had, by the delegation of the society, the declaring of the public will, are excluded from it, and others usurp the place, who have no such authority or delegation.

§ 213. This being usually brought about by such in the commonwealth who misuse the power they have, it is hard to consider it aright, and know at whose door to lay it, without knowing the form of government in which it happens. Let us suppose then the legislative placed in the concurrence of three distinct persons.

1. A single hereditary person, having the constant, supreme, executive power, and with it the power of convoking and dissolving the other two, within certain periods of time.

2. An assembly of hereditary nobility.

3. An assembly of representatives chosen, *pro tempore*,[3] by the people. Such a form of government supposed, it is evident,

§ 214. First, That when such a single person, or prince, sets up his own arbitrary will in place of the laws, which are the will of the society, declared by the legislative, then the legislative is changed: for that being in effect the legislative, whose rules and laws are put in execution, and required to be obeyed; when other laws are set up, and other rules pretended, and enforced, than what the legislative, constituted by the society, have enacted, it is plain that the

3. For a limited time.

legislative is changed. Whoever introduces new laws, not being thereunto authorized by the fundamental appointment of the society, or subverts the old; disowns and overturns the power by which they were made, and so sets up a new legislative.

§ 215. Secondly, When the prince hinders the legislative from assembling in its due time, or from acting freely, pursuant to those ends for which it was constituted, the legislative is altered: for it is not a certain number of men, no, nor their meeting, unless they have also freedom of debating, and leisure of perfecting, what is for the good of the society, wherein the legislative consists: when these are taken away or altered, so as to deprive the society of the due exercise of their power, the legislative is truly altered: for it is not names that constitute governments, but the use and exercise of those powers that were intended to accompany them; so that he, who takes away the freedom, or hinders the acting of the legislative in its due seasons, in effect takes away the legislative, and puts an end to the government.

§ 216. Thirdly, When, by the arbitrary power of the prince, the electors, or ways of election, are altered, without the consent, and contrary to the common interest of the people, there also the legislative is altered: for if others than those whom the society hath authorized thereunto, do choose, or in another way than what the society hath prescribed, those chosen are not the legislative appointed by the people.

§ 217. Fourthly, The delivery also of the people into the subjection of a foreign power, either by the prince or by the legislative, is certainly a change of the legislative, and so a dissolution of the government: for the end why people entered into society being to be preserved one entire, free, independent society, to be governed by its own laws; this is lost, whenever they are given up into the power of another.

§ 218. Why, in such a constitution as this, the disolution of the government in these cases is to be imputed to the prince, is evident; because he, having the force, treasure, and offices of the state to employ, and often persuading himself, or being flattered by others, that as supreme magistrate he is uncapable of control; he alone is in a condition to make great advances toward such changes, under pretence of lawful authority, and has it in his hands to terrify or suppress opposers, as factious, seditious, and enemies to the government: whereas no other part of the legislative, or people, is capable by themselves to attempt any alteration of the legislative, without open and visible rebellion, apt enough to be taken notice of; which, when it prevails, produces effects very little different from foreign conquest. Besides, the prince in such a form of government having the power of dissolving the other parts of the legislative, and thereby rendering them private persons, they can never in opposition to him, or without his concurrence, alter the legislative by a law, his consent being necessary to give any of their decrees that sanction. But yet, so far as the other parts of the legislative any way contribute to any attempt upon the government, and do either promote, or not (what lies in them) hinder such designs; they are guilty, and partake in this, which is certainly the greatest crime men can be guilty of one towards another.

§ 219. There is one way more whereby such a government may be dissolved, and that is, when he who has the supreme executive power, neglects and abandons that charge, so that the laws already made can no longer be put in execution.[4] This is demonstratively to reduce all to anarchy, and so effectually to dissolve the government: for laws not being made for themselves, but to be, by their execution, the bonds of the society, to keep every part of the body politic in its due place and function; when that totally ceases, the government visibly ceases, and the people become a confused multitude, without order or connexion. Where there is no longer the administration of justice, for the securing of men's rights, nor any remaining power within the community to direct the force, or provide for the necessities of the public; there certainly is no government left. Where the laws cannot be executed, it is all one as if there were no laws; and a government without laws is, I suppose, a mystery in politics, inconceivable to human capacity, and inconsistent with human society.

§ 220. In these and the like cases, when the government is dissolved, the people are at liberty to provide for themselves, by erecting a new legislative, differing from the other, by the change of persons, or form, or both, as they shall find it most for their safety and good: for the society can never, by the fault of another, lose the native and original right it has to preserve itself; which can only be done by a settled legislative, and a fair and impartial execution of the laws made by it. But the state of mankind is not so miserable that they are not capable of using this remedy, till it be too late to look for any. To tell people they may provide for themselves, by erecting a new legislative, when by oppression, artifice, or being delivered over to a foreign power, their old one is gone, is only to tell them, they may expect relief when it is too late, and the evil is past cure. This is in effect no more than to bid them first be slaves, and then to take care of their liberty; and when their chains are on, tell them they may act like freemen. This, if barely so, is rather mockery than relief; and men can never be secure from tyranny, if there be no means to escape it till they are perfectly under it; and therefore it is, that they have not only a right to get out of it, but to prevent it.

4. This paragraph and paragraph 220 were inserted after the overthrow of James II in 1688.

§ 221. There is therefore, secondly, another way whereby governments are dissolved, and that is, when the legislative, or the prince,
either of them, act contrary to their trust.

First, the legislative acts against the trust reposed in them, when
they endeavour to invade the property of the subject, and to make
themselves, or any part of the community, masters, or arbitrary disposers of the lives, liberties, or fortunes of the people.

§ 222. The reason why men enter into society is the preservation
of their property; and the end why they choose and authorize a legislative is, that there may be laws made, and rules set, as guards
and fences to the properties of all the members of the society: to
limit the power, and moderate the dominion, of every part and
member of the society: for since it can never be supposed to be the
will of the society that the legislative should have a power to destroy that which every one designs to secure by entering into society, and for which the people submitted themselves to legislators of
their own making; whenever the legislators endeavour to take away
and destroy the property of the people, or to reduce them to slavery
under arbitrary power, they put themselves into a state of war with
the people, who are thereupon absolved from any farther obedience, and are left to the common refuge, which God hath provided
for all men, against force and violence. Whensoever therefore the
legislative shall transgress this fundamental rule of society; and either by ambition, fear, folly, or corruption, endeavour to grasp
themselves, or put into the hands of any other, an absolute power
over the lives, liberties, and estates of the people; by this breach of
trust they forfeit the power the people had put into their hands for
quite contrary ends, and it devolves to the people, who have a right
to resume their original liberty, and, by the establishment of a new
legislative, (such as they shall think fit) provide for their own safety
and security, which is the end for which they are in society. What I
have said here, concerning the legislative in general, holds true also
concerning the supreme executor, who having a double trust put in
him, both to have a part in the legislative, and the supreme execution of the law, acts against both, when he goes about to set up his
own arbitrary will as the law of the society. He acts also contrary to
his trust, when he either employs the force, treasure, and offices of
the society to corrupt the representatives, and gain them to his purposes; or openly pre-engages the electors, and prescribes to their
choice, such, whom he has, by solicitations, threats, promises, or
otherwise, won to his designs; and employs them to bring in such,
who have promised beforehand what to vote, and what to enact.
Thus to regulate candidates and electors, and new-model the ways
of election, what is it but to cut up the government by the roots,
and poison the very fountain of public security? For the people hav-

ing reserved to themselves the choice of their representatives, as the fence to their properties, could do it for no other end, but that they might always be freely chosen, and so chosen, freely act, and advise, as the necessity of the commonwealth and the public good should, upon examination and mature debate, be judged to require. This, those who give their votes before they hear the debate, and have weighed the reasons on all sides, are not capable of doing. To prepare such an assembly as this, and endeavour to set up the declared abettors of his own will, for the true representatives of the people, and the law-makers of the society, is certainly as great a breach of trust, and as perfect a declaration of a design to subvert the government, as is possible to be met with. To which if one shall add rewards and punishments visibly employed to the same end, and all the arts of perverted law made use of, to take off and destroy all that stand in the way of such a design, and will not comply and consent to betray the liberties of their country, it will be past doubt what is doing. What power they ought to have in the society, who thus employ it contrary to the trust that went along with it in its first institution, is easy to determine; and one cannot but see, that he, who has once attempted any such thing as this, cannot any longer be trusted.

§ 223. To this perhaps it will be said, that the people being ignorant, and always discontented, to lay the foundation of government in the unsteady opinion and uncertain humour of the people, is to expose it to certain ruin; and no government will be able long to subsist, if the people may set up a new legislative, whenever they take offence at the old one. To this I answer, quite the contrary. People are not so easily got out of their old forms, as some are apt to suggest. They are hardly to be prevailed with to amend the acknowledged faults in the frame they have been accustomed to. And if there be any original defects, or adventitious ones introduced by time, or corruption; it is not an easy thing to get them changed, even when all the world sees there is an opportunity for it. This slowness and aversion in the people to quit their old constitutions, has in the many revolutions, which have been seen in this kingdom, in this and former ages, still kept us to, or, after some interval of fruitless attempts, still brought us back again to, our old legislative of king, lords, and commons: and whatever provocations have made the crown be taken from some of our princes' heads, they never carried the people so far as to place it in another line.

§ 224. But it will be said, this hypothesis lays a ferment for frequent rebellion. To which I answer.

First, No more than any other hypothesis: for when the people are made miserable, and find themselves exposed to the ill usage of arbitrary power, cry up their governors as much as you will, for sons of Jupiter; let them be sacred and divine, descended, or authorized from heaven; give them out for whom or what you please, the same will happen. The people generally ill-treated, and contrary to right, will be ready upon any occasion to ease themselves of a burden that sits heavy upon them. They will wish, and seek for the opportunity, which in the change, weakness, and accidents of human affairs, seldom delays long to offer itself. He must have lived but a little while in the world, who has not seen examples of this in his time; and he must have read very little, who cannot produce examples of it in all sorts of governments in the world.

§ 225. Secondly, I answer, such revolutions happen not upon every little mismanagement in public affairs. Great mistakes in the ruling part, many wrong and inconvenient laws, and all the slips of human frailty will be born by the people without mutiny or murmur. But if a long train of abuses,[5] prevarications, and artifices, all tending the same way, make the design visible to the people, and they cannot but feel what they lie under, and see whither they are going; it is not to be wondered, that they should then rouse themselves, and endeavour to put the rule into such hands which may secure to them the ends for which government was at first erected; and without which, ancient names, and specious forms, are so far from being better, that they are much worse, than the state of nature, or pure anarchy; the inconveniencies, being all as great and as near, but the remedy farther off and more difficult.

§ 226. Thirdly, I answer, that this doctrine of a power in the people of providing for their safety anew, by a new legislative, when their legislators have acted contrary to their trust, by invading their property, is the best fence against rebellion, and the probablest means to hinder it: for rebellion being an opposition, not to persons, but authority, which is founded only in the constitutions and laws of the government; those, whoever they be, who by force break through, and by force justify their violation of them, are truly and properly rebels: for when men, by entering into society and civil government, have excluded force, and introduced laws for the preservation of property, peace, and unity amongst themselves; those who set up force again in opposition to the laws, do *rebellare*, that is, bring back again the state of war, and are properly rebels: which they who are in power, (by the pretence they have to authority, the temptation of force they have in their hands, and the flattery of those about them) being likeliest to do; the properest way to prevent the evil is to show them the danger and injustice of it, who are under the greatest temptation to run into it.

5. These words, "a long train of abuses," appear in the U.S. Declaration of Independence.

§ 227. In both the fore-mentioned cases, when either the legislative is changed, or the legislators act contrary to the end for which they were constituted, those who are guilty are guilty of rebellion: for if any one by force takes away the established legislative of any society, and the laws by them made pursuant to their trust, he thereby takes away the umpirage, which every one had consented to, for a peaceable decision of all their controversies, and a bar to the state of war amongst them. They, who remove, or change the legislative, take away this decisive power, which nobody can have but by the appointment and consent of the people; and so destroying the authority which the people did, and nobody else can set up, and introducing a power which the people hath not authorized, they actually introduce a state of war, which is that of force without authority; and thus, by removing the legislative established by the society (in whose decisions the people acquiesced and united, as to that of their own will) they untie the knot, and expose the people anew to the state of war. And if those, who by force take away the legislative, are rebels, the legislators themselves, as has been shown, can be no less esteemed so; when they, who were set up for the protection and preservation of the people, their liberties and properties, shall by force invade and endeavour to take them away; and so they putting themselves into a state of war with those who made them the protectors and guardians of their peace, are properly, and with the greatest aggravation, *rebellantes*, rebels.

§ 228. But if they, who say, it lays a foundation for rebellion mean that it may occasion civil wars, or intestine broils, to tell the people they are absolved from obedience when illegal attempts are made upon their liberties or properties, and may oppose the unlawful violence of those who were their magistrates, when they invade their properties contrary to the trust put in them; and that therefore this doctrine is not to be allowed, being so destructive to the peace of the world: they may as well say, upon the same ground, that honest men may not oppose robbers or pirates, because this may occasion disorder or bloodshed. If any mischief come in such cases, it is not to be charged upon him who defends his own right, but on him that invades his neighbour's. If the innocent honest man must quietly quit all he has, for peace sake, to him who will lay violent hands upon it, I desire it may be considered, what a kind of peace there will be in the world, which consists only in violence and rapine; and which is to be maintained only for the benefit of robbers and oppressors. Who would not think it an admirable peace betwixt the mighty and the mean, when the lamb, without resistance, yielded his throat to be torn by the imperious wolf? Polyphemus's den gives us a perfect pattern of such a peace, and such a government, wherein Ulysses and his companions had nothing to do, but quietly to suffer themselves to be devoured.[6] And no doubt Ulysses, who was a prudent man, preached up passive obedience, and exhorted them to a quiet submission, by representing to them of what concernment peace was to mankind; and by showing the inconveniencies might happen, if they should offer to resist Polyphemus, who had now the power over them.

§ 229. The end of government is the good of mankind: and which is best for mankind, that the people should be always exposed to the boundless will of tyranny; or that the rulers should be sometimes liable to be opposed, when they grow exorbitant in the use of their power, and employ it for the destruction, and not the preservation of the properties of their people?

§ 230. Nor let any one say, that mischief can arise from hence, as often as it shall please a busy head, or turbulent spirit, to desire the alteration of the government. It is true, such men may stir, whenever they please; but it will be only to their own just ruin and perdition: for till the mischief be grown general, and the ill designs of the rulers become visible, or their attempts sensible to the greater part, the people, who are more disposed to suffer than right themselves by resistance, are not apt to stir. The examples of particular injustice or oppression, of here and there an unfortunate man, moves them not. But if they universally have a persuasion, grounded upon manifest evidence, that designs are carrying on against their liberties, and the general course and tendency of things cannot but give them strong suspicions of the evil intention of their governors, who is to be blamed for it? Who can help it, if they, who might avoid it, bring themselves into this suspicion? Are the people to be blamed, if they have the sense of rational creatures, and can think of things no otherwise than as they find and feel them? And is it not rather their fault, who put things into such a posture, that they would not have them thought to be as they are? I grant, that the pride, ambition, and turbulency of private men have sometimes caused great disorders in commonwealths, and factions have been fatal to states and kingdoms. But whether the mischief hath oftener begun in the people's wantonness, and a desire to cast off the lawful authority of their rulers, or in the rulers' insolence, and endeavours to get and exercise an arbitrary power over their people; whether oppression, or disobedience, gave the first rise to the disorder; I leave it to impartial history to determine. This I am sure, whoever, either ruler or subject, by force goes about to invade the rights of either prince or people, and lays the foundation for overturning the constitution and frame of any just government,

6. Homer's *Odyssey*, book IX (the story of Cyclops).

is guilty of the greatest crime, I think, a man is capable of; being to answer for all those mischiefs of blood, rapine, and desolation, which the breaking to pieces of governments bring on a country. And he who does it, is justly to be esteemed the common enemy and pest[7] of mankind, and is to be treated accordingly.

§ 231. That subjects or foreigners, attempting by force on the properties of any people, may be resisted with force, is agreed on all hands. But that magistrates, doing the same thing, may be resisted, hath of late been denied: as if those who had the greatest privileges and advantages by the law, had thereby a power to break those laws, by which alone they were set in a better place than their brethren: whereas their offence is thereby the greater, both as being ungrateful for the greater share they have by the law, and breaking also that trust, which is put into their hands by their brethren.

§ 232. Whosoever uses force without right, as everyone does in society, who does it without law, puts himself into a state of war with those against whom he so uses it; and in that state all former ties are cancelled, all other rights cease, and every one has a right to defend himself, and to resist the aggressor. This is so evident, that Barclay himself, that great assertor of the power and sacredness of kings,[8] is forced to confess, that it is lawful for the people, in some cases, to resist their king; and that too in a chapter, wherein he pretends to show, that the divine law shuts up the people from all manner of rebellion. Whereby it is evident, even by his own doctrine, that, since they may in some cases resist, all resisting of princes is not rebellion. His words are these.[9]

*   *   *

In English thus:

§ 233. "But if any one should ask, Must the people then always lay themselves open to the cruelty and rage of tyranny? Must they see their cities pillaged and laid in ashes, their wives and children exposed to the tyrant's lust and fury, and themselves and families reduced by their king to ruin, and all the miseries of want and oppression; and yet sit still? Must men alone be debarred the common privilege of opposing force with force, which nature allows so freely to all other creatures for their preservation from injury? I answer: Self-defence is a part of the law of nature; nor can it be de-

---

7. Plague.
8. William Barclay defended royal absolutism against those he called monarchomachs (king killers), especially Buchanan (see p. 120, n. 1). Locke possessed Barclay's book in 1681.
9. Latin text omitted.

nied the community, even against the king himself: but to revenge themselves upon him, must by no means be allowed them; it being not agreeable to that law. Wherefore if the king should show an hatred, not only to some particular persons, but sets himself against the body of the commonwealth, whereof he is the head, and shall, with intolerable ill usage, cruelly tyrannise over the whole, or a considerable part of the people, in this case the people have a right to resist and defend themselves from injury: but it must be with this caution, that they only defend themselves, but do not attack their prince: they may repair the damages received, but must not for any provocation exceed the bounds of due reverence and respect. They may repulse the present attempt, but must not revenge past violences: for it is natural for us to defend life and limb; but that an inferior should punish a superior, is against nature. The mischief which is designed them the people may prevent before it be done: but when it is done, they must not revenge it on the king, though author of the villany. This therefore is the privilege of the people in general, above what any private person hath; that particular men are allowed by our adversaries themselves (Buchanan[1] only excepted) to have no other remedy but patience; but the body of the people may with reverence resist intolerable tyranny; for, when it is but moderate, they ought to endure it."[2]

§ 234. Thus far that great advocate of monarchical power allows of resistance.

§ 235. It is true, he has annexed two limitations to it, to no purpose:

First, He says, it must be with reverence.

Secondly, It must be without retribution, or punishment; and the reason he gives is, "Because an inferior cannot punish a superior."

First, How to resist force without striking again, or how to strike with reverence, will need some skill to make intelligible. He that shall oppose an assault only with a shield to receive the blows, or in any more respectful posture, without a sword in his hand, to abate the confidence and force of the assailant, will quickly be at an end of his resistance, and will find such a defence serve only to draw on himself the worse usage. This is as ridiculous a way of resisting, as Juvenal thought it of fighting; "ubi tu pulsas, ego vapulo tantum."[3] And the success of the combat will be unavoidably the same he there describes it:

1. George Buchanan, a Scottish Calvinist theologian, argued for an individual right of resistance in *De Jure Regni apud Scotos* (*On the law of the kingdom of the Scots*) (1579).
2. Barclay's *Contra Monarchomachos, De Regino et Regali Potestati*, III.8.
3. "When you hit me, I just take it" (Juvenal's *Satires*, III:289–890).

"Libertas pauperis hæc est:
Pulsatus rogat, et pugnis concisus, adorat,
Ut liceat paucis cum dentibus inde reverti."[4]

This will always be the event[5] of such an imaginary resistance, where men may not strike again. He therefore who may resist, must be allowed to strike. And then let our author, or anybody else, join a knock on the head, or a cut on the face, with as much reverence and respect as he thinks fit. He that can reconcile blows and reverence, may, for aught I know, deserve for his pains a civil, respectful cudgelling, wherever he can meet with it.

Secondly, As to his second,[6] "An inferior cannot punish a superior;" that is true, generally speaking, whilst he is his superior. But to resist force with force, being the state of war that levels the parties, cancels all former relation of reverence, respect, and superiority: and then the odds that remains, is, that he, who opposes the unjust aggressor, has this superiority over him, that he has a right, when he prevails, to punish the offender, both for the breach of the peace, and all the evils that followed upon it. Barclay therefore, in another place, more coherently to himself, denies it to be lawful to resist a king in any case. But he there assigns two cases, whereby a king may unking himself. His words are.[7]

*   *   *

Which in English runs thus:

§ 237. "What then, can there no case happen wherein the people may of right, and by their own authority, help themselves, take arms, and set upon their king, imperiously domineering over them? None at all, whilst he remains a king. 'Honour the king, and he that resists the power, resists the ordinance of God,'[8] are divine oracles that will never permit it. The people therefore can never come by a power over him, unless he does something that makes him cease to be a king: for then he divests himself of his crown and dignity, and returns to the state of a private man, and the people become free and superior, the power which they had in the interregnum, before they crowned him king, devolving to them again. But there are but few miscarriages which bring the matter to this state. After considering it well on all sides, I can find but two. Two cases there are, I say, whereby a king, *ipso facto*, becomes no king, and loses all

---

4. "After being beaten and cut in the fight, a poor man is free to kneel down and beg to be left with a few teeth" (Juvenal's *Satires*, III:299–301).
5. Outcome.
6. limitation.
7. Latin text omitted.
8. 1 Peter 2:13; Paul 13:2.

power and regal authority over his people; which are also taken notice of by Winzerus."[9]

"The first is, if he endeavour to overturn the government, that is, if he have a purpose and design to ruin the kingdom and commonwealth, as it is recorded of Nero, that he resolved to cut off the senate and people of Rome, lay the city waste with fire and sword, and then remove to some other place—And of Caligula, that he openly declared, that he would be no longer a head to the people or senate, and that he had it in his thoughts to cut off the worthiest men of both ranks, and then retire to Alexandria; and he wished that the people had but one neck, that he might despatch them all at a blow. Such designs as these, when any king harbours in his thoughts, and seriously promotes, he immediately gives up all care and thought of the commonwealth; and consequently forfeits the power of governing his subjects, as a master does the dominion over his slaves whom he hath abandoned."

§ 238. "The other case is, when a king makes himself the dependent of another, and subjects his kingdom which his ancestors left him, and the people put free into his hands, to the dominion of another, for however perhaps it may not be his intention to prejudice the people, yet because he has hereby lost the principal part of regal dignity, viz. to be next and immediately under God supreme in his kingdom; and also because he betrayed or forced his people, whose liberty he ought to have carefully preserved, into the power and dominion of a foreign nation. By this, as it were, alienation of his kingdom he himself loses the power he had in it before, without transferring any the least right to those on whom he would have bestowed it; and so by this act sets the people free, and leaves them at their own disposal. One example of this is to be found in the Scottish Annals."[1]

§ 239. In these cases Barclay, the great champion of absolute monarchy, is forced to allow that a king may be resisted, and ceases to be a king. That is, in short, not to multiply cases, in whatsoever he has no authority, there he is no king, and may be resisted: for wheresoever the authority ceases, the king ceases too, and becomes like other men who have no authority and these two cases he instances differ little from those above-mentioned to be destructive to governments, only that he has omitted the principle from which his doctrine flows; and that is, the breach of trust, in not preserving the form of government agreed on, and in not intending the end of government itself, which is the public good and preservation of

---

9. Ninian Winzerus (Wingate), Scottish Benedictine monk, who opposed Buchanan's theory.
1. Barclay's *Contra Monarchomachos*, III.16.

property. When a king has dethroned himself, and put himself in a
state of war with his people, what shall hinder them from prosecuting him who is no king, as they would any other man, who has put
himself into a state of war with them; Barclay and those of his
opinion would do well to tell us. This farther I desire may be taken
notice of out of Barclay, that he says, "The mischief that is designed
them, the people may prevent before it be done: whereby he allows
resistance when tyranny is but in design. Such designs as these
(says he) when any king harbours in his thoughts and seriously promotes, he immediately gives up all care and thought of the commonwealth;" so that, according to him, the neglect of the public
good is to be taken as an evidence of such design, or at least for a
sufficient cause of resistance. And the reason of all he gives in
these words, "Because he betrayed or forced his people, whose liberty he ought carefully to have preserved." What he adds, "into the
power and dominion of a foreign nation," signifies nothing, the
fault and forfeiture lying in the loss of their liberty, which he ought
to have preserved, and not in any distinction of the persons to
whose dominion they were subjected. The people's right is equally
invaded, and their liberty lost, whether they are made slaves to any
of their own, or a foreign nation; and in this lies the injury, and
against this only have they the right of defence. And there are instances to be found in all countries, which show that it is not the
change of nations in the persons of their governors, but the change
of government, that gives the offence. Bilson, a bishop of our
church, and a great stickler for the power and prerogative of
princes, does, if I mistake not, in his *Treatise of Christian Subjection*, acknowledge that princes may forfeit their power, and their title to the obedience of their subjects; and if there needed authority
in a case where reason is so plain, I could send my reader to Brac-
ton, Fortescue, and the author of the Mirror,[2] and others, writers
that cannot be suspected to be ignorant of our government, or enemies to it. But I thought Hooker alone might be enough to satisfy
those men, who relying on him for their ecclesiastical polity, are by
a strange fate carried to deny those principles upon which he builds
it. Whether they are herein made the tools of cunninger workmen,
to pull down their own fabric, they were best look. This I am sure,
their civil policy is so new, so dangerous, and so destructive to both
rulers and people, that as former ages never could bear the broach-

2. Andrew Home's *A Book of Mirrors*, a fourteenth-century treatise, republished in 1640
(Locke 1988:426). Bilson, (sixteenth century), Anglican bishop who published *The True
Difference between Christian Subjection and Unchristian Rebellion* in 1585. Henry Brac-
ton, (thirteenth century), jurist who wrote *On the Laws and Customs of England*, which
argued for the superiority of the law over the monarch. Sir John Fortescue (fifteenth
century), wrote the treatise, *In Praise of the Laws of England*, which compared England
favorably to France because the English king was subject to the law.

ing of it; so it may be hoped those to come, redeemed from the im-
positions of these Egyptian under-task-masters, will abhor the
memory of such servile flatterers, who, whilst it seemed to serve
their turn, resolved all government into absolute tyranny, and
would have all men born to, what their mean souls fitted them for,
slavery.

§ 240. Here, it is like, the common question will be made, Who
shall be judge, whether the prince or legislative act contrary to their
trust? This, perhaps, ill-affected and factious men may spread
amongst the people, when the prince only makes use of his due
prerogative. To this I reply, The people shall be judge; for who shall
be judge whether his trustee or deputy acts well, and according to
the trust reposed in him, but he who deputes him, and must, by
having deputed him, have still a power to discard him, when he
fails in his trust? If this be reasonable in particular cases of private
men, why should it be otherwise in that of the greatest moment,
where the welfare of millions is concerned, and also where the evil,
if not prevented, is greater, and the redress very difficult, dear, and
dangerous?

§ 241. But farther, this question, (Who shall be judge?) cannot
mean, that there is no judge at all: for where there is no judicature
on earth, to decide controversies amongst men, God in heaven is
judge. He alone, it is true, is judge of the right. But every man is
judge for himself, as in all other cases, so in this, whether another
hath put himself into a state of war with him, and whether he
should appeal to the supreme Judge, as Jephthah did.

§ 242. If a controversy arise betwixt a prince and some of the
people, in a matter where the law is silent or doubtful and the thing
be of great consequence, I should think the proper umpire, in such
a case, should be the body of the people: for in cases where the
prince hath a trust reposed in him, and is dispensed from the common ordinary rules of the law; there, if any men find themselves aggrieved, and think the prince acts contrary to, or beyond that trust,
who so proper to judge as the body of the people, (who, at first,
lodged that trust in him) how far they meant it should extend? But
if the prince or whoever they be in the administration, decline that
way of determination, the appeal then lies nowhere but to Heaven;
force between either persons, who have no known superior on
earth, or which permits no appeal to a judge on earth, being properly a state of war, wherein the appeal lies only to Heaven; and in
that state the injured party must judge for himself, when he will
think fit to make use of that appeal, and put himself upon it.

§ 243. To conclude, The power that every individual gave the society, when he entered into it, can never revert to the individuals
again as long as the society lasts, but will always remain in the

community, because without this there can be no community, no commonwealth, which is contrary to the original agreement: so also when the society hath placed the legislative in any assembly of men, to continue in them and their successors, with direction and authority for providing such successors the legislative can never revert to the people whilst that government lasts because, having provided a legislative with power to continue for ever, they have given up their political power to the legislative, and cannot resume it. But if they have set limits to the duration of their legislative and made this supreme power in any person, or assembly, only temporary; or else, when by the miscarriages of those in authority it is forfeited; upon the forfeiture, or at the determination of the time set, it reverts to the society, and the people have a right to act as supreme and continue the legislative in themselves; or erect a new form, or under the old form place it in new hands as they think good.

A Letter Concerning Toleration†

To the Reader

The ensuing Letter concerning Toleration, first printed in Latin this very year, in Holland, has already been translated both into Dutch and French. So general and speedy an approbation may therefore bespeak its favourable reception in England. I think indeed there is no nation under heaven, in which so much has already been said upon that subject as ours. But yet certainly there is no people that stand in more need of having something further both said and done amongst them, in this point, than we do.

Our government has not only been partial in matters of religion, but those also who have suffered under that partiality, and have therefore endeavoured by their writings to vindicate their own rights and liberties, have for the most part done it upon narrow principles, suited only to the interests of their own sects.

This narrowness of spirit on all sides has undoubtedly been the principal occasion of our miseries and confusions. But whatever have been the occasions, it is now high time to seek for a thorough cure. We have need of more generous remedies than what have yet been made use of in our distemper. It is neither declarations of indulgence, nor acts of comprehension, such as have yet been practised or projected amongst us, that can do the work. The first will but palliate, the second increase our evil.

Absolute liberty, just and true liberty, equal and impartial liberty, is

†From www.constitution.org.

the thing that we stand in need of. Now, though this has indeed been much talked of, I doubt it has not been much understood; I am sure not at all practised, either by our governors towards the people in general, or by any dissenting parties of the people towards one another.

I cannot, therefore, but hope that this discourse, which treats of that subject, however briefly, yet more exactly than any we have yet seen, demonstrating both the equitableness and practicableness of the thing, will be esteemed highly seasonable by all men who have souls large enough to prefer the true interest of the public, before that of a party.

It is for the use of such as are already so spirited, or to inspire that spirit into those that are not, that I have translated it into our language. But the thing itself is so short, that it will not bear a longer preface. I leave it, therefore, to the consideration of my countrymen; and heartily wish they may make the use of it that it appears to be designed for.

William Popple

Honoured Sir,
Since you are pleased to inquire what are my thoughts about the mutual toleration of Christians in their different professions of religion, I must needs answer you freely [*briefly*][1] that I esteem that toleration to be the chief characteristic mark of the true church. For whatsoever some people boast of the antiquity of places and names, or of the pomp of their outward worship; others, of the reformation of their discipline; all, of the orthodoxy of their faith, for everyone is orthodox to himself: these things, and all others of this nature, are much rather marks of men's striving for power and empire over one another, than of the church of Christ. Let anyone have ever so true a claim to all these things, yet if he be destitute of charity, meekness, and goodwill in general towards all mankind, even to those that are not Christians, he is certainly yet short of being a true Christian himself. "The kings of the Gentiles exercise lordship over them," said our Saviour to his disciples, "but ye shall not be so", (Luke 22: 25, 26). The business of true religion is quite another thing. It is not instituted in order to the erecting (of) an external pomp, nor to the obtaining of ecclesiastical dominion, nor to the exercising of compulsive force; but to the regulating of men's lives according to the rules of virtue and piety. Whosoever will list himself under the banner of Christ [*enlist in the church*] must, in

---

1. When the translator, William Popple, departs from the Latin text, the literal translation from the Latin is set in italics. (For Latin text, see Mavio Montouri, ed., *John Locke, A Letter on Toleration* (The Hague: Martinus Nishoff, 1963). All notes are the editor's unless otherwise specified.

the first place, and above all things, make war upon his own lusts and vices. It is in vain for any man to usurp the name of Christian, without holiness of life, purity of manners, and benignity and meekness of spirit. "Let everyone that nameth the name of Christ depart from iniquity," (2 Tim. 2: 19). "Thou, when thou art converted, strengthen thy brethren," said our Lord to Peter, (Luke 22: 32). It would indeed be very hard for one that appears careless about his own salvation, to persuade me that he were extremely concerned for mine. For it is impossible that those should sincerely and heartily apply themselves to make other people Christians, who have not really embraced the Christian religion in their own hearts. If the Gospel and the apostles may be credited, no man can be a Christian without charity, and without that faith which works, not by force, but by love. Now I appeal to the consciences of those that persecute, torment, destroy, and kill other men upon pretence of religion, whether they do it out of friendship and kindness towards them, or no: and I shall then indeed, and not till then, believe they do so, when I shall see those fiery zealots correcting, in the same manner, their friends and familiar acquaintance, for the manifest sins they commit against the precepts of the Gospel; when I shall see them prosecute with fire and sword the members of their own communion that are tainted with enormous vices, and without amendment are in danger of eternal perdition; and when I shall see them thus express their love and desire of the salvation of their souls by the infliction of torments, and exercise of all manner of cruelties. For if it be out of a principle of charity, as they pretend, and love to men's souls, that they deprive them of their estates, maim them with corporal punishments, starve and torment them in noisome prisons, and in the end even take away their lives; I say, if all this be done merely to make men Christians, and procure their salvation, why then do they suffer "whoredom, fraud, malice, and such like enormities," which, according to the Apostle, (Romans 1), manifestly relish of heathenish corruption, to predominate so much and abound amongst their flocks and people? These, and such like things, are certainly more contrary to the glory of God, to the purity of the church, and to the salvation of souls, than any conscientious dissent from ecclesiastical decision, or separation from public worship, whilst accompanied with innocency of life. Why then does this burning zeal for God, for the church, and for the salvation of souls; burning, I say, literally with fire and faggot; pass by those moral vices and wickednesses, without any chastisement, which are acknowledged by all men to be diametrically opposite to the profession of Christianity, and bend all its nerves either to the introducing of ceremonies, or to the establishment of opinions, which for the most part are about nice and intricate matters, that exceed the capacity of ordinary understandings? Which of the parties contending about these things is in the right, which of them is guilty of schism, or heresy, whether those that domineer or those that suffer, will then at last be manifest, when the cause of their separation comes to be judged of. He certainly that follows Christ, embraces his doctrine, and bears his yoke, though he forsake both father and mother, separate from the public assemblies and ceremonies of his country, or whomsoever, **or whatsoever else**[2] he relinquishes, will not then be judged an heretic.

Now, though the divisions that are amongst sects should be allowed to be ever so obstructive of the salvation of souls, yet, nevertheless, "adultery, fornication, uncleanness, lasciviousness, idolatry, and such like things, cannot be denied to be works of the flesh;" concerning which the apostle has expressly declared, that "they who do them shall not inherit the kingdom of God," (Gal. 5: 21). Whosoever, therefore, is sincerely solicitous about the kingdom of God, and thinks it his duty to endeavor the enlargement of it amongst men, ought to apply himself with no less care and industry to the rooting out of these immoralities, than to the extirpation of sects. But if anyone do otherwise, and, whilst he is cruel and implacable towards those that differ from him in opinion, he be indulgent to such iniquities and immoralities as are unbecoming the name of a Christian, let such a one talk ever so much of the church, he plainly demonstrates by his actions, that it is another kingdom he aims at, and not the advancement of the kingdom of God.

That any man should think fit to cause another man, whose salvation he heartily desires, to expire in torments, and that even in an unconverted estate, would, I confess, seem very strange to me, and, I think, to any other also. But nobody, surely, will ever believe that such a carriage can proceed from charity, love, or goodwill. If anyone maintain that men ought to be compelled by fire and sword to profess certain doctrines, and conform to this or that exterior worship, without any regard had unto their morals; if anyone endeavor to convert those that are erroneous unto the faith, by forcing them to profess things that they do not believe, and allowing them to practice things that the Gospel does not permit; it cannot be doubted, indeed, that such a one is desirous to have a numerous assembly joined in the same profession with himself; but that he principally intends by those means to compose a truly Christian church, is altogether incredible. It is not therefore to be wondered at, if those who do not really contend for the advancement of the true religion, and of the church of Christ, make use of arms that do

2. Popple's additions to Locke's text appear in boldface.

not belong to the Christian warfare [*the army of Christ*]. If, like the Captain of our salvation, they sincerely desired the good of souls, they would tread in the steps and follow the perfect example of that Prince of Peace, who sent out his soldiers to the subduing of nations, and gathering them into his church, not armed with the sword, or other instruments of force, but prepared with the Gospel of peace, and with the exemplary holiness of their conversation [*conduct*], This was his method. Though if infidels were to be converted by force, if those that are either blind or obstinate were to be drawn off from their errors by armed soldiers, we knew very well that it was much more easy for him to do it with armies of heavenly legions, than for any one of the church, however potent soever, with all his dragoons.

The toleration of those that differ from others in matters of religion, is so agreeable to the Gospel *of* **Jesus Christ**, and to the genuine reason **of mankind**, that it seems monstrous for men to be so blind, **as not to perceive the necessity and advantage of it in**, *to* so clear a light. I will not here tax the pride and ambition of some, the passion and uncharitable zeal of others. These are faults from which human affairs can perhaps scarce ever be perfectly freed; but yet such as nobody will bear the plain imputation of, without covering them with some specious color; and so pretend to commendation **whilst they are carried away by their own irregular passion**. But, **however**, that some may not color their spirit of persecution and unchristian cruelty with a pretence of care of the public weal, and observation of the laws, and that others, under pretence of religion, may not seek impunity for their libertinism and licentiousness; in a word, that none may impose either upon himself or others, by the pretences of loyalty and obedience to the prince, or of **tenderness and** sincerity in the worship of God; I esteem it above all things necessary to distinguish *exactly* the business of civil government from that of religion, and to settle the *just* bounds that lie between the one and the other. If this be not done, there can be no end put to the controversies that will be always arising between those that have, or at least pretend to have, on the one side, a concernment for the interest of men's souls, and, on the other side, a care of the commonwealth.

The commonwealth seems to me to be a society of men constituted only for **the procuring**, preserving, and advancing their own civil interests.

Civil interest I call life, liberty, health, and indolency[3] of body; and the possession of outward things, such as money, lands, *houses*, furniture, and the like.

---

3. comfort.

It is the duty of the civil magistrate, by the impartial execution of equal laws, *by laws imposed equally on all* to secure unto all the people in general, and to everyone of his subjects in particular, the just possession of these things belonging to this life. If anyone presume to violate the laws of public justice and equity, **established for the preservation of these things**, his presumption is to be checked by the fear of punishment, consisting in the deprivation or diminution of those **civil interests, or** goods, which otherwise he might and ought to enjoy. But seeing no man does willingly suffer himself to be punished by the deprivation of any part of his goods, and much less of his liberty or life, therefore is the magistrate armed with the force and strength of all his subjects, in order to the punishment of those that violate any other man's rights.

Now that the whole jurisdiction of the magistrate reaches only to these civil concernments; and that all civil power, right, and dominion, is bounded and confined to the only care of promoting these things; and that it neither can nor ought in any manner to be extended to the salvation of souls; these following considerations seem unto me **abundantly** to demonstrate.

First, Because the care of souls is not committed to the civil magistrate, any more than to other men. It is not committed unto him. **I say**, by God; because it appears not that God has ever given any such authority to one man over another, as to compel anyone to his religion. Nor can any such power be vested in the magistrate by the consent of the people; because no man can so far abandon the care of his own salvation as **blindly** to leave it to the choice of any other, whether prince or subject, to prescribe to him what faith or worship he shall embrace. For no man can, if he would, conform his faith to the dictates of another. All the life and power of true religion consists in **the inward persuasion of the mind; and** faith **is not faith without believing**. Whatever profession we [*you*][4] make, to whatever outward worship we conform, if we are not fully satisfied in our own mind that the one is true, and the other well-pleasing unto God, such profession and such practice, far from being any furtherance, are indeed great obstacles to our salvation. For in this manner, instead of expiating other sins by the exercise of religion, I say, in offering thus unto God Almighty such a worship as we esteem to be displeasing unto him, we add unto the number of our other sins, those also of hypocrisy, and contempt of his Divine Majesty.

In the second place. The care of souls cannot belong to the civil magistrate, because his power consists only in outward force: but true and saving religion consists in the inward persuasion of the

---

4. Here and subsequently Popple translates *you* as "we."

mind, without which nothing can be acceptable to God. And such is the nature of the understanding, that it cannot be compelled to the belief of anything by outward force. Confiscation of estate, imprisonment, torments, nothing of that nature can have any such efficacy as to make men change the inward judgment that they have framed of things.

It may indeed be alleged that the magistrate may make use of arguments, and thereby draw the heterodox into the way of truth, and procure their salvation. I grant it; but this is common to him with other men. In teaching, instructing, and redressing the erroneous by reason, he may certainly do what becomes any good man to do. Magistracy does not oblige him to put off either humanity or Christianity. But it is one thing to persuade, another to command; one thing to press with arguments, another with penalties. This[5] the civil power alone has a right to do; to the other, good-will is authority enough. Every man has commission to admonish, exhort, convince another of error, and by reasoning to draw him into truth: but to give laws, receive obedience, and compel with the sword, belongs to none but the magistrate. And upon this ground I affirm, that the magistrate's power extends not to the establishing of any articles of faith, [or *dogmas*,] or forms of worship, by the force of his laws. For laws are of no force at all without penalties, and penalties in this case are absolutely impertinent; because they are not proper to convince the mind. Neither the profession of any articles of faith, [or *dogmas*], nor **the conformity to** any outward form of worship, as has been already said, can be available to the salvation of souls, unless the truth of the one, and the acceptableness of the other unto God, be thoroughly believed by those that so profess and practice. But penalties are no ways capable to produce such belief. It is only light and evidence that can work a change in men's opinions; and that light can in no manner proceed from corporal sufferings **or any other outward penalties**.

In the third place, the care of the salvation of men's souls cannot belong to the magistrate; because, though the rigor of laws and the force of penalties were capable to **convince and** change men's minds, yet would not that help at all to the salvation of their souls. For, there being but one truth, one way to heaven; what hopes is there that more men would be led into it, if they had no other rule to follow but the religion of the court [*the prince*] and were put under the necessity to quit [*the light of*] their own reason and [*to oppose*,] the dictates of their own consciences, and blindly to resign up themselves to the will of their governors [the prince], and to the religion **which either ignorance, ambition, or superstition had**

5. The use of force.

chanced to establish[ed] in the countries where they were born? In the variety and contradiction of opinions in religion, wherein the princes of the world are as much divided as in their secular interests, the narrow way [to heaven] would be much straitened; one country alone would be in the right **and all the rest of the world put under the obligation of following their princes in the ways that lead to destruction** and that which heightens the absurdity, and very ill suits the notion of a Deity, men would owe their eternal happiness or misery to the places of their nativity.

These considerations, to omit many others that might have been urged to the same purpose, seem unto me sufficient to conclude, that all the power of civil government relates only to men's civil interests, is confined to the care of the things of this world, and hath nothing to do with the world to come.

Let us now consider what a church is. A church then I take to be a voluntary [*free*] society of men, joining themselves together of their own accord, in order to the public worshipping of God, in such a manner as they judge acceptable to him **and effectual** to the salvation of their souls.

I say, it is a free and voluntary society. Nobody is born a member of any church; otherwise the religion of parents would descend unto children, by the same right of inheritance as their temporal estates, and everyone would hold his faith by the same tenure he does his lands; than which nothing can be imagined more absurd. Thus therefore that matter stands. No man by nature is bound unto any particular church or sect, but everyone joins himself voluntarily to that society in which he believes he has found that profession and worship which is truly acceptable to God. The hopes of salvation, as it was the only cause of his entrance into that communion, so it can be the only reason of his stay there. For if afterwards he discover anything either erroneous in the doctrine, or incongruous in the worship of that society to which he has joined himself, why should it not be as free for him to go out as it was to enter? No member of a religious society can be tied with any other bonds but what proceed from the certain expectation of eternal life. A church then is a society of members voluntarily uniting to this end.

It follows now that we consider what is the power of this church, and unto what laws it is subject.

Forasmuch as no society, how free so ever, or upon whatsoever slight occasion instituted, (whether of philosophers for learning, of merchants for commerce, or of men of leisure for mutual conversation and discourse) no church or company, I say, can in the least subsist and hold together, but will presently dissolve and break to pieces, unless it be regulated by some laws. Place and time of meeting must be agreed on; rules for admitting and excluding members must be established; distinction of officers, and putting things into a regular course, and such like, cannot be omitted. But since the joining together of several members into this church-society, as has already been demonstrated, is absolutely free and spontaneous, it necessarily follows, that the right of making its laws can belong to none but the society itself, or at least, which is the same thing, to those whom the society by **common** consent has authorized thereunto.

Some perhaps may object, [*But you say*] that no such society can be said to be a true church, unless it have in it a bishop, or presbyter, with ruling authority derived from the very apostles, and continued down unto the present time by an uninterrupted succession.

To these I answer. In the first place, [**let them**] show me the edict by which Christ has imposed that law upon his church. And let not any man think me impertinent, if, in a thing of this consequence, I require that the terms of that edict be [*very*] express and positive. For the promise he has made us, that wheresoever two or three are gathered together in his name, he will be in the midst of them, (Matth. 18: 20), seems to imply the contrary. Whether such an assembly want anything necessary to a true church, pray do you consider. Certain I am, that nothing can be there wanting unto the salvation of souls, which is sufficient for our purpose.

Next, pray observe how great have always been the divisions amongst even those who lay so much stress upon the **divine** institution [*by Christ*], and continued succession of a certain order of rulers in the church. Now their very dissension unavoidably puts us upon a necessity of deliberating, and consequently allows a liberty of choosing that, which upon consideration we prefer.

And, in the last place [*Thirdly*]. I consent that these men have a ruler of their church, established by such a long series of succession as they judge necessary, provided I may have liberty at the same time to join myself to that society, in which I am persuaded those things are to be found which are necessary to the salvation of my soul. In this manner ecclesiastical liberty will be preserved on all sides, and no man will have a legislator imposed upon him, but whom himself has chosen.

But since men are so solicitous about the true church, I would only ask them here by the way, if it be not more agreeable to the church of Christ to make the conditions of her communion consist in such things, and such things only, as the Holy Spirit has in the Holy Scriptures declared, in express words, to be necessary to salvation? **I ask, I say**, whether this be not more agreeable to the church of Christ, than for men to impose their own inventions and interpretations upon others, as if they were of divine authority; and to establish by ecclesiastical laws, as absolutely necessary to the profession of Christianity such things as the holy Scriptures do either not mention, or at least not expressly command? Whosoever requires those things **in order to** (*for*) ecclesiastical communion, which Christ does not require **in order to** [*for*] life eternal, he may perhaps indeed constitute a society accommodated to his own opinion, and his own advantage; but how that can be called the church of Christ, which is established upon laws that are not his, and which excludes such persons from its communion as he will one day receive into the kingdom of heaven **I understand not.** But this being not a proper place to inquire into the marks of the true church, I will only mind those that contend so earnestly for the decrees of their own society, and that cry out continually the CHURCH, the CHURCH, with as much noise, and perhaps upon the same principle, as the Ephesian silversmiths did for their Diana, this, I say, I desire to mind them of, that the Gospel frequently declares, that the true disciples of Christ must suffer persecution; but that the church of Christ should persecute others, and force others by fire and sword to embrace her faith and doctrine, I could never yet find **in any of the books of** the New Testament.

The end of a religious society, as has already been said, is the public worship of God, and by means thereof the acquisition of eternal life. All discipline ought therefore to tend to that end, and all ecclesiastical laws to be thereunto confined. Nothing ought, nor can be transacted in this society, relating to the possession of civil and wordly goods. No force is here to be made use of, upon any occasion whatsoever: for force belongs wholly to the civil magistrate, and the possession of all outward goods is subject to his jurisdiction.

But it may be asked, by what means then shall ecclesiastical laws be established, if they must be thus destitute of all compulsive power? I answer they must be established by means suitable to the nature of such things, whereof the external profession and observation, if not proceeding from a thorough conviction and approbation of the mind, is altogether useless and unprofitable. The arms by which the members of this society are to be kept within their duty, are exhortations, admonitions, and advice. If by these means the offenders will not be reclaimed, and the erroneous convinced, there remains nothing farther to be done, but that such stubborn and obstinate persons, who give no ground to hope for their reformation, should be cast out and separated from the society. This is the last and utmost force of ecclesiastical authority: no other punishment can thereby be inflicted, than that the relation ceasing between the body and the member which is cut off, the person so condemned ceases to be a part of that church.

These things being thus determined, let us inquire, in the next place, how far the duty of toleration extends, and what is required from everyone by it.

At first, I hold that no church is bound by the duty of toleration to retain any such person in her bosom, as after admonition continues obstinately to offend against the laws of the society. For these being the condition of communion, and the bond of society, if the breach of them were permitted without any animadversion, the society would immediately be thereby dissolved. But nevertheless, in all such cases care is to be taken that the sentence of excommunication, and the execution thereof, carry with it no rough usage, of word or action, whereby the ejected person may any ways be damnified [*injured*] in body or estate. For all force, as has often been said, belongs only to the magistrate, nor ought any private persons, at any time, to use force; unless it be in self-defense against unjust violence. Excommunication neither does nor can deprive the excommunicated person of any of those civil goods that he formerly possessed. All those things belong to the civil government, and are under the magistrate's protection. The whole force of excommunication consists only in this, that the resolution of the society in that respect being declared, the union that was between the body and some member, comes thereby to be dissolved; and that relation ceasing, the participation of some certain things, which the society communicated to its members, and unto which no man has any civil right, comes also to cease. For there is no civil injury done unto the excommunicated person, by the church minister's refusing him that bread and wine, in the celebration of the Lord's supper, which was not bought with his, but other men's money.

Secondly: No private person has any right in any manner to prejudice another person in his civil enjoyments, because he is of another church or religion. All the rights and franchises that belong to him as a man, or as a denizen[6] are inviolably to be preserved to him. These are not the business of religion. No violence nor injury is to be offered him, whether he be Christian or pagan. Nay, we must not content ourselves with the narrow measures of bare justice: charity, bounty, and liberality must be added to it. This the Gospel enjoins, this reason directs, and this that natural fellowship we are born into requires of us. If any man err from the right way, it is his own misfortune, no injury to thee: nor therefore art thou to punish him in the things of this life, because thou supposest he will be miserable [*perish*] in that which is to come.

What I say concerning the mutual toleration of private persons differing from one another in religion, I understand also of particu-

6. Inhabitant.

lar churches; which stand as it were in the same relation to each
other as private persons among themselves; nor has anyone of them
any manner of jurisdiction over any other, no, not even when the
civil magistrate, as it sometimes happens, comes to be of this or the
other communion. For the civil government can give no new right
to the church, nor the church to the civil government. So that
whether the magistrate join himself to any church, or separate from
it, the church remains always as it was before, a free and voluntary
society. It neither acquires the power of the sword by the magistrate's coming to it, nor does it lose the right of instruction and excommunication by his going from it. This is the fundamental and
immutable right of a spontaneous society, that it has to remove any
of its members who transgress the rules of its institution: but it
cannot, by the accession of any new members, acquire any right of
jurisdiction over those that are not joined with it. And therefore
peace, equity, and friendship, are always mutually to be observed by
particular churches, in the same manner as by private persons,
without any pretence of superiority or jurisdiction over one another.

That the thing may be made yet clearer by an example; let us
suppose two churches, the one of Arminians, the other of Calvinists, residing in the city of Constantinople. Will anyone say, that either of these churches has right to deprive the members of the
other of their estates and liberty, [or punish them through exile or
death], as we see practiced elsewhere, because of their differing
from it in some doctrines or ceremonies; whilst the Turks in the
meanwhile silently stand by, and laugh to see with what inhuman
cruelty Christians thus rage against Christians? But if one of these
churches hath this power of treating the other ill, I ask which of
them it is to whom that power belongs, and by what right? It will be
answered, undoubtedly, that it is the orthodox church which has
the right of authority over the erroneous or heretical. This is, in
great and specious words, to say just nothing at all. For every
church is orthodox to itself; to others, erroneous or heretical.
Whatsoever any church believes, it believes to be true; and the contrary thereunto it pronounces to be error. So that the controversy
between these churches about the truth of their doctrines, and the
purity of their worship, is on both sides equal; nor is there any
judge, either at Constantinople, or elsewhere upon earth, by whose
sentence it can be determined. The decision of that question belongs only to the Supreme Judge of all men, to whom also alone belongs the punishment of the erroneous. In the meanwhile, let those
men consider how heinously they sin, who, adding injustice, if not
to their error, yet certainly to their pride, do rashly and arrogantly

take upon them to misuse the servants of another master, who are
not at all accountable to them.

Nay, further: if it could be manifest which of these two dissenting churches were in the right way, there would not accrue thereby
unto the orthodox any right of destroying the other. For churches
have neither any jurisdiction in worldly matters, nor are fire and
sword any proper instruments wherewith to convince men's minds
of error, and inform them of the truth [*and convert them*]. Let us
suppose, nevertheless, that the civil magistrate is inclined to favor
one of them, and to put his sword into their hands, that, by his consent, they might chastise the dissenters as they pleased. Will any
man say that any right can be derived unto a Christian church, over
its brethren, from a Turkish emperor? An infidel, who has himself
no authority to punish Christians for the articles of their faith, cannot confer such an authority upon any society of Christians, nor
give unto them a right which he has not himself. **This would be
the case at Constantinople.** And the reason of the thing is the
same in any Christian kingdom. The civil power is the same in
every place: nor can that power, in the hands of a Christian prince,
confer any greater authority upon the church, than in the hands of
a heathen; which is to say, just none at all.

Nevertheless, it is worthy to be observed, and lamented, that the
most violent of these defenders of the truth, the opposers of error,
the exclaimers against schism, do hardly ever let loose this their
zeal for God, with which they are so warmed and inflamed, unless
where they have the civil magistrate on their side. But so soon as
ever court favor has given them the better end of the staff, and they
begin to feel themselves the stronger; then presently peace and
charity are to be laid aside: otherwise they are religiously to be observed. **Where they have not the power to carry on persecution,
and to become masters, there they desire to live upon fair
terms, and preach up toleration.** When they are not strengthened
with the civil power, then they can bear most patiently, and un-
movedly, the contagion of idolatry, superstition, and heresy, in their
neighborhood; of which, on other occasions, the interest of religion
makes them to be extremely apprehensive. They do not forwardly
attack those errors which are in fashion at court, or are countenanced by the government. Here they can be content to spare their
arguments: which yet, with their leave, is the only right method of
propagating truth; which has no such way of prevailing, as when
strong arguments and **good** reason are joined with the softness of
civility and good usage.

Nobody therefore, in fine, neither single persons, nor churches,
nay, nor even commonwealths, have any just title to invade the civil

rights and worldly goods of each other, upon pretence of religion. Those that are of another opinion, would do well to consider with themselves how pernicious a seed of discord and war, how powerful a provocation to endless hatreds, rapines, and slaughters, they thereby furnish unto mankind. No peace and security, no, not so much as common friendship, can ever be established or preserved amongst men, so long as this opinion prevails, that dominion is founded in grace, and that religion is to be propagated by force of arms.

In the third place: Let us see what the duty of toleration requires from those who are distinguished from the rest of mankind, from the laity, as they please to call us, by some ecclesiastical character and office; whether they be bishops, priests, presbyters, ministers, or however else dignified or distinguished. It is not my business to inquire here into the original of the power or dignity of the clergy. This only I say, that whence soever their authority be sprung, since it is ecclesiastical, it ought to be confined within the bounds of the church, nor can it in any manner be extended to civil affairs; because the church itself is a thing absolutely separate and distinct from the commonwealth. The boundaries on both sides are fixed and immoveable. He jumbles heaven and earth together, the things most remote and opposite, who mixes these societies, which are, in their original, end, business, and in everything, perfectly distinct, and infinitely different from each other. No man therefore, with whatsoever ecclesiastical office he be dignified, can deprive another man, that is not of his church and faith, either of liberty, or of any part of his worldly goods, upon the account of that difference which is between them in religion. For whatsoever is not lawful to the whole church cannot, by any ecclesiastical right, become lawful to any of its members.

But this is not all. It is not enough that ecclesiastical men abstain from violence and rapine, and all manner of persecution. He that pretends to be a successor of the apostles, and takes upon him the office of teaching, is obliged also to admonish his hearers of the duties of peace and good-will towards all men; as well towards the erroneous as the orthodox; towards those that differ from them in faith and worship, as well as towards those that agree with them therein: and he ought industriously to exhort all men, whether private persons or magistrates, if any such there be in his church, to charity, meekness, and toleration, and diligently endeavor to allay and temper all that heat, and unreasonable averseness of mind, which either any man's fiery zeal for his own **religion or** sect, or the craft of others, has kindled against dissenters. I will not undertake to represent how happy and how great would be the fruit, both in church and state, if the pulpits everywhere sounded with this

doctrine of peace and toleration; lest I should seem to reflect too
severely upon those men whose dignity I desire not to detract from,
nor would have it diminished either by others or themselves. But
this I say, that thus it ought to be. And if anyone that professes
himself to be a minister of the word of God, a preacher of the
Gospel of peace, teach otherwise; he either understands not, or
neglects the business of his calling, and shall one day give account
thereof unto the Prince of Peace. If Christians are to be admon-
ished that they abstain from all manner of revenge, even after repeated provocations and multiplied **seventy times seven** injuries;
how much more ought they who suffer nothing, who have had no
harm done them, to forbear violence, and abstain from all manner
of ill usage towards those from whom they have received none! This
caution and temper they ought certainly to use towards those who
mind only their own business, and are solicitous for nothing but
that, whatever men think of them, they may worship God in that
manner which they are persuaded is acceptable to him, and in
which they have the strongest hopes of eternal salvation. In private
domestic affairs, in **the management of estates**, in the conservation of bodily health, every man may consider what suits his own
conveniency, and follow what course he likes [*judges*] best. No man
complains of the ill management of his neighbor's affairs. No man
is angry with another for an error committed in sowing his land, or
in marrying his daughter. Nobody corrects a spendthrift for con-
suming his substance in taverns. Let any man pull down, or build,
or make whatsoever expenses he pleases, nobody murmurs, nobody
controls him; he has his liberty. But if any man do not frequent the
church, if he do not there conform his behavior exactly to the accustomed ceremonies, or if he brings not his children to be initiated in the sacred mysteries of this or the other congregation; this
immediately causes an uproar, and the neighborhood is filled with
noise and clamor. Everyone is ready to be the avenger of so great a
crime. And the zealots hardly have patience to refrain from violence
and rapine, so long till the cause be heard, and the poor man be,
according to form, condemned to the loss of liberty goods [or *life*.]
Oh that our ecclesiastical orators, of every sect, would apply themselves, with all the strength of argument that they are able, to the
confounding of men's errors! But let them spare their persons. Let
them not supply their want of reasons with the instruments of
force, which belong to another jurisdiction, and do ill become a
churchman's hands. Let them not call in the magistrate's authority
to the aid of their eloquence or learning; lest perhaps, whilst they
pretend only love for the truth, this their intemperate zeal, breath-
ing nothing but fire and sword, **betray their ambition, and** show
that what they desire is temporal dominion. For it will be very diffi-

cult to persuade men of sense, that he, who with dry eyes, and satisfaction of mind, can deliver his brother unto the executioner, to
be burnt alive, does sincerely and heartily concern himself to save
that brother from the flames of hell in the world to come.

In the last place, let us now consider what is the magistrate's
duty in the business of toleration: which is certainly very considerable. We have already proved, that the care of souls does not belong
to the magistrate: not a magisterial care, I mean, if I may so call it,
which consists in prescribing by laws, and compelling by punishments. But a charitable care, which consists in teaching, admon-
ishing, and persuading, cannot be denied unto any man. The care
therefore of every man's soul belongs unto himself, and is to be left
unto himself. But what if he neglect the care of his soul? I answer,
what, [*you say*] if he neglect the care of his health, or of his estate;
which things are nearlier related to the government of the magistrate than the other? Will the magistrate provide by an express law,
that such an one shall not become poor or sick? Laws provide, as
much as is possible, that the goods and health of subjects be not injured by the fraud or violence of others; they do not guard them
from the negligence or ill husbandry of the possessors themselves.
No man can be forced to be rich or healthful, whether he will or
no. Nay, God himself will not save men against their wills. Let us
suppose, however, that some prince were desirous to force his subjects to accumulate riches, or to preserve the health and strength of
their bodies. Shall it be provided by law, that they must consult
none but Roman physicians, and shall everyone be bound to live
according to their prescriptions? What, shall no potion, no broth be
taken, but what is prepared either in the Vatican, suppose, or in a
Geneva shop? Or to make these subjects rich, shall they all be
obliged by law to become merchants, or musicians? Or, shall everyone turn victualler, or smith, because there are some that maintain
their families plentifully, and grow rich in those professions? But it
may be said there are a thousand ways to wealth, but one only way
to heaven. It is well said indeed, especially by those that plead for
compelling men into this or the other way; for if there were several
ways that lead thither, there would not be so much as a pretence
left for compulsion. But now, if I be marching on with my utmost
vigor, in that way which, according to the sacred geography, leads
straight to Jerusalem; why am I beaten and ill used by others, because **perhaps**, I wear not buskins[7] because my hair is not of the
right cut; because, perhaps, I have not been dipped in the right
fashion; because I eat flesh upon the road, or some other food
which agrees with my stomach; because I avoid certain by-ways,

7. Boots.

which seem unto me to lead into briars or precipices; because, amongst the several paths that are in the same road, I choose that to walk in which seems to be the straightest and cleanest; because I avoid to keep company with some travelers that are less grave, and others that are more sour than they ought to be; or in fine, because I follow a guide that either is, or is not, clothed in white, and crowned with a miter? Certainly, if we consider right, we shall find that for the most part they are such frivolous things as these, that, without any prejudice to religion or the salvation of souls, if not accompanied with superstition or hypocrisy, might either be observed or omitted. **I say they are such like things as these, which breed implacable enmities among Christian brethren, who are all agreed in the substantial and truly fundamental part of religion.**

But let us grant unto these zealots, who condemn all things that are not of their mode, that from these circumstances arise different ends [*roads*]. What shall we conclude from thence? There is only one of these [*thousands*] which is the true way to eternal happiness. But, in this great variety of ways that men follow, it is still doubted which is this right one. Now, neither the care of the commonwealth, nor the right of enacting laws, does discover this way that leads to heaven more certainly to the magistrate, than every private man's search and study discovers it unto himself. I have a weak body, sunk under a languishing disease, for which I suppose there is only one remedy, but that unknown: does it therefore belong unto the magistrate to prescribe me a remedy, because there is but one, and because it is unknown? Because there is but one way for me to escape death, will it therefore be safe for me to do whatsoever the magistrate ordains? Those things that every man ought sincerely to inquire into himself, and by meditation, study, search, and his own endeavors, attain the knowledge of, cannot be looked upon as the peculiar profession of anyone sort of men. Princes, indeed, are born superior unto other men in power, but in nature equal. Neither the right, nor the art of ruling, does necessarily carry along with it the certain knowledge of other things; and least of all of the true religion; for if it were so, how could it come to pass that the lords of the earth should differ so vastly as they do in religious matters? But let us grant that it is probable the way to eternal life may be better known by a prince than by his subjects; or, at least, that in this incertitude of things, the safest and most commodious way for private persons is to follow his dictates. You will say, what then? If he should bid you follow merchandise for your livelihood, would you decline that course, for fear it should not succeed? I answer, I would turn merchant upon the prince's command, because in case I should have ill success in trade, he is abundantly able to make up my loss some other way. If it be true, as he pretends, that he desires I should thrive and grow rich, he can set me up again when unsuccessful voyages have broken me. But this is not the case in the things that regard the life to come. If there I take a wrong course, if in that respect I am once undone, it is not in the magistrate's power to repair my loss, to ease my suffering, or to restore me in any measure, much less entirely, to a good estate. What security can be given for the kingdom of heaven?

Perhaps **some** [*you*] will say that they do not suppose this infallible judgment, that all men are bound to follow in the affairs of religion, to be in the civil magistrate, but in the church. What the church has determined, that the civil magistrate orders to be observed; and he provides by his authority, that nobody shall either act or believe, in the business of religion, otherwise than the church teaches; so that the judgment of those things is in the church. The magistrate himself yields obedience thereunto, and requires the like obedience from others. I answer, Who sees not how frequently the name of the church, which was so venerable in the time of the apostles, has been made use of to throw dust in people's eyes, in following ages? But, however, in the present case it helps us not. The one only narrow way which leads to heaven is not better known to the magistrate than to private persons, and therefore I cannot safely take him for my guide, who may probably be as ignorant of the way as myself, and who certainly is less concerned for my salvation than I myself am. Amongst so many kings of the Jews, how many of them were there whom any Israelite, thus blindly following, had not fallen into idolatry, and thereby into destruction? Yet, nevertheless, you bid me be of good courage, and tell me that all is now safe and secure, because the magistrate does not now enjoin the observance of his own decrees in matters of religion, but only the decrees of the church. Of what church, I beseech you? Of that which certainly **likes him best** [*pleases the prince*]. As if he that compels me by laws and penalties [*and coercion*] to enter into this or the other church, did not interpose his own judgment in the matter. What difference is there whether he lead me himself, or deliver me over to be led by others? I depend both ways upon his will, and it is he that determines both ways of my eternal state. Would an Israelite, that had worshipped Baal upon the command of his king, have been in any better condition, because somebody had told him that the king ordered nothing in religion upon his own head, nor commanded anything to be done by his subjects in divine worship, but what was approved by the counsel of priests, and declared to be of divine right by the doctors of the church? If the religion of any church become, therefore, true and saving, because the head of that sect, the prelates and priests, and those of that tribe, do all

of them, with all their might, extol and praise it, **and command it
as they can to their subjects**; and what religion can ever be accounted erroneous, false, and destructive? I am doubtful concerning the doctrine of the Socinians,[8] I am suspicious of the way of
worship practiced by the Papists or Lutherans; will it be ever *a jot*
the safer for me to join either unto the one or the other of those
churches, upon the magistrate's command, because he commands
nothing in religion but by the authority and counsel of the doctors
of that church?

But to speak the truth, we must acknowledge that the church, if
a convention of clergymen, making canons, must be called by that
name, is for the most part more apt to be influenced by the court,
than the court by the church. How the church was under the vicis-
situde of orthodox and Arian[9] emperors is very well known. Or if
those things be too remote, [*our*] modern English history affords us
fresher examples, in the reigns of Henry VIII, Edward VI, Mary,
and Elizabeth, how easily and smoothly the clergy changed their
decrees, their articles of faith, their form of worship, everything,
according to the inclination of those kings and queens. Yet were
those kings and queens of such different minds, in points of religion, and enjoined thereupon such different things, that no man in
his wits, I had almost said none but an atheist, will presume to say
that any sincere and upright worshipper of God could, with a safe
conscience, obey their several decrees. To conclude, it is the same
thing whether a king that prescribes laws to another man's religion
pretend to do it by his own judgment, or by the ecclesiastical authority and advice of others. The decisions of churchmen, whose
differences and disputes are sufficiently known, cannot be any
sounder or safer than his: nor can all their suffrages joined together
add any new strength unto the civil power. Though this also must
be taken notice of, that princes seldom have any regard to the suffrages of ecclesiastics that are not favorers of their own faith and
way of worship.

But after all, the principal consideration, and which absolutely
determines this controversy, is this: although the magistrate's opinion in religion be sound, and the way that he appoints be truly
evangelical, yet if I be not thoroughly persuaded thereof in my own
mind, there will be no safety for me in following it. No way whatsoever that I shall walk in against the dictates of my conscience, will
ever bring me to the mansions of the blessed. I may grow rich by an
art that I take not delight in; I may be cured of some disease by

8. The followers of the teachings of the sixteenth-century Italian Faustus Socinius, who denied the divinity of Christ. Today's Unitarians trace their ancestry to the Socinians.
9. Early Christian emperors who embraced the doctrines of Arius, who denied the divinity
of Christ.

remedies that I have not faith in; but I cannot be saved by a religion that I distrust, and by a worship that I abhor. It is in vain for an unbeliever to take up the outward show of another man's profession. Faith **only** and inward sincerity, are the things that procure acceptance with God. The most likely and most approved remedy can have no effect upon the patient, if his stomach reject it as soon as taken; and you will in vain cram a medicine down a sick man's throat, which his particular constitution will be sure to turn into poison. In a word, whatsoever may be doubtful in religion, yet this at least is certain, that no religion, which I believe not to be true, can be either true or profitable unto me. In vain, therefore, do princes compel their subjects to come into their church-communion, under pretence of saving their souls. If they believe, they will come of their own accord; if they believe not, their coming will nothing avail them. How great, soever, in fine, may be the pretence of good-will and charity, and concern for the salvation of men's souls, men cannot be forced to be saved whether they will or no; and therefore, when all is done, they must be left to their own consciences.

Having thus at length freed men from all dominion over one another in matters of religion, let us now consider what they are to do. All men know and acknowledge that God ought to be publicly worshipped. Why otherwise do they compel one another unto the public assemblies? Men, therefore, constituted in this liberty are to enter into some religious society, that they may meet together, not only for mutual edification, but to own to **the world** [*the people*] that they worship God, and offer unto his divine majesty such service as they themselves are not ashamed of, and such as they think not unworthy of him, nor unacceptable to him; and finally, that by the purity of doctrine, holiness of life, and decent form of worship, they may draw others unto the love of the true religion, and perform such other things in religion as cannot be done by each private man apart.

These religious societies I call churches: and these I say the magistrate ought to tolerate: for the business of these assemblies of the people is nothing but what is lawful for every man in particular to take care of; I mean the salvation of their souls: nor, in this case. is there any difference between the national church and other separated congregations.

But as in every church there are two things especially to be considered; the outward form and rites of worship, and the **doctrines and** articles of faith; these things must be handled each distinctly, that so the whole matter of toleration may the more clearly be understood.

Concerning outward worship, I say, in the first place, that the magistrate has no power to enforce by law, either in his own church, or much less in another, the use of any rites or ceremonies whatsoever in the worship of God, **and this** not only because these churches are free societies, but because whatsoever is practiced in the worship of God is only so far justifiable as it is believed by those that practice it to be acceptable unto him. Whatsoever is not done with that assurance of faith, is neither well in itself, nor can it be acceptable to God. To impose such things, therefore, upon any people, contrary to their own judgment, is, in effect, to command them to offend God; **which**, considering that the end of all religion is to please him, and that liberty is essentially necessary to that end (*is repugnant*) **appears to be absurd beyond expression**.

But perhaps it may be concluded from hence, that I deny unto the magistrate all manner of power about indifferent things; which, if it be not granted, the whole subject matter of law-making is taken away. No, [*I answer*] I readily grant that indifferent things, and perhaps none but such, are subjected to the legislative power.

But it does not therefore follow, that the magistrate may ordain whatsoever he pleases concerning anything that is indifferent. The public good is the rule and measure of all law-making. If a thing be not useful to the commonwealth, though it be ever so indifferent, it may not presently be established by law.

But further things ever so indifferent in their own nature, when they are brought into the church and worship of God, are removed out of the reach of the magistrate's jurisdiction, because in that use they have no connection at all with civil affairs. The only business of the church is the salvation of souls: and it no ways concerns the commonwealth, or any member of it, that this or the other ceremony be there made use of. Neither the use, nor the omission, of any ceremonies in those religious assemblies does [*or can*] **either advantage or** prejudice the life, liberty, or estate, of any man. For example: Let it be granted, that the washing of an infant with water is in itself an indifferent thing: let it be granted also, that if the magistrate understand such washing to be profitable to the curing or preventing of any disease that children are subject unto, and esteem the matter weighty enough to be taken care of by a law, in that case he may order it to be done. But will anyone, therefore, say, that the magistrate has the same right to ordain, by law, that all children shall be baptized by priests, in the sacred font, in order to the purification of their souls, **or that they be initiated by other sacred rites**? The extreme difference of these two cases is visible to everyone at first sight. Or let us apply the last case to the child of a Jew, and the thing will speak itself: for what hinders but a Christian magistrate may have subjects that are Jews? Now, if we acknowledge that such an injury may not be done unto a Jew, as to compel

him, against his own opinion, to practice in his religion a thing that
is in its nature indifferent, how can we maintain that anything of
this kind may be done to a Christian?

Again: Things in their own nature indifferent, cannot, by any
human authority, be made any part of the worship of God, for
this very reason, because they are indifferent. For since indifferent
things are not capable, by any virtue of their own, to propitiate the
Deity, no human power or authority can confer on them so much
dignity and excellency as to enable them to do it. In the common
affairs of life, that use of indifferent things which God has not forbidden is free and lawful; and therefore in those things human authority [*and will*] has place. But it is not so in matters of religion.
Things indifferent are not otherwise lawful in the worship of God
than as they are instituted by God himself; and as he, by some positive command, has ordained them to be made a part of that worship which he will vouchsafe to accept of at the hands of poor
sinful men. Nor when an incensed **Deity** [*God*] shall ask us, "Who
has required these or such like things at your hands?" will it be
enough to answer him, that the magistrate commanded them. If
civil jurisdiction extended thus far, what might not lawfully be introduced into religion? What hodge-podge of ceremonies, what su-
perstitious inventions, built upon the magistrate's authority, might
not, against conscience, be imposed upon the worshippers of God!
For the greatest part of these ceremonies and superstitions consists
in the religious use of such things as are in their own nature indifferent: nor are they sinful upon any other account, than because
God is not the author of them. The sprinkling of water, and use of
bread and wine, are both in their own nature, and in the ordinary
occasions of life, altogether indifferent. Will any man, therefore,
say that these things could have been introduced into religion, and
made a part of divine worship, if not by divine institution? If any
human authority or civil power could have done this, why might it
not also enjoin the eating of fish, and drinking of ale, in the holy
banquet, as a part of divine worship? Why not the sprinkling of the
blood of beasts in churches, and expiations by water or fire, and
abundance more of this kind? But these things, how indifferent so
ever they be in common uses, when they come to be annexed unto
divine worship, without divine authority, they are as abominable to
God as the sacrifice of a dog. **And why a dog so abominable?**
What difference is there between a dog and a goat, in respect of
the divine nature, equally and infinitely distant from all affinity
with matter; unless it be that God required the use of the one in his
worship, and not of the other? We see, therefore, that indifferent
things, how much so ever they be under the power of the civil magistrate, yet cannot, upon that pretence, be introduced into religion,

and imposed upon religious assemblies; because in the worship of God they wholly cease to be indifferent. He that worships God, does it with design to please him, and procure his favor: but that cannot be done by him, who, upon the command of another, offers unto God that which he knows will be displeasing to him because not commanded by himself. This is not to please God, or appease his wrath, but willingly and knowingly to provoke him, by a manifest contempt; which is a thing absolutely repugnant to the nature **and end** of worship.

But it will here be asked, If nothing belonging to divine worship be left to human discretion, how is it then that churches themselves have the power of ordering anything about the time and place of worship, and the like? To this I answer; that in religious worship we must distinguish between what is part of the worship itself, and what is but a circumstance. That is a part of the worship which is believed to be appointed by God, and to be well pleasing to him; and therefore that is necessary. Circumstances are such things which, though in general they cannot be separated from worship, yet the particular instances or modifications of them are not determined; and therefore they are indifferent. Of this sort are the time and place of worship, the habit [*dress*], and posture of him that worships. **These are circumstances, and perfectly indifferent**, where God has not given any express command about them. For example: amongst the Jews, the time and place of their worship, and the habits of those that officiated in it, were not mere circumstances, but a part of the worship itself; in which, if anything were defective, or different from the institution, they could not hope that it would be accepted by God. But these, to Christians, under the liberty of the Gospel, are mere circumstances of worship which the prudence of every church may bring into such use as shall be judged most subservient to the end of order, decency, and edification. Though even under the Gospel also, those who believe **the first or seventh** [*the Lord's*] day to be set apart by God, and consecrated still to his worship, to them that portion of time is not a simple circumstance, but a real part of divine worship, which can neither be changed nor neglected.

In the next place: *As* the magistrate has no power **to impose, by his laws, the use of any rites or ceremonies in any church; so neither has he any power** to forbid the use of such rites and ceremonies as are already received, approved, and practiced by any church: because, if he did so, he would destroy the church itself; the end of whose institution is only to worship God with freedom, after its own manner.

You will say, by this rule, if some congregations should have a mind to sacrifice infants, or, as the primitive Christians were falsely accused, lustfully pollute themselves in promiscuous uncleanness, or practice any other such heinous enormities, is the magistrate obliged to tolerate them, because they are committed in a religious assembly? I answer, No. These things are not lawful in the ordinary course of life, nor in any private house; and, therefore, neither are they so in the worship of God, or in any religious meeting. But, indeed, if any people congregated upon account of religion, should be desirous to sacrifice a calf, I deny that that ought to be prohibited by a law. Meliboeus, whose calf it is, may lawfully kill his calf at home, and burn any part of it that he thinks fit: for no injury is thereby done to anyone, no prejudice to another man's goods. And for the same reason he may kill his calf also in a religious meeting. Whether the doing so be well-pleasing to God or no, it is their part to consider that do it. The part of the magistrate is only to take care that the commonwealth receive no prejudice, and that there be no injury done to any man, either in life or estate. And thus what may be spent on a feast may be spent on a sacrifice. But if, peradventure, such were the state of things, that the interest of the commonwealth required all slaughter of beasts should be forborn for some while, in order to the increasing of the stock of cattle, that had been destroyed by some extraordinary murrain[1]; who sees not that the magistrate, in such a case, may forbid all his subjects to kill any calves for any use whatsoever? Only it is to be observed, that in this case the law is not made about a religious, but a political matter: nor is the sacrifice, but the slaughter of calves thereby prohibited.

By this we see what difference there is between the church and the commonwealth. Whatsoever is lawful in the commonwealth, cannot be prohibited by the magistrate in the church. Whatsoever is permitted unto any of his subjects for their ordinary use, neither can nor ought to be forbidden by him to any sect of people for their religious uses. If any man may lawfully take bread or wine, either sitting or kneeling, in his own house, the law ought not to abridge him of the same liberty in his religious worship; though in the church the use of bread and wine be very different, and be there applied to the mysteries of faith, and rites of divine worship. But those things that are prejudicial to the commonweal of a people in their ordinary use, and are therefore forbidden by laws, those things ought not to be permitted to churches in their sacred rites. Only the magistrate ought always to be very careful that he do not misuse his authority, to the oppression of any church, under pretence of public good. [*What is commonly allowed elsewhere cannot be forbidden by law in divine worship and holy places*].

It may be said, What if a church be idolatrous, is that also to be

---

1. Disease.

tolerated by the magistrate? In answer, I ask, what power can be given to the magistrate for the suppression of an idolatrous church, which may not, in time and place, be made use of to the ruin of an orthodox one? For it must be remembered, that the civil power is the same everywhere, and the religion of every prince is orthodox to himself. If, therefore, such a power be granted unto the civil magistrate in spirituals, as that at Geneva, for example; he may extirpate, by violence and blood, the religion which is there reputed idolatrous; by the same rule, another magistrate, in some neighboring country, may oppress the **reformed** [*orthodox*] religion; and, in India, the Christian. The civil power can either change everything in religion, according to the prince's pleasure, or it can change nothing. If it be once permitted to introduce anything into religion, by the means of laws and penalties, [*by force*] there can be no bounds put to it; but it will, in the same manner, be lawful to alter everything, according to that rule of truth which the magistrate has framed unto himself. No man whatsoever ought therefore to be deprived of his terrestrial enjoyments, upon account of his religion. Not even Americans[2], subjected unto a Christian prince, are to be punished either in body or goods, for not embracing our faith and worship. If they are persuaded that they please God in observing the rites of their own country, and that they shall obtain happiness [*salvation*] by that means, they are to be left unto God and themselves.

Let us trace this matter to the bottom. Thus it is: an inconsiderable and weak number of Christians, destitute of everything, arrive in a pagan country; these foreigners beseech the inhabitants, by the bowels of humanity, that they would succur them with the necessaries of life; those necessaries are given them, habitations are granted, and they all join together, and grow up into one body of people. The Christian religion by this means takes root in that country, and spreads itself; but does not suddenly grow the strongest. While things are in this condition, peace, friendship, faith, and equal justice, are preserved amongst them. At length the magistrate becomes a Christian, and by that means their party becomes the most powerful. Then immediately all compacts are to be broken, all civil rights to be violated, that idolatry may be extirpated: and unless these innocent pagans, strict observers of the rules of equity and the law of nature [*a man to man*], and no ways offending against the laws of the society, I say unless they will forsake their ancient religion, and embrace a new and strange one, they are to be turned out of the lands and possessions of their forefathers, and perhaps deprived of life itself. Then at last it appears what zeal for the church, joined with the desire of dominion, is capable to produce: and how

2. i.e., American Indians.

easily the pretence of religion, and of the care of souls, serves for a cloak to covetousness, rapine, and ambition.

Now, whosoever maintains that idolatry is to be rooted out of any place by laws, punishments, fire, and sword, may apply this story to himself: for the reason of the thing is equal, both in America and Europe. And neither pagans there, nor any dissenting Christians here, can with any right be deprived of their worldly goods by the predominating faction of a court-church; nor are any *civil* rights to be either changed or violated upon account of religion in one place more than another.

But idolatry, say some, is a sin, and therefore not to be tolerated. If they said it were therefore to be avoided, the inference were good. But it does not follow, that because it is a sin, it ought therefore to be punished by the magistrate. For it does not belong unto the magistrate to make use of his sword in punishing everything, indifferently, that he takes to be a sin against God. Covetousness, uncharitableness, idleness, and many other things are sins, by the consent of all men, which yet no man ever said were to be punished by the magistrate. The reason is, because they are not prejudicial to other men's rights, nor do they break the public peace of societies. Nay, even the sins of lying and perjury are nowhere punishable by laws; unless in certain cases, in which the real turpitude of the thing, and the offence against God, are not considered, but only the injury done unto men's neighbors, and to the commonwealth. And what if, in another country, to a Mohammedan or a pagan prince, the Christian religion seem false and offensive to God; may not the Christians, for the same reason, and after the same manner, be extirpated there?

But it may be urged farther, that by the law of Moses idolaters were to be rooted out. True indeed, by the law of Moses; but that is not obligatory to us Christians. Nobody pretends that everything, generally, enjoined by the law of Moses, ought to be practiced by Christians. But there is nothing more frivolous than that common distinction of moral, judicial, and ceremonial law, which men ordinarily make use of: for no positive law whatsoever can oblige any people but those to whom it is given. "Hear, O Israel," sufficiently restrains the obligation of the law of Moses only to that people. And this consideration alone is answer enough unto those that urge the authority of the law of Moses, for the inflicting of capital punishments upon idolaters. But however I will examine this argument a little more particularly.

The case of idolaters, in respect of the Jewish commonwealth, falls under a double consideration. The first is of those, who, being initiated in the Mosaic rites, and made citizens of that commonwealth, did afterwards apostatize from the worship of the God of Israel. These were proceeded against as traitors and rebels, guilty of no less than high treason; for the commonwealth of the Jews, different in that from all others, was *an absolute* theocracy: nor was there, or could there be, [*as after the birth of Christ*], any difference between that commonwealth and the church. The laws established there concerning the worship of one invisible Deity, were the civil laws of that people, and a part of their political government, in which God himself was the legislator. Now if anyone can show me where there is a commonwealth, at this time, constituted upon that foundation, I will acknowledge that the ecclesiastical laws do there unavoidably become a part of the civil; and that the subjects of that government both may, and ought to be, kept in strict conformity with that church, by the civil power. But there is absolutely no such thing, under the Gospel, as a Christian commonwealth. There are, indeed, many cities and kingdoms that have embraced the faith of Christ; but they have retained their ancient forms of government, with which the law of Christ hath not at all meddled. He, indeed, hath taught men how, by faith and good works, they may attain eternal life. But he instituted no commonwealth; he prescribed unto his followers no new and peculiar form of government; nor put he the sword into any magistrate's hand, with commission to make use of it in forcing men to forsake their former religion, and receive his.

Secondly, foreigners, and such as were strangers to the commonwealth of Israel, were not compelled by force to observe the rites of the Mosaic law: but, on the contrary, in the very same place where it is ordered that an Israelite that was an idolater should be put to death, there it is provided that strangers should not be "vexed nor oppressed," (Exod. 22: 21). I confess that the seven nations that possessed the land which was promised to the Israelites were utterly to be cut off. But this was not *simply* because they were idolaters; for if that had been the reason, why were the Moabites and other nations to be spared? No; the reason is this: God being in a peculiar manner the King of the Jews, he could not suffer the adoration of any other deity, which was properly an act of high treason against himself, in the land of Canaan, which was his kingdom; for such a manifest revolt could no ways consist with his dominion, which was perfectly political, in that country. All idolatry was therefore to be rooted out of the bounds of his kingdom; because it was an acknowledgment of another God [*king*], that is to say, another king [*God*], against the laws of empire. The inhabitants were also to be driven out, that the entire possession of the land might be given to the Israelites. And for the like reason the Emims and the Horims were driven out of their countries by the children of Esau and Lot; and their lands, upon the same grounds, given by God to the in-

vaders, Deut. 2: 12. But though all idolatry was thus rooted out of
the land of Canaan, yet every idolater was not brought to execution. [*Joshua spared*] The whole family of Rahab, the whole nation
of the Gideonites, **articled with Joshua and were allowed** by
treaty; and there were many captives amongst the Jews, who were
idolaters. David and Solomon subdued many countries without the
confines of the Land of Promise, and carried their conquests as far
as the Euphrates river. Amongst so many captives taken, of so many
nations reduced under their obedience, we find not one man forced
into the Jewish religion, and the worship of the true God, and punished for idolatry, though all of them were certainly guilty of it. If
anyone indeed, becoming a proselyte, desired to be made a denizen
of their commonwealth, he was obliged to submit unto their laws;
that is, to embrace their religion. But this he did willingly, on his
own accord, not by constraint. He did not unwillingly submit, to
show his obedience; but he sought and solicited for it, as a privilege; and as soon as he was admitted, he became subject to the
laws of the commonwealth, by which all idolatry was forbidden
within the borders of the land of Canaan. But that law, as I have
said, did not reach to any of those regions, however subjected unto
the Jews, that were situated without those bounds.

Thus far concerning outward worship. Let us now consider **articles of** faith.

The articles of religion [*church dogmas*] are some of them practical, and some speculative. Now, though both sorts consist in the
knowledge of truth, yet these terminate simply in the understanding, those influence the will and manners. Speculative opinions,
therefore, and articles of faith, as they are called, which are required only to be believed, cannot be imposed on any church by the
law of the land; for **it is absurd**, [*how is it possible*] that things
should be enjoined by laws which are not in men's power to perform; and to believe this or that to be true does not depend upon
our will. But of this enough has been said already. But, **will some
say** let men at least profess that they believe. A sweet religion, indeed, that obliges men to dissemble, and tell lies both to God and
man, for the salvation of their souls! If the magistrate thinks to save
men thus, he seems to understand little of the way of salvation; and
if he does it not in order to save them, why is he so solicitous about
the articles of faith as to enact them by a law?

Further, the magistrate ought not to forbid the preaching or pro-
fessing of any speculative opinions in any church, because they
have no manner of relation to the *civil* rights of the subjects. If **a
Roman Catholic** [*papist*] believe that to be really the body of
Christ, which another man calls bread, he does no injury thereby to
his neighbor. If a Jew does not believe the New Testament to be the

word of God, he does not thereby alter anything in men's civil
rights. If a heathen doubt of both Testaments, he is not therefore to
be punished as a pernicious citizen. The power of the magistrate,
and the estates of the people, may be equally secure, whether any
man believe these things or no. I readily grant that these opinions
are false and absurd; but the business of laws is not to provide for
the truth of opinions, but for the safety and security of the commonwealth, and of every particular man's goods **and person**. And
so it ought to be; for truth certainly would do well enough, if she
were once left to shift for herself. She seldom has received, and I
fear never will receive, much assistance from the power of great
men, to whom she is but rarely known, and *more* rarely welcome.
She is not taught by laws, nor has she any need of force to procure
her entrance into the minds of men. Errors indeed prevail by the
assistance of foreign and borrowed succors. But if truth makes not
her way into the understanding by her own light, she will be but the
weaker for [*she cannot do so through*] any borrowed force violence
can add to her. Thus much for speculative opinions. Let us now
proceed to the practical ones.

A good life, in which consists not the least part of religion and
true piety, concerns also the civil government: and in it lies the
safety both of men's souls and of the commonwealth. Moral actions
belong therefore to the jurisdiction both of the outward and inward
court; both of the civil and domestic governor; I mean, both of the
magistrate and conscience. Here therefore is great danger, lest one
of these jurisdictions entrench upon the other, and discord arise
between the keeper of the public peace and the overseers of souls.
But if what has been already said concerning the limits of both
these governments be rightly considered, it will easily remove all
difficulty in this matter.

Every **man** [*mortal*] has an immortal soul, capable of eternal happiness or misery; whose **happiness depending** [*salvation depends*]
upon his believing and doing those things in this life, which are
necessary to the obtaining of God's favor, and are prescribed by
God to that end: it follows from thence, first, that the observance of
these things is the highest obligation that lies upon mankind, and
that our utmost care, application, and diligence, ought to be exercised in the search and performance of them; because there is
nothing in this world that is of any consideration in comparison
with eternity. Secondly, that seeing one man does not violate the
right of another, by his erroneous opinions, and undue manner of
worship, nor is his perdition any prejudice to another man's affairs;
therefore the care of each man's salvation belongs only to himself.
But I would not have this understood, as if I meant hereby to condemn all charitable admonitions, and affectionate endeavors to

reduce men from errors; which are indeed the greatest duty of a Christian. Anyone may employ as many exhortations and arguments as he pleases, towards the promoting of another man's salvation. But all force and compulsion are to be forborn. Nothing is to be done imperiously [*by the government*]. Nobody is obliged in that manner to yield obedience unto the admonitions or injunctions of another, farther than he himself is persuaded. Every man, in that, has the supreme and absolute authority of judging for himself; and the reason is, because nobody else is concerned in it, nor can receive any prejudice from his conduct therein.

But besides their souls, which are immortal, men have also their temporal lives here upon earth; the state whereof being frail and fleeting, and the duration uncertain, they have need of several outward conveniencies to the support thereof, which are to be procured or preserved by pains and industry; for those things that are necessary to the comfortable support of our lives, are not the spontaneous products of nature, nor do offer themselves fit and prepared for our use. This part, therefore, draws on another care **and necessarily gives another employment**. But the pravity[3] of mankind being such, that they had rather injuriously prey upon the fruits of other men's labors than take pains to provide for themselves; the necessity of preserving men in the possession of what honest industry has already acquired, and also of preserving their liberty and strength **whereby they may acquire what they further want**, obliges men to enter into society with one another; that by mutual assistance and joint force, they may secure unto each other their properties, in the things that contribute to the comforts and happiness of this life; leaving in the meanwhile to every man the care of his own eternal happiness, the attainment whereof can neither be facilitated by another man's industry, nor can the loss of it turn to another man's prejudice, nor the hope of it be forced from him by any external violence. But forasmuch as men thus entering into societies, grounded upon their mutual compacts of assistance, for the defense of their temporal goods, may nevertheless be deprived of them, either by the rapine and fraud of their fellow-citizens, or by the hostile violence of foreigners: the remedy of this evil consists in arms, riches, and multitudes of citizens: the remedy of others in laws: and the care of all things relating both to the one and the other is committed by the society to the civil magistrate. This is the original, this is the use, and these are the bounds of the legislative, which is the supreme power in every commonwealth. I mean, that provision may be made for the security of each man's private possessions; for the peace, riches, and public commodities

3. Depravity.

of the whole people, and, as much as possible, for the increase of their **inward** strength against foreign invasions.

These things being thus explained, it is easy to understand to what end the legislative power ought to be directed, and by what measures regulated, and that is the temporal good and outward prosperity of the society, which is the sole reason of men's entering into society, and the only thing they seek and aim at in it; and it is also evident what liberty remains to men in reference to their eternal salvation, and that is, that everyone should do what he in his conscience is persuaded to be acceptable to the Almighty, on whose good pleasure and acceptance depends his eternal **happiness** [*salvation*]; for obedience is due in the first place to God, and afterwards to the laws.

But some may ask, "What if the magistrate should enjoin anything by his authority, that appears unlawful to the conscience of a private person?" I answer, that if government be faithfully administered, and the counsels of the magistrate be indeed directed to the public good, this will seldom happen. But if perhaps it do so fall out, I say, that such a private person is to abstain from the actions that he judges unlawful; and he is to undergo the punishment, which is not unlawful for him to bear; for the private judgment of any person concerning a law enacted in political matters, for the public good, does not take away the obligation of that law, nor deserve **a dispensation** [*toleration*] But if the law indeed be concerning things that lie not within the verge of the magistrate's authority; as, for example, that the people, or any party amongst them, should be compelled to embrace a strange religion, and join in the worship and ceremonies of another church; men are not in these cases obliged by that law, against their consciences; for the political society is instituted for no other end, but only to secure every man's possession of the things of this life. The care of each man's soul, and of the things of heaven, which neither does belong to the commonwealth, nor can be subjected to it, is left entirely to every man's self. Thus the safeguard of men's lives, and of the things that belong unto this life, is the business of the commonwealth; and the preserving of those things unto their owners is the duty of the magistrate; and therefore the magistrate cannot take away these worldly things from this man, or party, and give them to that; nor change property amongst fellow **subjects** [*citizens*], no, not even by a law, for a cause that has no relation to the end of civil government; I mean for their religion; which, whether it be true or false, does no prejudice to the worldly concerns of their fellow **subjects** [*citizens*], which are the things that only belong unto the care of the commonwealth.

But what if the magistrate believe such a law as this to be for the public good? I answer: as the private judgment of any particular person, if erroneous, does not exempt him from the obligation of law, so the private judgment, as I may call it, of the magistrate, does not give him any new right of imposing laws upon his subjects, which neither was in the constitution of the government granted him, nor ever was in the power of the people to grant: and least of all, if he make it his business to enrich and advance his followers and fellow-sectaries with the spoils of others. But what if the magistrate believe that he has a right to make such laws, and that they are for the public good; and his subjects believe the contrary? Who shall be judge between them? I answer, God alone; for there is no judge upon earth between the supreme magistrate and the people. God, I say, is the only judge in this case, who will retribute unto everyone at the last day according to his deserts; that is, according to his sincerity and uprightness in endeavouring to promote piety, and the public weal and peace of mankind. But what shall be done in the meanwhile? I answer: the principal and chief care of everyone ought to be of his own soul first, and, in the next place, of the public peace: though yet there are few will think it is peace there, where they see all laid waste. There are two sorts of contests amongst men; the one managed by law, the other by force: and they are of that nature, that where the one ends, the other always begins. But it is not my business to inquire into the power of the magistrate in the different constitutions of nations. I only know what usually happens where controversies arise, without a judge to determine them. You will say then the magistrate being the stronger will have his will, and carry his point. Without doubt. But the question is not here concerning the doubtfulness of the event, but the rule of right [*conduct*].

But to come to particulars. I say, first, No **opinions** [*doctrines*] contrary to human society, or to those moral rules which are necessary to the preservation of civil society, are to be tolerated by the magistrate. But of those indeed examples in any church are rare. For no sect can easily arrive to such a degree of madness, as that it should think fit to teach, for doctrines of religion, such things as manifestly undermine the foundations of society, and are therefore condemned by the judgment of all mankind: because their own interest, peace, reputation, *everything* would be thereby endangered.

Another more secret evil, but more dangerous to the commonwealth, is when men arrogate to themselves, and to those of their own sect, some peculiar prerogative, covered over with a specious show of deceitful words, but in effect opposite to the civil [*law*] **rights of the community**. For example: we cannot find any sect that teaches expressly and openly, that men are not obliged to keep their promise; that princes may be dethroned by those that differ

from them in religion; or that the dominion of all things belongs
only to themselves. For these things, proposed thus nakedly and
plainly, would soon draw on them the eye and hand of the magistrate, and awaken all the care of the commonwealth to a watch-
fulness against the spreading of so dangerous an evil. But
nevertheless, we find those that say the same things in other words.
What else do they mean, who teach that faith is not to be kept with
heretics.[4] Their meaning, forsooth, is, that the privilege of breaking
faith belongs unto themselves: for they declare all that are not of
their communion to be heretics, or at least may declare them so
whensoever they think fit. What can be the meaning of their assert-
ing that kings excommunicated forfeit their crowns and kingdoms?
It is evident that they thereby arrogate unto themselves the power
of deposing kings: because they challenge the power of excommunication as the peculiar right of their hierarchy. That dominion is
founded in grace, is also an assertion by which those that maintain
it do plainly lay claim to the possession of all things. For they are
not so wanting to themselves as not to believe, or at least as not to
profess, themselves to be the truly pious and faithful. These therefore, and the like, who attribute unto the faithful, religious, and
orthodox, that is, in plain terms, unto themselves, any peculiar privilege or power above other mortals, in civil concernments; or who,
upon pretence of religion, do challenge any manner of authority
over such as are not associated with them in their ecclesiastical
communion; I say these have no right to be tolerated by the magistrate; as neither those that will not **own and** teach the duty of tol-
erating all men in matters of mere **religion** [*religious dissent*]. For
what do all these and the like doctrines signify, but that they may,
and are ready upon any occasion to seize the government, and possess themselves of the estates and fortunes of their fellow **subjects**
[*citizens*]; and that they only ask leave to be tolerated by the magistrates so long, until they find themselves strong enough to effect it.

Again: That church can have no right to be tolerated by the magistrate, [*in*] which **is constituted on such a bottom that** all those
who enter into it, do thereby, ipso facto, deliver themselves up to
the protection and service of [*dependence on, and obedience to*]
another prince. For by this means the magistrate would give way to
the settling of a foreign jurisdiction in his own country, and suffer
his own people to be listed, as it were, for soldiers against his own
government. Nor does the frivolous and fallacious distinction between the court and the church afford any remedy to this incon-

---

4. A reference to the teaching of the Jesuits, e.g., Robert Bellarmine, that Catholic subjects
   are released from their oaths of allegiance to heretical rulers. English citizens were required on many occasions to swear oaths of allegiance to the monarch.

venience; especially when both the one and the other are equally
subject to the absolute authority of the same person; who has not
only power to persuade the members of his church to whatsoever
he lists, either as purely religious, or as in order thereunto; but can
also enjoin it them on pain of eternal fire. It is ridiculous for anyone to profess himself to be a Mahometan only in religion, but in
everything else a faithful subject to a Christian magistrate, while at
the same time he acknowledges himself bound to yield blind obedience to the mufti of Constantinople; who himself is entirely obedient to the Ottoman emperor, and frames the famed oracles of that
religion according to his pleasure. But this Mahometan, living
amongst Christians, would yet more apparently renounce their government, if he acknowledged the same person to be head of his
church, who is the supreme magistrate in the state.[5]

Lastly, those are not at all to be tolerated who deny **the being of
God** [*the Deity*]. Promises, covenants, and oaths, which are the
bonds of human society, can have no hold upon an atheist. The taking away of God, though but even in thought, dissolves all. Besides
also, those that by their atheism undermine *and destroy* all religion,
can have no pretence of religion whereupon to challenge the privilege of a toleration. As for other practical opinions, though not absolutely free from all error, yet if they do not tend to establish
domination over others, or civil impunity to the church in which they
are taught, there can be no reason why they should not be tolerated.

It remains that I say something concerning those assemblies,
which being vulgarly called, and perhaps having sometimes been
conventicles, and nurseries of factions and seditions, are thought to
afford the strongest matter of objection against this doctrine of toleration. But this has not happened by anything peculiar unto the
genius of such assemblies, but by the unhappy circumstances of an
oppressed or ill-settled liberty. These accusations would soon cease,
if the law of toleration were once so settled, that all churches were
obliged to lay down toleration as the foundation of their own liberty;
and teach that liberty of conscience is every man's natural right,
equally belonging to dissenters as to themselves [*religious dissenters
are to be tolerated*] and that nobody ought to be compelled in matters of religion either by law or force. The establishment of this one
thing would take away all ground of complaints and tumults upon
account of conscience. And these causes of discontents and and an-
imosities being once removed, there would remain nothing in these
assemblies that were not more peaceable, and less apt to produce

---

5. Despite the references to Islam, Locke is speaking of Roman Catholic obedience to the
   pope.

disturbance of state, than in any other meetings whatsoever. But let us examine particularly the heads of these accusations.

You will say that assemblies and meetings endanger the public peace, and threaten the commonwealth. I answer: if this be so, why are there daily such numerous meetings in **markets** [*associations*] and courts of judicature? Why are crowds **upon the Exchange and a concourse of people, in cities** suffered? You will reply, these are civil assemblies; but those we object against are ecclesiastical. I answer: it is a likely thing indeed, that such assemblies as are altogether remote from civil affairs should be most apt to embroil them. O, but civil assemblies are composed of men that differ from one another in matters of religion: but these ecclesiastical meetings are of persons that are all of one opinion. [*I answer:*] As if an agreement in matters of religion were in effect a conspiracy against the commonwealth: or as if men would not be so much the more warmly unanimous in religion, the less liberty they had of assembling. But it will be urged still, that civil assemblies are open, and free for anyone to enter into; whereas religious conventicles are more private, and thereby give opportunity to clandestine machinations. I answer that this is not strictly true: for many civil assemblies are not open to everyone. And if some religious meetings be private, who are they, I beseech you, that are to be blamed for it, those that desire, or those that forbid their being public? Again: you will say, that religious communion does exceedingly unite men's minds and affections to one another, and is therefore the more dangerous. But [*I answer,*] if this be so, why is not the magistrate afraid of his own church; and why does he not forbid their assemblies, as things dangerous to his government? You will say, because he himself is a part, and even the head of them. As if he were not also a part of the commonwealth, and the head of the whole people.

Let us therefore deal plainly. The magistrate is afraid of other churches, but not of his own; because he is kind and favorable to the one, but severe and cruel to the other. These he treats like children, and indulges them even to wantonness. Those he uses as slaves; and how blamelessly so ever they demean themselves, recompenses them no otherwise than by galleys, prisons, confiscations, and death. These he cherishes and defends: those he continually scourges *and oppresses*. Let him turn the tables: or let those dissenters enjoy but the same privileges in **civils** [*civil affairs*] as his other subjects, and he will quickly find that these religious meetings will be no longer dangerous. For if men enter into seditious conspiracies, it is not religion inspires them to it in their meetings, but their sufferings and oppressions **that make them willing to ease themselves.** Just and moderate governments are everywhere quiet, everywhere safe. But oppression raises ferments, and makes men struggle **to cast off an uneasy and tyrannical yoke**. I know that seditions are very frequently raised upon pretence of religion. But it is as true, that, for religion, subjects are frequently ill treated, and live miserably. Believe me, the stirs that are made proceed not from any peculiar temper of this or that church or religious society; but from the common disposition of all mankind, who, when they groan under any heavy burden, endeavour naturally to shake off the yoke that galls their necks. Suppose this business of religion were let alone, and that there were some other distinction made between men and men, upon account of their different complexions, shapes, and features, so that those who have black hair, for example, or gray eyes, should not enjoy the same privileges as other citizens; that they should not be permitted either to buy or sell, or live by their callings; that parents should not have the government and education of their own children; that they should either be excluded from the benefit of the laws, or meet with partial judges: can it be doubted but these persons, thus distinguished from others by the color of their hair and eyes, and united together by one common persecution, would be as dangerous to the magistrate, as any others that had associated themselves merely upon the account of religion? Some enter into company for trade and profit: others, for want of business, have their clubs for **claret** [*enjoyment*]. Neighborhood joins some, and religion others. But there is one thing only which gathers people into seditious commotions, and that is oppression.

You will say; what, will you have people to meet at divine service against the magistrate's will? I answer; why, I pray, against his will? Is it not both lawful and necessary that they should meet? Against his will, do you say? That is what I complain of. That is the very root of all the mischief. Why are assemblies less sufferable in a church than in a theater or market? Those that meet there are not either more vicious, or more turbulent, than those that meet elsewhere. The business in that is, that they are ill used, and therefore they are not to be suffered. Take away the partiality that is used towards them in matters of common **right** [*law*]; change the laws, take away the penalties unto which they are subjected, and all things will immediately become safe and peaceable: nay, those that are averse to the religion of the magistrate, will think themselves so much the more bound to maintain the peace of the commonwealth, as their condition is better in that place than elsewhere; and all the several **separate** [*dissident*] congregations, like so many guardians of the public peace, will watch one another, that nothing may be innovated or changed in the form of the government: because they can hope for nothing better than what they already enjoy; that is, an equal condition with their fellow-subjects, under a just and moderate government. Now if that church, which agrees in religion with the prince, be esteemed the chief support of any civil government, and that for no other reason, as has already been shown, than because the prince is kind, and the laws are favorable to it; how much greater will be the security of a government, where all good subjects, of whatsoever they be, without any distinction upon account of religion, enjoying the same favor of the prince, and the same benefit of the laws, shall become the common support and guard of it; and where none will have any occasion to fear the severity of the laws, but those that do injuries to their neighbors, and offend against the civil peace!

That we may draw towards a conclusion. The sum of all we drive at is that every man enjoy the same rights that are granted to others. Is it permitted to worship God in the Roman manner? Let it be permitted to do it in the Geneva[6] form also. Is it permitted to speak Latin in the market-place? Let those that have a mind to it, be permitted to do it also in the church. Is it lawful for any man in his own house to kneel, stand, sit, or use any other posture; and clothe himself in white or black, in short or in long garments? Let it not be made unlawful to eat bread, drink wine, or wash with water in the church. In a word: whatsoever things are left free by law in the common occasions of life, let them remain free unto every church in divine worship. Let no man's life, or body, or house, or estate, suffer any manner of prejudice upon these accounts. Can you allow of the presbyterian discipline? Why should not the episcopal also have what they like?[7] Ecclesiastical authority, whether it be administered by the hands of a single person, or many, is everywhere the same; and neither has any jurisdiction in things civil, nor any manner of power of compulsion, nor anything at all to do with riches and revenues.

Ecclesiastical assemblies and sermons, are justified by daily experience **and public allowance**. These are allowed to people of some one **persuasion** [*church or sect*]: why not to all? If anything pass in a religious meeting seditiously, and contrary to the public peace, it is to be punished in the same manner, and no otherwise, than as if it had happened in a fair or market. These meetings ought not to be sanctuaries of factious and flagitious fellows: nor ought it to be less lawful for men to meet in churches than in halls: nor are one part of the **subjects** [*citizens*] to be esteemed more blamable for their meeting together than others. Everyone is to be accountable for his own actions; and no man is to be laid under a suspicion, or odium,

6. i.e., Calvinist.
7. Those who believe that the church should be governed by bishops (i.e., the Anglicans) and those who favor the rule of elders or presbyters (i.e., the Presbyterians).

for the fault of another. Those that are seditious, murderers, thieves, robbers, [*rapists*], adulterers, slanderers, etc, of whatsoever church, whether **national** [*established*] or not, ought to be punished and suppressed. But those whose doctrine is peaceable, and whose manners are pure and blameless, ought to be upon equal terms with their fellow-subjects. Thus if solemn assemblies, observations of festivals, public worship, be permitted to anyone sort of professors; all these things ought to be permitted to the **Presbyterians, Independents, Anabaptists, Arminians, Quakers, and others,** [*Remonstrants, Anti-Remonstrants, Lutherans, Anabaptists, Unitarians, etc.*][8] with the same liberty. Nay, if we may openly speak the truth, and as becomes one man to another, neither pagan, nor Mahometan, nor Jew, ought to be excluded from the civil rights of the commonwealth, because of his religion. The Gospel commands no such thing. The church, "which judgeth not those that are without," (1 Cor. 5:11), wants it not. And the commonwealth, which embraces indifferently all men that are honest, peaceable, and industrious, requires it not. Shall we suffer a pagan to deal and trade with us, and shall we not suffer him to pray unto and worship God? If we allow the Jews to have private houses and dwellings amongst us, why should we not allow them to have synagogues? Is their doctrine more false, their worship more abominable, or is the civil peace more endangered, by their meeting in public, than in their private houses? But if these things may be granted to Jews and pagans, surely the condition of any Christians ought not to be worse than theirs, in a Christian commonwealth.

You will say, perhaps, yes, it ought to be: because they are more inclinable to factions, tumults, and civil wars. I answer: is this the fault of the Christian religion? If it be so, truly the Christian religion is the worst of all religions, and ought neither to be embraced by any particular person, nor tolerated by any commonwealth. For if this be the genius, this the nature of the Christian religion, to be turbulent and destructive of the civil peace, that church itself which the magistrate indulges will not always be innocent. But far be it from us to say any such thing of that religion, which carries the greatest opposition to covetousness, ambition, discord, contention, and all manner of inordinate desires; and is the most modest and peaceable religion that ever was. We must therefore seek another cause of those evils that are charged upon religion. And if we consider right, we shall find it consist wholly in the subject that

8. Popple replaced Locke's list of Protestant denominations on the Continent, which was appropriate for the audience of his Latin letter, with those more prevalent in England. Remonstrants and Arminians were Calvinist sects that disagreed with orthodox Calvinist doctrine on predestination.

I am treating of. It is not the diversity of opinions, which cannot be avoided; but the refusal of toleration to those that are of different opinions, which might have been granted, that has produced all the bustles and wars, that have been in the Christian world, upon account of religion. The heads and leaders of the church, moved by avarice and insatiable desire of dominion, making use of the immoderate ambition of magistrates, and the **credulous** superstition of the **giddy** multitude, have incensed and animated them against those that dissent from themselves, by preaching unto them, contrary to the laws of the Gospel, and to the precepts of charity, that schismatics and heretics are to be outed of their possessions, and destroyed. And thus have they mixed together, and confounded two things, that are in themselves most different, the church and the commonwealth. Now as it is very difficult for men patiently to suffer themselves to be stripped of the goods, which they have got by their honest industry; and contrary to all the laws of equity, both human and divine, to be delivered up for a prey to other men's violence and rapine; especially when they are otherwise altogether blameless; and that the occasion for which they are thus treated does not at all belong to the jurisdiction of the magistrate, but entirely to the conscience of every particular man, for the conduct of which he is accountable to God only; what else can be expected, but that these men, growing weary of the evils under which they labor, should in the end think it lawful for them to resist force with force, and to defend their **natural** rights [*created by nature and God*], which are not forfeitable upon account of religion, with arms as well as they can? That this has been hitherto the ordinary course of things, is abundantly evident in history: and that it will continue to be so hereafter, is but too apparent in reason. It cannot indeed be otherwise, so long as the principle of persecution for religion shall prevail, as it has done hitherto, with magistrate and people; and so long as those that ought to be the preachers of peace and concord, shall continue, with all their art and strength, to excite men to arms, and sound the trumpet of war. But that magistrates should thus suffer these incendiaries, and disturbers of the public peace, might justly be wondered at, if it did not appear that they have been invited by them unto a participation of the spoil, and have therefore thought fit to make use of their covetousness and pride, as means whereby to increase their own power. For who does not see that these good men are indeed more ministers of the government than ministers of the Gospel; and that by flattering the ambition, and favouring the dominion of princes and men in authority, they endeavour with all their might to promote that tyranny in the commonwealth, which otherwise they should not be able to establish in the church? This is the unhappy agreement that we see between the church and the state.

Whereas if each of them would contain itself within its own bounds, the one attending to the worldly welfare of the commonwealth, the other to the salvation of souls, it is impossible that any discord should ever have happened between them . . . *Sed pudet haec opprobria etc.*[9] God Almighty grant, I beseech him, that the Gospel of peace may at length be preached, and that civil magistrates, growing more careful to conform their own consciences to the law of God, and less solicitous about the binding of other men's consciences by human laws, may, like fathers of their country, direct all their counsels and endeavors to promote universally the civil welfare of all their children; except only of such as are arrogant, ungovernable, [*unjust*,] and injurious to their brethren; and that all ecclesiastical men, who boast themselves to be the successors of the apostles, walking peaceably and modestly in the apostles' steps, without intermeddling with state affairs, may apply themselves wholly to promote the salvation of souls. Farewell.

Postscriptum

Perhaps it may not be amiss to add a few things concerning heresy and schism.[1] A **Turk** [*Mohammedan*] is not, nor can be either heretic or schismatic to a Christian; and if any man fall off from the Christian faith to Mohammedanism [*Islam*], he does not thereby become a heretic, or a schismatic, but an apostate and an infidel. This nobody doubts of. And by this it appears that men of different religions cannot be heretics or schismatics to one another.

We are to inquire, therefore, what men are of the same religion: concerning which, it is manifest that those who have one and the same rule of faith and worship are of the same religion, and those who have not the same rule of faith and worship are of different religions. For since all things that belong unto that religion are contained in that rule, it follows necessarily, that those who agree in one rule are of one and the same religion; and vice versa. Thus Turks and Christians are of different religions; because these take the Holy Scriptures to be the rule of their religion, and those the Koran. And for the same reason, there may be different religions also, even amongst Christians. The Papists and the Lutherans, though both of them profess faith in Christ, and are therefore called Christians, yet are not both of the same religion: because

9. "But it is shameful that these reproaches can be directed at us and we cannot answer" Ovid's *Metamorphoses*, I:758.
1. The Postscript was added to defend Locke's Arminian Dutch friends from the charge by other Dutch Calvinists that they were heretics or schismatics.

these acknowledge nothing but the Holy Scriptures to be the rule and foundation of their religion; those take in also traditions and decrees of popes, and of all these together make the rule of their religion. And thus the Christians of St. John,[2] as they are called, and the Christians of Geneva are of different religions: because these also take only the Scriptures, and those, I know not what traditions, for the rule of their religion.

This being settled, it follows, first, that heresy is a separation made in ecclesiastical communion between men of the same religion, for some opinions no way contained in the rule itself.

And secondly, that amongst those who acknowledge nothing but the Holy Scriptures to be their rule of faith, heresy is a separation made in their Christian communion, for opinions not contained in the express words of Scripture.

Now this separation may be made in a twofold manner:

First, when the greater part, or, by the magistrate's patronage, the stronger part, of the church separates itself from others, by excluding them out of her communion, because they will not profess their belief of certain **opinions** [*doctrines*] which are not to be found in the express words of Scripture. For it is not the paucity of those that are separated, not the authority of the magistrate, that can make any man guilty of heresy; but he only is an heretic who divides the church into parts, introduces names and marks of distinction, and voluntarily makes a separation because of such opinions.

Secondly, when anyone separates himself from the communion of a church, because that church does not publicly profess some certain **opinions** [*doctrines*] which the Holy Scriptures do not expressly teach.

Both these are heretics, because they err in fundamentals, and they err obstinately against knowledge. For when they have determined the Holy Scriptures to be the only foundation of faith, they nevertheless lay down certain propositions as fundamental, which are not in the Scripture; and because others will not acknowledge these additional opinions of theirs, nor build upon them as if they were necessary and fundamental, they therefore make a separation in the church, either by withdrawing themselves from the others, or expelling the others from them. Nor does it signify anything for them to say that their confessions and symbols are agreeable to Scripture, and to the analogy of faith: for if they be conceived in the express words of Scripture, there can be no question about them; because those are acknowledged by all Christians to be of divine inspiration, and therefore fundamental. But if they say that

2. The Knights of Malta.

the articles which they require to be professed are consequences deduced from the Scripture, it is undoubtedly well done of them to believe and profess such things as seem unto them so agreeable to the rule of faith: but it would be very ill done to obtrude those things upon others, unto whom they do not seem to be the indubitable doctrines of the Scripture. And to make a separation for such things as these, which neither are nor can be fundamental, is to become heretics. For I do not think there is any man arrived to that degree of madness, as that he dare give out his consequences and interpretations of Scripture as divine inspirations, and compare [equate] the articles of faith, that he has framed according to his own fancy, with the authority of the Scripture. I know there are some propositions so evidently agreeable to Scripture, that nobody can deny them to be drawn from thence: but about those therefore there can be no difference. This only I say, that however clearly we may think this or the other doctrine to be deduced from Scripture, we ought not therefore to impose it upon others as a necessary article of faith, because we believe it to be agreeable to the rule of faith; unless we would be content also that other doctrines should be imposed upon us in the same manner; and that we should be compelled to receive and profess all the different and contradictory **opinions** [dogmas] of Lutherans, Calvinists, Remonstrants, Anabaptists, and other sects, which the contrivers of symbols, systems, and confessions, are accustomed to deliver unto their followers as genuine and necessary deductions from the Holy Scripture. I cannot but wonder at the extravagant arrogance of those men who think that they themselves can explain things necessary to salvation more clearly than the Holy Ghost, the eternal and infinite wisdom of God.

Thus much concerning heresy; which word in common use is applied only to the doctrinal part of religion. Let us now consider schism, which is a crime near akin to it: for both those words seem unto me to signify an ill-grounded separation in ecclesiastical communion, made about things not necessary. But since use, which is the supreme law in matter of language, has determined that heresy relates to errors in faith, and schism to those in worship or discipline, we must consider them under that distinction.

Schism then, for the same reasons that have already been alleged, is nothing else but a separation made in the communion of the church, upon account of something in divine worship, or ecclesiastical discipline, that is not any necessary part of it. Now nothing in worship or discipline can be necessary to Christian communion, but what Christ our legislator, or the apostles, by inspiration of the Holy Spirit, have commanded in express words.

In a word: he that denies not anything that the Holy Scriptures teach in express words, nor makes a separation upon occasion of anything that is not manifestly contained in the sacred text; however he may be **nicknamed** [*badly received*] by any sect of Christians, and declared by some, or all of them, to be utterly void of true Christianity; yet in deed and in truth this man cannot be either a heretic or schismatic.

These things might have been explained more largely, and more advantageously; but it is enough to have hinted at them, thus briefly, to a person of your parts.

FINIS

BACKGROUND
SELECTIONS

Essays on the Law of Nature (1663–64)

Locke's early lectures on natural law were published only in 1954, but they provide important information on Locke's intellectual development. After receiving his B.A. and M.A. at Oxford in 1656 and 1658, he remained at Christ Church, as a tutor, reader in Greek (1660), reader in rhetoric (1662), and censor of moral philosophy (1664); and his studentship (fellowship) continued until it was terminated for political reasons in 1683. Two notebooks from this period with Latin drafts of lectures on natural law were among the large collection of books and papers bequeathed to Locke's cousin Peter King and sold to Oxford in 1947 by his descendant the earl of Lovelace. The second and larger set, copied in another hand but corrected by Locke is dated 1663, although one of its final lectures is dated 1664. It may have been prepared for use in connection with his duties as censor of moral philosophy, a post he held for a year beginning in December 1663. The Latin version and an English translation titled *Essays on the Law of Nature*, along with an extensive introduction were published by W. von Leyden (Locke 1954). Another Latin text and a new English translation, restoring the original numbering of the lectures and retitled *Questions on the Law of Nature* (because the lectures, in the tradition of the medieval scholastic disputations are structured around a series of questions), was published by Jenny Strauss Clay and Diskin Clay with an introduction by Robert Horwitz in 1990 (Locke 1990). I use the von Leyden edition because it has become standard in the literature and because the Clay translation is not significantly better than that of von Leyden (The von Leyden introduction is also much superior from a scholarly point of view. See the highly critical review by M. A. Stewart, 1992, which ridicules Horwitz's claim that Locke was a crypto-atheist.)

The *Essays on the Law of Nature* are important for an understanding of the background of Locke's treatment of ethics in his *Essay Concerning Human Understanding*, the first versions of which were written in 1671 as a result of discussions "about morality and revealed religion." They also clarify his understanding of natural law in the *Two Treatises*. (The fact that a transcription of the *Essays*, perhaps with a view to their publication, was carried out by his servant at Locke's behest between 1687 and 1692—that is, around the time when he was publishing *The Two Treatises* [Locke 1954:13] argues against the view that Locke's views on natural law had changed.) They show that Locke was already familiar with Book I of Hooker's *Laws of Ecclesiastical Polity*, sharing its view of natural law as a reflection of the divine will in the created universe but disagreeing with Hooker on universal consent as an indication of its content. They also seem to reflect at least an indirect knowledge of Hobbes, perhaps through Samuel von Pufendorf's *Elements of Universal Jurisprudence*, which was published in Latin in 1660 and which clearly influenced the *Essays* (see, for example, von Leyden's footnotes to Essay VII). Although they use some of the same concepts—for example, the state of nature and the distinction between natural right and natural law—both Pufendorf and Locke specifically disagree with Hobbes on man's social obligations, casting doubt on the attempt of Leo Strauss (see p. 274 herein) and his followers to describe Locke as a crypto-Hobbesian (see John Yolton, p. 281 herein).

While the first essay speaks of the natural law as "implanted in our hearts" later essays anticipate Locke's denial of innate ideas in the *Essay Concerning Human Understanding,* and Essay III even uses the Latin words *tabula rasa* (blank slate) to describe in a similar way the initial state of the human mind. Their description of the action of reason on sense-experience in order to arrive at the principles of natural law, basing obligation on the structure and function of the human constitution as a reflection of the purposes of God and nature (see Essay IV) reproduces traditional Aristotelian and Thomistic arguments. It is not significantly different from many statements in the *Essay Concerning Human Understanding,* although the passages in the latter work about pleasure and pain, as well as its increased emphasis on sense-experience as the source of knowledge, have often been cited to argue that Locke's ethical theory had undergone a fundamental change. Like the *Second Treatise,* the *Essays* include the property right and self-preservation among the precepts of the natural law, but the justification of property through labor seems to have been a later development. The last essay on the relation of natural law to utility clearly refutes claims that Locke is a utilitarian—that is, derives morality from the calculation of pleasure and pain. Its argument that utility is the effect of virtue, rather than its cause, can also be used to understand the later role of pleasure and pain in the *Essay Concerning Human Understanding.*

From Essays on the Law of Nature†

From *I. Is There a Rule of Morals or Law of Nature Given to Us? Yes*

* * *

This law, denoted by these appellations, [the law of nature] ought to be distinguished from natural right: for right is grounded in the fact that that we have the free use of a thing, whereas law is what enjoins or forbids the doing of a thing.

Hence, this law of nature can be described as being the decree of the divine will discernible by the light of nature and indicating what is or what is not in conformity with rational nature, and for this very reason commanding or prohibiting. It appears to me less

† From *Essays on the Law of Nature,* ed. and trans. W. von Leyden (Oxford: Clarendon Press, 1954, 1958, 1988). Reprinted by permission of Oxford University Press.

correctly termed by some people the dictate of reason,[1] since reason does not so much establish and pronounce this law of nature as
search for it and discover it as law enacted by a superior power and
implanted in our hearts.

* * *

* * * I admit that all people are by nature endowed with reason,
and I say that natural law can be known by reason, but from this it
does not necessarily follow that it is known to any and every one.
For there are some who make no use of the light of reason but prefer darkness and would not wish to show themselves to themselves.
* * * In others, again, through natural defect the acumen of the
mind is too dull to be able to bring to light those secret decrees of
nature. For how few there are who in matters of daily practice or
matters easy to know surrender themselves to the jurisdiction of
reason or follow its lead, when either led astray by the violence of
passions or being indifferent through carelessness or degenerate
through habit, they readily follow the inducements of pleasure or
the urges of their base instincts rather than the dictates of reason.
Who, as I might almost say, is there in the commonwealth that
knows the law of his state, though they have been promulgated,
hung up in public places, are easy to read and understand, and are
everywhere exposed to view? And how much less will he be acquainted with the secret and hidden law of nature? Hence, in this
matter, not the majority of people should be consulted but those
who are more rational and perceptive than the rest.

* * *

From II. Can the Law of Nature Be Known by the Light of Nature? Yes

* * * We do not maintain that this law of nature, written as it
were on tablets, lies open in our hearts, and that, as soon as some
inward light comes near it (like a torch approaching a notice board
hung up in darkness), it is at length read, perceived, and noted by
the rays of that light. Rather, by saying that something can be
known by the light of nature, we mean nothing else but that there
is some sort of truth to the knowledge of which a man can attain by
himself and without the help of another, if he makes proper use of
the faculties he is endowed with by nature.

However, there are three kinds of knowledge which, without an
over-careful choice of terms, I may call inscription, tradition, and
sense-experience. To these may be added a fourth kind, namely su-

---

1. This is a reference to Grotius's definition. Following Pufendorf, Locke disagrees with
Grotius's view that the rational character of the natural law is sufficient to give it binding force. All notes are the editor's unless otherwise specified.

pernatural and divine revelation, but this is no part of our present argument. For we do not investigate here what a man can experience who is divinely inspired, or what a man can behold who is illuminated by a light from heaven, but what a man who is endowed with understanding, reason, and sense-experience, can by the help of his own nature and his own sagacity search out and examine. * * *

* * *

(1) As regards inscription, there are some who are of the opinion that this law of nature is inborn in us and is so implanted by nature in the minds of all, that there is none who comes into the world whose mind does not carry these innate characters and marks of his duty engraved upon it. * * * Whether in fact there is any such imprint of the law of nature in our hearts, and whether it becomes known to mankind in the manner described, will perhaps be discussed at another place. As regards the present question, it will suffice to have proved that, if man makes use properly of his reason and of the inborn faculties with which nature has equipped him, he can attain to the knowledge of this law without any teacher instructing him in his duties, and monitor reminding him of them. * * *

(2) * * * [T]hat the law of nature, in so far as it is a law, does not become known to us by means of tradition, is shown, if I mistake not, by the following arguments.

First, in the presence of so much variety among conflicting traditions it would be impossible to determine what the law of nature is, and it would be difficult to decide completely what is true and what is false, what is law and what is opinion, what is commanded by nature and what by utility, what advice reason gives and what instructions are given by society. * * *

* * *

(3) The last way of knowledge that remains to be discussed is sense-perception, which we declare to be the basis of our knowledge of the law of nature. However, this must not be understood in the sense that the law of nature appears somewhere so conspicuously that we can either read it off with our eyes, examine it with our hands, or hear it proclaiming itself. But since we are searching now for the principle and origin of the knowledge of this law and for the way in which it becomes known to mankind, I declare that the foundation of all knowledge of it is derived from those things which we perceive through our senses. From these things, then, reason and power of arguing, which are both distinctive marks of man, advance to the notion of the maker of these things (there being no lack of arguments in this direction such as are necessarily derived from the matter, motion, and visible structure and arrange-

ment of this world) and at last they conclude and establish for themselves as certain that some Deity[2] is the author of all these things. As soon as this is laid down, the notion of a universal law of nature binding on all men necessarily emerges. * * *

* * *

From III [IV].[3] Is the Law of Nature Inscribed in the Minds of Men? No

* * *

(1) It has been only an empty assertion and no one has proved it until now, although many have laboured to this end, that the souls of men when they are born are something more than empty tablets[4] capable of receiving all sorts of imprints but having none stamped on them by nature.

(2) If this law of nature were stamped by nature upon the minds of men as a whole at their very birth, how does it come about that human beings, who would have their souls furnished with that law, do not forthwith all to a man agree about it without hesitation and show readiness to obey it? * * *

(3) If this law of nature is inscribed in the minds of men, how does it happen that younger boys, illiterate people, and those primitive races which, having no institutions, laws, and knowledge, are said to live in accordance with nature, do not best of all know and understand this law? They are all free from notions coming from without which may divert the minds elsewhere; they do not imbibe opinions borrowed from some other source, which can either corrupt, or blot out or destroy the dictates of nature; for they have no other teachers than themselves and follow nothing but nature. * * * Thus the law of nature does not appear to be written in the hearts of men, if those who have no other guide than nature itself and among whom the decrees of nature are least spoiled by arbitrary customs live in such ignorance of every law, as though there were no principle of rightness and goodness to be had at all.

* * *

From IV [V]. Can Reason Attain to the Knowledge of Natural Law through Sense-Experience? Yes

* * * [S]ince, as has been shown elsewhere, this light of nature is neither tradition nor some inward moral principle written in our minds by nature, there remains nothing by which it can be defined

---

2. *Deum*; god.
3. Locke's original numbering of the essays appears in brackets. In some cases the essays are identified only by title.
4. *Rasae tabulae.*

but reason and sense-perception. For only these two faculties appear to teach and educate the minds of men to provide what is characteristic of the light of nature, namely that things otherwise wholly unknown and hidden in darkness should be able to come before the mind and be known and as it were looked into. As long as these two faculties serve one another, sensation furnishing reason with the ideas of particular sense-objects and supplying the subject-matter of discourse, reason on the other hand guiding the faculty of sense, and arranging together the images of things derived from sense-perception, thence forming others and composing new ones, there is nothing so obscure, so concealed, so removed from any meaning that the mind, capable of everything, could not apprehend it by reflection and reasoning, if it is supported by these faculties. * * * The foundations, however, on which rests the whole of that knowledge which reason builds up and raises as high as heaven are the objects of sense-experience; for the senses primarily supply the entire as well as the chief subject-matter of discourse and introduce it into the deep recesses of the mind. * * * But in order that we may know how sense-experience and reason, as long as they assist one another mutually, can lead us to the knowledge of natural law, certain facts must first be set forth, because they are necessarily presupposed in the knowledge of any and every law. First, in order that anyone may understand that he is bound by a law, he must know beforehand that there is a law-maker, i.e. some superior power to which he is rightly subject. Secondly, it is also necessary to know that there is some will on the part of that superior power with respect to the things to be done by us, that is to say, that the law-maker, whoever he may prove to be, wishes that we do this but leave off that, and demands of us that the conduct of our life should be in accordance with his will. * * *

*   *   *

Secondly, we say that the mind, after more carefully considering in itself the fabric of this world perceived by the senses and after contemplating the beauty of the objects to be observed, their order, array, and motion, thence proceeds to an inquiry into their origin, to find out what was the cause, and who the maker, of such an excellent work, for it is surely undisputed that this could not have come together casually and by chance into so regular and in every respect so perfect and ingeniously prepared structure. Hence it is undoubtedly inferred that there must be a powerful and wise creator of all these things, who has made and built this whole universe and us mortals who are not the lowest part of it. * * *

*   *   *

* * * [S]ince on the evidence of the senses it must be concluded that there is some maker of all these things, whom it is necessary to

recognize as not only powerful but also wise, it follows from this that he has not created this world for nothing and without purpose. For it is contrary to such great wisdom to work with no fixed aim. * * * Hence it is quite evident that God intends man to do something, and this was the second of the two things required for the knowledge of any and every law, namely, the will on the part of a superior with respect to the things to be done by us; that is, God wills that we do something. But what it is that is to be done by us can be partly gathered from the end in view for all things. For since these derive their origin from a gracious divine purpose and are the work of a most perfect and wise maker, they appear to be intended by Him for no other end than His own glory, and to this all things must be related. Partly also we can infer the principle and a definite rule of our duty from man's own constitution and the faculties with which he is equipped. For since man is neither made without design nor endowed to no purpose with these faculties which both can and must be employed, his function appears to be that which nature has prepared him to perform. * * * Further, he feels himself not only to be impelled by life's experience and pressing needs to procure and preserve a life in society with other men, but also to be urged to enter into society by a certain propensity of nature, and to be prepared for the maintenance of society by the gift of speech and through the intercourse of language, in fact as much as he is obliged to preserve himself.[5] * * *

From V [VII]. Can the Law of Nature Be Known from the General Consent of Men? No

'The voice of the people is the voice of God.' Surely, we have been taught by a most unhappy lesson how doubtful, how fallacious this maxim is, how productive of evils, and with how much party spirit and with what cruel intent this ill-omened proverb has been flung wide [lately] among the common people. Indeed if we should listen to this voice as if it were the herald of divine law, we should hardly believe that there was any God at all. * * *

* * *

* * * [T]o take an example, it is evident that the agreement among envoys having safe passage * * * is positive and does not imply a law of nature, precisely because according to the law of nature all men alike are friends of one another and bound together by common interests unless (as is maintained by some[6]) there is in the

---

5. The obligation of self-preservation is cited in St. Thomas Aquinas's *Suma Theologial*, I–II, qu. 94.a.2. The argument from speech for the social nature of man appears in Aristotle's *Politics*, book I.
6. Hobbes.

state of nature a general war and perpetual and deadly hatred among men. * * *

* * *

* * * [I]f we would review each class of virtues and vices—and nobody doubts that this classification is the actual law of nature—it will easily appear that there is none of them of which men do not form different opinions buttressed by public authority and custom. Hence, if the general consent of men is to be regarded as the rule of morality, there will either be no law of nature at all or it will vary from place to place, a thing being morally good in one place and wrong in another, and the vices themselves will become duties. But this no one will maintain. * * *

* * *

What is one to say of modesty and chastity, if among the Assyrians women were accustomed and encouraged to take part in banquets stark naked and exposed to the view of all present, while among other nations it is unlawful for women to go out in public, even though veiled, or to show the face, or be seen by strangers? Among others it is lawful for unmarried girls to live dissolutely, and it is thought that chastity belongs only to married women, and that females are restrained from lust only by matrimony. * * *

* * *

But if any law of nature would seem to be established among all as sacred in the highest decree, which the whole of mankind, it seems, is urged to observe by a certain natural instinct and by its own interest, surely this is self-preservation, and therefore some lay this down as the chief and fundamental law of nature. But in fact the power of custom and of opinion based on traditional ways of life is such as to arm men even against their own selves, so that they lay violent hands upon themselves and seek death as eagerly as others shun it. Subjects have been met with who not only worship and defend their king while alive but also follow him into death. And there are slaves who attend their masters beyond the grave and desire to discharge their duty of obedience in a place where all are equal. * * *

It would be tedious to describe further instances. Nor is it surprising that men think so differently about what is right and good, since they differ even in the first principles, and doubt is thrown upon God and the immortality of souls. Even if God and the soul's immortality are not moral propositions and laws of nature, nevertheless they must be necessarily presupposed if natural law is to exist. For there is no law without a law-maker, and a law is to no purpose without punishment. * * *

* * *

From VII [X]. Is the Binding Force of the Law of Nature Perpetual and Universal? Yes

* * *

* * * [The law of nature] is a fixed and permanent rule of morals which reason itself pronounces, and which persists, being a fact so firmly rooted in the soil of human nature. Hence human nature must needs be changed before this law can either be altered or annulled. * * * [S]ince man has been made such as he is, equipped with reason and his other faculties and destined for this mode of life, there necessarily result from his inborn constitution some definite duties for him, which cannot be other than they are. In fact it seems to me to follow just as necessarily from the nature of man that, if he is a man, he is bound to love and worship God and also to fulfil other things appropriate to the rational nature, i.e. to observe the law of nature, as it follows from the nature of a triangle that, if it is a triangle, its three angles are equal to two right angles, although perhaps very many men are so ignorant and so thoughtless that for want of attention they ignore both these truths, which are so manifest that nothing could be plainer. * * *

* * *

From VIII [XI]. Is Every Man's Own Interest[7] the Basis of the Law of Nature? No

There are some who in their attack upon natural law have adopted the following argument: 'It is on the basis of utility that men have laid down for themselves legal codes varying in accordance with their manners and customs, and often changed with changing times among the same people; there is, however, no law of nature, for all men as well as other living creatures are driven by innate impulse to seek their own interests; and there is likewise no such thing as a natural law of justice, or, if it exists, it is the height of folly, inasmuch as to be mindful of the advantages of others is to do harm to oneself.'[8] * * *

* * *

* * * [W]hen we say that each man's personal interest is not the basis of natural law, we do not wish to be understood to say that the common rules of human equity and each man's private interest are opposed to one another, for the strongest protection of each man's private property is the law of nature, without the observance of which it is impossible for anybody to be master of his property and

7. *Utilitas.*
8. The view of Carneades in Cicero's *On the Republic*, summarized in Grotius's *On the Law of War on Peace.*

to pursue his own advantage. Hence it will be clear to anyone who candidly considers for himself the human race and the practices of men, that nothing contributes so much to the general welfare of each and so effectively keeps men's possessions safe and secure as the observance of the natural law. Nevertheless we do deny that each person is at liberty to do what he himself, according to circumstances, judges to be of advantage to him. You have certainly no reason for holding that each person's own interest is the standard of what is just and right, unless you let every single man be judge in his own case and himself determine what is in his own interest, seeing that no one can be a fair and just appraiser of another's advantages; and you deceive a man with what is only a semblance of utility, if you say he is permitted to do what is useful and yet would let another man have the power to determine what is and is not useful. Hence the point of the question is precisely this: Is it true that what each individual in the circumstances judges to be of advantage to himself and his affairs is in accordance with natural law, and on that account is not only lawful for him but also unavoidable, and that nothing in nature is binding except so far as it carries with it some immediate personal advantage? It is this we deny, for three reasons:

First, it is impossible for something to be the basis of natural law or to be the principal law, which is not the ground of the binding force of other, less universal, laws of that same nature. But the binding force of other laws does not rest on the principle of utility as its foundation, for if you should run over all the dutiful actions of human life, you will find none that arises out of mere utility and is binding for the sole reason that it is advantageous. In fact a great number of virtues, and the best of them, consist only in this: that we do good to others at our own loss. * * *

Secondly, it is impossible that the primary law of nature is such that its violation is unavoidable. Yet, if the private interest of each person is the basis of that law, the law will inevitably be broken, because it is impossible to have regard for the interests of all at one and the same time. In point of fact, the inheritance of the whole of mankind is always one and the same, and it does not grow in proportion to the number of people born. Nature has provided a certain profusion of goods for the use and convenience of men, and the things provided have been bestowed in a definite way and in a predetermined quantity; they have not been fortuitously produced nor are they increasing in proportion with what men need or covet. Clothes are not born with us, nor do men, like tortoises, possess and carry about shelters that have originated with them and are growing up together with them. Whenever either the desire, or the need of property increases among men, there is no extension, then and there, of the world's limits. Victuals, clothes, adornments, riches, and all other good things of life are provided for common use. And so, when any man snatches for himself as much as he can, he takes away from another man's heap the amount he adds to his own, and it is impossible for anyone to grow rich except as the expense of someone else. * * *

* * *

* * * The duties of life are not at variance with one another, nor do they arm men against one another—a result which, secondly, follows of necessity from the preceding assumption, for upon it men are, as they say, by the law of nature in a state of war;[9] so all society is abolished and all trust, which is the bond of society. For what reason is there for the fulfillment of promises, what safeguard of society, what common life of man with man, when equity and justice are one and the same utility? What else indeed can human intercourse be than fraud, violence, hatred, robbery, murder, and such like, when every man not only may, but must, snatch from another by any and every means what the other in his turn is obliged to keep safe.

Hence there arises a third argument, namely, that it is impossible for any principle to be the basis of natural law, whereby, if it is laid down as true, all justice, friendship, and generosity are taken away from life. For what justice is there where there is no personal property or right of ownership, or what personal property where a man is not only allowed to possess his own, but what he possesses is his own, merely because it is useful to him. * * *

* * *

* * * An objector, however, might say that if the observance of natural law and of every duty of life always leads to what is useful and if whatever we do according to the law of nature cannot but create, either directly or indirectly, great advantages, then the basis of natural law is each man's own interest. But (he goes on) the truth of the minor premise is evident, for the observance of this law gives rise to peace, harmonious relations, friendship, freedom from punishment, security, possession of our property, and—to sum it all up in one word—happiness. Our answer to the objector is this: Utility is not the basis of the law or ground of obligation, but the consequence of obedience to it. Surely, it is one thing for an action of itself to yield some profit, another for it to be useful because it is in accordance with the law, so that if the law were abolished it would have in it no utility whatever: for example, to stand by one's promise, though it were to one's own hindrance. In fact we must

9. A reference to and criticism of Hobbes's *Leviathan* (see p. 244 herein). There is a similar veiled reference in *Essay V* [VII].

distinguish between an action as such and obedient action, for action itself can be inexpedient—for example, the restitution of a trust that diminishes our possessions—whereas obedient action is useful in so far as it averts the penalty due to crime. But this penalty would not be due and hence need not be shunned, if the standard of rightness were immediate advantage. And thus the rightness of an action does not depend on its utility; on the contrary, its utility is a result of its rightness.

Thus thought

1664   J. Locke

An Essay Concerning Human Understanding
(1671–90)

An Essay Concerning Human Understanding, published in December 1689, but dated 1690, was the work that made Locke famous. That fame was mainly related to its criticism of traditional theories of knowledge, especially Aristotelian conceptions of science that relied on real essences and inherent purposes in nature, and to its emphasis on reason operating on sense-experience as the sole means, other than divine revelation, by which human beings acquire knowledge. It began, as Locke says in his introduction, with a group of "five or six friends meeting at my chamber and discoursing on a subject very remote from this" (according to one of the participants, "morality and revealed religion") leading to Locke's realization that "it was necessary to examine our own abilities, and see what objects our understandings were, or were not, fitted to deal with." That meeting took place in 1671, and Locke worked on several drafts of the *Essay* in the intervening years. The *Essay Concerning Human Understanding* was so successful when it was published that four editions appeared during Locke's lifetime, and a fifth in 1706 after his death.

The work is divided into four books—a critique of innate ideas, an analysis of ideas or "modes of thinking," "words or language in general," and "knowledge and opinion." The selections printed here are concerned with the aspects of his theories that relate to his political and ethical thought. They develop the criticism of innate ideas and an argument about the derivation of knowledge from sense-experience that had already been anticipated in the *Essays on the Law of Nature*. A passing reference (in 1.3.5) also indicates that Locke knew Hobbes's political theory and contrasted it with Christian and classical ideas of virtue, but there is no indication that he shared Hobbes's views. A single sentence about individuals giving up the use of force in favor of the rule of law while retaining their ability to criticize the government (in 2.28.10) also reflects the argument of the *Second Treatise*.

The *Essay*'s frequent references to pleasure and pain as the sources of our knowledge of good and evil led some of his critics, then and now, to accuse him of a hedonistic and materialistic approach to morality, what his contemporaries called "Hobbism." However, given his repeated arguments that revelation, reason, and long-run pleasure and pain are mutually reinforcing by divine intention, it is difficult to make this argument except by ignoring his explicit statements. Moreover, the pleasure and pain that results from the performance of good or evil acts includes eternal happiness in heaven or misery in hell, which he variously described as certain and as possible. (He also described the immortality of the soul as "a strong probability, amounting almost to certainty"; see Marshall, 1994:152. On the importance of God, angels, and spirits in the *Essay*, see Yolton, 2004.) In addition, reflecting an alternative view that he later developed further, he also allowed for the possibility of the annihilation of evildoers at death (see 2.21.60, 61, and 70). In response to the criticism that he was a "Hobbist"—that is, a materialist and determinist who equated morality with calculations of self-interest—he added to the second edition, published in 1694, a description of divine law, as "promulgated . . . by the light of reason or the voice of revelation," describing them as "the only true touchstone of moral rectitude" (2.28.8), and he added a new section to the chapter "On Power" (2.20) that argued for moral choice and free will.

For Locke, pleasure and pain are ways in which we know what God has designated as good and evil, and acting morally produces good results if not in this world, then in the next. They are not, however, the reasons why we should act morally. The principles of morality are revealed by God through revelation and through reason, including "natural religion," which demonstrates God's existence and his will for his creatures. It is true that pleasure and pain, as indications but not as constituents of virtue and vice, receive more emphasis in the *Essay Concerning Human Understanding* than in the earlier *Essays on the Law of Nature*, but already in the last of the *Essays* Locke had argued that "utility is not the basis of the law, nor the ground of obligation, but the consequence of obedience to it," a description that can also be applied to his discussions of pleasure and pain in the *Essay Concerning Human Understanding*.

A more general criticism based on Locke's epistemology, argues that Locke's empiricism makes it impossible for him to believe in a natural law morality. It is true that Locke believed human beings are not "fitted by nature" to know "the beings of things themselves" in the physical world, thus breaking with the Aristotelian–Thomistic beliefs in the human capacity to perceive forms, essences, and final causes in the physical world. However, he repeatedly aaserts that God has given man the ability to reason to God's existence and know the "precise real essence of the things that moral words stand for" (3.11.16), in a way that is comparable to our knowledge of the principles of mathematics or geometry. (The selections printed here include several comparisons of the demonstrability of ethics to our knowledge of the properties of a triangle.) Moreover, in his attacks on innate ideas, he distinguishes innate law from the law of nature, which, he says, we "may attain to the knowledge of, by the use and application of our natural faculties" (1.3.13).

While Locke was clearly a theist, and like Aquinas believed that faith confirms and supplements reason in a purposive universe governed by divine providence, he was much more inclined to subject religious doctrines to the critical standards of reason. He was critical of those who claimed special insight into the divine will and repeatedly argued that reason should be the final judge of what is and is not divine revelation. Yet in areas that are beyond or not contrary to reason, and even in those where we only have probable knowledge, we should defer, he says, to revelation, provided we are sure that a given proposition is indeed included in revelation. The relation of faith and reason continued to concern him. To understand the next step in his discussion of their relationship, see *The Reasonableness of Christianity* (p. 207 herein).

From Essay Concerning Human Understanding†

From *Book 1. Of Innate Notions*

FROM CHAPTER I. *INTRODUCTION*

*   *   *

5. *Our capacity united to our state and concerns.* * * * Men have reason to be well satisfied with what God hath thought fit for them. * * * How short soever their knowledge may come of an universal or comprehensive knowledge of whatever is, yet it secures their great concernments that they have light enough to lead them to the knowledge of their Maker and the sight of their own duties. * * * We shall not have much reason to complain of the narrowness of our minds if we will but employ them about what may be of use to us, for of that they are very capable; and it will be an unpardonable as well as childish peevishness if we undervalue the advantages of our knowledge and neglect to improve it for the ends for which it was given us because there are some things that are set out of reach of us. It will be no excuse to an idle and untoward servant who would not attend his business by candlelight to plead that he had not broad sunshine. The candle that is set up in us shines bright enough for all our purposes. * * *

6. *Knowledge of our capacity, a cure of skepticism and idleness.* * * * It is of great use to the sailor to know the length of his line, though he cannot with it fathom all the depths of the ocean. It is well that he knows it is long enough to reach the bottom at such places as are necessary to direct his voyage, and to caution him against shoals that may ruin him. Our business here is not to know

---

† From *The Works of John Locke*, Thomas Tegg et al. (London, 1823; rpnt. Aalen: Scientia Verlag, 1963). Numbering has been changed from Roman to Arabic numerals to conform to present usage.

all things, but those which concern our conduct. If we can find out those measures whereby a rational creature, put in the state in which man is in this world, may and ought to govern his opinions and actions, depending thereon, we need not to be troubled that some other things escape our knowledge.

* * *

FROM CHAPTER 2. *NO INNATE PRINCIPLES IN THE MIND*

* * *

15. *The Steps by which the Mind attains several Truths.* The senses at first let in particular ideas, and furnish the yet empty cabinet, and, the mind by degrees growing familiar with some of them, they are lodged in the memory, and names got to them. Afterwards the mind, proceeding farther, abstracts them, and by degrees learns the use of general names. In this manner the mind comes to be furnished with ideas and language, the materials about which to exercise its discursive faculty: And the use of reason becomes daily more visible, as these materials, that give it employment, increase. But though the having of general ideas, and the use of general words and reason, usually grow together; yet I see not how this any way proves them innate. * * *

* * *

FROM CHAPTER 3. *NO INNATE PRACTICAL PRINCIPLES*

1. *No moral principles so clear and so generally received as the forementioned speculative principles.* * * * [M]oral principles require reasoning and discourse and some exercise of the mind to discover the certainty of their truth. They lie not open as natural characters engraven in the mind. * * * But this is no derogation of their truth and certainty, no more than it is to the truth and certainty of the three angles of a triangle being equal to two rights ones because it is not so evident as 'the whole is bigger than the part,' nor so apt to be assented to on first hearing. It may suffice that these moral rules are capable of demonstration, and therefore it is our own faults if we come not to a certain knowledge of them. * * *

* * *

3. *Objection. Though men deny them in their practice, yet they admit them in their thoughts, answered.* * * * Nature, I confess, has put into man a desire of happiness, and an aversion to misery: These indeed are innate practical principles, which (as practical principles ought) do continue constantly to operate and influence all our actions without ceasing. These may be observed in all persons and all ages, steady and universal; but these are inclinations of

the appetite to good, not impressions of truth on the understanding. I deny not, that there are natural tendencies imprinted on the minds of men; and that, from the very first instances of sense and perception, there are some things that are grateful[1] and others unwelcome to them; some things, that they incline to, and others that they fly: But this makes nothing for innate characters on the mind, which are to be principles of knowledge, regulating our practice. * * *

                              *   *   *

5. *Instance in keeping compacts.* * * * That men should keep their compacts, is certainly a great and undeniable rule in morality. But yet, if a Christian, who has the view of happiness and misery in another life, be asked why a man must keep his word, he will give this as a reason; because God, who has the power of eternal life and death, requires it of us. But if a Hobbist[2] be asked why, he will answer, because the public requires it, and the Leviathan will punish you if you do not. And if one of the old philosophers had been asked,[3] then he would have answered, because it was dishonest, below the dignity of man, and opposite to virtue, the highest perfection of human nature, to do otherwise.

6. *Virtue generally approved, not because innate, but because profitable.* Hence naturally flows the great variety of opinions concerning moral rules, which are to be found among men, according to the different sorts of happiness they have a prospect of, or propose to themselves: which could not be if practical principles were innate, and imprinted in our minds immediately by the hand of God. I grant the existence of God is so many ways manifest, and the obedience we owe him so congruous to the light of reason, that a great part of mankind give testimony to the law of nature; but yet I think it must be allowed, that several moral rules may receive from mankind a very general approbation, without either knowing or admitting the true ground of morality; which can only be the will and law of a God, who sees men in the dark, has in his hand rewards and punishments, and power enough to call to account the proudest offender. For God having, by an inseparable connection, joined virtue and public happiness together, and made the practice thereof necessary to the preservation of society, and visibly beneficial to all with whom the virtuous man has to do; it is no wonder, that everyone should not allow, but recommend and magnify those rules to others, from whose observance of them he is sure to reap advantage to himself.

---

1. Agreeable. All notes are the editor's unless otherwise specified.
2. A follower of the political theory of Thomas Hobbes's *Leviathan* (see p. 241 herein).
3. Locke is referring to Cicero.

* * *

10. *Men have contrary practical principles.* He that shall carefully peruse the history of mankind; and look abroad into the several tribes of men, and with indifferency survey their actions, will be able to satisfy himself that there is scarce that principle of morality to be named, or rule of virtue to be thought on (those only excepted that are absolutely necessary to hold society together which commonly are neglected between societies) which is not, somewhere or other, slighted and condemned by the general fashion of whole societies of men, governed by practical opinions and rules of living quite opposite to others.

* * *

12. * * * But what duty is cannot be understood without a law, nor a law be known or supposed without a lawmaker or without reward and punishment, so that it is impossible for * * * any * * * practical principle to be innate, i.e., be imprinted on the mind as a duty without supposing the ideas of God, of law, of obligation, of punishment, or a life after this, innate. * * *

13. * * * There is a great deal of difference between an innate law and a law of nature; between something imprinted on our minds in their very original, and something that we being ignorant of, may attain to the knowledge of, by the use and due application of our natural faculties. And I think they equally forsake the truth who, running into contrary extremes, either affirm an innate law, or deny that there is a law knowable by the light of nature, i.e. without the help of positive revelation.

* * *

FROM CHAPTER 4. *OTHER CONSIDERATIONS CONCERNING INNATE PRINCIPLES, BOTH SPECULATIVE AND PRACTICAL*

* * *

12. *Suitable to God's goodness that all men should have an idea of him, therefore naturally imprinted by him answered.* * * * But the goodness of God hath not been wanting to men without such original impressions of knowledge, or ideas stamped on the mind; since he hath furnished man with those faculties, which will serve for the sufficient discovery of all things requisite to the end of such a being. And I doubt not but to show that a man, by the right use of his natural abilities, may, without any innate principles, attain a knowledge of a God, and other things that concern him. God having endued[4] man with those faculties of knowledge which he hath, was no more obliged by his goodness to plant those innate notions in

4. Endowed.

his mind, than that having given him reason, hands, and materials, he should build him bridges, or houses; which some people in the world, however, of good parts, do either totally want, or are but ill provided of, as well as others are wholly without ideas of God, and principles of morality, or at least have but very ill ones. The reason in both cases being, that they have never employed their parts, faculties, and powers industriously that way, but contend themselves with the opinions, fashions, and things of their country, as they found them, without looking any farther.

*   *   *

22. *Differences of men's discoveries depends on the different application of their faculties.* * * * The great difference that is to be found in the notions of mankind is from the different use they put their faculties to; while some (and those the most) taking things upon trust, misemploy their power of assent by lazily enslaving their minds to the dictates and dominion of others in doctrines, which it is their duty carefully to examine, and not blindly, with an implicit faith, to swallow. Others, employing their thoughts only about some few things, grow acquainted sufficiently with them, attain great degrees of knowledge of them, and are ignorant of all other, having never let their thoughts loose in the search of other enquiries. Thus, that the three angles of a triangle are quite equal to two right ones, is a truth as certain as anything can be, and I think more evident than many of those propositions that go for principles; and yet there are millions, however expert in other things, who know not this at all, because they never set their thoughts on work about such angles; and he that certainly knows this proposition may yet be utterly ignorant of the truth of other propositions in mathematics itself which are as clear and evident as this; because, in his search of those mathematical truths, he stopped his thoughts short, and went not so far. The same may happen concerning the notions we have of the being of a deity: For though there be no truth which a man may more evidently make out to himself than the existence of God, yet he that shall content himself with things as he finds them in this world, as they minister to his pleasures and passions, and not make enquiry a little farther into their causes, ends, and admirable contrivances, and pursue the thoughts thereof with diligence and attention, may live long without any notion of such a being.

*   *   *

23. *Men must think and know for themselves.* * * * Nor is it a small power it gives one man over another, to have the authority to be dictator of principles and teacher of unquestionable truths, and to make a man swallow that for an innate principle which may

serve to his purpose who teaches them. Whereas had they examined the ways whereby men came to the knowledge of many universal truths, they would have found them to result in the minds of men from the beings of things themselves, when duly considered, and that they were discovered by the application of those faculties that were fitted by nature to receive and judge of them, when duly applied about them.

From *Book 2. Of Ideas*

FROM CHAPTER 2. *OF IDEAS IN GENERAL AND THEIR ORIGIN*

*   *   *

2. *All ideas come from sensation or reflection.* Let us then suppose the mind to be, as they say, a white paper, void of all characters, without any ideas; how comes it to be furnished? Whence comes it by that vast store which the busy and boundless fancy of man has painted on it with an almost endless variety? Whence has it all the materials of reason and knowledge? To this I answer in one word, from experience; in that all our knowledge is founded and from that it ultimately derives itself. Our observation employed either about external sensible objects or about the internal objects of our minds, perceived and reflected upon by ourselves, is that which supplies our understandings with all the materials of thinking. These two are the fountains of knowledge from whence all the ideas we have or can naturally have do spring.

*   *   *

FROM CHAPTER 20. *OF MODES OF PLEASURE AND PAIN*

*   *   *

2. *Good and Evil, what.* Things then are good or evil, only in reference to pleasure or pain. That we call good, which is apt to cause or increase pleasure, or diminish pain in us; or else to procure or preserve us the possession of any other good, or absence of any evil. And on the contrary, we name that evil, which is apt to produce or increase any pain, or diminish any pleasure in us; or else to procure us any evil, or deprive us of any good. By pleasure and pain, I must be understood to mean of body or mind, as they are commonly distinguished; though in truth they be only different constitutions of the mind, sometimes occasioned by disorder in the body, sometimes by thoughts of the mind.

*   *   *

15. *Pleasure and pain what.* By *pleasure* and *pain*, delight and uneasiness I must all along be understood (as I have above intimated)

to mean, not only bodily pleasure and pain, but whatsoever *delight* or *uneasiness* is felt by us, whether arising from any grateful or acceptable sensation or reflection. * * *

*   *   *

18. I would not be mistaken here, as if I meant this as a discourse of the passions; they are many more than those I have named * * * I have only mentioned these here as so many instances of modes of pleasure and pain resulting in our minds from various considerations of good and evil. I might perhaps have instanced in other modes of pleasure and pain more simple than these, as the pain of hunger and thirst, and the pleasure of eating and drinking to remove them; the pain of tender eyes and the pleasure of music; pain from uninstructive wrangling and the pleasure of rational conversation with a friend, or of well-directed study in the search and discovery of truth. * * *

FROM CHAPTER 21. *OF POWER*

*   *   *

42. *Happiness, what.* Happiness then in its full extent is the utmost pleasure we are capable of, and misery the utmost pain and the lowest grade of what can be called happiness is so much ease from all pain, and so much present pleasure, as without which anyone cannot be content. Now because pleasure and pain are produced in us by operation of certain objects, either in our minds or our bodies, and in different degrees; therefore what has an aptness to produce pleasure in us is that we call good, and what is apt to produce pain in us, we call evil, for no other reason, but for its aptness to produce pleasure and pain in us, wherein consists our happiness and misery. * * *

*   *   *

47. * * * The mind, having in most cases, as is evident from experience, a power to suspend the execution and satisfaction of any its desires, and so all, one after another, is at liberty to consider the objects of them, examine them on all sides and weigh them with others. In this lies the liberty man has, and from not using it right comes all the variety of mistakes, errors, and faults which we run into in the conduct of our lives and our endeavors after happiness, whilst we precipitate the determinations of our wills and engage too soon before due examination. To prevent this we have a power to suspend the prosecution of this or that desire, as everyone daily may experiment in himself. This seems to me the source of all liberty; in this seems to consist that which is (as I think improperly) called free will. * * *

*   *   *

55. *How men come to pursue different purposes.* The mind has a different relish, as well as the palate; and you will fruitlessly endeavour to delight all men with riches or glory (which yet some men place their happiness in) as you would to satisfy all men's hunger with cheese or lobsters; which, though very agreeable and delicious fare to some, are to others extremely nauseous and offensive. And many people would with reason prefer the griping of a hungry belly to those dishes which are feast to others. Hence it was, I think, that the philosophers of old did in vain enquire, whether *summun bonum*[5] consisted in riches or bodily delights, or virtue, or contemplation. And they might have as reasonably disputed, whether the best relish were to be found in apples, plums, or nuts; and have divided themselves in sects upon it. For as pleasant tastes depend not on the things themselves, but on their agreeableness to this or that particular palate, wherein there is great variety: So the greatest happiness consists in the having those things which produce the greatest pleasure, and in the absence of those which cause any disturbance, any pain. * * * [I]f there be no prospect beyond the grave, the inference is certainly right, 'let us eat and drink,' let us enjoy what we delight in, 'for tomorrow we die.' * * *

56. *How men come to choose ill.* * * * (A) man may be justly punished * * * because; by a too hasty choice of his own making, he has imposed on himself wrong measures of good and evil. * * * The eternal law and nature of things must not be altered to comply with his ill-ordered choice. * * *

*   *   *

60. *From a wrong judgement what makes a necessary part of their happiness.* * * * To him * * * who hath a prospect of the different state of perfect happiness or misery that attends all men after this life, depending on their behavior here, the measures of good and evil that govern his choice are mightily changed. For since nothing of pleasure and pain in this life can bear any proportion to the endless happiness or eternal misery of an immortal soul hereafter, actions in his power will have their preference not according to the transient pleasure or pain that accompanies or follows them here, but as they serve to secure that perfect durable happiness hereafter. * * *

61. *A more particular account of wrong judgement.* But to account more particularly for the misery that men often bring on themselves, notwithstanding that they do all in earnest pursue happiness, we must consider how things come to be represented to our desires, under deceitful appearances: And that is by the judgement pronouncing wrongly concerning them. To see how far this

5. The highest good.

reaches, and what are the causes of wrong judgement, we must remember that things are judged good or bad in a double sense.

First, that which is properly good or bad, is nothing but bare
pleasure or pain.

Secondly, but because not only present pleasure and pain, but
that also which is apt by its efficacy or consequences to bring it
upon us at a distance, is a proper object of our desires, and apt to
move a creature that has foresight; therefore things also that draw
after them pleasure and pain, are considered as good and evil.

*   *   *

63. *In comparing present and future.* Therefore, as to present
pleasure and pain, the mind, as has been said, never mistakes that
which is really good or evil; that which is the greater pleasure, or
the greater pain, is really just as it appears. But though present
pleasure and pain show their difference and degrees so plainly as
not to leave room for mistake; yet when we compare present pleasure or pain with future, (which is usually the case in most important determinations of the will) we often make wrong judgements
of them, taking measures of them in different positions of distance.
Objects, near or in view, are apt to be thought greater than those of
a larger size, that are more remote; and so it is with pleasure and
pains; the present is apt to carry it, and those at a distance have the
disadvantage in the comparison. *   *   *

*   *   *

70. *Preference of vice over virtue a manifest wrong judgement.* *   *   *
Morality established in its true foundations cannot but determine
the choice in anyone who will but consider, and he that will not be
so far a rational creature as to reflect seriously upon infinite happiness or misery must needs condemn himself as not making that use
of his understanding he should. The rewards and punishments of
another life which the Almighty has established as the enforcements of his law are of weight enough to determine the choice
against whatever pleasure or pain this life can show, when the eternal state is considered but in its bare possibility, which nobody can
make any doubt of. He that will allow exquisite and endless happiness to be but the possible consequence of a good life here and the
contrary state the possible reward of a bad one *   *   * must own
himself to judge very amiss if he does not conclude that a virtuous
life with the certain expectation of everlasting bliss which may
come is to be preferred to a vicious one with the fear of that dreadful state of misery which, it is very possible, may overtake the
guilty; or at best the terrible uncertain state of annihilation. *   *   *

*   *   *

*   *   *

12. *Our faculties of discovery suited to our state.* * * * The infinitely wise contriver of us and all things about us, hath fitted our senses, faculties and organs to the conveniencies of life, and the business we have here. * * * But it appears not that God intended we should have a perfect, clear, and adequate knowledge of them; that perhaps is not in the comprehension of any finite being. We are furnished with faculties (dull and weak as they are) to discover enough in the creatures to lead us to the knowledge of the Creator and the knowledge of our duty. * * *

*   *   *

FROM CHAPTER 27. OF IDENTITY AND DIVERSITY

*   *   *

26. *Person a forensic term.* Person, as I take it, is the name for this self. Wherever a man finds what he calls himself, there I think another may say is the same person. It is a forensic term appropriating actions and their merit; and so belongs only to intelligent agents capable of a law, and happiness or misery. This personality extends itself beyond present existence to what is past only by consciousness, whereby it becomes concerned and accountable, owns and imputes to itself past action, just upon the same ground, and for the same reason that it does the present: all of which is founded in a concern for happiness, the unavoidable concomitant of consciousness; that which is conscious of pleasure and pain desiring that that self that is conscious should be happy. * * *

FROM CHAPTER 28. OF OTHER RELATIONS

*   *   *

5. *Moral Good and Evil.* Good and evil, as hath been shown, (B 2, chap. 20, paragraph 2, and chap. 21 paragraph 42) are nothing but pleasure and pain, or that which occasions pleasure or pain to us. Moral good and evil then is only the conformity or disagreement of our voluntary actions to some law, whereby good or evil is drawn on us by the will and power of the law-maker; which good and evil, pleasure or pain, attending our observance, or breach of the law, by the decree of the law-maker, is that [which] we call reward and punishment.

6. *Moral Rules.* Of these moral rules, or laws, to which men generally refer, and by which they judge of the rectitude or pravity[6] of their actions, there seem to me to be three sorts, with their three

6. Depravity.

different enforcements, or rewards and punishments. For since it would be utterly in vain to suppose a rule set to the free actions of men, without annexing to it some enforcement of good and evil to determine his will, we must, wherever we suppose a law, suppose also some reward or punishment annexed to that law. It would be in vain for one intelligent being to set a rule to the actions of another, if he had it not in his power to reward the compliance with, and punish deviation from his rule, by some good and evil, that is not the natural product and consequence of the action itself. For that being a natural convenience or inconvenience, would operate of itself without a law. This, if I mistake not, is the true nature of all law, properly so-called.

7. *Laws.* The laws that men generally refer their actions to, to judge of their rectitude or obliquity,[7] seem to me to be these three. (1) The divine law. (2) The civil law. (3) The law of opinion or reputation, if I may so call it. By the relation they bear to the first of these, men judge whether their actions are sins or duties; by the second, whether they be criminal or innocent; and by the third, whether they be virtues ovices.

8. *Divine Law and the Measure of Sin and Duty.* First the divine law, whereby I mean that law which God has set to the actions of men, whether promulgated to them by the light of nature or the voice of revelation.[8] That God has given a rule whereby men should govern themselves, I think there is nobody so brutish as to deny. He has a right to do it, [for] we are his creatures: He has goodness and wisdom to direct our actions to that which is best; and he has power to enforce it by rewards and punishments, of infinite weight and duration in another life: For nobody can take us out of his hands. This is the only touchstone of moral rectitude[9] and, by comparing them to this law it is that men judge of the most considerable moral good or evil of their actions: That is, whether as duties or sins, they are like to procure them happiness or misery from the hands of the Almighty.

* * *

10. *Philosophical Law the Measure of Virtue and Vice.* * * * Virtue and vices are names pretended and supposed everywhere to stand for actions in their own nature right and wrong; and as far as they really are so applied, they so far are coincident with the divine law above-mentioned. * * * [T]hough men uniting into politic societies have resigned up to the public the disposing of all their force, so that they cannot employ it against fellow-citizens any farther

---

7. Perversity.
8. "Whether . . . voice of revelation": added in the second edition (1694).
9. "This is . . . moral rectitude": added in the second edition.

than the law of the country directs; yet they retain still the power of thinking well or ill, approving or disapproving of the actions of those whom they live amongst, and converse with: And by this approbation and dislike they establish amongst themselves what they will call virtue and vice.

From *Book 3. Of Words*

FROM CHAPTER I. *OF WORDS OR LANGUAGE IN GENERAL*

1. *Man fitted to fitted to form articulate sounds.* God having designed man for a sociable creature, made him not only with an inclination and under the necessity to have fellowship with those of his own kind, but furnished him with language which was to be the great instrument and common tie of society, man therefore had by nature his organs so fashioned as to be fit to frame articulate sounds which we call words. * * *

* * *

FROM CHAPTER 6. *OF THE NAMES OF SUBSTANCES*

* * *

2. *The essence of each sort is the abstract idea.* The measure and boundary of each sort or species whereby is constituted that particular sort and distinguished from others is that we call its essence, which is nothing but that abstract idea to which the name is annexed, so that everything contained in that idea is essential to that sort. Thus, though it be all the essence of natural substances that we know or by which we distinguish them into sorts, yet I call it by a peculiar name, the nominal essence, to distinguish it from the real constitution of substances upon which depends this nominal essence and the properties of that sort, which, therefore, as has been said, may be called the real essence. For example, the nominal essence of gold is that complex idea the word, gold, stands for: let it be, for instance, a body yellow, of a certain weight, malleable, fusible, and fixed. But the real essence is the constitution of the insensible parts of that body on which those qualities and all the other properties of gold depend. How far these two are different, though they both be called essences, is obvious at first sight to discover.

3. *The nominal and real essence different.* For though perhaps voluntary motion with sense and reason, joined to a body of a certain shape, be the complex idea to which I and others annex the name, man, and so be the nominal essence of the species so called, yet nobody will say that complex idea is the real essence and source of all those operations which are to be found in any individual of

that sort. The foundation of all those qualities which are the ingre-
dients of our complex idea is something different; and had we such
a knowledge of the constitution of man from which his faculties of
moving, sensation and reasoning, and other powers flow, and on
which his so regular shape depends, as it is possible angels have
and it is certain that his Maker has, we should have quite another
idea of his essence than what is now contained in our definition of
that species.

* * *

12. *Whereof*[1] *there are probably numberless species.* * * * And
when we consider the infinite power and wisdom of the Maker, we
have reason to think that it is suitable to the magnificent harmony
of the universe, and the great design and infinite goodness of the
architect, that the species of creatures should also by gentle degrees ascend upward from us toward his infinite perfection, as we
see they gradually descend from us downwards; which if it be probable, we have more reason then to be persuaded that there are far
more species of creatures above us than beneath; we being in degrees of perfection much more remote from the infinite being of
God than we are from the lowest state of being. * * *

* * *

27. * * * The real essence of that[2] or any other sort of substances, it is evident we know not, and therefore are so undetermined in our nominal essences, which we make ourselves, that if
several men were to be asked concerning some oddly-shaped fetus
as soon as born, whether it were a man or no, it is past doubt one
should meet with different answers, which could not happen if the
nominal essences whereby we limit and distinguish the species of
substances were not made by man with some liberty, but were exactly copies from precise boundaries set by nature.

* * *

FROM CHAPTER 9. *OF THE IMPERFECTIONS OF WORDS*

* * *

23. The volumes of interpreters and commentators on the Old
and New Testament are but too manifest proofs of this. Though
everything said in the text be infallibly true, yet the reader may be,
nay cannot choose but be, very fallible in the understanding of it.
Nor is it to be wondered, that the will of God, when clothed in
words, should be liable to that doubt and uncertainty, which unavoidably attends that sort of conveyance; when even his Son,
whilst clothed in flesh, was subject to all the frailties and inconve-

1. Spirits.
2. i.e., the human species.

niences of human nature, sin excepted. And we ought to magnify his goodness that he hath spread before all the world such legible characters of his works and providence, and given all mankind so sufficient a light of reason, that they to whom this written word never came, could not (whenever they set themselves to search) either doubt of the being of a God, or of the obedience due to him. Since then the precepts of natural religion are plain, and very intelligible to mankind, and seldom come to be controverted; and other revealed truths, which are conveyed to us by books and languages, are liable to the common and natural obscurities and difficulties incident to words; methinks it would become us to be more careful and diligent in observing the former, and less magisterial, positive, and imperious, in imposing our own sense and interpretations of the latter.[3]

*   *   *

FROM CHAPTER II. OF THE REMEDIES OF THE FOREGOING IMPERFECTIONS AND ABUSES

*   *   *

15. [*To make known their meaning*] *in Mixed Modes by Definition.* Secondly mixed modes especially those belonging to morality, being most of them such combinations of ideas as the mind puts together of its own choice, and whereof there are not always standing patterns to be found existing, the signification of their names cannot be made known, as those of simple ideas, by any showing, but in recompense thereof may be perfectly and exactly defined. * * * Since the precise signification of the names of mixed modes, or, which is all one, the real essence of each species is to be known, they being not of nature's making but of man's, it is a great negligence and perverseness to discourse of moral things with uncertainty and obscurity. * * *

16. *Morality capable of demonstration.* Upon this ground it is that I am bold to think that morality is as capable of demonstration as well as mathematics, since the precise real essence of the things moral words stand for may be precisely known, and so the congruity or incongruity of the things themselves be certainly discovered, in which consists perfect knowledge. * * * As to substances, when concerned with moral discourses, their divers nature are not so much inquired into, as supposed, e.g. when we say that man is subject to law, we mean nothing by man but a corporeal rational creature; what the real essence or other qualities of that creature are in this case in no way considered. And therefore whether a

---

3. In *The Reasonableness of Christianity* (1695) Locke argued that belief in Jesus as the Messiah and the need for repentance are doctrines that are accessible to all.

child or changeling be a man in the physical sense may among the naturalists be as disputable as it will, it concerns not at all the moral man, as I may call him, which is this immoveable unchangeable idea, a corporeal rational being. For were there a monkey or any other creature to be found that has the use of reason to such a degree as to be able to understand general signs and to deduce consequences about general ideas, he would no doubt be subject to law and in that senses be a man, how much soever he differed in shape from others of that name. * * *

17. *Definitions can make moral discourse clear.* * * * [A] definition is the only way whereby the precise meaning of moral words may be known, and yet a way whereby their meaning can be known certainly and without leaving any room for any contest about it. And therefore the negligence or perverseness of mankind cannot be excused if their discourses in morality be not much clearer than those in natural philosophy, since they are about ideas in the mind which are none of them false or disproportionate, they having no external beings for the archetypes which they are referred to and must correspond with. * * *

*   *   *

From *Book 4. Of Knowledge and Opinion*

FROM CHAPTER 3. *OF THE EXTENT OF HUMAN KNOWLEDGE*

1. *No farther than we have ideas.* Knowledge, as has been said, lying in the perception of the agreement or disagreement of any of our ideas, it follows from hence that, first, we can have knowledge no farther than we have ideas.

2. *Nor farther than we can perceive their agreement and disagreement.* Secondly that we have no knowledge farther than we can have perception of their agreement or disagreement. Which perception being. 1. Either by intuition or the immediate comparing any two ideas; or 2. By reason, examining the agreement or disagreement of two ideas by the intervention of some others, or 3. By sensation, perceiving the existence of particular things. * * *

*   *   *

6. *Our knowledge therefore narrower than our ideas.* * * * [T]he state we are at present in not being that of vision, we must in many things content ourselves with faith and probability; and in the present question about the immateriality of the soul, if our faculties cannot arrive at demonstrative certainty, we need not think it strange. All the great ends of morality and religion are well enough secured without philosophical proofs of the soul's immateriality; since it is evident that he who made us at the beginning to subsist

here sensible intelligent beings, and for several years continued us in such a state, can and will restore us to the like state of sensibility in another world and make us capable there to receive the retribution he has designed men according to their doings in this life. * * * It is past controversy that we have in us something that thinks; our very doubts about what it is confirms the certainty of its being though we must content ourselves in the ignorance of what kind of being it is. * * * Other spirits who see and know the nature and inward constitution of things, how much they exceed us in knowledge! To which if we add larger comprehension which enables them at one glance to see the connexion and agreement of many ideas and readily supplies to them the intermediate proofs which we by single and slow steps and long poring in the dark, hardly at last find out, and are often ready to forget one before we have hunted out another; we may guess at some part of the happiness of superior ranks of spirits who have a quicker and more penetrating sight as well as a larger field of knowledge. * * *

* * *

18. *Morality capable of demonstration.* The idea of a Supreme Being, infinite in power, goodness, and wisdom, whose workmanship we are and on whom we depend, and the idea of ourselves as understanding rational beings being such as are clear to us, would, I suppose, if duly considered and pursued, afford such foundations of our duty and rules of action as might place morality amongst the sciences that are capable of demonstration, wherein I doubt not but from self-evident propositions; by necessary consequences as incontestable as those in mathematics, the measures of right and wrong might be made out to anyone that will apply himself with the same indifferency and attention to the one as he does to the other of the sciences. * * *

FROM CHAPTER 4. *OF THE REALITY OF KNOWLEDGE*

* * *

6. *The reality of mathematical knowledge.* I doubt not but it will be easily granted that the knowledge we have of mathematical truths is not only certain but real knowledge * * * and yet if we will consider, we shall find that it is only of our own ideas. The mathematician considers the truth and the properties belonging to a rectangle or circle only as they are in idea in his own mind. For it is possible he found neither of them existing mathematically, i.e. precisely true, in his life. But yet the knowledge he has of any truths or properties belonging to the circle or any mathematical figure are nevertheless true and certain, even of real things existing. * * *

7. *And of moral.* And hence it follows that moral knowledge is as

capable of certainty as mathematics. For certainty being the perception of the agreement or disagreement of our ideas, and demonstration nothing but the perception of such agreement by the intervention of other ideas or mediums, our moral ideas, as well as mathematical, being archetypes themselves, and so adequate and complete ideas, all the agreement or disagreement we shall find in them will produce real knowledge as well as in mathematical figures.

8. * * * *Existence not required to make abstract knowledge real.* All the discourse of mathematicians about the squaring of the circle, conic sections or any other parts of mathematics concerns not the existence of any of those figures, but their demonstrations which depend on their ideas are the same whether there be any square or circle existing in the world or no. In the same manner, the truth and certainty of moral discourses abstracts from the lives of men and the existence of those virtues in the world whereof they treat. * * *

9. *Nor will it be less true or certain because moral ideas are of our own making and naming.* * * * Just the same is it in moral knowledge; let a man have the idea of taking from others without their consent what their honest industry has possessed them of, and call this justice if he please. He that takes the name here without the idea put to it will be mistaken by joining another idea of his own to that name. * * *

* * *

FROM CHAPTER 10. *OF OUR KNOWLEDGE OF THE EXISTENCE OF GOD*

1. *We are capable of knowing certainly that there is a God.* Though God has given us no innate ideas of himself, though he has stamped no original characters on our minds, wherein we may read his being, yet having furnished us with those faculties our minds are endowed with, he hath not left himself without witness; since we have sense, perception, and reason, and cannot want a clear proof of him, as long as we carry ourselves about us. Nor can we justly complain of our ignorance in this great point, since he has so plentifully provided us with the means to discover and know him, so far as is necessary to the end of our being, and the great concernment of our happiness. But, though this be the most obvious truth that reason discovers, and though its evidence be (if I mistake not) equal to mathematical certainty, yet it requires thought and attention; and the mind must apply itself to a regular deduction of it from some part of our intuitive knowledge, or else we shall be as uncertain and ignorant of this as of other propositions, which are

in themselves capable of clear demonstration. To show, therefore, that we are capable of *knowing*, i.e. *being certain* that there is a God, and how we may come by this certainty, I think we need go no further than ourselves, and that undoubted knowledge we have of our own existence.

* * *

3. *He knows also that Nothing cannot produce a Being; therefore Something eternal.* * * * If * * * we know there is some real being, and that nonentity cannot produce any real being, it is an evident demonstration that from eternity there has been something; since what was not from eternity had a beginning, and what had a beginning must be produced by something else.

* * *

5. *And [that eternal Being must be] most knowing.* Again, a man finds in himself perception and knowledge. We have then got one step further; and we are certain now that there is not only some being. but some knowing, intelligent being in the world. * * * For it is as repugnant to the idea of senseless matter that it should put into itself sense, perception, and knowledge, as it is repugnant to the idea of a triangle that it should put into itself greater angles than two right ones.

6. *And Therefore God.* Thus, from the consideration of ourselves, and what we infallibly find in our own constitutions, our reason leads us to the knowledge of this certain and evident truth. That there is an eternal, most powerful, and most knowing being; which whether anyone please to call God, it matters not. The thing is evident; and from this idea duly considered, will easily be deduced all those other attributes, which we ought to ascribe to this eternal Being.

* * *

10. * * * For I judge it as certain and clear a truth as can anywhere be delivered that the invisible things of God are clearly seen from the creation of the world, being understood by the things that are made, his eternal power and Godhead. * * * [O]ur own being furnishes us, as I have shown, with an evident and uncontestable proof of a deity—and I believe nobody can avoid the cogency of it * * * this being so fundamental a truth, and of that consequence, that all religion and genuine morality depend thereon. * * *

* * *

12. * * * [T]his discovery of the necessary existence of an eternal Mind does sufficiently lead us to the knowledge of God, since it will hence follow that all other knowing beings that have a beginning must depend on him. And have no other ways of knowledge or extent of power than what he gives them; and therefore if he made

those, he made also the less excellent pieces of the universe, all inanimate being whereby his ominiscience, power, and providence will be established, and all other attributes necessarily follow. * * *

*   *   *

FROM CHAPTER 12. *OF THE IMPROVEMENT OF OUR KNOWLEDGE*

*   *   *

8. *By which Morality also may be made clearer.* * * * [M]orality is capable of demonstration, as well as mathematics. For the ideas that ethics are conversant about, being real essences, and such as I imagine have a discoverable connection and agreement one with another; so far as we can find their habitudes[4] and relations, so far we shall be possessed of certain, real, and general truths. And I doubt not, but if a right method were taken, a great part of morality might be made out with that clearness, that could leave, considering man, no more reason to doubt, than he could have to doubt of the truth of propositions in mathematics which have been demonstrated to him.

*   *   *

11. *We are fitted for moral knowledge and natural improvements.* From whence it is obvious to conclude, that since our faculties are not fitted to penetrate into the internal fabric and real essences of bodies; but yet plainly discover to us the being of a God, and the knowledge of ourselves, enough to lead us into a full and clear discovery or our duty and great concernment, it will become us, as rational creatures, to employ those faculties we have about what they are most adapted to, and follow the direction of nature, where it seems to point us out the way. For it is rational to conclude that our proper employment lies in those inquiries, and in that sort of knowledge which is most suited to our natural capacities, and carries in it our greatest interest, i.e. the condition of our eternal estate. Hence I think I may conclude, that morality is the proper science and business of mankind in general; (who are both concerned, and fitted to search out their *summum bonum*[5]) as several arts, conversant about several parts of nature, are the lot and private talent of particular men, for the common use of human life, and their own particular subsistence in this world.

*   *   *

4. Characteristics.
5. The highest good. Cf. with the implied criticism of our search for the highest good in 1.21. 55.

FROM CHAPTER 14. *OF JUDGEMENT*

*   *   *

2. *What is to be made of this twilight state?* Therefore as God has set some things in broad daylight, as he has given us some certain knowledge, though limited in comparison, probably as a taste of what intellectual creatures are capable of, to excite in us the desire; and endeavour after a better state, in the greatest part of our concernment, he had afforded us only the twilight, as I may say, of *probability*, suitable, I presume, to that; state of mediocrity and probationership he has been pleased to place us in here, wherein to check our over-confidence and presumption, we might by every day's experience be made sensible of our short sightedness and error; the sense whereof might be a constant admonition to us to spend the days of this our pilgrimage with industry and care, in the search and following of the way which may lead us to greater perfection—it being; highly rational to think, even were revelation silent in the case, that as men employ those talents God has given them here, they shall accordingly receive their rewards at the close of the day when their sun shall set and night shall put an end to their labors.

*   *   *

FROM CHAPTER 16. *OF THE DEGREES OF ASSENT*

*   *   *

13. *One case where contrary experience lessens not the testimony.* Though the common experience and the ordinary course of things have justly a mighty influence on the minds of men to make them give or refuse credit to anything proposed to their belief: yet there is one case wherein the strangeness of the fact lessens not the assent to a fair testimony given of it. For where supernatural events are suitable to the ends aimed at by him who has the power to change the course of nature, there under such circumstances they may be the fitter to procure belief, however much they are beyond or contrary to ordinary observation. This is the proper case of miracles which, well attested, do not only find credit themselves, but give it also to other truths which need such confirmation.

14. *The bare testimony of revelation is the highest certainty.* Besides those we have hitherto mentioned, there is one sort of propositions that challenge the highest degree of our assent upon bare testimony, whether the thing proposed agree or disagree with common experience and the ordinary course of things, or no. The reason whereof is because the testimony is of such an one as cannot deceive, nor be deceived; and that is of God himself. This carries with it assurance beyond doubt, evidence beyond exception. This is

called by a peculiar name, revelation; and our assent to it, faith, which as absolutely determines our minds, and as perfectly excludes all wavering, as our knowledge itself; and we may as well doubt of our own being, as we can, whether any revelation from God be true. So that faith is a settled and sure principle of assent and assurance, and leaves no manner of room for doubt or hesitation. Only we must be sure, that it be a divine revelation, and that we understand it right: Else we shall expose ourselves to all extravagancy of enthusiasm, and all error of wrong principles, if we have faith and assurance in what is not divine revelation. And therefore, in those cases, our assent can be rationally no higher than the evidence of its being a revelation.

*   *   *

FROM CHAPTER 17. OF REASON

*   *   *

2. *Wherein Reasoning consists.* If general knowledge as has been shown, consists in a perception of the agreement or disagreement of our own ideas, and the knowledge of the existence of all things without us (except only of God, whose existence every man may certainly know and demonstrate to himself from his own existence) be had only from the senses, what room is there for the exercise of any faculty but outward sense and perception.? What need is there of reason? Very much, both for the enlargement of knowledge and regulating our assent. * * * Sense and intuition reach but a very little way. The greatest part of our knowledge depends on deductions and intermediate ideas; and in those cases where we are fain to substitute assent instead of knowledge, and take propositions for true without being certain that they are so, we have need to find out, examine, and compare the grounds of their probability. In both these cases, the faculty which finds out the means and rightly applies them to discover certainty in the one, and probability in the other, is that which we call *reason.* * * *

*   *   *

24. *Reason and faith not opposite.* * * * [F]aith is nothing but a firm assent of the mind; which, if it be regulated as is our duty, cannot be afforded to anything but upon good reason, and so cannot be opposite to it. * * * [H]e that makes use of the light and faculties that God has given him and seeks sincerely to discover truth by those helps and abilities he has, may have this satisfaction in doing his duty as a rational creature that, though he should miss the truth, he will not miss the reward of it. * * * He that doth otherwise transgresses against his own light, and misuses those facilities

which were given to him to no other end but to search and follow the clearer evidence and greater probability. * * *

* * *

FROM CHAPTER 18. *OF FAITH AND REASON, AND THEIR DISTINCT PROVINCES*

* * *

2. *Faith and Reason, what, as contradistinguished.* * * * Reason therefore here, as contradistinguished to faith, I take to be the discovery of the certainty or probability of such propositions or truths, which the mind arrives at by deduction made from such ideas, which it has got by the use of its natural faculties; viz. by sensation or reflection.

Faith, on the other side, is the assent to any proposition, not thus made out by the deductions of reason; but upon the credit of the proposer, as coming from God, in some extraordinary way of communication. This way of discovering truths to men we call revelation.

* * *

5. *Revelation cannot be admitted against the clear evidence of the senses.* In propositions then whose certainty is built upon the clear perception of the agreement or disagreement of our ideas attained either by immediate intuition, as in self-evident propositions, or by evident deductions of reason in demonstrations, we need not the assistance of revelation as necessary to gain our assent. * * *

6. *Traditional revelation much less.* * * * In all things, therefore, in which we have clear evidence of our ideas, and those principles of knowledge I have above-mentioned, reason is the proper judge; and revelation, though it may in consenting with it confirm its dictates, yet cannot in such cases invalidate its decrees: Nor can we be obliged, where we have the clear and evident sentence of reason, to quit it for the contrary opinion, under the pretense that it is a matter of faith; which can have no authority against the plain and clear dictates of reason.

7. *Things above Reason.* But, there being many things, wherein we have very imperfect notions, or none at all; and other things, of whose past, present, or future existence, by the natural use of our faculties, we can have no knowledge at all; these, as being beyond the discovery of our natural faculties, and above reason, are, when revealed, the proper matter of faith. Thus, that part of the angels rebelled against God, and thereby lost their happy state; and that the dead shall rise, and live again; these and the like, being beyond the discovery of reason, are purely matters of faith; with which reason has directly nothing to do.

8. *Or not contrary to Reason, if revealed, are Matter of Faith.* But since God in giving us the light of reason has not thereby tied up his own hands from affording us, when he thinks fit, the light of revelation in any of those matters, wherein our natural faculties are able to give a probable determination; revelation, where God has pleased to give it, must carry it against the probable conjectures of reason. Because the mind not being certain of the truth of that it does not evidently know, but only yielding to the probability that appears to it, is bound to give up its assent to such testimony; which, it is satisfied, comes from one who cannot err, and will not deceive. But yet it still belongs to reason to judge of the truth of its being a revelation, and of the signification of the words wherein it is delivered. Indeed, if anything shall be thought revelation, which is contrary to the plain principles of reason, and the evident knowledge the mind has of its own clear and distinct ideas; there reason must be hearkened to, as to a matter within its province.

* * *

FROM CHAPTER 20. *OF WRONG ASSENT, OR ERROR*

* * *

2. *Want of proofs.* * * * [A] great part of mankind are, by the natural and unalterable state of things in this world and the constitution of human affairs, unavoidably given over to invincible ignorance of those proofs on which others build and which are necessary to establish these opinions: the greatest part of men, having much to do to get the means of living, are not in a condition to look after those of learned and laborious inquiries.

3. *What shall become of those who want them answered.* What shall we say then? * * * Have the bulk of mankind no other guide but accident and blind chance to conduct them to their happiness or misery? Are the current opinions and licensed guides of every country sufficient evidence and security to every man to venture his great concernments on, nay, his everlasting happiness and misery? Or can those be the certain and infallible oracles and standard of truth which teach one thing in Christendom and another in Turkey? Or shall a poor countryman be eternally happy for having the chance to be born in Italy or a day-labourer be unavoidably lost because he had the ill luck to be born in England? * * * God has furnished man with faculties sufficient to direct them in the way they should take if they will but seriously employ them in that way when their ordinary vocations allow them the leisure. No man is so wholly taken up with the attendance on the means of living as to have no spare time at all to think of his soul and inform himself of religion. Were men as intent upon this as they are on things of

lower concernment, there are none so enslaved to the necessities of life who might not find vacancies that might be husbanded to this advantage of their knowledge.

4. Reason is natural revelation whereby the eternal Father of light and fountain of all knowledge communicates to mankind that portion of truth which he has laid within the reach of their natural faculties: revelation is natural reason enlarged by a new set of discoveries communicated by God immediately, which reason vouches the truth of by the testimony and proofs it gives that they come from God. So that he who takes away reason to make way for revelation puts out the light of both, and does much—what the same as if he would persuade a man to put out his eyes, the better to receive the remote light of an invisible star by a telescope.

* * *

The Reasonableness of Christianity (1695)

Locke was always interested in theology. Indeed late in his life, he described it as a science that is "incomparably above all the rest . . . that noble study which is every man's duty" (*On the Conduct of Understanding* [1697]; Locke 1996: 195 no. 23). Religious concerns were central to his political thought. The proofs for the existence of God were discussed in the early *Essays on the Law of Nature*, as well as in the *Essay Concerning Human Understanding*. A principal argument in the *Letter on Toleration* was that the nature of the Christian religion was such as to require toleration. The *First Treatise* was to a considerable extent an exercise in biblical interpretation, and the *Second Treatise* can be interpreted as an extended argument on the political implications of the divinely imposed duty to preserve ourselves and others. Near the end of his life Locke worked on *A Paraphrase and Notes upon the Epistles of St. Paul* (Locke 1987) which was published after his death.

Locke argued in the *Essay* that the propositions known by faith should be subjected to the judgments of reason but that revelation of truths beyond reason can be a genuine source of knowledge. He was brought up as a Calvinist and later thought of himself as a member of the Church of England; but he had books about, and personal friends who adhered to, Socinianism, the name given to the teachings of sixteenth-century theologian Faustus Socinus, who denied the divinity of Christ. (In Locke's lifetime, those who held such beliefs began to be called Unitarians.) He also had friends in the latitudinarian or "broad church" branch of Anglicanism who were interested in opening the church more widely by reducing the doctrines of Christianity to a broadly acceptable minimum. The *Reasonableness*, as he announces at the outset, is an attempt to steer a moderate course between the pessimism of traditional Calvinism that saw mankind as inevitably sinful as a result of Adam's sin, and the optimism of his Deist contemporaries

who believed that human reason, rather than religion, should be the
basis of morality. It argues that Christ came to save men from sin, and
proved by his miracles and those of his followers, that belief in him and
repentance for one's sins would lead to eternal life. Jesus' moral teachings confirmed and reinforced the law of nature, which could be
known but, in fact was not known, "all entire as a law" (no. 242) by
mankind, most of whom had fallen into polytheism and idolatry.

The *Reasonableness* was criticized as denying the doctrine of the
Trinity, a serious charge at that time since the 1689 Act of Toleration
was limited to Trinitarian Protestants. Locke was evasive in his reply
maintaining that he had "never denied" the Trinity. There is scholarly
debate over his actual beliefs concerning the Trinity, although the most
comprehensive reviews of the evidence conclude that he believed that
Christ was the Messiah sent by God, but not divine (Marshall 2000;
Nuovo in Stewart 2000). In the *Paraphrase and Notes* he also interpreted St. Paul as teaching that sin leads to the loss of immortality
("The wages of sin is death"), while in the *Reasonableness*, he refers
both to "the loss of immortality" (para. 11) and to "hell" as the punishment for sinners (para 245). (See also *Essay Concerning Human Understanding* 2.21.70, p. 192 herein, in which he asserts that evildoers
face either eternal punishment or annihilation.)

In keeping with his individualism, Locke denies inherited original
sin—that is, the imputation to all mankind of guilt and liability to
divine punishment because of Adam's sin—since he believed that it
was contrary to God's goodness to punish men for sins they did not
commit. Yet he had no illusions about man's tendency toward evil (see
W. M. Spellman on p. 365 herein) and argued that faith is necessary to
provide specific knowledge of the natural law and the incentives for
good conduct, which "supply the defect of full obedience." He also argued that before the coming of Jesus men had only vague notions of
the afterlife, but the resurrection and ascension of Jesus promised eternal happiness to the righteous so that virtue was not only "the perfection and excellence of our nature", but "by much the best bargain"
(para. 245).

His observation that most human beings lack the leisure or education to know the natural law has been seen by some commentators
(Zuckert 1994, 2002) as in contradiction to the *Second Treatise*, which
assumes that in making the social contract human beings know their
natural law rights and obligations. However, it should be noted that
Locke's argument is that the *entire body* of the natural law has not
been, and in all likelihood cannot be, arrived at without the help of
Christ's teaching. In the *Second Treatise*, basic natural law principles—
equality, freedom, and the duty to preserve oneself and all mankind—
can be known by all when they consent to the social contract, since
"reason . . . teaches all mankind, who will but consult it that being all
equal and independent, no one ought to harm another in his life,
health, liberty, and possessions" (6). However, "though the law of nature be plain and intelligible to all rational creatures, yet men [are] bi-
ased by their interest, as well as ignorant for want of study of it" (124).

THE REASONABLENESS OF CHRISTIANITY 209

Thus all human beings are able to recognize the moral basis for the social contract, but they still need Christianity to give them certainty
about morality and the motivation to observe it. Locke puts forward a
rationalist, even secular, basis for politics—our mutual recognition of
rights as moral beings—but he believes that, in practice, Christianity
provides a stronger foundation for moral conduct and liberal constitutionalism.

How can one describe Locke's religions beliefs? John Marshall's
(1994) classic study on the relation of his religious beliefs to his political theory describes him as "Unitarian heretic." Yet Locke attended
Anglican services and received the Sacrament on his death bed. His
numerous writings do not include any devotional materials, so that he
"could not be called a pious man," and yet he "was in his own way a
deeply religious man" (Locke 1999:cxiv). He rejected the classical
Calvinist insistence on God's grace as the sole way to salvation, although he was influenced by the more moderate interpretation of the
Arminian Calvinists that emphasized the importance of free cooperation with grace. He was sympathetic to latitudinarian Anglicanism, but
he was fiercely anticlerical, had doubts about the doctrine of the Trinity, and rejected the doctrine of the atonement—that Christ's death
was necessary to give satisfaction to God for Adam's sin. His view of
the Christian message as confirming natural law morality resembled
Deism, but he believed that Christ had a special divinely intended role
in providing the foundation of the virtuous life and announcing the
way to heaven. As he so often urged others to do, in the area of religion
Locke thought for himself and maintained throughout his life a belief,
which he considered rationally grounded, in the existence of God who
has revealed himself both through reason and revelation.

From The Reasonableness of Christianity†

1. It is obvious to anyone, who reads the New Testament, that the
doctrine of redemption, and consequently of the Gospel, is founded
upon the supposition of Adam's fall. To understand, therefore, that
we are restored by Jesus Christ, we must consider what the Scriptures show we lost by Adam. This I thought worthy of a diligent and
unbiased search: since I found the two extremes that men run into
on this point, either on the one hand shook the foundations of all
religion, or, on the other, made Christianity almost nothing: for
while some men would have all Adam's posterity doomed to eternal,
infinite punishment for the transgression of Adam, whom millions
had never heard of, and no one had authorized to transact for him
or be his representative; this seemed to others so little consistent

† From *The Works of John Locke*, 12th ed., vol. VII (London, 1823, reprint Aalen: Scientia
  Verlag, 1963). Paragraph numbers were added by T. R. Ramsey in the 1958 Stanford University Press edition. Roman numerals in biblical citations have been changed to Arabic.

with the justice or the goodness of the great and infinite God, that they thought there was no redemption necessary, and consequently that there was none; rather than admit of it upon a supposition so derogatory to the honour and attributes of that infinite Being; and so made Jesus Christ nothing but the restorer and preacher of pure natural religion; thereby doing violence to the whole tenor of the New Testament. And, indeed, both sides will be suspected to have trespassed this way against the written word of God by anyone who does but take it to be a collection of writings designed by God, for the instruction of the illiterate bulk of mankind in the way of salvation; and therefore, generally, and in necessary points, to be understood in the plain direct meaning of the words and phrases: such as they may be supposed to have had in the mouths of the speakers who used them according to the language of that time and country wherein they lived; without such learned, artificial, and forced senses of them as are sought out, and put upon them in most of the systems of divinity according to the notions that each one has been bred up in.

2. To one that, thus unbiased, reads Scriptures, what Adam fell from, is visible, was the state of perfect obedience, which is called justice in the New Testament; though the word, which in the original signifies justice, be translated righteousness: and by this fall he lost paradise, wherein was tranquility and the tree of life; i.e. he lost bliss and immortality. * * *

*   *   *

7. Adam being thus turned out of paradise, and all his posterity born out of it, the consequence of it was, that all men should die, and remain under death forever, and so be utterly lost.

8. From this estate of death, Jesus Christ restores mankind to life; 1 Cor. 15: 22, 'As in Adam all die, so in Christ shall all be alive.' How this shall be, the same apostle tells us in the foregoing verse 21, 'By man death came, by man also came the resurrection from the dead.' And so our Saviour himself tells us, John 5. 21, 'For as the Father raiseth up the dead and makes them alive, even so the Son maketh alive whom he will.' Whereby it appears, that the life, which Jesus Christ restores to all men, is that life, which they receive again at the resurrection. Then they recover from death, which otherwise all mankind should have continued under, lost for ever; as appears by St. Paul's arguing, 1 Cor. 15 concerning the resurrection.

9. And thus men are, by the second Adam, restored to life again; that so by Adam's sin they may none of them lose anything, which by their own righteousness they might have a title to: for righteousness, or an exact obedience to law, seems, by the Scripture, to have a claim of right to eternal life.

* * *

11. Here then we have the standing measures of life and death. Immortality and bliss belong to the righteous; those who have lived in exact conformity to the law of God, are out of the reach of death; but an exclusion from paradise and loss of immortality is the portion of sinners; all of those, who have any way broke that law, and failed of complete obedience to it, by the guilt of any one transgression. And thus mankind by the law, are put upon issues of life or death, as they are righteous or unrighteous, just or unjust; i.e. exact performers or transgressors of the law.

12. But yet, 'All having sinned,' Romans 3: 23, 'and come short of the glory of God,' i.e. the kingdom of God in heaven (which is often called his glory) 'both Jews and Gentiles;' ver. 22, so that, 'by the deeds of the law,' no one could be justified, ver. 20, it follows, that no one could then have eternal life and bliss.

13. Perhaps it will be demanded, Why did God give so hard a law to mankind, that, to the apostle's time, no one of Adam's issue had kept it? As appears by Rom. 3 and Galatians 3: 21–22.

14. Answer. It was such a law as purity of God's nature required, and must be the law of such a creature as man; unless God would have made him a rational creature, and not required him to have lived by the law of reason; but would have countenanced in him irregularity and disobedience to that light which he had, and that rule which was suitable to his nature; which would have been to have authorized disorder, confusion, and wickedness in his creatures: for that this law was the law of reason, or, as it is called, of nature, we shall see by and by; and if rational creatures will not live up to the rule of their reason, who shall excuse them?

* * *

22. The rule, therefore, of right, is the same that ever was; the obligation to observe it is also the same: the difference between the law of works, and the law of faith, is only this: that the law of works makes no allowance for failing on any occasion. Those that obey are righteous; those that in any part disobey, are unrighteous, and must not expect life, the reward of righteousness. But, by the law of faith, faith is allowed to supply the defect of full obedience; and so the believers are admitted to life and immortality, as if they were righteous. Only here we must take notice, that when St. Paul says, that the Gospel establishes the law, he means the moral part of the law of Moses; for that he could not mean the ceremonial, or political part of it, is evident, by what I quoted out of him just now, where he says, 'The Gentiles do, by nature, the things contained in the law, their consciences bearing witness.'[1] For the Gentiles nei-

---

1. Romans 2:15. All notes are the editor's unless otherwise specified.

ther did, nor thought of, the judicial or ceremonial institutions of Moses; it was only the moral part their consciences were concerned in. * * *

* * *

26. What we are now required to believe to obtain eternal life, is plainly set down in the Gospel. St. John tells us, John 3: 36, 'He that believeth on the Son, hath eternal life; and he that believeth not the Son, shall not see life.' * * *

27. * * * [B]elieving on the Son is the believing that Jesus was the Messiah; giving credit to the miracles he did, and the profession he made of himself. * * *

* * *

231. * * * But though there were many * * * to whom the promise of the Messiah never came and so were never in a capacity to believe or reject that revelation, yet God had by the light of reason revealed to all mankind who would make use of this light that he was good and merciful. The same spark of the divine nature and knowledge in man which, making him a man, showed him the law he was under as a man, showed him also the way of atoning the merciful, kind, compassionate Author and Father of him and his being when he transgressed that law. He that made use of this candle of the Lord so far as to find what was his duty, could not miss to find also the way to reconciliation and forgiveness when he failed of his duty. * * *

* * *

236. * * * The great and many advantages we receive by the coming of Jesus the Messiah will show that it was not without need that he was sent in the world.

237. The evidence of our Saviour's mission from heaven is so great, in the multitude of miracles he did before all sorts of people, that what he delivered cannot but be received as the oracles of God, and unquestionable verity. For the miracles he did were so ordered by the divine providence and wisdom, that they never were, nor could be denied by any of the enemies or opposers of Christianity.

238. Though the works of nature, in every part of them, sufficiently evidence a Deity; yet the world made so little use of their reason, that they saw him not, where, even by the impressions of himself, he was easy to be found. Sense and lust blinded their minds in some, and a careless inadvertency in others, and fearful apprehensions in most (who either believed there were, or could not but suspect there might be, superior unknown beings) gave them up into the hands of the priests, to fill their heads with false notions of the Deity, and their worship with foolish rites, as they pleased: and what dread or craft once began, devotion soon made

sacred, and religion immutable. In this state of darkness and ignorance of the true God, vice and superstition held the world. Nor
could any help be had or hoped for from reason; which could not
be heard, and was judged to have nothing to do in the case; the
priests, everywhere, to secure their empire, having excluded reason
from having anything to do in religion. And in the crowd of wrong
notions, and invented rites, the world had almost lost sight of the
one only true God. The rational and thinking part of mankind, it is
true, when they sought after him, they found the one supreme, invisible God; but if they acknowledged and worshipped him, it was
only in their own minds. They kept this truth locked up in their
own breasts as a secret, nor ever durst venture it amongst the people; much less amongst the priests, those wary guardians of their
own creeds and profitable inventions. Hence we see, that reason,
speaking ever so clearly to the wise and virtuous, had never authority enough to prevail on the multitude; and to persuade the societies of men, that there was but one God, that alone was to owned
and worshipped. * * *

239. In this state of darkness and error, in reference to the "true
God," our Saviour found the world. But the clear revelation he
brought with him dissipated this darkness; made the 'one invisible
true God' known to the world: and that with such evidence and
energy, that polytheism and idolatry have nowhere been able to
withstand it: but wherever the preaching of the truth he delivered,
and the light of the Gospel hath come those mists have been dis-
pelled.

*   *   *

241. Next to the knowledge of one God, Maker of all things, a
clear knowledge of their duty was wanting to mankind. This part of
knowledge, though cultivated with some care by some heathen
philosophers, yet got little footing among the people. All men, indeed, under pain of displeasing the gods, were to frequent the tem-
ples: everyone went to their sacrifices and services: but the priests
made it not their business to teach them virtue. If they were diligent in their observations and ceremonies; punctual in their feasts
and solemnities, and the tricks of religion; the holy tribe assured
them the gods were pleased, and they looked no farther. Few went
to the schools of the philosophers to be instructed in their duties,
and to know what was good and evil in their actions. The priests
sold the better pennyworths, and therefore had all the custom.[2]
Lustrations[3] and processions were much easier than a clean conscience, and a steady course of virtue; and an expiatory sacrifice,

2. Customers.
3. Offerings.

that atoned for the want of it, was much more convenient than a strict holy life. No wonder then, that religion was everywhere distinguished from, and preferred to virtue; and that it was dangerous heresy and profaneness to think the contrary. So much virtue as was necessary to hold societies together, and to contribute to the quiet of governments, the civil laws of commonwealths taught, and forced upon men that lived under magistrates. But these laws being for the most part made by such who had no other aims but their own power, reached no farther than those things that would serve to tie men together in subjection; or at most were directly to conduce to the prosperity and temporal happiness of any people. But natural religion, in its full extent, was nowhere, that I know, taken care of, by the force of natural reason. It should seem, by the little that has hitherto been done in it, that it is too hard a task for unassisted reason to establish morality in all its parts, upon its true foundation, with a clear convincing light. And it is at least a surer and shorter way, to the apprehensions of the vulgar, and mass of mankind, that one manifestly sent from God, and coming with visible authority from him, should, as a king and law-maker, tell them their duties, and require their obedience, than leave it to the long and sometimes intricate deductions of reason, to be made out to them. Such trains of reasoning the greatest part of mankind have neither leisure to weigh, nor, for want of education and use, skill to judge. * * * Experience shows, that the knowledge of morality, by mere natural light, (how agreeable soever it be to it) makes but a slow progress, and little advance in the world. And the reason of it is not hard to be found in men's necessities, passions, vices, and mistaken interests; which turn their thoughts another way: and the designing leaders, as well as following herd, find it not to their purpose to employ much of their meditations this way. Or whatever else was the cause, it is plain, in fact, that human reason unassisted failed men in its great and proper business of morality. It never from unquestionable principles, by clear deductions, made out an entire body of the 'law of nature.' And he that shall collect all the moral rules of the philosophers, and compare them with those contained in the New Testament, will find them to come short of the morality delivered by our Saviour, and taught by his apostles; a college made up, for the most part, of ignorant, but inspired fishermen.

242. * * * It is true, there is a law of nature; but who is there that ever did, or undertook to give it us all entire, as a law; no more, nor no less, than what was contained in, and showed the world their obligation? Where was there any such code, that mankind might have recourse to, as their unerring rule, before our Saviour's time? If there was not, it is plain there was need of one to give us

such a morality; such a law, which might be the sure guide of those who had a desire to go right; and, if they had a mind, need not mistake their duty, but might be certain when they had performed, when failed in it. Such a law of morality Jesus Christ hath given us in the New Testament; but by the latter of these ways, by revelation. We have from him a full and sufficient rule for our direction, and conformable to that reason. But the truth and obligation of its precepts have their force, and are put past doubt to us, by the evidence of his mission. He was sent by God: his miracles show it; and the authority of God in his precepts cannot be questioned. Here morality has a sure standard, that revelation vouches, and reason cannot gainsay, nor question; but both together witness to come from God, the great lawmaker. And such an one as this, out of the New Testament, I think the world never had, nor can anyone say, is anywhere else to be found. * * *

243. A great many things which we have been bred up in the belief of from our cradles (and are notions grown familiar with, and, as it were, natural to us, under the gospel) we take for unquestionable obvious truths, and easily demonstrable, without considering how long we might have been in doubt or ignorance of them, had revelation been silent. It is no diminishing to revelation, that reason gives its suffrage too to the truths revelation has discovered. But it is our mistake to think, that because reason confirms them to us, we had the first certain knowledge of them from thence; and in that clear evidence we now possess them. The contrary is manifest, in the defective morality of the Gentiles, before our Saviour's time; and the want of reformation in the principles and measures of it, as well as practice. Philosophy seemed to have spent its strength, and done its utmost; or if it should have gone farther, as we see it did not, and from undeniable principles given us ethics in a science like mathematics, in every part demonstrable; this yet would not have been so effectual to man in this imperfect state, nor proper for the cure. The greatest part of mankind want leisure or capacity for demonstration; nor can carry a train of proofs, which in that way they must always depend upon convictions, and cannot be required to assent to, until they see demonstration. Wherever they stick, the teachers are always put upon proof, and must clear the doubt by a thread of coherent deductions from the first principle, how long, or how intricate soever they be. And you may as soon hope to have all the day-labourers and tradesmen, the spinsters and dairy-maids, perfect mathematicians, as to have them perfect in ethics this way. Hearing plain commands is the sure and only course to bring them to obedience and practice. The greatest part cannot know, and therefore they must believe. And I ask, whether one coming from heaven in the power of God, in full and clear evidence and demon-

stration of miracles, giving plain and direct rules of morality and obedience be not likelier to enlighten the bulk of mankind, and set them right in their duties, and bring them to do them, than by reasoning with them from general notions and principles of human reason? And were all the duties of human life clearly demonstrated, yet I conclude, when well considered, that method of teaching men their duties would be thought proper only to a few, who had much leisure, improved understandings, and were used to abstract reasonings. But the instruction of the people were best still left to the precepts and principles of the Gospel. The healing of the sick, the restoring sight to the blind by word, the raising and being raised from the dead, are matters of fact, which they can without difficulty conceive, and that he who does such things, must do them by the assistance of a divine power. These things lie level to the ordinaries apprehension; he that can distinguish between sick and well, lame and sound, dead and alive, is capable of this doctrine. To one who is once persuaded that Jesus Christ was sent by God to a King, and a Saviour of those who believe in him; all his commands become principles; there needs no other proof for the truth of what he says, but that he said it. And then there needs no more, but to read the inspired books, to be instructed: all the duties of morality lie there clear, and plain, and easy to be understood.

* * *

245. * * * Before our Saviour's time, the doctrine of a future state, though it were not wholly hid, yet it was not clearly known in the world. It was an imperfect view of reason, or perhaps, the decayed remains of an ancient tradition, which seemed rather to float on men's fancies, than sink into their hearts. It was something, they knew not what, between being and not being. Something in a man they imagined might escape the grave; but a perfect complete life, of eternal duration, after this, was what entered little into their thoughts, and less into their persuasions. And they were so far from being clear herein, that we see no nation of the world publicly professed it, and built upon it: no religion taught it; and it was nowhere made an article of faith and principle of religion until Jesus Christ came; of whom it is truly said, that he, at his appearing, 'brought life and immortality to light.'[4] And that not only in the clear revelation of it, and in instances shown of men raised from the dead; but he has given us an unquestionable assurance and pledge of it in his own resurrection and ascension into heaven. How has this one truth changed the nature of things in the world, and given the advantage to piety over all that could tempt or deter men from it! The philosophers, indeed, showed the beauty of

4. 1 Timothy 1:10.

virtue; they set her off so, as drew men's eyes and approbation to her; but leaving her unendowed, few were willing to espouse her. The generality could not refuse her their esteem and commendation; but still turned their backs on her, and forsook her, as a match not for their turn. But now there being put into the scales on her side, 'an exceeding and immortal weight of glory;'[5] interest is come about to her, and virtue now is visibly the most enriching purchase, and by much the best bargain. That she is the perfection and excellency or our nature; that she is herself a reward, and will recommend our names to future ages, is not all that can now be said for her. It is not strange that the learned heathens satisfied not many with such airy commendations. It has another relish and efficacy to persuade men, that if they live well here, they shall be happy hereafter. Open their eyes upon the endless, unspeakable joys of another life, and their hearts will find something solid and powerful to move them. The view of heaven and hell will cast a slight upon the short pleasures and pains of this present state, and give attractions and encouragements to virtue, which reason and interest, and the cares of ourselves, cannot but allow and prefer. Upon this foundation, and upon this only, morality stands firm, and may defy all competition. This makes it more than a name; a substantial good, worth all our aims and endeavors; and thus the Gospel of Jesus Christ has delivered it to us.

5. 2 Corinthians 4:17.

SOURCES

RICHARD HOOKER

Richard Hooker (1554–1600) was an Anglican clergyman who wrote *The Laws of Ecclesiastical Polity* (1593) in defense of Anglicanism as a middle way between Catholicism and Calvinism. The selection printed here from book I includes Hooker's discussion of the types of law, which was strongly influenced by a similar discussion by St. Thomas Aquinas in his *Summa Theologiae* (I, II, qu. 90–97). It also argues that government and law are based on consent, since in "those times wherein there were no civil societies" (when Locke quotes this passage, he adds, "i.e. in the state of nature"), men "growing into composition and agreement" consent to government and the rule of law because of conflicts created by human partiality in applying law of nature. Locke appealed to Hooker in support of government by consent, but it should be noted that contrary to Locke's conception of individual consent, consent is given in Hooker's theory by the community as a whole. In contrast to Locke, Hooker (in a passage that Locke omits when he quotes from the preceding sentences) says that community consent, even given five hundred years ago, binds succeeding generations because "corporations are immortal" (I.10.8). Hooker, like Locke argues for an individual right of self-defense before the formation of society and also like Locke notes that one of its shortcomings is that one tends to favor oneself. In a passage quoted by Locke, he also describes men as "equal in nature," and like him, argues for the rule of law—but without, as in Locke's case, provisions for individual or collective action in cases of violation of the law by the ruler.

Leo Strauss and his followers (e.g. Robert Horwitz et al. in their translation of Locke's [1990] early *Essays*, which, because it takes the form of a classic scholastic disputation, is called *Questions on the Law of Nature*) arguing for the Hobbesian character of Locke's political theory have emphasized the differences between Locke and Hooker. They stress in particular Locke's denial that the law of nature can be demonstrated by universal consent to its precepts. It is true that Locke, was more aware of cultural differences in moral norms, but the selection here shows that Hooker also recognized culturally based departures from the natural law (see I.10). They also argue that Locke's conception of the relation of natural law and scripture was different from that of Hooker (see Leo Strauss, p. 274 herein and John Yolton, p. 281 herein). Yet a comparison of Locke's *Essays on the Law of Nature* (1663–64), his additions to the second edition of the *Essay Concerning Human Understanding* (1689), and the later *Reasonableness of Christianity* (1695) demonstrates that, for Locke as for Hooker, they are two related ways in which God has revealed the moral law. It is true, of course, that it could not be said of Hooker's prepolitical state that "all men are naturally in that state and remain so, till by their own consent they make themselves members of some politic society" (*Second Treatise* 15). As in Locke's theory, however, they agree to overcome the conflicts in the prepolitical state by establishing law and government, in the English case, a monarchy under laws adopted by Parliament in which the king also has a legislative role.

Locke referred to the "learned and reverend Mr. Hooker" in the English version of his early (1660) *Tract on the Civil Magistrate* (Locke 1967) and quoted from Hooker's definition of law in the 1662 Latin version (Locke, 1997:50, 62). He used Hooker's paraphrase of Aquinas on the eternal law in *Essay I* of his *Essays on the Law of Nature* (1663–64) and cited him in his journal. On June 13, 1681, he bought a copy of the *Ecclesiastical Polity* and quoted from it sixteen times in the text and footnotes of the *Second Treatise*, while at the same time entering additional extracts in his notebooks, one of Laslett's arguments that Locke was writing *The Second Treatise* in 1681. He cited Hooker in defense of his argument for consent, a somewhat dubious procedure since, as noted earlier, Locke maintained that legitimate government required explicit or tacit consent by the individual rather than by the community. He also cited Hooker's argument that the Church is based on consent (of the community) in his journal in 1682 in support of a very different conception of the Church as a voluntary society, a crucial part of his later argument in the *Letter on Toleration* (1685). Hooker provided one of Locke's major arguments for *The Reasonableness of Christianity* (1695), that the Bible gives us certainty about the principles of the natural law that can only be known with difficulty by the unaided reason. Locke had three editions of Hooker in his library; and in 1703, shortly before his death, Locke recommended "the first book of Mr. Hooker's *Ecclesiastical Polity*" in *Some Thoughts for Reading and Study for a Gentleman*.

From Of the Laws of Ecclesiastical Polity (1593)†

From *Book I*

I. The law which natural agents have given them to observe, and their necessary manner of keeping it.

I am not ignorant that by law eternal the learned for the most part do understand the order, not which God hath eternally purposed himself in all his works to observe, but rather that which himself he hath set down as expedient to be kept by all his creatures, according to the several conditions wherewith he hath endued them. They who thus are accustomed to speak apply the name of *Law* unto that only rule of working which superior authority imposeth; whereas we somewhat more enlarging the sense thereof term any kind of rule or canon, whereby actions are framed, a law. Now that law which, as it is laid up in the bosom of

---

† From *Of the Laws of Ecclesiastical Polity*, Book I, ed. R. W. Church (Oxford: Clarendon Press, 1905).

God, they call *etemal*, receiveth according unto the different kinds
of things which are subject unto it different and sundry kinds of
names. That part of it which ordereth natural agents we call usually
nature's law; that which Angels do clearly behold and without any
swerving observe is a law *celestial* and heavenly; the law of *reason*,
that which bindeth creatures reasonable in this world, with which
by reason they may most plainly perceive themselves bound; that
which bindeth them, and is not known but by special revelation
from God, *Divine* law; *human* law, that which out of the law either
of reason or of God men probably gathering to be expedient, they
make it a law. All things therefore, which are as they ought to be,
are conformed unto *this second law eternal;* and even those things
which to this eternal law are not conformable, are notwithstanding
in some sort ordered by *the first eternal law.* For what good or evil is
there under the sun, what action correspondent or repugnant unto
the law which God hath imposed upon his creatures, but in or
upon it God doth work according to the law which himself hath
eternally purposed to keep; that is to say, the *first law eternal.* So
that a twofold law eternal being thus made, it is not hard to conceive how they both take place in all things.[1]

2. Wherefore to come to the law of nature: albeit thereby we
sometimes mean that manner of working which God hath set for
each created thing to keep; yet forasmuch as those things are
termed most properly natural agents, which keep the law of their
kind unwittingly, as the heavens and elements of the world, which
can do no otherwise than they do; and forasmuch as we give unto
intellectual natures the name of voluntary agents, that so we may
distinguish them from the other; expedient it will be, that we sever
the law of nature observed by the one from that which the other is
tied unto.

* * *

**VIII. Of the natural way of finding out laws by reason to guide
the will unto that which is good.**
3. * * * The general and perpetual voice of men is as the sentence
of God himself. For that which all men have at all times learned,
nature herself must needs have taught; and God being the author
of nature, her voice is but his instrument. By her from him we receive whatsoever in such sort we learn. Infinite duties there are, the
goodness whereof is by this rule sufficiently manifested, although
we had no other warrant besides to approve them. The Apostle St.
Paul having speech concerning the Heathen saith of them, *They are*

1. 'All that is done among created things is the matter of eternal law.' Thomas Aquinas,
   Summa Theologiae, I–II, qu 93, a. 4. 'In no way does anything evade the laws of that
   most high creator and orderer, by whom the peace of the universe is administered.' St.
   Augustine, *The City of God*, Bk. 19, ch. 12 [Hooker's note].

a law unto themselves.[2] His meaning is, that by force of the light of reason, wherewith God illuminateth every one which cometh into the world, men being enabled to know truth from falsehood, and good from evil, do thereby learn in many things what the will of God is; which himself not revealing by any extraordinary means unto them, but they by natural discourse attaining the knowledge thereof, seem the makers of those laws which indeed are his, and they but only the finders of them out.

4. A law therefore generally taken, is a directive rule unto goodness of operation. The rule of divine operations outward, is the definitive appointment of God's own wisdom set down within himself. The rule of natural agents that work by simple necessity, is the determination of the wisdom of God, known to God himself the principal director of them, but not unto them that are directed to execute the same. The rule of natural agents which work after a sort of their own accord, as the beasts do, is the judgement of common sense of fancy concerning the sensible goodness of those objects wherewith they are moved. The rule of ghostly or immaterial natures, as spirits and Angels, is their intuitive intellectual judgment concerning the amiable beauty and high goodness of that object, which with unspeakable joy and delight doth set them on work. The rule of voluntary agents on earth is the sentence that reason giveth concerning the goodness of those things which they are to do. And the sentences which reason giveth are some more, some less, general before it come to define in particular actions what is good.

5. The main principles of reason are in themselves apparent. For to make nothing evident of itself unto man's understanding were to take away all possibility of knowing anything.

*   *   *

7. Touching the several grand mandates, which being imposed by the understanding faculty of the mind must be obeyed by the will of man, they are by the same method found out, whether they import our duty towards God or towards man.

Touching the one, I may not here stand to open by what degrees of discourse the minds even of mere natural men have attained to know, not only that there is a God, but also what power, force, wisdom, and other properties that God hath, and how all things depend on him. This being therefore presupposed, from that known relation which God hath unto us as unto children, and unto all good things as unto effects whereof himself is the principal cause these axioms and laws natural concerning our duty have arisen.

*   *   *

2. Romans 2:14. All notes are the editor's unless otherwise specified.

[T]he like natural inducement hath brought men to know that it is their duty no less to love others than themselves. For seeing those things which are equal must needs all have one measure; if I cannot but wish to receive all good, even as much at every man's hand as any man can wish unto his own soul, how should I look to have any part of my desire herein satisfied, unless myself be careful to satisfy the like desire which is undoubtedly in other men, we all being of one and the same nature? To have anything offered them repugnant to this desire must needs in all respects grieve them as much as me: so that if I do harm I must look to suffer; there being no reason that others should show greater measure of love to me than they have by me showed unto them. My desire therefore to be loved of my equals in nature as much as possible may be, imposeth upon me a natural duty of bearing to them-ward fully the like affection. From which relation of equality between ourselves and them that are as ourselves, what several rules and canons natural reason hath drawn for direction of life no man is ignorant.

* * *

8. * * * [A] law is properly that which reason in such sort defineth to be good that it must be done. And the law of reason or human nature is that which men by discourse of natural reason have rightly found out themselves to be all forever bound unto in their actions.

9. Laws of reason have these marks to be known by: Such as keep them resemble most lively in their voluntary actions that very manner of working which nature herself doth necessarily observe in the course of the whole world. The works of nature are all behoveful,[3] beautiful, without superfluity or defect; even so theirs, if they be framed according to that which the law of reason teacheth. Secondly, those laws are investigable by reason, without the help of revelation supernatural and divine. Finally, in such sort they are investigable, that the knowledge of them is general, the world hath always been acquainted with them. * * * It is not agreed upon by one, or two, or few, but by all: which we may not so understand, as if every particular man in the whole world did know and confess whatsoever the law of reason doth contain; but this law is such that being proposed no man can reject it as being unreasonable and unjust. Again, there is nothing in it but any many (having natural perfection of wit and ripeness of judgement) may by labour and travail, find out. And to conclude, the general principles thereof are as such, as it is not easy to find men ignorant of them. Law rational therefore, which men commonly use to call the law of nature, meaning thereby the law which human nature knoweth itself in

3. Useful.

reason universally bound unto, which also for that cause may be termed most fitly the law of reason; this law, I say, comprehendeth all those things which men by the light of their natural understanding evidently know, or at leastwise may know, to be beseeming or unbeseeming, virtuous or vicious, good or evil for them to do.

*   *   *

11. If then it be here demanded, by what means it should come to pass (the greatest part of the law moral being so easy for all men to know) that so many thousands of men notwithstanding have been ignorant even of principal moral duties, not imagining a breach of them to be sin, I deny not but lewd and wicked custom beginning perhaps at the first amongst few, afterwards spreading into greater multitudes, and so continuing from time to time, may be of force even in plain things to smother the light of natural understanding; because men will not bend their wits to examine whether things wherewith they have been accustomed be good or evil.

*   *   *

X. How reason doth lead men unto the making of human laws whereby politic societies are governed; and to agreement about laws whereby the fellowship or communion of independent societies standeth.

1. * * * The laws which have been hitherto mentioned do bind men absolutely even as they are men, although they have never any settled fellowship, never any solemn agreement amongst themselves what to do or not to do. But forasmuch as we are not by ourselves sufficient to furnish ourselves with competent store of things needful for such a life as our nature doth desire, a life fit for the dignity of man; therefore to supply those defects and imperfections which are in us living single and solely by ourselves, we are naturally induced to seek communion and fellowship with others. This was the cause of men's uniting themselves at the first in politic societies; which societies could not be without government, nor government without a distinct kind of law from that which hath been already declared. Two foundations there are which bear up public societies; the one, a natural inclination, whereby all men desire sociable life and fellowship; the other, an order expressly or secretly[4] agreed upon touching the manner of their union in living together. The latter is that which we call the law of a commonweal, the very soul of a politic body, the parts whereof are by law animated, held together, and set on work in such actions as the common good requireth. Laws politic, ordained for external order and regiment amongst men, are never framed as they should be, unless presuming the will of man to be inwardly obstinate, rebellious, and averse

4. Tacitly.

from all obedience unto the sacred laws of his nature; in a word, unless presuming man to be in regard of his depraved mind little better than a wild beast, they do accordingly provide notwithstanding so to frame his outward actions, that they be no hindrance unto the common good for which societies are instituted: unless they do this, they are not perfect.

*   *   *

3. * * * We all make complaint of the iniquity of our times: not unjustly; for the days are evil. But compare them with those times wherein there were no civil societies, with those times wherein there was as yet no manner of public regiment established, with those times wherein there were not above eight persons righteous living upon the face of the earth;[5] and we have surely good cause to think that God hath blessed us exceedingly, and hath made us behold most happy days.

4. To take away all such mutual grievances, injuries, and wrongs, there was no way but only by growing unto composition and agreement amongst themselves, by ordaining some kind of government public, and by yielding themselves subject thereunto; that unto whom they granted authority to rule and govern, by them the peace, tranquility, and happy estate of the rest might be procured. Men always knew that when force and injury was offered they might be defenders of themselves; they knew that howsoever men may seek their own commodity, yet if this were done with injury unto others it was not to be suffered, but by all men and by all good means to be withstood; finally they knew that no man might in reason take upon him to determine his own right, and according to his own determination proceed in maintenance thereof, inasmuch as every man is towards himself and them whom he greatly affecteth partial; and therefore that strifes and troubles would be endless, except they gave their common consent all to be ordered by some whom they should agree upon: without which consent there was no reason that one man should take upon him to be lord or judge another; because, although there be according to the opinion of some very great and judicious men a kind of natural right in the noble, wise, and virtuous, to govern them which are of servile disposition;[6] nevertheless for manifestation of this their right, and men's more peaceable contentment on both sides, the assent of them who are to be governed seemeth necessary.

To fathers within their private families nature hath given a supreme power; for which cause we see throughout the world even from the foundation thereof, all men have ever been taken as lords

---

5. 2 Peter 2:5, referring to Noah and his family after the Flood.
6. Aristotle's *Politics*, I:5.

and lawful kings in their own houses. Howbeit over a whole grand multitude having no such dependency upon anyone, and consisting of so many families as every politic society in the world doth, impossible it is that any should have complete lawful power, but by consent of men, or immediate appointment of God; because not having the natural superiority of fathers, their power must needs be either usurped, and then unlawful; or, if lawful, then either granted or consented unto by them over whom they exercise the same, or else given extraordinarily from God, unto whom all the world is subject. It is no improbable opinion therefore which the Arch-philosopher,[7] was of, that as the chiefest person in every household was always as it were a king, so when numbers of households joined themselves in civil society together, kings were the first kind of governors amongst them. Which is also (as it seemeth) the reason why the name of Father continued still in them, who of fathers were made rulers; as also the ancient custom of governors to do as Melchisedec[h] and being kings to exercise the office of priests, which fathers did at the first, grew perhaps by the same occasion.

Howbeit not this the only kind of regiment that hath been received in the world. The inconveniences of one kind have caused sundry other to be devised. So that in a word all public regiment of what kind soever seemeth evidently to have risen from deliberate advice, consultation, and composition between men, judging it conve-nient and behoveful there being no impossibility in nature considered by itself, but that men might have lived without any public regiment. Howbeit, the corruption of our nature being presupposed, we do not deny but that the law of nature doth now require of necessity some kind of regiment; so that to bring things unto the first course they were in, and utterly to take away all kind of public government in the world, were apparently to overturn the whole world.

5. The case of man's nature standing therefore as it doth, some kind of regiment the law of nature doth require; yet the kinds thereof being many, nature tieth not to anyone, but leaveth the choice as a thing arbitrary. At the first when some certain kind of regiment was once approved, it may be that nothing was then further thought upon for the manner of governing, but all permitted unto their wisdom and discretion which were to rule; till by experience they found this for all parts very inconvenient, so as the thing which they had devised for a remedy did indeed but increase the sore which it should have cured. They saw that to live by one man's will became the cause of all men's misery. This constrained them to come unto laws, wherein all men might see their duties beforehand, and know the penalties of transgressing them.

7. Aristotle's *Politics*, I:2.

* * *

6. And because the greatest part of men are such as prefer their own private good before all things, even that good which is sensual before whatsoever is most divine; and for that the labour of doing good, together with the pleasure arising from the contrary, doth make men for the most part slower to the one and proner to the other, then that duty prescribed them by law can prevail sufficiently with them: therefore unto laws that men do make for the benefit of men it hath seemed always needful to add rewards, which may more allure unto good than any hardness deterreth from it, and punishments, which may deter from evil than any sweetness thereto allureth. Wherein as the generality is natural, *Virtue rewardable and vice punishable,* so the particular determination of the reward or punishment belongeth unto them by whom laws are made. Theft is naturally punishable, but the kind of punishment is positive, and such lawful as men shall think with discretion convenient by law to appoint.

7. * * * Laws do not only teach what is good, but they enjoin it, they have in them a certain constraining force. And to constrain men unto any thing inconvenient doth seem unreasonable. Most requisite therefore it is that to devise laws which all men shall be forced to obey none but wise men be admitted. Laws are matters of principal consequence; men of common capacity and but ordinary judgement are not able (for how should they?) to discern what things are fittest for each kind and state of regiment.

* * *

8. Howbeit laws do not take their constraining force from the quality of such a devise them, but from that power which doth give them the strength of laws. That which we spake before concerning the power of government must here be applied unto the power of making laws whereby to govern; which power God hath over all: and by the natural law, whereunto he hath made all subject, the lawful power of making laws to command whole politic societies of men belongeth so properly unto the same entire societies, that for any prince or potentate of what kind soever upon earth to exercise the same of himself, and not either by express commission immediately and personally received from God, or else by authority derived at the first from their consent upon whose persons they impose laws, it is no better than mere tyranny.

Laws they are not therefore which public approbation hath not made so. But approbation not only they give who personally declare their assent by voice, sign, or act, but also when others do it in their names by right originally at the least derived from them. As in parliaments, councils, and the like assemblies, although we be not personally ourselves present, notwithstanding our assent is, by reason

of others, agents there in our behalf. And what we do by others, no
reason but that it should stand as our deed, no less effectually to
bind us than if ourselves had done it in person.

*   *   *

Of this point therefore we are to note, that since men naturally
have no full and perfect power to command whole politic multitudes of men, therefore utterly without our consent we could in
such sort be at no man's commandment living. And to be commanded we do consent, when that society whereof we are part hath
at any time before consented, without revoking the same after by
the like universal agreement. Wherefore as any man's deed past is
good as long as himself continueth; so the act of a public society of
men done five hundred years sithence standeth as theirs who
presently are of the same societies, because corporations are immortal; we were then alive in our predecessors, and they in their
successors do live still by.[8] Laws therefore human, of what kind soever, are available by consent.

**XII. The cause why so many natural or rational laws are set
down in holy scripture.**

2. * * * The first principles of the law of nature are easy; hard it
were to find men ignorant of them. But concerning the duty which
nature's law doth require at the hands of men in a number of things
particular, so far hath the natural understanding even of sundry
whole nations been darkened, that they have not discerned no not
gross iniquity to be sin. Again, being so prone as we are to fawn
upon ourselves, and to be ignorant as much as may be of our
own deformities, without the feeling sense whereof we are most
wretched; even so much the more, because not knowing them we
cannot so much as desire to have them taken away; how should our
festered sores be cured, but that God hath delivered a law as sharp
as the two-edged sword, piercing the very closest and most un-
searchable corners of the heart, which the law of nature can hardly,
human laws by no means possible, reach unto? Hereby we know
even secret concupiscence to be sin, and are made fearful to offend
though it be but in a wandering cogitation. Finally, of those things
which are for direction of all parts of our life needful, and not impossible to be discerned by the light of nature itself, are there not
many which few men's natural capacity, and some which no man's
hath been able to find out? They are, saith St. Augustine,[9] but a few
and they endued[1] with great ripeness of wit and judgement, free
from all such affairs as might trouble their meditations, instructed

---

8. This sentence was omitted by Locke in the paragraph quoted in his footnote to *Second
Treatise* 134.
9. *On the Trinity*, xii.22.
1. Endowed.

in the sharpest and the subtlest points of learning, who have, and
that very hardly, been able to find out but only the immortality of
the soul. The resurrection of the flesh what man did ever at any
time dream of, having not heard it otherwise than from the school
of nature? Whereby it appeareth how much we are bound to yield
unto our creator, the father of all mercy, eternal thanks, for that he
hath delivered his law unto the world, a law wherein so many
things are laid open, clear and manifest, as a light which otherwise
would have been buried in darkness, not without the hazard, or
rather not with the hazard but with the certain loss, of infinite
thousands of souls most undoubtedly now saved.

3. We see, therefore, that our sovereign good is desired naturally;
that God the author of that natural desire had appointed natural
means whereby to fulfil it; that man having utterly disabled his nature unto those means hath had other revealed from God, and hath
received from heaven a law to teach him how that which is desired
naturally must now supernaturally be attained: finally, we see that
because those later exclude not the former quite and clean as
unnecessary, therefore together with such supernatural duties as
could not possibly have been otherwise known to the world, the
same law that teacheth them, teacheth also with them such natural
duties as could not by light of nature easily have been known.

*   *   *

XVI. A Conclusion

*   *   *

5. * * * [L]et us place man in some public society with others,
whether civil or spiritual; and in this case there is no remedy but we
must add yet a further law. For although even here likewise the laws
of nature and reason be of necessary use, yet somewhat over and
above them is necessary, namely human and positive laws, together
with that law which is of commerce between grand societies, the
law of nations, and of nations Christian. For which cause the law of
God likewise said, 'Let every soul be subject to the higher power.'[2]
The public power of all societies is above every soul contained in
the same societies. And the principal use of that power is to give
laws unto all that are under it; which laws in such case we must
obey, unless there be reason showed which may necessarily enforce
that the law of reason or of God doth enjoin the contrary. * * *

2. Romans 13:1.

HUGO GROTIUS

Hugo Grotius (in Dutch, de Groot) (1583–1645) was a Dutch lawyer, theologian, and diplomat whose book *On the Law of War and Peace* (*De Jure Belli et Pacis*) is regarded as the founding document of modern international law. *On the Law of War and Peace*, published in 1625, was written to provide a set of moral and legal principles to regulate the conduct of the European states in the period of religious warfare known as the Thirty Years War (1618–48). It outlined a system of international law, based on the natural law, that was intended to transcend religious differences. Emphasizing man's rational and social nature, Grotius transmitted to Protestant Europe a revised version of the natural law tradition that had been developed in medieval and early modern Catholic ("scholastic") philosophy.

Grotius's statement that the natural law would still oblige, even if God did not exist, was related to his effort to construct legal principles that would apply to the relations of independent states despite the lack of a superior coercive force to implement them. Regarded by some historians of political theory as a new doctrine that contributed to the secularization of moral and political thought, it repeated statements that were often made by the defenders of the rationality of natural law in the late medieval debate on the relative importance of reason vs. the will of a superior (in this case, God) as the foundation of natural law. Grotius also discussed the general principles of government, developing a contractual theory that both accepted the popular origin of political authority and allowed the people to surrender themselves unconditionally and irrevocably to their rulers. His book was very widely read; and besides his arguments about natural and international law, his discussions of the origins of private property, the contractual basis of government, and the justification for slavery were familiar to seventeenth-century scholars, including both Hobbes (who borrowed his distinction between law and rights) and Locke.

Locke knew Grotius's works, both religious and political. Locke's *Essays on the Law of Nature* (1663–64) quote Grotius, without naming him, on the definition of natural law and on universal consent as a proof of its existence—in both cases in order to question Grotius's theories. Like Pufendorf (p. 251 herein) Locke also derives the obligation of natural law from the will of God, challenging Grotius's emphasis on its intrinsic rationality as the source of obligation, while, both in the *Essays on the Law of Nature* and in the *Essay Concerning Human Understanding*, insisting on its rational content. The argument for utility attributed to Carneades in *Essay VIII* of Locke's *Essays on the Law of Nature* is also likely to have been drawn from, or at least suggested by Grotius's reference to the argument at the beginning of his book on international law. In the *First Treatise of Civil Government*, Locke mentions the (inaccurate) citations from Grotius on parental authority in Filmer's *Patriarcha* and develops an argument on the conventional nature of the laws of inheritance that is similar to that of Grotius. In the *Second Treatise*, Locke also discusses the social contract and the natural law basis of property in ways that, as he must have recognized, differ from Grotius's arguments for the irrevocable submission of the people to the monarch and for the conventional character of property.

Locke's theory places more emphasis on individual rights and consent than does Grotius's, but, contrary to some views, it shares his belief in the social nature of man (*Second Treatise*, 77). Grotius also describes an individual right to enforce the law of nature before rules are made by society in a way that is similar to what Locke argues is his "strange" doctrine (*Second Treatise*, 9), and he makes an identical argument from human partiality for the need for common judges (see II.XX.9).

Those who argue that Locke provides a different conception of moral obligation from that of writers like Grotius, who derive the precepts of natural law from man's social nature (e.g. Zuckert, 1994:chap. 5), ignore Locke's references to man's obligation to "preserve himself and the rest of mankind" (*Second Treatise*, 129) as God's workmanship (*Second Treatise*, 6), his reference, citing Hooker, to "the obligation to mutual love amongst men" (*Second Treatis*, 5), as well as his claim that in the state of nature, men "are quickly driven into society" (*Second Treatise*, 127).

Locke's library had fifteen books by Grotius, two of them editions of *On the Law of War and Peace* and the others on theology and biblical interpretation (Harrison and Laslett, 1971: nos. 1329–40). In his *Some Thoughts Concerning Education* (1693) Lake recommended *On the Law of War and Peace* but said that Pufendorf's later work (p. 251 herein) on natural law was "perhaps better."

From On the Law of War and Peace (1625)†

From *Prolegomena*

8. The maintenance of the social order which we have roughly sketched and which is consonant with human intelligence is the source of law properly so called. To this sphere of law belong the abstaining from that which is another's, the restoration to another of anything of his which we may have, together with any gain which we may have received from it, the obligation to fulfil promises, the making good of a loss incurred through our fault and the inflicting of penalties upon men according to their deserts.

*   *   *

11. What we have been saying would have a degree of validity even if we should concede that which cannot be conceded without the utmost wickedness, that there is no God or that the affairs of men are of no concern to Him. The very opposite of this view has been implanted in us, partly by reason, partly by unbroken tradition, and

† From *The Law of War and Peace*, trans. Francis W. Kelsey, et al. (Oxford: Oxford University Press, 1925), pp. 34, 35, 38–39, 40, 42, 53–54, 103–4, 109–10, 111, 191–92, 193, 470–71, 472–73, 475, 476.

confirmed by many proofs as well as by miracles attested by all ages. Hence it follows that we must without exception render obedience to God as our Creator, to Whom we owe all that we are and have; especially since in manifold ways He has shown Himself supremely good and supremely powerful, so to those who obey Him He is able to give supremely great rewards, even rewards which are eternal, since He himself is eternal.

* * *

From *Book I*

FROM CHAPTER I. WHAT IS WAR? WHAT IS LAW?

III. Law is considered a rule of action * * *

* * * Law in our use of the term here means nothing else than what is just, and that too rather in a negative sense than in an affirmative sense, that being lawful which is not unjust. * * *

IV. A body of rights * * *

There is another meaning of law viewed as a body of rights, different from the one just defined but growing out of it, which has reference to a person. In this sense a right becomes a moral quality of a person, making it possible to have or do something lawfully. * * *

X. Definitions of the law of nature, division, and distinction from things which are not properly so called

1. The law of nature is a dictate of right reason, which points out that an act, according as it is or is not in conformity with rational nature, has in it a quality of moral baseness or moral necessity; and that, in consequence, such an act is either forbidden or enjoined by the author of nature, God.

2. The acts in regard to which such a dictate exists are, in themselves, either obligatory or not permissible, and so it is understood that necessarily they are enjoined or forbidden by God. In this characteristic the law of nature differs not only from human law, but also from volitional divine law; for volitional divine law does not enjoin or forbid those things which in themselves and by their own nature are obligatory or not permissible, but by forbidding things it makes them unlawful, and by commanding things it makes them obligatory.

* * *

5. The law of nature, again, is unchangeable—even in the sense that it cannot be changed by God. Measureless as is the power of

God, nevertheless it can be said that there are certain things over which that power does not extend; for things of which this is said are spoken only, having no sense corresponding with reality and being mutually contradictory. Just as even God, then, cannot cause that two times two should not make four, so he cannot cause that that which is intrinsically evil be not evil.

* * *

7. Furthermore, some things belong to the law of nature not through simple relation but as well as a result of a particular combination of circumstances. Thus the use of things in common was in accordance with the law of nature so long as ownership by individuals was not introduced; and the right to use force in obtaining one's own existed before laws were promulgated.

XII. In what way the existence of the law of nature is proved

1. In two ways men are wont to prove something is according to the law of nature, from that which is antecedent and from that which is consequent. Of the two lines of proof the former is more subtle, the latter more familiar.

Proof *a priori* consists in demonstrating the necessary agreement or disagreement of anything with a rational and social nature; proof *a posteriori*, in concluding, if not with absolute assurance, at least with every probability, that that is according to the law of nature which is believed to be such among all nations, or among all those that are more advanced in civilization. For an effect that is universal demands a universal cause; and the cause of such an opinion can hardly be anything else than the feeling which is called the common sense of mankind.

* * *

FROM CHAPTER II. WHETHER IT IS EVER LAWFUL TO WAGE WAR

I. That war is not in conflict with the law of nature is proved by several considerations

* * *

5. Right reason, moreover, and the nature of society * * * do not prohibit all use of force, but only that use of force which is in conflict with society, that is which attempts to take away the rights of another. For society has in view this object, that through community of resource and effort each individual be safeguarded in the possession of what belongs to him.

It is easy to understand that this conclusion would hold even if private ownership (as we now call it) had not been introduced; for

life, limbs, and liberty would in that case be the possessions belonging to each, and no attack could be made upon these by another without injustice. Under such conditions the first one taking
possession would have the right to use things not claimed and to
consume them up to the limit of his needs, and anyone depriving
him of that right would commit an unjust act. But now that private
ownership has assumed a definite form, the matter is much easier
to understand.

* * *

FROM CHAPTER III. DISTINCTION BETWEEN PUBLIC AND PRIVATE WAR;
EXPLANATION OF SOVEREIGNTY

* * *

VIII. The opinion that sovereignty always resides in the people is rejected, and arguments are answered

1. At this point first of all the opinion of those must be rejected
who hold that everywhere and without exception sovereignty re-
sides in the people, so that it is permissible for the people to restrain and punish kings whenever they make a bad use of their
power. How many evils this opinion has given rise to, and can even
now give rise to if it sinks deep into men's minds, no wise person
fails to see. We refute it by means of the following arguments.

To every man it is permitted to enslave himself to anyone he
pleases for private ownership, as is evident both from Hebraic and
from Roman Law. Why, then, would it not be permitted to a people
having legal competence to submit itself to some one person, or to
several persons, in such a way as plainly to transfer to him the legal
right to govern, retaining no vestige of that right itself? And you
should not say that such a presumption is not admissible; for we
are not trying to ascertain what the presumption should be in case
of doubt, but what can legally be done.

It is idle, too, to bring up the inconveniences which result, or
may result, from such a procedure; for no matter what form of government you may devise, you will never be free from difficulties
and dangers. * * *

2. Just as, in fact, there are many ways of living, one being better
than another, and out of so many ways of living each is free to select that which he prefers, so also a people can select that form of
government which it wishes; and the extent of its legal right in the
matter is not to be measured by the superior excellence of this or
that form of government, in regard to which different men hold different views, but by its free choice.

3. In truth it is possible to find not a few causes which may impel a people wholly to renounce the right to govern itself and to vest this in another, as, for example, if a people threatened with destruction cannot induce anyone to defend it on any other condition; again, if a people pinched by want can in no other way obtain the supplies needed to sustain life.

* * *

13. The arguments which are presented on the other side it is not hard to meet. For, in the first place, the assertion, that he who vests some one with authority is superior to him upon whom the authority is conferred, holds true only of a relationship the effect of which is continually dependent on the will of the constituent authority; it does not hold true of a situation brought about by an act of will, from which a compulsory relationship results, as in case of a woman giving authority to a husband, whom she must ever after obey. * * *

14. Another argument men take from saying of the philosophers, that all government was established for the benefit of those who are governed, not of those who govern; from this they think it follows that, in view of the worthiness of the end they who are governed are superior to him who governs.

But it is not universally true, that all government was constituted for the benefit of the governed. For some types of governing in and of themselves have in view only the advantage of him who governs; such as the exercise of power by the master, the advantage of the slave being extrinsic and incidental, just as the earnings of a physician bear no relation to medicine as the art of healing. Other types of governing have in view a mutual advantage, as that of marriage. Thus some imperial governments may have been constituted for the benefit of kings, as those which have been secured through victory, and yet are not on that account to be called tyrannical, since tyranny, at any rate as the word is now understood, connotes injustice. Some, again, may have in view as much advantage of him who governs as of those who are governed, as when a people powerless to help itself places itself in subjection to a powerful king for its own protection.

* * *

IX. The argument that there is always a relation of mutual dependence between king and people, is refuted

1. Some imagine that between king and people there is a relation of mutual dependence, so that the whole people ought to obey the king who governs well, while the king who governs badly should be made subject to the people. If they who hold his opinion should say

that anything which is manifestly wrong should not be done because the king commanded it, they would be saying what is true and acknowledged among all good men; but such a refusal implies no curtailing of power or any right to exercise authority. If it had been the purpose of any people to divide the sovereign power with a king (on this point something will need to be said below), surely such limits ought to have been assigned to the power of each as could easily be discerned from a difference in places, persons, and affairs.

2. The moral goodness or badness of an action, especially in matters relating to the state, is not suited to division into parts; such qualities frequently are obscure, and difficult to analyze. In consequence the utmost confusion would prevail in case the king on one side, and the people on the other, under pretext that an act is good or bad, should be trying to take cognizance of the same matter, each by virtue of its power. To introduce so complete disorder into its affairs has not, so far as I know, occurred to any people.

*　*　*

From *Book II*

FROM CHAPTER II. OF THINGS WHICH BELONG TO MEN IN COMMON

*　*　*

IV. That unoccupied lands become property of the individuals who become occupants of them, unless they have been taken over as a whole people

Let us proceed to the things which can be made subject of private ownership, but have not yet become private property. Of such sort are many places hitherto uncultivated, islands in the sea, wild animals, fish, and birds.

In this connection two points must be noted. Possession may be taken in two ways, either of an undivided whole, or by means of individual allotments. The first method is ordinarily employed by a people, or by the ruler of a people; the second, by individuals. Possession by individual allotments, nevertheless, is more often taken in consequence of a grant than by free occupation.

If, however, anything which has been occupied as a whole has not yet been assigned to individual owners, it ought not on that account to be considered as unoccupied property; for it remains subject to the ownership of the first occupant, whether a people or a king. To this class ordinarily rivers, lakes ponds, forests, and rugged mountains belong.

VI. That in case of necessity men have the right to use things which have become the property of another, and whence this right comes

1. Now let us see whether men in general possess any right over things which have already become the property of another.

Some perchance may think it strange that this question should be raised, since the right of private ownership seems completely to have absorbed the right which had its origin in a state of community of property. Such, however, is not the case. We must, in fact, consider what the intention was of those who first introduced individual ownership; and we are forced to believe that it was their intention to depart as little as possible from natural equity. For as in this sense even written laws are required to be interpreted, much more should such a point of view prevail in the interpretation of usages which are not held to be exact statements by the limitations of a written form.

2. Hence it follows, first, that in direct need the primitive right of user revives, as if community of ownership had remained, since in respect to all human laws—the law of ownership included—supreme necessity seems to have been expected.

3. Hence it follows, again, that on a voyage, if provisions fail, whatever each person has ought to be contributed to the common stock. Thus, again, if fire has broken out, in order to protect a building belonging to me I can destroy a building of my neighbour. I can, furthermore, cut the ropes or nets in which my ship has been caught, if it cannot be freed. None of these rules was introduced by the civil law, but they have all come into existence through interpretations of it.

4. Even among theologians the principle has been accepted that, if a man under stress of such necessity takes from the property of another what is necessary to preserve his own life, he does not commit a theft.[1]

The reason which lies back of this principle is not, as some allege, that the owner of a thing is bound by the rule of love to give to him who lacks; it is, rather, that all things seem to have been distributed to individual owners with a benign reservation in favor of the primitive right. For if those who made the original distribution had been asked what they thought about this matter they would have given the same answer that we do.

---

1. Cf. Locke's similar discussion in the *First Treatise*, 41. On the earlier history of this limit on property, see Swanson, 1996. All notes are the editor's unless otherwise specified.

CHAPTER XX. ON PUNISHMENTS

VII. Proof that punishment for the good of the wrong-doer; may be exacted by anyone at all according to the law of nature

1. The punishment which serves this end is by nature permitted to anyone of sound judgement who is not subject to vices of the same kind or of equal seriousness. * * * However in the case of corporeal chastisement and other punishments that contain an element of compulsion the distinction between those who may or may not apply them is not made by nature * * * but by the laws. * * *

VIII. Likewise for the good of him who has been wronged, where it concerns vengeance permitted by universal common law.

* * *

4. But since; in our private affairs and in those of our kinsmen, we are liable to partiality, as soon as families were united at a common point, judges were appointed and to them alone was given the power to avenge the injured, while others were deprived of the freedom of action wherewith nature endowed them. * * *

IX. Likewise for the good of the whole

1. The good of mankind in general which is the third object of punishment involves the same problems as those presented by the good of one who has been wronged. For in this case the punishment may be inflicted to prevent the man who has injured one person from injuring others, which is accomplished by removing him or weakening him or restraining him so that he cannot do harm, or by reforming him. * * *

4. But since both the inquiry into the fact often demands great care and the evaluation of the punishment requites much prudence and fairness, to prevent strife arising from each man claiming too much for himself, which others refuse to yield, in communities animated by a sense of right, men have agreed to select as arbiters those who they think are the best and wisest, or hope that they will prove to be such. * * *

THOMAS HOBBES

Thomas Hobbes (1588–1679), an English philosopher and political theorist, published the *Leviathan* in 1651, shortly after the end of the English civil wars. In it he attempted to develop a deductive geometry of politics, arguing from the equal capacity of men to kill each other and the competitiveness and insecurity in the "natural condition of mankind" (the state of nature) where life is "solitary, nasty, brutish, and short," to the need for the establishment of a covenant or social contract "of every man with every man." All the parties to the contract are to agree that whoever is chosen as sovereign by a majority should be given absolute power in exchange for providing protection and physical security for all. Reformulating the traditional understanding of natural law of Hooker and Aquinas, he distinguished between natural right and natural law, defining natural right as the liberty to do whatever is necessary, including killing, to preserve oneself, and natural law as the rules or laws that can best promote self-preservation if, and only if, generally adopted and enforced. In contrast to Locke's *Letter Concerning Toleration*, Hobbes was critical of the rights of conscience as a source of conflict in the commonwealth and favored complete subordination of the church to the sovereign.

Because he defined morality in hedonistic terms, Hobbes's writings were attacked as materialistic and atheistic, but all subsequent writers were required to take account of them. Locke lent out his copy of the *Leviathan* in 1674 and did not get it back until 1691 (Locke, 1988:71) after he had written and published the *Two Treatises* and the *Essay on Human Understanding*. In the *Second Treatise*, Locke begins his analysis with individuals in "the state of nature" (a term used by Pufendorf and others, but not by Hobbes, who called it the "natural condition of mankind"), who then contract to establish government by majority rule. However, in section 19 of the *Second Treatise* he explicitly distinguishes the state of nature from the state of war "which some men have confounded." The state of nature is a state of peace, governed by the moral law, "the law of nature," and it is only because of its "inconveniences," primarily the need for a common judge of disputes arising from human partiality, that the individuals contract to leave the state of nature. The contract is a decision to act by majority rule to establish— not an absolute sovereign, as in Hobbes—a government in which the legislature and executive are (partially in the case of England) separated and that is limited by natural rights of life, liberty, and property as well as the possibility of "the appeal to heaven" (i.e, revolution) if those rights are repeatedly violated. Both the *Essays on the Law of Nature* and the *Second Treatise* describe self-preservation, which is central to Hobbes's theory, as part of the natural law, but St. Thomas Aquinas had also done so in his discussion of natural law (*Summa Theologiae*, I–II, qu. 93). In contrast to Hobbes, Locke insists that the law of nature requires that man must respect the "life, health, liberty, and possessions" of others who are free and equal creatures of God and is obliged not only to preserve himself but also "when his own preservation comes not in competition to preserve the rest of mankind" (*Second Treatise*, 6). Indeed there are so many differences between Hobbes and Locke that, until Laslett convincingly argued for an earlier date of composition, the *Second Treatise* was widely believed to be an answer to Hobbes rather than a reply to Filmer.

Yet beginning in the 1950s, the link between good and evil and pleasure and pain that Locke describes in the *Essay on Human Understanding* was used by Leo Strauss and his followers to argue that Locke was a Hobbesian in disguise, a view that was subsequently rejected by most commentators (see Leo Strauss, p. 274 herein, John, Yolton, p. 281, and A. John Simmons, p. 286). Even in his own times Locke was several times accused of Hobbesianism, each time replying in ways that implied little or no familiarity with what he called Hobbes's "justly decried" writings (Locke, 1988:74).

Did Locke ever read Hobbes? In his early *Essays on the Law of Nature*, Locke criticized—without naming him—Hobbes's definition of the law of nature as "a dictate of reason" (*Essay I*, 1954:111). He quoted Hobbes directly only once, in 1668 before he lent out his copy of the *Leviathan*, and his other critical reference to Hobbes's doctrines—the discussion of the ethics of the "Hobbist" in the *Essay Concerning Human Understanding* (1.3.5)—reflects a more general familiarity with his thought. Locke had in his library and was influenced by the natural law theories of Pufendorf (p. 250 herein), who like Locke used ideas that resembled Hobbes's. But Pufendorf was even more explicitly critical of Hobbes's theories. We may conclude that Locke knew Hobbes's main theories directly and through intermediaries, and although he used concepts such as the state of nature that Hobbes (and Pufendorf) used, there were important and fundamental differences between them, beginning, although not ending, with his understanding of natural law and the nature and source of moral obligation.

From Leviathan†

From *Part I. Of Man*

FROM CHAPTER 6. OF THE INTERIOR BEGINNINGS OF VOLUNTARY MOTIONS; COMMONLY CALLED THE PASSIONS; AND SPEECHES BY WHICH THEY ARE EXPRESSED

* * * [B]ecause the constitution of a man's body is in continual motion, it is impossible that all the same things should always cause in him the same appetites, and aversions: much less can all men consent, in the desire of almost any one and the same object.

---

† From William Molesworth, ed., *The English Works of Thomas Hobbes* (Aalen: Scientia Verlag, 1966).

But whatsoever is the object of any man's appetite or desire, that is it which he for his part calleth *good*: and the object of his hate and aversion, *evil*; and of his contempt, *vile* and *inconsiderable*. For these words of good, evil, and contemptible, are ever used with relation to the person that useth them: there being nothing simply and absolutely so; nor any common rule of good and evil, to be taken from the nature of objects themselves; but from the person of the man (where there is no commonwealth;) or, (in a commonwealth,) from the person that representeth it; or from an arbitrator or judge, whom men disagreeing shall by consent set up, and make his sentence the rule thereof.

*   *   *

FROM CHAPTER 13. OF THE NATURAL CONDITION OF MANKIND AS CONCERNING THEIR FELICITY, AND MISERY

Nature hath made men so equal, in their faculties of body, and mind; as though there be found one man sometimes manifestly stronger in body, or of quicker mind than another; yet when all is reckoned together, the difference between man and man, is not so considerable, as that one man can thereupon claim himself any benefit, to which another may not pretend, as well as he. For as to the strength of body, the weakest has strength enough to kill the strongest, either by secret machinations, or by confederacy with others that are in the same danger with himself.

And as to the faculties of the mind, (setting aside the arts grounded upon words, and especially that skill of proceeding upon general, and infallible rules, called science which very few have, and but in a few things; as being not a native faculty, born with us; nor attained, (as prudence) while we look after somewhat else,) I find yet a greater equality amongst men, than that of strength. For prudence is but experience; which equal time equally bestows on all men, in those things they equally apply themselves unto. That which may perhaps make such equality incredible, is but vain conceit of one's own wisdom, which almost all men think they have in a greater degree than the vulgar; that is, than all men but themselves, and a few others, whom by fame, or for concurring with themselves, they approve. For such is the nature of men, that howsoever they may acknowledge many others to be more witty, or more eloquent, or more learned; yet they will hardly believe there be many so wise as themselves: For they see their own wit at hand, and others men's at a distance. But this proveth rather that men are in that point equal, than unequal. For there is not ordinarily a greater sign of equal distribution of any thing, than that man is contented with his share.

From this equality of ability, ariseth equality of hope in the attaining of our ends. And therefore if any two men desire the same thing, which nevertheless they cannot both enjoy, they become enemies; and in the way to their end, which is principally their own conservation, and sometimes their delectation only, endeavor to destroy, or subdue one another. And from hence it comes to pass that where an invader hath no more to fear than another man's single power; if one plant, sow, build, or possess a convenient seat, others may probably be expected to come prepared with forces united to dispossess, and deprive him, not only of the fruit of his labour, but also of his life, or liberty. And the invader again is in the like danger. of another.

*   *   *

* * * [I]n the nature of man, we find three principal causes of quarrel. First, competition; secondly, diffidence;[1] thirdly, glory.

The first, maketh men invade for gain; the second, for safety; and the third, for reputation. The first use violence, to make themselves masters of other men's persons, wives, children, and cattle; the second, to defend them; the third, for trifles, as a word, a smile, a different opinion, and any other sign of undervalue, either direct in their persons, or by reflection in their kindred, their friends, their nations, their profession, or their name.

Hereby it is manifest, that during the time men live without a common power to keep them all in awe, they are in that condition which is called war; and such a war, as is of every man, against every man. For war, consisteth not in battle only, or the act of fighting; but in tract of time, wherein the will to contend by battle is sufficiently known: and therefore the notion of *time* is to be considered in the nature of war; as it is in the nature of weather. For as the nature of foul weather, lieth not in a shower or two of rain; but in an inclination thereto of many days together; so the nature of war, consisteth not in any actual fighting; but in the known disposition thereto, during all the time there is no assurance to the contrary. All other time is peace.

Whatsoever therefore is consequent to a time of war, where every man is enemy to every man; the same is consequent to the time, wherein men live without other security, than what their own strength, and their own invention shall furnish them withal. In such condition, there is no place for industry; because the fruit thereof is uncertain: and consequently no culture of the earth; no navigation, nor use of the commodities that may be imported by sea; no commodious building; no instruments of moving, and removing such things as require much force; no knowledge of the

---

1. Distrust. All notes are the editor's unless otherwise specified.

face of the earth; no account of time; no arts; no letters; no society; and which is worst of all, continual fear, and danger of violent death; and the life of man, solitary, poor, nasty, brutish, and short.

* * *

It may peradventure be thought, there was never such a time, nor condition of war as this; and I believe it was never generally so over all the world: but there are many places, where they live so now. For the savage people in many places of America, except the government of small families, the concord whereof dependeth on natural lust, have no government at all; and live at this day in that brutish manner, as I said before. Howsoever, it may be perceived what manner of life there would be, where there were no common person to fear; by the manner of life, which men that have formerly lived under a peaceful government use to degenerate into in a civil war.

But though there had never been any time, wherein particular men were in a condition of war one against another; yet in all times, kings, and persons of sovereign authority, because of their independency, are in continual jealousies, and in the state and posture of gladiators; having their weapons pointing, and their eyes fixed on one another; that is, their forts, garrisons, and guns upon frontiers of their kingdoms; and continual spies upon their neighbours; which is a posture of war. But because they uphold thereby, the industry of their subjects; there does not follow from it, that misery, which accompanies the liberty of particular men.

To this war of every man against every man, this is also consequent; that nothing can be unjust. The notions of right and wrong, justice and injustice have there no place. Where there is no common power, there is no law: where no law, no injustice. * * *

* * *

The passions that incline men to live in peace, are fear of death; desire of such things as are necessary for commodious living; and a hope by their industry to obtain them. And reason suggesteth convenient articles of peace, upon which men may be drawn to agreement. These articles, are they, which otherwise are called the Laws of Nature: whereof I shall speak more particularly, in the following chapters.

FROM CHAPTER 14. OF THE FIRST AND SECOND NATURAL LAWS, AND OF CONTRACTS

The RIGHT OF NATURE, which writers commonly call *jus naturale*, is the liberty each person hath, to use his own power, as he will himself, for the preservation of his own nature; that is to say, of his own life; and consequently, of doing anything, which in his own judgement, and reason, he shall conceive to be the aptest means thereunto.

By LIBERTY, is understood, according to the proper signification of the word, the absence of external impediments: which impediments, may oft take away part of a man's power to do what he would; but cannot hinder him from using the power left him, according as his judgement, and reason shall dictate to him.

A LAW OF NATURE, (*lex naturalis*,) is a precept, or general rule, found out by reason, by which a man is forbidden to do that which is destructive of his life, or taketh away the means of preserving the same; and to omit that, by which he thinketh it may be best preserved. For though they that speak of this subject, use to confound *jus*, and *lex*, *right* and *law*; yet they ought to be distinguished; because RIGHT, consisteth in liberty to do, or to forbear; whereas LAW determineth, and bindeth to one of them: so that law, and right, differ as much, as obligation, and liberty; which in one and the same matter are inconsistent.

And because the condition of man, (as hath been declared in the precedent chapter) is a condition of war of every one against every one; in which case every one is governed by his own reason; and there is nothing he can make use of, that may not be a help unto him, in preserving his life against enemies; it followeth, that in such a condition, every man has a right to every thing; even to one another's body. And therefore, as long as this natural right of every man to every thing endureth, there can be no security to any man, (how strong or wise soever he be) of living out the time, which nature ordinarily alloweth men to live. And consequently it is a precept, or general rule of reason, *that every man, ought to endeavor peace, as far as he has hope of obtaining it; and when he cannot obtain it, that he may seek, and use, all helps, and advantages of war.* The first branch of which rule, containeth the first, and fundamental law of nature; which is, *to seek peace, and follow it.* The second, the sum of the right of nature; which is, *by all means we can, to defend ourselves.*

From this fundamental law of nature, by which men are commanded to endeavour to peace, is derived this second law; *that a man be willing, when others are so too, as far-forth, as for peace, and defence of himself he shall think necessary, to lay down this right to all things; and be contented with so much liberty against other men, as he would allow other men against himself.* For as long as every man holdeth this right, of doing any thing he liketh; so long are all men in the condition of war. But if other men will not lay down their right, as well as he; then there is no reason for any one, to divest himself of his: for that were to expose himself to prey, (which no man is bound to) rather than to dispose himself to peace * * *

*   *   *

From *Part II*. Of Commonwealth

*   *   *

* * * [T]he laws of nature, as *justice, equity, modesty, mercy,* and, in sum, *doing to others, as we would be done to,* of themselves, without terror of some power, to cause them to be observed, are contrary to our natural passions, that carry us to partiality, pride, revenge, and the like. And covenants, without the sword, are but words, and of no strength to secure a man at all. Therefore notwithstanding the laws of nature, which every one hath then kept, when he has the will to keep them, when he can do so safely, if there be no power erected, or not great enough for our security; every man will, and may lawfully rely on his own strength and art, for caution against all other men. And in all places, where men have lived by small families, to rob and spoil one another has been a trade, and so far from being reputed against the law of nature, that the greater spoils they gained, the greater was their honour; and men observed no other laws therein, but the law of honour; that is, to abstain from cruelty, leaving men their lives, and instruments of husbandry. And as small farms did then; so now do cities and kingdoms which are but greater families, for their own security, enlarge their dominions, upon all pretences of danger, and fear of invasion, or assistance that may be given to invaders, endeavour as much as they can, to subdue, or weaken their neighbours, by open force, and secret arts, for want of other caution, justly; and are remembered for it in after ages with honour.

*   *   *

The only way to erect such a common power, as may be able to defend them from the invasion of foreigners, and the injuries of one another, and thereby to secure them in such sort, as that by their own industry, and by the fruits of the earth they may nourish themselves and live contentedly; is, to confer all their power and strength upon one man, or assembly of men, that may reduce all their wills, by plurality of voices, unto one will: which is as much as to say, to appoint one man, or assembly of men, to bear their person; and every one to own, and acknowledge himself to be author of whatsoever he that so beareth their person, shall act, or cause to be acted, in those things which concern the common peace and safety and therein to submit their wills, every one to his will, and their judgements, to his judgement. This is more than consent, or concord; it is a real unity of them all, in one and the same person, made by covenant of every man with every man, is such manner, as if every man should say to every man, *I authorize and give up my right of governing myself, to this man, or assembly of men, on this condition, that thou give up thy right to him, and authorize all his actions in like manner*. This done, the multitude so united in one person, is called a COMMONWEALTH, in Latin CIVITAS. This is the generation of that great LEVIATHAN, or rather, to speak more reverently, of that *mortal god*, to which we owe under the *immortal God*, our peace and defence. For by this authority, given him by every particular man in the commonwealth, he hath the use of so much power and strength conferred on him, that by terror thereof, he is enabled to form the wills of them all, to peace at home, and mutual aid against their enemies abroad. And in him consisteth the essence of the commonwealth; which (to define it,) is *one person, of whose acts a great multitude, by mutual covenants one with another, have made themselves every one the author, to the end he may use the strength and means of all, as he shall think expedient, for their peace and common defence*. And he that carrieth this person, is called SOVEREIGN, and said to have sovereign power; and every one besides, his SUBJECT.

The attaining to this sovereign power, is by two ways. One, by natural force; as when a man maketh his children, to submit themselves and their children to his government, as being able to destroy them if they refuse; or by war subdueth his enemies to his will, giving them their lives on that condition. The other, is when men agree amongst themselves, to submit to some man, or assembly of men, voluntarily, on confidence to be protected by him against all others. This latter, may be called a political commonwealth, or commonwealth by *institution*; and the former, a commonwealth by *acquisition*.

FROM CHAPTER 18. OF THE RIGHTS OF SOVEREIGNS BY INSTITUTION

A *commonwealth* is said to be *instituted* when a *multitude* of men do agree and *covenant, every one with every one*, that to whatsoever *man* or *assembly of men* shall be given by the major part the *right* to *present* the person of them all, that is to say, to be their *representative*, every one,—as well he that *voted for it*, as that *voted against it*, shall *authorize* all the actions and judgements of that man or assembly of men, in the same manner as if they were his own, to the end to live peaceably amongst themselves, and be protected against other men.

From this institution of a commonwealth are derived all the

rights and *faculties* of him, or them, on whom the sovereign power is conferred by the consent of the people assembled.

* * *

FROM CHAPTER 21. OF THE LIBERTY OF SUBJECTS

* * *

* * * Seeing there is no commonwealth in this world wherein there be enough rules set down for the regulating of all the actions and words of men (as being a thing impossible) it followeth necessarily that in all kinds of actions by the laws pretermitted[2] men have the liberty of doing what their own reasons shall suggest for the most profitable to themselves'.

* * *

* * * As for other liberties, they depend on the silence of the law. In cases where the sovereign has prescribed no rule, there the subject hath the liberty to do or forbear according to his own discretion. * * *

SAMUEL VON PUFENDORF

Samuel von Pufendorf (1632–94) was a German jurist, historian, and professor of law whose works on natural and international law were very widely read in the seventeenth and eighteenth centuries but are little known today. His earliest work, *The Elements of Natural Jurisprudence*, was published in 1660. Locke possessed a copy of the 1660 edition, and it probably influenced his early *Essays on the Law of Nature*, where he follows Pufendorf in distinguishing (as Hobbes had done earlier) between natural right (*jus naturale*) and natural law (*lex naturalis*), and in deriving the obligation of natural law from the divine will, rather than, as in Grotius, from reason. Locke recorded in his journals the purchase in 1678 of the Latin text of Pufendorf's *On the Duty of Man and the Citizen* (Lough, 1984:213) and he purchased *On the Law of Nature and Nations* as well as a second copy of the *Elements* in 1681, while he was working on the *Second Treatise* (Locke, 1954:38–39). At his death, Locke's library included the two editions of the *Elements of Jurisprudence*, two copies of the 1672 edition of *On the Law of Nature and of Nations*, and the 1673 edition of *On the Duty of Man and the Citizen* (all in the original Latin).

There are numerous resemblances—as well as important differences—between Pufendorf's political and legal theories and those of Locke, and he was an important influence on Locke's political theory (Tuck, 1999:176–181). Pufendorf was a strong critic of Hobbes but,

2. Omitted.

like him, begins with free and equal individuals in the state of nature in developing his social contract theory. However, unlike Hobbes, he insists that, while they have the right to take measures to preserve themselves, they must respect the rights of others, particularly the right to self-preservation. He argues, as Locke does in the last of his *Essays on the Law of Nature*, that individual self-interest (*utilitas*) cannot be used as a moral standard since it leads to conflicting conclusions in society. Pufendorf's state of nature is not a state of war. As in Locke, it is ruled by natural law, which can be perceived by human reason as obligatory because it is a decree of the divine will. Men have both selfish and sociable tendencies, and, as in Locke's theory, the disputes and conflicts caused by human selfishness lead them to establish government and law. As in Locke's case, the movement from original freedom and equality in the state of nature requires consent, either express or tacit, "of every individual with every other one" to make decisions by majority rule on the form of government and the ruler. An important difference from Locke's consent theory is that for Pufendorf, the original consent to government binds both the contractors and their successors without the necessity of additional acts of consent. In addition, Pufendorf claims that the citizens have a right of emigration, while Locke denies it to those who have given express consent (*Second Treatise*, 121)

Pufendorf bases property on agreement among men rather than on labor, although he discusses the role of labor in giving rise to property, and both he and Locke use the example of the appropriation of an acorn in their arguments. He makes the father's role much more important than does Locke, and he justifies slavery by consent (which Locke denies) and as punishment for participation in an unjust war (which Locke accepts). His argument for resistance by the people in cases of extreme injury—that no one would, or is permitted to, contract away his life—is similar to one made by Locke (*Second Treatise*, 168). For Pufendorf, however, the people (i.e. the community) determine whether the contract has been violated, whereas for Locke "any single man" may do so (*Second Treatise*, 168), although he must try to persuade the majority of the justice of his cause (*Second Treatise*, 209, 233).

Locke often recommended Pufendorf's works on natural law. In his *Thoughts on Education*, published in 1693, among his recommendations for a gentleman's education, he suggested that after reading "Tully's *Offices*" (Cicero, *On Duties*) "and Pufendorf's *De Officio Hominis et Civis*" (On the duty of man and the citizen), "it may be seasonable to set him upon Grotius, *De Jure Belli et Pacis*" (On the law of war and peace), "or which perhaps is the better of the two, Pufendorf, *De Jure Naturae et Gentium*" (On the law of nature and nations) "wherein he will be instructed in the natural rights of men and the original and foundations of society." (Locke 1996:139, no. 186) In 1703 at the end of a similar list "on the original of societies, and the rise and extent of political power" Locke recommended *On the Law of Nature and Nations*, adding "which last is the best book of that kind." Locke was being modest since he also included in the list, giving the date of publication, but not the name of the author, The *Two Treatises of Government* (Locke 1997: 349).

On the Law of Nature and of Nations†

From *Book I. Chapter 6. On Law in General*

3. Now since the term "right" often signifies the same thing as law¹ especially when it is used for a complex of laws, care ought to be taken that we do not use it in place of law itself, when it means the power, given or left by laws, to do something. * * * The word, "right", means merely liberty, while the word, law, denotes some bond by which our natural liberty is restrained.²

4. In general a law is most conveniently defined as a decree by which a superior obligates a subject to adapt his actions to the former's command. * * * The dictate of reason teaches us not only that the observance of natural law is profitable to the race of men but that God also wills and commands mortals to guide their actions by the rule of law, and this is enough for the essence of law. * * *

From *Book II. Chapter 2. On the Natural State of Man*

1. By the natural state of man we do not understand that condition which nature intended should be the most perfect and for his greatest good, but that condition for which man is understood to be constituted by the mere fact of his birth, all inventions and institutions, either of man or suggested to him from above, being disregarded. * * * To get a more distinct idea of this state we will consider it *in itself*, especially as to what advantages and rights accompany it; that is, what would have been the condition of individual men had mankind discovered no civilization and introduced no arts or commonwealths; and secondly, *in relation to other men*, whether it bears a resemblance to peace or to war; that is, whether men who live in a state of mutual natural liberty, wherein no man is subject to another, and they have no common master, should be considered foes or friends.

* * *

3. Now the rights attendant to this natural state of man can be easily gathered, in the first place from the desire common to all ani-

† From Samuel Pufendorf, *On the Law of Nature and of Nations*, trans. C. W. and W. A. Oldfeather (Oxford: Clarendon Press, 1934), pp. 89, 154, 158, 207–8, 211, 213–14, 215, 217–19, 330, 333, 340–42, 344, 536, 537, 539–40, 553–54, 914, 915–17, 935, 937, 974, 994, 1111–12.
1. The Latin original uses *lex* for "law" and *jus for* "right." All notes are the editor's unless otherwise specified.
2. Cf. Hobbes's *Leviathan* (pp. 245–46 herein).

mals whereby they cannot but use every means to preserve their
body and life, and to avert everything that would destroy them, and
in the second place, from the fact that those who enjoy this state
are subject to no man's orders. For it follows from the first consideration that men, constituted in a natural state, may use and enjoy
everything that is open to them, and may secure and do everything
that will lead to their preservation, in so far as no injury is done to
the right of others. And from the second, that they may use their
own judgement and decision, provided, of course, that it is framed
on this natural law, just as they use their own strength to secure
their own defence and preservation. And in this respect also the
state of nature has come to be described as a natural liberty since
every man, antecedent to any act of man, is understood to be under
his own right and power, and to be subject to the power of no other
man. And so every man is considered the equal of every other man,
since neither is subject of the other.

From *Book II. Chapter 3. On the Law of Nature in General*

*   *   *

15. After the preceding remarks it is easy to find the basis of natural law. It is quite clear that man is an animal extremely desirous of
his own preservation, in himself exposed to want, unable to exist
without the help of his fellow-creatures, fitted in a remarkable way
to contribute to the common good, and yet at all times malicious,
petulant, and easily irritated, as well as quick and powerful to do
injury. For such an animal to live and enjoy the good things that in
this world attend his condition, it is necessary that he be sociable,
that is, be willing to join himself with others like him, and conduct
himself towards them in such a way that, far from having any cause
to do him harm, they may feel that there is reason to preserve and
increase his good fortune.

*   *   *

16. When * * * each man decides to seek his own advantage to the
hurt of others, all manner of confusion arises, where the race of
man is divided into warring groups. To avoid such a state of affairs
the care of one's own safety commands that the laws of a sociable
attitude be observed, since without the latter the former cannot be
secure. As for the demonstration whereby Hobbes very adroitly de-
duces the laws of nature from the desire for self-preservation we
should observe at the outset that such a method of proof shows, indeed, most clearly how conducive it is to the safety of men for them
to lead their life in accordance with such dictates of reason. But
the conclusion should not be drawn, without more ado, that man
has a right to use such dictates as means for his preservation, and

that therefore he is also bound to observe them as by some law; if those dictates of reason are to have the effect of laws they must certainly be drawn from some other principle.

In the next place great care should also be taken to prevent any one from concluding that when he feels he has made his own safety perfectly sure he need take no thought of others, or that he may do despite[3] at his pleasure to anybody that contributes nothing to my safety, or has not the strength to work it harm. For we called man a sociable creature because men are so constituted as to render mutual help more than any other creature, just as no creature can suffer more injury from man than can man himself. Nay, man's eminence and perfection stand out all the more as they contribute to the advantage of others, and deeds of such a nature are considered most noble and indicative of the greatest wisdom, while on the other hand any worthless fellow and a fool can bother and injure others. Furthermore, if it be proper to consider a man's own advantage his one end of life, then when several persons decide that their greatest advantage is concerned with the same thing it will follow either that the ends of several people, involving a contradiction, are said to agree at the said time with right reason, which is absurd; or, since no one can claim that his end should be preferred to that of another, it will have to be admitted that man should not propose his own advantage as his end unless he also takes into consideration the advantage of others.

*   *   *

18. But, although by the wisdom of the Creator the natural law has been so adapted to the nature of man, that its observance is always connected with the profit and advantage of men, and therefore also this general love tends to man's greatest good, yet, in giving a reason for this fact, one does not refer to the advantage accruing therefrom, but to the common nature of all men. For instance, if a reason must be given why a man should not injure another, you do not say, because it is to his advantage, although it may, indeed, be most advantageous, but because the other person also is a man, that is, an animal related by nature, whom it is a crime to injure.

19. [I]f these dictates of reason are to have the force of laws, it is necessary to presuppose the existence of God and His providence, whereby all things are governed, and primarily mankind. For we cannot agree with Grotius, when he says in his Prolegomena that natural laws 'will have some place, even if we should grant—what can only be done with the greatest impiety—that there is no God, or that He does not concern himself with the affairs of men.' For if some man should devise such an impious and idiotic theory, and

3. Injury.

imagine that mankind had sprung from itself, then the dictates of reason could in no possible way have the force of law, since law necessarily support a superior.

*　*　*

18. It must, therefore, under all circumstances be maintained that the obligation of natural law is of God, the creator and final governor of mankind, who by his authority has bound men, his creatures, to observe it. And this assertion can be proved by the light of reason. Inasmuch as it has long since been established by men of discernment, and no God-fearing man disputes it, we now assume that God is the maker and controller of this universe. Since He so formed the nature of the world and man that the latter cannot exist without leading a social life, and for this reason gave him a mind capable of grasping the ideas that lead to this end, and since He suggests these ideas to men's minds by the course of natural events as they come from Him as the first cause, and represent clearly their necessary relationship and truth, it is surely to be recognized that He also willed for man to regulate his actions by the native endowment which God Himself appears to have given him in a special way above the beasts. And since this end cannot be attained in any other way than by the observance of natural law, it is understood that man has been obligated also by the Creator to observe this law, as a means not elaborated by the wish of men, and changeable at their pleasure, but as expressly ordained by the Creator Himself to secure this end. For whoever has the authority to enjoin some end upon another is also understood to have obligated such a person to use the means without which that end cannot be secured.

*　*　*

Now the laws of nature would have had full power to obligate men, even if God had never proclaimed them again in his revealed word, for man was bound to obey his Creator, whatever the way in which he might reveal his will to him. Nor was a special revelation absolutely necessary, in order that a rational creature might recognize that he was subject to the command of the final judge of things. No one, indeed, would deny that even those to whom the Sacred Scriptures were not known have sinned against the law of nature—a statement which could not be made, if it acquired the force of law only through its pronouncement in the Scriptures.

From Book III. Chapter 2. All Men Are Accounted as Naturally Equal

1. Now since human nature belongs equally to all men, and no one can live a social life with a person by whom he is not rated as at

least a fellow man, it follows, as a precept of natural law, that
'Every man should esteem and treat another man as his equal by
nature, or as much a man as he is himself.'

*   *   *

2. And this equality we can call an *equality of right*, which has its
origin in the fact that an obligation to cultivate a social life is
equally binding upon all men, since it is an integral part of human
nature as such.

8. A further conclusion to be drawn from what has been said is that
the old idea handed down from the Greeks, to the effect that certain men are slaves by nature, merits complete disapproval.

*   *   *

* * * [I]t would be most absurd to believe that nature herself has,
in fact, given to the more prudent rule over the more dull, or even
any such a right, whereby the former can force the latter to serve
them against their will. For if sovereignty is established in fact,
some human agency must precede, and a natural aptitude for ruling does not of itself give a man the rule over him who is constituted by nature only for servitude. Nor can I, without more ado,
use force in imposing upon another what is good for him. For men
enjoy an equal natural liberty, and if they are to allow it to be cur-
tailed, their consent must be secured, whether that consent be express, or tacit, or interpretative, or else they must have done
something whereby others have secured the right to deprive them
of their equality, even against their will.

9. A few remarks should be made, at this point, on that equality
which is a consequence of a natural state, and which we can call
equality of power or *of liberty*. By this all men are recognized to be
naturally equal, in so far as no one, apart from an antecedent deed
or agreement of man, has any power over another, but every man is
the governor of his acts or power. This equality was afterwards removed by a civil state, wherein, since one or more persons received
the power to give order to others, the rest were put under the necessity of obedience, resulting in the greatest inequality imaginable
between rulers and subjects.

*   *   *

From *Book IV. Chapter 4. On the Origin of Dominion*[4]

4. * * * [D]ominion presupposes absolutely an act of man and an
agreement, whether tacit or express. It is true that God allowed
man to turn the earth, its products, and its creatures to his own use
and convenience, that is he gave men an indefinite right to them,

---

4. Property.

yet the manner, intensity, and extent of this power were left to the judgement and disposition of men. * * *

5. * * * [I]t is clear that before any conventions of men existed there was a community of all things, not, indeed, such as we have called positive, but a negative one, that is, that all things lay open to all men, and belonged no more to one than to another. But since things are of no use to men unless at least their fruits may be appropriated, and this is impossible if others as well can take what we have already by our own act selected for our uses, it follows that the first convention between men was about these very concerns, to the effect that whatever one of these things which were left open to all, and of their fruits, a man had laid his hands upon, with intent to turn it to his uses, could not be taken from him by another.

6. The causes of things passing into proprietorship, and the order which they followed can, I think, be understood on these considerations: Most things which are of use to men immediately and are employed to nourish them and protect their bodies, are not produced everywhere by nature and without cultivation in such abundance that they fully suffice for every one. Therefore, an occasion for quarrels and wars lay ready at hand, if two or more men needed the same thing, and individuals tried to appropriate for themselves them same thing, when it was not enough for all. Moreover, most things require labour and cultivation by men to produce them and make them fit for use. But in such cases it was improper that a man who had contributed no labour should have a right to things equal to this by whose industry a thing had been raised or rendered fit for service. Therefore, it was advantageous to peace among men that, as soon as men multiplied, there should be introduced dominion of mobile things, especially such as require labor and cultivation by men, and, among immobile things, dominion of those which are of immediate use to men such as places for dwelling; that, in other words, the substance of these objects might belong separately to individuals, or, when several were concerned, to those who by special convention had agreed to a positive community in such things.

* * *

But regarding the immobile things produced by nature without the labour of man, such as fields, they were so extensive that they abundantly provided for the small number of early men, and for that reason at first only so much of them was occupied as men judged to be suitable for their uses, while the rest was left in a state of original negative community, so that every man who wished to was free in the future to take it. And hence it is understood that a pact was agreed upon, to the effect that such fields as had been assigned to one person by the express convention of the rest of men, or such as the rest could be held tacitly to have withdrawn from, in view of the fact that one man alone had been allowed to enjoy them in peace, while they had claimed for themselves other fields on the same basis—that such fields should belong to those who cultivated them. And finally, that what was left should pass to those who would hereafter occupy the fields.

*   *   *

13. [P]rimitive community is one thing, before any deed of man and the use of any thing, when each thing merely belongs no more to one man than to another, and in this way belongs quite as well to neither; but it is another thing when men begin to make use of things open to all. For then, whatever each man has seized for his own uses becomes proper to him by a previous pact, since without such, men would have to refrain from the use of all things. Therefore, in this, as it were, limited community the bodies of things belong to no one, but their fruits after gathering are proper. Such a tempering of primitive community with proprietorship, I feel, is comprehensible even by men of ordinary intelligence. An oak-tree belonged to no man, but the acorns that fell to the ground were his who had gathered them.[5]

*   *   *

From *Book VI. Chapter 2. On Paternal Power*

*   *   *

4. [T]he right of parents over children is based upon a two-fold claim: First, because the very law of nature, by reason of its command that man be sociable, has laid upon parents the care of children, and, to provide against its neglect, has at the same time implanted in them the most tender affection for their offspring. For unless you provide that parents rear their offspring, it is impossible to conceive of a social life. But that care cannot properly be exercised unless parents have power to direct the actions of their children to their good, which is not yet recognized by the children because of their immature judgement. And so for this very reason nature enjoins upon parents that they exercise sufficient sovereignty over their children to attain that end. For whoever obligates a man to an end is understood to have conferred upon him at the same time the power to avail himself of the means without which it cannot be obtained. Furthermore, this power of parents, resulting from the command to care for one's children, necessarily lays upon children the obligation to submit themselves to the direction of their parents, since this direction without the former obligation is to no purpose.

---

5. See Locke, *Second Treatise*, 28.

* * *

5. When the further question is raised, as to which parent has the greater right over the offspring, the matter may be cleared up by drawing a distinction at the outset. For they either live within or without a state; and there is or there is not a pact between them. If the parents live without a state, in natural liberty, the offspring belongs to the mother, in case they joined themselves without any lasting pact. For in that state the father cannot be known but on the evidence of the mother, at least with such certainty as matters of fact usually require, it being permissible in such a state for the mother to accept the services of other men as well.

* * *

[W]here males establish states, just as they are regularly the heads of the families, so the private sovereignty over children lies with the fathers, and hence the orders of the mothers have of themselves only the force of advice, and usually have full authority to obligate the children only as they borrow the power from the father. For just as it is advantageous for wives to be admitted to a share in the administration of the household, so the sovereignty of the father does not exclude the mother's care over the children.

* * *

From *Book VI. Chapter 3. On the Power of a Master*

* * *

4. Our idea on the origin of slavery is as follows. When in early days men departed from their original simple manner of living and began to devote more efforts to the elaboration of life, and to turn their attention to increasing their possessions, it is highly probable that the more sagacious and more wealthy invited the more sluggish and the poorer sort to hire themselves out to them. Then when both parties came to realize the advantage of this, the latter sort were gradually led to attach themselves permanently to the families of their employers, on condition that the latter should provide sustenance and all other necessities of life, and the former take care of all the work about the establishment as the owners might order. And so the first beginnings of slavery followed upon the willing consent of men of poorer condition, and a contract of the form of "goods for work": I will always provide for you, if you will always work for me.[6]

* * *

5. Now after the convenience of performing one's labours by the hand of others was recognized * * * and when wars began to grow

6. Cf. Locke, *Second Treatise*, 85, which has a different view.

common, it gradually became customary to grant captives in war their life and bodily liberty, provided they served their captors for their lifetime. * * * Once having been introduced it was extended, even on a relatively slight excuse, also to the children of such captives, or to such as had been acquired by purchase.

* * *

6. In this pact the one who has been conquered receives some good, that is, the present of life, which could have been taken by the right of war, while the good which he in turn promises is service and obedience, and the latter, so far as is possible, absolute. * * *

* * *

From *Book VII. Chapter 2. On the Internal Structure of the State*

* * *

7. The number and the nature of those pacts by the intervention of which a state is built up are discovered in the following manner. If we imagine to ourselves a multitude of men endowed with natural liberty and equality[7] who voluntarily set about to establish a new state, it is necessary for the future citizens, as the first step, to enter into an agreement, every individual with every other one, that they are desirous of entering into a single and perpetual group, and of administrating the considerations of their safety and security by common council and leadership (although in such a pact the individuals usually reserve to themselves the privilege of emigration).

Such a pact is entered into either absolutely or conditionally. Absolutely, when a man pledges himself to remain with the group, whatever form of government the majority may finally decide upon. Conditionally, when he stipulates that the form of government be such as he approves of. Furthermore, when this pact is entered into, it is necessary for each and all to give their consent. Whoever does not do so, for so long as he continues in the same place with the rest, remains outside the future state, nor is he required by the agreement of the rest, however numerous they be, to join their group at all; but he continues in his natural liberty, wherein he will be permitted to decide matters of his safety according to his own judgement.

But after such a group, already taking on the rudiments and beginning of a state, has been formed by the pact mentioned, it is yet further necessary for a decree to be passed upon the form of gov-

---

7. A description of what earlier (II.2.1) Pufendorf had called the state of nature (*status naturalis*). The term is associated with Hobbes, who called it "the natural condition of mankind," but had been used earlier by the sixteenth-century Spanish writers on international law. The concept of a prepolitical state was also present in Grotius and Hooker.

ernment that shall be introduced. For until this decision is reached, it will be impossible to take consistent action on matters concerning the common safety. At this step those who have joined themselves to the group absolutely, will be forced by the agreement of the majority to consent to that form of government which these latter have agreed upon, although they might have preferred another, if, indeed, they wish to remain in the spot where the group is fixed. For in making no exception to the pact, they are understood to have submitted themselves to the will of the majority, at least in that point, for they can have no grounds for demanding that all the others prefer the judgement of a few to their own. But he who has joined the group conditionally will not become a member of the future state, nor obligated by the agreement of the majority, unless he has expressly agreed to the form of government to be introduced.

8. After the decree upon the form of government, a new pact will be necessary when the individual or body is constituted that receives the government of the group, by which pact the rulers bind themselves to the care of the common security and safety, and the rest to render them obedience, and in which there is that subjection and union of wills, by reason of which a state is looked upon as a single person. From this pact there finally comes a finished state.

*   *   *

20. When a state has been formed in the way described, the person or persons on whom devolves the sovereignty, is called a monarch, senate, or people, according as this sovereignty resists in a single man, one council, composed of a few members, or of all the citizens; while all others are known as subjects. Here we must observe that man may become a member of any state in two ways: by an expressed or by a tacit pact. For those who establish states in the first place are surely not held to have done so with the thought that they would cease with the death of their founders, but they had before their eyes the obtaining in this way of advantages which would be lasting and perpetual, and would be a source of gratification to their children and all their posterity. Therefore, it is held that they also had in mind that their children and descendants should upon birth enjoy the common advantages and rewards of the state; and since these cannot be secured without sovereignty, which is, as it were, the soul of a state, all who are born in a state are also understood to have subjected themselves to that sovereignty. Hence it is that those who have once accepted the sovereignty in a state are under no necessity of requiring anew an express subjection from each newly-born child, although all of those who first conferred sovereignty upon them may be dead.

Furthermore, since every state is situated upon some certain part of the surface of the earth, in which the citizens have gathered themselves and their property for safety, and since this safety would be easily imperilled, if men could come and go there who did not recognize the sovereignty of the state, it is understood as a common law of all states, that, whoever has passed into the territory of any state, and all the more if he wishes to enjoy its advantages, is held to have given up his natural liberty, and to have subjected himself to the sovereignty of that state, at least for so long a time as he desires to remain there.

*   *   *

From *Book VII. Chapter 8. On the Sanctity of the Supreme Sovereign in States*

*   *   *

7. What we have said does not differ greatly from the position of Grotius.[8] * * * He is right in suggesting, among other things, that it can be decided, first, from the nature of supreme sovereignty, and then, from the presumed will of those who were the first to unite to form a state, whether an extreme injury by a supreme sovereign can be repelled with violence. For surely it is by no means repugnant to the nature of supreme sovereignty that it should direct the acts of all citizens to the public safety, and that it should hold the severest punishment before him who flaunts its decrees, without also having the power to slay anyone at its pleasure, and allow him no degree of resistance. Nor is there any natural connection between the absolute power to secure a man's safety, and the absolute power to slay him at pleasure. And it cannot be shown that such a power in a sovereign, or that such an obligation in citizens, can contribute to the peace and security of a state. * * * Grotius is right in saying that if those who at the outset gave rise to supreme sovereignty by gathering into states had been questioned as to whether they wished to lay upon all the burden that they shall choose to die rather than under any circumstances to repel with arms the unjust violence of superiors, they would never have replied that they wanted anything of the sort. For that would have been a greater hardship than what they were trying to avoid in the establishment of the state. * * *

---

8. Grotius's *On the Law of War and Peace*, I.4.7. (p. 232 herein).

SIR ROBERT FILMER

Sir Robert Filmer (1583–1653) was a member of the English landed gentry and a defender of absolute monarchy. In the 1640s and 1650s, during and after the English civil wars, he published several works on English constitutional history and political theory, defending royal power against parliamentary claims. However, his most important royalist work, *Patriarcha*, which was composed earlier, probably in the late 1620s and early 1630s (Filmer, 1991: xxii–xxiv) remained unpublished until 1680, when it was printed as part of the controversy over Parliament's right to exclude, because of his conversion to Catholicism, the duke of York (the future James II) from succeeding Charles II as king. As the title implies, Filmer derives the authority of kings from their succession to the divinely instituted patriarchal authority of Adam and attacks those who conclude from a theory of original natural freedom that the king's authority is based on the consent of "the multitude."

Filmer has three arguments against consent as the basis for the legitimacy of government: (1) Historically it was not consent based on original freedom that established political communities, (2) original freedom and equality if they exist cannot be surrendered to a majority, and (3) if the consent of the people is tacit it can justify any existing government. Filmer also criticizes the theory of consent on historical, and in the English case, constitutional grounds, arguing that Parliament's role in legislation was a concession by the king and that it was called and dissolved at his discretion.

Locke was familiar with Filmer's other works in 1667 (Locke, 1988:33), and in the *Second Treatise* he quotes from a collection of Filmer's writings that was published in 1679. When the *Patriarcha* appeared in 1680, Locke bought a copy and quoted from it frequently by page number in the *First Treatise*, which he wrote as a response to its publication. The *Second Treatise*, a more general attack on absolutism and a defense of original freedom and equality relies primarily on philosophical arguments rather than, as in the *First Treatise*, on scripture and history. Both treatises were slightly revised and updated after the overthrow of James II in 1688 and were published in 1690 as a defense of William III's accession to the throne, at a time when Filmer's arguments were no longer compelling.

Patriarcha, or the Natural Power of King Defended against the Unnatural Liberty of the People (1680)†

From *Chapter I. That the First Kings Were Fathers of Families*

1. SINCE the time that school divinity began to flourish there hath been a common opinion maintained, as well by divines as by divers[e] other learned men, which affirms:

> "Mankind is naturally endowed and born with freedom from all subjection, and at liberty to choose what form of government it please, and that the power which any one man hath over others was at first bestowed according to the discretion of the multitude."

This tenet was first hatched in the schools,[1] and hath been fostered by all succeeding Papists for good divinity.[2] The divines, also, of the Reformed Churches[3] have entertained it, and the common people everywhere tenderly embrace it as being most plausible to flesh and blood, for that it prodigally distributes a portion of liberty to the meanest of the multitude, who magnify liberty as if the height of human felicity were only to be found in it, never remembering that the desire of liberty was the first cause of the fall of Adam.

But howsoever this vulgar opinion hath of late obtained a great reputation, yet it is not to be found in the ancient fathers and doctors of the primitive Church. It contradicts the doctrine and history of the Holy Scriptures, the constant practice of all ancient monarchies, and the very principles of the law of nature. It is hard to say whether it be more erroneous in divinity or dangerous in policy.

Yet upon the ground of this doctrine, both Jesuits and some other zealous favourers of the Geneva discipline have built a perilous conclusion, which is, that the people or multitude have power to punish or deprive the prince if he transgress the laws of the kingdom. * * *

This desperate assertion whereby kings are made subject to the censures and deprivations of their subjects follows—as the authors of it conceive—as a necessary consequence of that former position of the supposed natural equality and freedom of mankind, and liberty to choose what form of government it please.

* * *

If such as maintain the natural liberty of mankind take offence at the liberty I take to examine it, they must take heed that they do

---

† From *Patriarcha* (The Constitution Society, www.constitution.org/eng/patriarcha).
1. i.e., medieval universities. All notes are the editor's unless otherwise specified.
2. Theology.
3. Churches espousing the teachings of John Calvin (1509–1564), who headed the Calvinist church in Geneva.

not deny by retail that liberty which they affirm by wholesale. For if the thesis be true, the hypothesis will follow that all men may examine their own charters, deeds, or evidences by which they claim and hold the inheritance or freehold of their liberties.[4]

* * *

3. I come now to examine that argument which is used by Bellarmine, and is the one and only argument I can find produced by my author for the proof of the natural liberty of the people. It is thus framed: "That God hath given or ordained power, is evident by Scripture; but God hath given it to no particular person, because by nature all men are equal, therefore he hath given power to the people or multitude."[5]

* * * Adam was lord of his children, so his children under him had a command and power over their own children, but still with subordination to the first parent, who is lord-paramount over his children's children to all generations, as being the grandfather of his people.

4. I see not then how the children of Adam, or of any man else, can be free from subjection to their parents. And this subjection of children being the fountain of all regal authority, by the ordination of God himself; it follows that civil power not only in general is by divine institution, but even the assignment of it specifically to the eldest parents, which quite takes away that new and common distinction which refers only power universal and absolute to God, but power respective in regard of the special form of government to the choice of the people.

This lordship which Adam by command had over the whole world, and by right descending from him the patriarchs did enjoy, was as large and ample as the absolutest dominion of any monarch which hath been since the creation. * * *

* * *

7. [W]e may trace this paternal government unto the Israelites coming into Egypt, where the exercise of supreme patriarchal jurisdiction was intermitted[6] because they were in subjection to a stronger prince. After the return of these Israelites out of bondage, God, out of a special care of them, chose Moses and Joshua successively to govern as princes in the place and stead of the supreme fathers; and after them likewise for a time He raised up judges to defend His people in tune of peril. But when God gave the Israelites kings, He re-established the ancient and prime right of lin-

4. I.e., all property rights.
5. Cardinal Robert Bellarmine (1543–1621), Italian Jesuit who wrote *De Potestate Summi Pontificis* (On the power of the supreme pontiff) (1610), from which the reference is taken.
6. Interrupted.

eal succession to paternal government. And whensoever He made choice of any special person to be king, He intended that the issue[7] also should have benefit thereof, as being comprehended sufficiently in the person of the father, although the father only was named in the grant.

8. It may seem absurd to maintain that kings now are the fathers of their people, since experience shows the contrary. It is true, all kings be not the natural parents of their subjects, yet they all either are, or are to be reputed, the next heirs to those first progenitors who were at first the natural parents of the whole people, and in their right succeed to the exercise of supreme jurisdiction; and such heirs are not only lords of their own children, but also of their brethren, and all others that were subject to their fathers. * * *

As long as the first fathers of families lived, the name of patriarchs did aptly belong unto them; but after a few descents, when the true fatherhood itself was extinct, and only the right of the father descends to the true heir, then the title of prince or king was more significant to express the power of him who succeeds only to the right of that fatherhood which his ancestors did naturally enjoy. By this means it comes to pass that many a child, by succeeding a king, hath the right of a father over many a greyheaded multitude, and hath the title of *Pater Patriae*.[8]

* * *

10. In all kingdoms or commonwealths in the world, whether the prince be the supreme father of the people or but the true heir of such a father, or whether he come to the crown by usurpation, or by election of the nobles or of the people, or by any other way whatsoever, or whether some few or a multitude govern the commonwealth, yet still the authority that is in any one, or in many, or in all these, is the only right and natural authority of a supreme father. There is and always shall be continued to the end of the world a natural right of a supreme father over every multitude, although, by the secret will of God, many at first do most unjustly obtain the exercise of it.

To confirm this natural right of regal power, we find in the Decalogue[9] that the law which enjoins obedience to kings is delivered in the terms of "Honour thy father," as if all power were originally in the father.[1] * * *

7. Offspring.
8. Father of his country.
9. The Ten Commandments.
1. Locke notes in the *First Treatise* (66) that the commandment reads "Honour thy father and mother."

From *Chapter II. It Is Unnatural for the People to Govern or Choose Governors*

*   *   *

5. But let us condescend a while to the opinion of Bellarmine and Suarez,[2] and all those who place supreme power in the whole people, and ask them if their meaning be that there is but one and the same power in all the people of the world, so that no power can be granted except all the men upon the earth meet and agree to choose a governor.

*   *   *

* * * Can they show or prove that ever the whole multitude met and divided this power which God gave them in gross by breaking into parcels and by appointing a distinct power to each several commonwealth? Without such a compact I cannot see—according to their own principles—how there can be any election of a magistrate by any commonwealth, but by a mere usurpation upon the privilege of the whole world. If any think that particular multitudes at their own discretion had power to divide themselves into several commonweals, those that think so have neither reason nor proof for so thinking, and thereby a gap is opened for every petty factious multitude to raise a new commonwealth, and to make more commonwealths than there be families in the world. But let this also be yielded them, that in each particular commonwealth there is a distinct power in the multitude. Was a general meeting of a whole kingdom ever known for the election of a prince? Is there any example of it ever found in the whole world? To conceit[3] such a thing is to imagine little less than an impossibility, and so by consequence no one form of government or king was ever established according to this supposed law of nature.

6. It may be answered by some that if either the greatest part of a kingdom, or if a smaller part only by themselves, and all the rest by proxy, or if the part not concurring in election do after, by a tacit assent, ratify the act of others, that in all these cases it may be said to be the work of the whole multitude.

As to the acts of the major part of a multitude, it is true that by politic human constitutions it is oft ordained that the voices of the most shall overrule the rest; and such ordinances bind, because where men [are] assembled by a human power, that power that doth assemble them can also limit and direct the manner of the execution of that power, and by such derivative power, made known by law or custom, either the greater part, or two thirds, or three

---

2. Francisco Suarez (1548–1617), Spanish Jesuit who wrote *The Treatise on the Laws and God the Lawgiver* (1611).
3. Conceive.

parts of five, or the like, have power to oversway the liberty of their opposites. But in assemblies that take their authority from the law of nature, it cannot be so; for what freedom or liberty is due to any man by the law of nature no inferior power can alter, limit or diminish; no one man nor a multitude can give away the natural right of another. The law of nature is unchangeable, and howsoever one man may hinder another in the use or exercise of his natural right, yet thereby no man loseth the right of itself; for the right and the use of the right may be distinguished, as right and possession are oft distinct. Therefore, unless it can be proved by the law of nature that the major or some other part have power to overrule the rest of the multitude, it must follow that the acts of multitudes not entire are not binding to all but only to such as consent unto them.

7. As to the point of proxy, it cannot be shown or proved that all those that have been absent from popular elections did ever give their voices to some of their fellows. I ask but one example out of the history of the whole world: let the commonweal be but named wherever the multitude or so much as the greatest part of it consented, either by voice or by procuration,[4] to the election of a prince. The ambition sometimes of one man, sometimes of many, or the faction of a city or citizens, or the mutiny of an army, hath set up or put down princes; but they have never tarried for this pretended order by proceeding of the whole multitude.

Lastly, if the silent acceptation of a governor by part of the people be an argument of their concurring in the election of him, by the same reason the tacit assent of the whole commonwealth may be maintained; from whence it follows that every prince that comes to a crown, either by succession, conquest, or usurpation, may be said to be elected by the people, which inference is too ridiculous; for in such cases the people are so far from the liberty of specification that they want even that contradiction.[5]

* * *

17. If it be unnatural for the multitude to choose their governors, or to govern or to partake in the government, what can be thought of that damnable conclusion which is made by too many that the multitude may correct or depose their prince if need be? Surely the unnaturalness and injustice of this position cannot sufficiently be expressed; for admit that a king make a contract or paction with his people, either originally in his ancestors or personally at his coronation—for both these pactions some dream of but cannot offer any proof for either—yet by no law of any nation can a contract be thought broken, except that first a lawful trial be had by the ordi-

4. representation.
5. I.e., not only do the people have no role in designating the king but they cannot oppose him.

nary judge of the breakers thereof, or else every man may be both party and judge in his own case, which is absurd once to be thought, for then it will lie in the hands of the headless multitude when they please to cast off the yoke of government—that God hath laid upon them—to judge and punish him, by whom they should be judged and punished themselves. * * *

*   *   *

From Chapter III. Positive Laws Do Not Infringe the Natural and Fatherly Power of Kings

1. Hitherto I have endeavoured to show the natural institution of regal authority, and to free it from subjection to an arbitrary election of the people. It is necessary also to inquire whether human laws have a superiority over princes, because those that maintain the acquisition of royal jurisdiction from the people do subject the exercise of it to positive laws. But in this also they err; for *as kingly power is by the law of God, so it hath no inferior law to limit it.*[6]

*   *   *

5. *The reason why laws have been also made by kings was this: when kings were either busied with wars, or distracted with public cares, so that every private man could not have access to their persons to learn their wills and pleasure, then of necessity were laws invented, that so every particular subject might find his prince's pleasure deciphered to him in the tables of his laws.* * * *

6. * * * *General laws made in Parliament may, upon known respects to the king, by his authority be mitigated or suspended upon causes only known to him.* * * *

*   *   *

[14.] * * * [I]n the former parliaments, instituted and continued since King Henry I's[7] time, is not to be found the usage of any natural liberty of the people; for all those liberties that are claimed in parliament are the liberties of grace from the king, and not the liberties of nature to the people; for if the liberty were natural, it would give power to the multitude to assemble themselves when and where they please, to bestow sovereignty, and by pactions[8] to limit and direct the exercise of it. Whereas the liberties of favour and grace which are claimed in parliaments are restrained both for time, place, persons, and other circumstances, to the sole pleasure of the king, the people cannot assemble themselves, but the king, by his writs, calls them to what place he pleases; and then again

6. Sentences in italics were quoted by Locke in his *First Treatise*.
7. King Henry I ruled 1100–35.
8. Agreement.

scatters them with his breath at an instant, without any other cause
shown than his will. * * *

* * *

15. [I]n parliament all statutes or laws are made properly by the
king alone, at the rogation[9] of the people, as his Majesty King
James, of happy memory, affirms in his True Law of Free Monarchy, and, as Hooker teacheth us, "That laws do not take their constraining force from the quality of such as devise them, but from
the power that doth give them the strength of laws."[1] Le roy le veult
("the king will have it so") is the interpretive phrase pronounced at
the king's passing of every Act of Parliament. And it was the ancient
custom for a long time, till the days of Henry V,[2] that the kings,
when any Bill was brought unto them that had passed both Houses,
to take and pick out what they liked not, and so much as they chose
was enacted for a law; but the custom of the later kings hath been
so gracious as to allow always of the entire Bill as it hath passed
both Houses.

16. The parliament is the king's court, for so all the oldest
statutes called it, "the king in his parliament." But neither of the
two Houses are that supreme court, nor yet both of them together;
they are only members and a part of the body whereof the king is
the head and ruler. The king's governing of this body of the parliament we may find most significantly proved, both by the statutes
themselves as also by such precedents as expressly show us how the
king, sometimes by himself, sometimes by his council, and other
times by his judges, hath overruled and directed the judgments of
the Houses of Parliament. For the king, we find that Magna Carta[3]
and the Charter of Forests, and many other statutes about those
times, had only the form of the king's letters-patents, or grants under the great seal, testifying those great liberties to be the sole act
and bounty of the king. * * *

* * *

9. Request.
1. James I (1566–1625) published this work in defense of the divine right of kings in 1598.
   Hooker in *Laws of Ecclesiastical Polity* (I.10) argues that the power of law comes from
   consent; the opposite of Filmer's argument.
2. King of England from 1413 to 1422.
3. A charter of liberties signed in 1215.

INTERPRETATIONS

Locke as Hobbesian Hedonist

In the 1950s, Leo Strauss, a German émigré who taught at the University of Chicago, developed an approach to the history of political theory that profoundly affected later interpretations of Locke's thought. Strauss divided that history into the classic period of "natural right" theory, beginning with Plato, and the modern period of natural rights, beginning with Hobbes. He had also argued earlier that many writers in the past concealed their true beliefs because of fear of persecution. In the selection printed here from his classic book *Natural Right and History* (1953), he applied his theory to Locke, arguing that Locke's apparent adherence to traditional natural law theory disguised his true "teaching," which was basically a modified version of that of Hobbes. In order to make this argument he quoted selected texts from Locke's writings to conclude that rather then espousing, as he appeared to do, a version of the natural law theory of Richard Hooker, Locke really shared Hobbes's views on the centrality of self-preservation as a human desire and the only natural right and on the state of nature as a state of war.

In 1958, John W. Yolton vigorously attacked Strauss's view in *The Philosophical Review*. After observing that Locke's early *Essays on the Law of Nature*, written in 1663 but published only in 1954, after Strauss's book appeared, proved that he espoused a more or less traditional view of natural law, Yolton criticized Strauss's reading of Locke as "violently distorted" and "grossly misleading," noting that in a number of cases his quotations omitted or misrepresented statements by Locke that refuted his view. He argued that Locke's view of natural law was not a deductive one, as in Hobbes, but one based on intuitions of the purposes of nature and God. He also analyzed Locke's statements about the relation of pleasure and pain to good and evil, which had been quoted by Strauss as proving Locke's adhesion to Hobbesian hedonism, Yolton maintained that pleasure and pain were, in Locke's view, the motives for virtuous conduct but not the source of moral obligation, which in Locke's view was God and the rational moral order he created. Despite the rejection of Strauss's view by scholars of Locke, his interpretation of Locke's thought as secular, hedonist, relativist, and egoist continues to be influential, especially among conservatives. (For a response to Yolton by a follower of Strauss, see Zuckert 2002:39–41, 98–100.)

In the selection included here, A. John Simmons, the author of several books on Locke's political thought, attempts to resolve the controversies about the place of God, natural law, and pleasure and pain in Locke's moral thinking by arguing that Locke's theory was based on "more than one foundational stance." Locke, he argues, believed that we can know by reason that God had created the laws of nature (natural theology) and designed them in a way that they would bring the best results over the long run (rule-utilitarianism), including man's long-run pleasure and pain (hedonism), and made them available to men as rational and moral beings who are aware that they are free and equal (Kantianism). Where others have found contradictions in Locke, Simmons finds "moral overdetermination but not conceptual incoherence," so that the secular and religious aspects of his thought are separable but not opposed. Seeing Locke as a transitional figure between two "pictures of our moral condition"—earlier theocentric theories based on obligations to God and more modern anthropocentric ones based on the mutual recognition of moral equality—Simmons concludes that there is no obvious incoherence in combining them as Locke does. Simmons also links the religious elements in his thinking to more communitarian and socially oriented interpretations of his work. He also argues that more secular views of Locke, which ignore his theistically grounded belief in moral and social obligations to others, have led to the more individualistic and libertarian interpretations that have been given to his thought in recent years.

LEO STRAUSS

From Natural Right and History†

*   *   *

At first glance Locke seems to reject altogether Hobbes's notion of natural law and to follow the traditional teaching. He certainly speaks of man's natural rights as if they were derivative from the law of nature, and he accordingly speaks of the law of nature as if it were a law in the strict sense of the term. The law of nature imposes perfect duties on man as man, regardless of whether he lives in the state of nature or in civil society. "The law of nature stands as an eternal rule to all men," for it is "plain and intelligible to all rational creatures." It is identical with "the law of reason." It is "knowable by the light of nature; that is, without the help of positive revelation." Locke considers it entirely possible for the law of nature or the moral law to be raised to the rank of a demonstrative science. That science would make out "from self-evident propositions, by necessary consequences . . . the measures of right and wrong." Man would thus become able to elaborate "a body of ethics, proved to be the law of nature, from principles of reason,

---

† From *Natural Right and History* (Chicago: University of Chicago Press, 1953). Reprinted by permission of The University of Chicago Press.

and teaching all the duties of life," or "the entire body of the 'law of nature,' " or "complete morality," or a "code" which give us the law of nature "entire." That code would contain, among other things, the natural penal law. Yet Locke never made a serious effort to elaborate that code. His failure to embark on this great enterprise was due to the problem posed by theology.

The law of nature is a declaration of the will of God. It is "the voice of God" in man. It can therefore be called the "law of God" or "divine law" or even the "eternal law"; it is "the highest law." It is the law of God not only in fact. It must be known to be the law of God in order to be law. Without such knowledge man cannot act morally. For "the true ground of morality . . . can only be the will and law of a God." The law of nature can be demonstrated because the existence and the attributes of God can be demonstrated. This divine law is promulgated, not only in or by reason, but by revelation as well. In fact, it first became known to man in its entirely by revelation, but reason confirms this divine law thus revealed. This does not mean that God did not reveal to man some laws which are purely positive: the distinction between the law of reason, which obliges man as man, and the law revealed in the gospel, which obliges Christians, is preserved by Locke.

One may wonder whether what Locke says about the relation between the law of nature and the revealed law is free from difficulties. However this may be, his teaching is exposed to a more fundamental and more obvious difficulty, to a difficulty which seems to endanger the very notion of a law of nature. He says, on the one hand, that, in order to be a law, the law of nature must not only have been given by God, but it must in addition have as its sanctions divine "rewards and punishments, of infinite weight and duration, in another life." On the other hand, however, he says that reason cannot demonstrate that there is another life.[1] Only through revelation do we know of the sanctions for the law of nature or of "the only true touchstone of moral rectitude." Natural reason is therefore unable to know the law of nature as a law. This would mean that there does not exist a law of nature in the strict sense.

* * *

1. Strauss's confusing footnotes, which list many references for each section, have been omitted. They include a number of references to Locke's statements that certainty about morality can be achieved only through divine revelation of the existence of eternal rewards and punishments. They also include, however, a reference to Locke's 1694 addition to the *Essay Concerning Human Understanding* 2.28.8 (see p. 194 herein) that states that the divine law can be known by "the light of reason." For Locke's views on the afterlife, see the *Essay Concerning Human Understanding* 2.28.60 ("endless happiness or eternal misery"); 2.28.70 ("everlasting bliss . . . dreadful state of misery . . . or at best . . . annihilation"); 4.20.3 ("everlasting happiness or misery"). [see pp. 187, 188, and 197 herein]. All notes are the editor's unless otherwise specified.

Yet, however much Locke may have followed tradition in the *Treatise*, already a summary comparison of its teaching with the teachings of Hooker and of Hobbes would show that Locke deviated considerably from the traditional natural law teaching and followed the lead given by Hobbes. There is, indeed only one passage in the *Treatise* in which Locke explicitly notes that he deviates from Hooker. But the passage draws our attention to a radical deviation. After having quoted Hooker, Locke says: "But I, moreover, affirm that all men are naturally in [the state of nature]." He thus suggests that, according to Hooker, some men were in fact or accidentally in the state of nature. Actually, Hooker had not said anything about the state of nature: the whole doctrine of the state of nature is based on a break with Hooker's principles, i.e., with the principles of the traditional natural law doctrine.[2] * * *

* * *

The law of nature cannot be truly a law if it is not effective in the state of nature. It cannot be effective in the state of nature if the state of nature is not a state of peace. The law of nature imposes on everyone the perfect duty of preserving the rest of mankind, "as much as he can," but only "when his own preservation comes not in competition." If the state of nature were characterized by habitual conflict between self-preservation and the preservation of others, the law of nature which "willeth the peace and preservation of all mankind" would be ineffectual: the higher claim of self-preservation would leave no room for concern with others. The state of nature must therefore be "a state of peace, good-will, mutual assistance, and preservation." This means that the state of nature must be a social state; in the state of nature all men "make up one society" by virtue of the law of nature, although they have no "common superior on earth." Inasmuch as self-preservation requires food and other necessities, and scarcity of such things leads to conflict, the state of nature must be a state of plenty: "God has given us all things richly." The law of nature cannot be a law if it is not known; it must be known and therefore it must be knowable in the state of nature.

After having drawn or suggested this picture of the state of nature especially in the first pages of the *Treatise*, Locke demolishes it as his argument proceeds. The state of nature, which at first glance seems to be the golden age ruled by God or good demons, is literally a state without government, "pure anarchy." It could last forever, "were it not for the corruption and viciousness of degenerate

2. In a footnote Strauss cites but does not reproduce Locke's quotation from Hooker, in *Second Treatise* no. 15, that the laws of nature "do bind men absolutely, even as they are men, although they have never any settled fellowship, never any solemn agreement amongst themselves what to do or not do." Locke takes this to be a description of the state of nature.

men"; but unfortunately "the greater part" are "no strict observers of equity and justice." For this reason, to say nothing of others, the state of nature has great "inconveniences." Many "mutual griev-ances, injuries, and wrongs . . . attend men in the state of nature"; "strife and troubles would be endless" in it. It "is full of fears and continual dangers." It is "an ill condition." Far from being a state of peace, it is a state in which peace and quiet are uncertain. The state of peace is civil society; the state antedating civil society is the state of war. This is either the cause or the effect of the fact that the state of nature is a state not of plenty but of penury. Those liv-ing in it are "needy and wretched." Plenty requires civil society. Be-ing "pure anarchy," the state of nature is not likely to be a social state. In fact, it is characterized by "want of society." "Society" and "civil society" are synonymous terms. The state of nature is "loose." For "the first and strongest desire God planted in man" is not the concern with others, not even concern with one's offspring, but the desire for self-preservation.

* * *

What then is the status of the law of nature in Locke's doctrine? What is its foundation? There is no rule of the law of nature which is innate, "that is, . . . imprinted on the mind as a duty." This is shown by the fact that there are no rules of the law of nature, "which, as practical principles ought, do continue constantly to op-erate and influence all our actions without ceasing [and which] may be observed in all persons and all ages, steady and universal." However, "Nature . . . has put into man a desire of happiness, and an aversion to misery; these, indeed, are innate practical princi-ples": they are universally and unceasingly effective. The desire for happiness and the pursuit of happiness to which it gives rise are not duties. But "men . . . must be allowed to pursue their happi-ness, nay, cannot be hindered." The desire for happiness and the pursuit of happiness have the character of an absolute right, of a natural right. To understand how this is possible, one merely has to reformulate our last quotation: pursuit of happiness is a right, it "must be allowed," because "it cannot be hindered." It is a right an-tedating all duties for the same reason that, according to Hobbes, establishes as the fundamental moral fact the right of self-preservation: man must be allowed to defend his life against violent death because he is driven to do so by some natural necessity which is not less than that by which a stone is carried downward. Being universally effective, natural right, as distinguished from nat-ural duty, is effective in the state of nature: man in the state of na-ture is "absolute lord of his own person and possessions." Since the right of nature is innate, whereas the law of nature is not, the right

of nature is more fundamental than the law of nature and is the
foundation of the law of nature.

Since happiness presupposes life, the desire for life takes precedence over the desire for happiness in case of conflict. This dictate
of reason is at the same time a natural necessity: "the first and
strongest desire God planted in men, and wrought into the very
principles of their nature, is that of self-preservation." The most
fundamental of all rights is therefore the right of self-preservation.
While nature has put into man "a strong desire of preserving his
life and being," it is only man's reason which teaches him what is
"necessary and useful to his being." And reason—or, rather, reason
applied to a subject to be specified presently—is the law of nature.
Reason teaches that "he that is master of himself and his own life
has a right, too, to the means of preserving it." Reason further
teaches that, since all men are equal in regard to the desire, and
hence to the right, of self-preservation, they are equal in the decisive respect, notwithstanding any natural inequalities in other respects. From this Locke concludes, just as Hobbes did, that in the
state of nature everyone is the judge of what means are conducive
to his self-preservation, and this leads him, as it did Hobbes, to the
further conclusion that in the state of nature "any man may do
what he thinks fit."[3] No wonder, therefore, that the state of nature
is "full of fears and continual dangers." But reason teaches that life
cannot be preserved, let alone enjoyed, except in a state of peace:
reason wills peace. Reason therefore wills such courses of action as
are conducive to peace. Reason dictates, accordingly, that "no one
ought to harm another," that he who harms another—who therefore has renounced reason—may be punished by everyone and that
he who is harmed may take reparations. These are the fundamental
rules of the law of nature on which the argument of the *Treatise* is
based: the law of nature is nothing other than the sum of the dictates of reason in regard to men's "mutual security" or to "the peace
and safety" of mankind. Since in the state of nature all men are
judges in their own cases and since, therefore, the state of nature is
characterized by constant conflict that arises from the very law of
nature, the state of nature is "not to be endured": the only remedy
is government or civil society. Reason accordingly dictates how civil
society must be constructed and what its rights or bounds are:
there is a rational public law or a natural constitutional law. The
principle of that public law is that all social or governmental power

3. Strauss documents the quotation with a footnote to *Second Treatise*, no. 94. However, in
   a similar earlier passage (*Second Treatise*, 4), Locke says that in the state of nature, all
   men can "dispose of their possessions and their persons, as they think fit *within the
   bounds of the law of nature*" [emphasis added]. See also *Second Treatise*, no. 128, for a
   similar statement.

is derivative from powers which by nature belong to the individuals. The contract of the individuals actually concerned with their self-preservation—not the contract of the fathers qua fathers or divine appointment or an end of man that is independent of the actual wills of all individuals—creates the whole power of society: "the supreme power in every commonwealth [is] but the joint power of every member of the society."

Locke's natural law teaching can then be understood perfectly if one assumes that the laws of nature which he admits are, as Hobbes put it, "but conclusions, or theorems concerning what conduces to the conservation and defense" of man over against other men. And it must be thus understood, since the alternative view is exposed to the difficulties which have been set forth. The law of nature, as Locke conceives of it, formulates the conditions of peace or, more generally stated, of "public happiness" or "the prosperity of any people." There is therefore a kind of sanction for the law of nature in this world: the disregard of the law of nature leads to public misery and penury. * * *

* * *

Locke's teaching on property, and therewith his whole political philosophy, are revolutionary not only with regard to the biblical tradition but with regard to the philosophic tradition as well. Through the shift of emphasis from natural duties or obligations to natural rights, the individual, the ego, had become the center and origin of the moral world, since man—as distinguished from man's end—had become that center or origin. Locke's doctrine of property is a still more "advanced" expression of this radical change than was the political philosophy of Hobbes. According to Locke, man and not nature, the work of man and not the gift of nature, is the origin of almost everything valuable: man owes almost everything valuable to his own efforts. Not resigned gratitude and consciously obeying or imitating nature but hopeful self-reliance and creativity become henceforth the marks of human nobility. Man is effectively emancipated from the bonds of nature, and therewith the individual is emancipated from those social bonds which antedate all consent or compact, by the emancipation of his productive acquisitiveness, which is necessarily, if accidentally, beneficent and hence susceptible of becoming the strongest social bond: restraint of the appetites is replaced by a mechanism whose effect is humane. And that emancipation is achieved through the intercession of the prototype of conventional things, i.e., money. The world in which human creativity seems to reign supreme is, in fact, the world which has replaced the rule of nature by the rule of convention. From now on, nature furnishes only the worthless materials as in themselves; the forms are supplied by man, by man's free creation. For there are no natural forms, no intelligible "essences": "the abstract ideas" are "the inventions and creatures of the understanding, made by it for its own use." Understanding and science stand in the same relation to "the given" in which human labor, called forth to its supreme effort by money, stands to the raw materials. There are, therefore, no natural principles of understanding: all knowledge is acquired; all knowledge depends on labor and is labor.

Locke is a hedonist: "That which is properly good or bad, is nothing but barely pleasure or pain." But his is a peculiar hedonism: "The greatest happiness consists" not in enjoying the greatest pleasures but "in the having those things which produce the greatest pleasures." It is not altogether an accident that the chapter in which these statements occur, and which happens to be the most extensive chapter of the whole *Essay*, is entitled "Power." For if, as Hobbes says, "the power of a man . . . is his present means, to obtain some future apparent good," Locke says in effect that the greatest happiness consists in the greatest power. Since there are no knowable natures, there is no nature of man with reference to which we could distinguish between pleasures which are against nature, or between pleasures which are by nature higher and pleasures which are by nature lower: pleasure and pain are "for different mer . . . very different things." Therefore, "the philosophers of old did in vain inquire, whether *summum bonum* consisted in riches, or bodily delights, or virtue, or contemplation?" In the absence of a *summum bonum*, man would lack completely a star and compass for his life if there were no *summum malum*. "Desire is always moved by evil, to fly it." The strongest desire is the desire for self-preservation. The evil from which the strongest desire recoils is death. Death must then be the greatest evil: Not the natural sweetness of living but the terrors of death make us cling to life. What nature firmly establishes is that from which desire moves away, the point of departure of desire; the goal toward which desire moves is secondary. The primary fact is want. But this want, this lack, is no longer understood as pointing to something complete, perfect, whole. The necessities of life are no longer understood as necessary *for* the complete life or the good life, but as mere inescapabilities. The satisfaction of wants is therefore no longer limited by the demands of the good life but becomes aimless. The goal of desire is defined by nature only negatively—the denial of pain. It is not pleasure more or less dimly anticipated which elicits human efforts: "the chief, if not only, spur to human industry and action is uneasiness." So powerful is the natural primacy of pain that the active denial of pain is itself painful. The pain which removes pain is labor. It is this pain, and hence a defect, which gives man originally the most important of all rights: sufferings and defects, rather than merits or virtues, originate rights. Hobbes identifies the rational life with the life dominated by the fear of fear, by the fear which relieves us from fear. Moved by the same spirit, Locke identifies the rational life with the life dominated by the pain which removes pain. Labor takes the place of the art which imitates nature; for labor is, in the words of Hegel, a negative attitude toward nature. The starting point of human efforts is misery: the state of nature is a state of wretchedness. The way toward happiness is a movement away from the state of nature, a movement away from nature: the negation of nature is the way toward happiness. And if the movement toward happiness is the actuality of freedom, freedom is negativity. Just like the primary pain itself, the pain which relieves pain "ceaseth only in death." Since there are therefore no pure pleasures, there is no necessary tension between civil society as the mighty leviathan or coercive society, on the one hand, and the good life, on the other: hedonism becomes utilitarianism or political hedonism. The painful relief of pain culminates not so much in the greatest pleasures as "in the having those things which produce the greatest pleasures." Life is the joyless quest for joy.

JOHN YOLTON

Strauss on Locke's Law of Nature†

* * *

* * * The * * * rationale for a reappraisal of Locke on the law of nature is the violently distorted interpretation recently advanced by Leo Strauss. Strauss did not have access to the published edition of the early essays[1] nor did he consult the Lovelace Collection of Locke manuscripts.[2] He might not be expected to have as full a view of Locke's theory as we can now have. But Strauss has gone to very particular pains to say that Locke was really a genuine Hobbist in his social theory, a claim Strauss pretends to demonstrate by minute attention to and quotation from the Locke corpus. It is not so much the obvious incorrectness of Strauss's reading which calls for comment as it is the techniques employed in support of his reading. Strauss has an ulterior reason for dealing with Locke as he

---

† From "Locke on the Law of Nature," *The Philosophical Review* 67. 4 (October 1958), by permission.
1. *Essays on the Law of Nature*. All notes are the editor's unless otherwise specified.
2. Acquired by the Bodleian Library at Oxford in the 1940s.

does: he claims that Locke's real doctrine has been purposely hidden under the show of respectability. It is not surprising that the Strauss esotericism[3] turns out to be insupportable when applied to Locke, but it is startling to discover the flimsiness of the pretended support and the unscholarly nature of Strauss's analysis. Strauss's general esotericist thesis suffers a severe blow when we consult the techniques he employs. * * *

*   *   *

* * * Strauss strives to extract from the Locke corpus, [four main] propositions necessary for his Hobbesian reading of Locke. These can be formulated as follows. (1) Natural law is opposed to and different from Scriptural law and is man-made, not the will of God. (2) Natural law is based on an innate natural right for happiness or self-preservation, the natural law being that law required by man to protect his own self-interest. (3) The sanction for the natural law is pleasure and pain, rewards and punishments; natural law has a hedonistic basis. (4) The state of nature is full of conflict; every man can do what he wants. All four of these are Hobbesian principles and all except (3) were expressly rejected by Locke. * * *

*   *   *

If the Scripture contains the full law of nature, Locke should have written, Strauss claims, a politics taken from the Scripture. Since what he wrote was *Two Treatises*, he must have found it impossible to write the Scriptural politics. * * * The alternative to a Scriptural politics should have been, Strauss argues, a demonstrative politics; or at least the basis of political society, that is, natural law, should be capable of being demonstrated. Strauss's understanding of Locke at this point is rather naive. Truths are either *revealed* by Scripture or *demonstrated* by reason. But reason performs another important function for Locke: it intuits those self-evident truths embodied in the law of nature. The precise relation between the law of nature, positive law, and the rules for ethical actions are not always clear from what Locke says. The doctrine of the law of nature contains the body of rules or precepts necessary for making individual and social action moral. It is not entirely clear what Locke understood by a demonstrative ethics, but a listing of some of the rules claimed by him as knowable by the light of reason or as laws of nature strongly suggests that the moral rules which compose the law of nature could not be derived in any form, demonstrative or otherwise, from a general law.

The light of reason not only knows there is a God who is supreme lawmaker; it knows very specific rules as derivable from the law of nature. The following rules—by no means all that

3. Belief in hidden meanings.

STRAUSS ON LOCKE'S LAW OF NATURE   283

one can find—are taken from the early *Essays* and the *Second Treatise*.

(1) Love and respect and worship God (*Essays*, p. 195).
(2) Obey your superiors (*ibid.*, p. 129).
(3) Tell the truth and keep your promises (*ibid.*).
(4) Be mild and pure of character and be friendly (*ibid.*).
(5) Do not offend or injure, without cause, any person's health, life, or possessions (*ibid.*, p. 163; T II, 6).
(6) Be candid and friendly in talking about other people (*Essays*, p. 195).
(7) Do not kill or steal (*ibid.*).
(8) Love your neighbor and your parents (*ibid.*).
(9) Console a distressed neighbor (*ibid.*).
(10) Feed the hungry (*ibid.*).
(11) "Who so sheddeth man's blood, by man shall his blood be shed" (T II, 11).
(12) That property is mine which I have acquired through my labor, so long as I can use it before it spoils (T II, 29–30).
(13) Parents are to preserve, nourish, and educate their children (T II, 56).

It would seem a gross overstatement to argue that all of these concrete rules are derivable from a law of nature which is apprehended by the function of reason and sense. In fact, it is clearly impossible to derive these precepts from any single principle, whether it be innate, the light of reason, or a standard agreed upon by men. What these rules do is to disclose the moral framework in terms of which Locke examined society and civil government. Some of them are the same rules which his contemporaries claimed to be innate. All of them perform the same function as the principles said to be innate: they provide the moral foundation for his views on individuals and social action. Just as the line of argument for those who believed in innate ideas was that certain moral rules are correct because they are innate, so Locke's main defense for any moral rule is to say it is known to be true by the light of reason, that it is a law of nature. He nowhere formulates a general maxim which he calls "the law of nature." There is no such single and general law. The law of nature turns out to be a list of laws, all of which are apparent to the rational being. These laws are taken as finding their justification in God, as being God's will. All positive law must, to be justified, be a reinforcement of these natural moral laws.

*   *   *

Strauss is not quickly put down, however. In *Human Understanding*, Bk. I, ch. iii, sect. 3, Locke had said: "Nature, I confess, has put into man a desire of happiness and aversion to misery: these in-

deed are innate practical principles." This is enough to enable
Strauss to conclude that the foundation for the law of nature is an
innate natural right, the right to happiness. This is a right "antedating all duties. . . . Since the right of nature is more fundamental
than the law of nature and is the foundation of the law of nature"
(p. 227). But Strauss need only to have finished the sentence he
quotes to discover that Locke meant to contrast desires and aversions with impressions of truth upon the understanding. Only the
latter are properly called "innate practical principles." The rest of
the sentence clarifies his point by saying that the desire for happiness and the aversion to pain are "inclinations of the appetite." * * *
The whole point of this passage in *Human Understanding* is to draw
just this distinction. It is an odd kind of perversity on Strauss's part
which keeps him from finishing Locke's sentence and prevents his
readers from seeing the correct meaning of Locke's statements. The
laws of nature are innate in the dispositional sense but the instinct
and appetites of men are nowhere said by Locke to be innate, although they are natural to the organism. The only possible connection for Locke between the laws of nature and the desire for
happiness is that a life lived in accordance with the laws of nature
will be a happy life. God has, "by an inseparable connection, joined
virtue and public happiness together" (*Human Understanding*,
Bk. I, ch. ii, sect. 6 * * *). The laws are in no way a consequence
of what will make men happy.

*   *   *

* * * There is a clear difference for Locke between obligation
and motivation. The law of nature obligates because it is the will of
a superior. A right is the free use we have of something, while a law
is the rule which enjoins or forbids the doing of something. Rights
are those acts men are allowed to do by the precepts of the laws of
nature. The things these laws require are obligations. The relation
between right and obligation is that we are obliged to do what it is
right for someone to require us to do. It is the recognition of this
relation between right and obligation which should be the proper
moral sanction leading us to meet our obligations: "not fear of punishment, but a rational apprehension of right puts us under an obligation" (*Essays*, p. 185). But the rational apprehension of right is
insufficient to motivate us to action.

*   *   *

* * * [W]e may object to Locke's denial that obligation is sufficient by itself to motivate. * * * [According to Locke] it takes the
expectations of rewards and punishments to lead men to *obey* the
dictates of the law of nature. The laws of nature are not, as they
were for Hobbes, the *consequences* of the desire for rewards and
the fear of punishment.

* * *

In line with his Hobbesian distortion of Locke, Strauss has to make Locke's state of nature as nasty and brutish as Hobbes's. Accordingly, Strauss plays upon those phrases used by Locke which characterize the "uncertainties" and "inconveniences" of the state of nature (pp. 224–225). Locke meant to contrast the settled, just, and harmonious conditions of civil society with the disordered and uncertain conditions, even perversions of the laws, in the state of nature. But Strauss takes this contrast so far that he can say "the state antedating the civil society is the state of war" (p. 225). Most of the references Strauss gives at this point find Locke setting up the opposition between civil society and the state of war; Locke never identifies the state of war with the state of nature. Locke was not so naive as to believe all men act rationally all the time. He carefully makes his civil society a society of rational men. The theory of punishment, which seems so harsh, was motivated by his firm conviction that the laws of nature specify the conditions for humanity. To violate these laws is tantamount to renouncing one's humanity. Some men are perverse and self-seeking but it is a gross misreading of Locke to claim he really believed that life in the state of nature (at whatever level) resembles Hobbe's war of all against all. The reasonable man will discover the laws of nature and will strive to order his life in terms of them. The state of nature is characterized by the inconveniences of no written law, no just and reasonable administration of the law, even by whole groups seeking to interpret the law in their favor. The state of war "is a state of enmity and destruction; and therefore declaring by word or action, not a passionate and hasty, but sedate, settled design upon another man's life puts him in a state of war with him against whom he has declared such an intention" (T II, 16). The state of nature, even in its primitive forms, is not characterized by every man having these deliberate designs upon others. In his *Letter on Toleration*, Locke spoke of the "pravity of mankind being such, that they had rather injuriously prey upon the fruits of other men's labors than take pains to provide themselves." He even traces the need for civil society to this depravity of man. But the perversity of men was for Locke a deviation from the norm, the state of war was sharply and carefully differentiated from the state of nature, and the state of nature pertains to many complex political units organized on principles other than those of Locke's civil polity. There is no ground at all for equating Locke's concept of the state of nature with that in Hobbes. * * *

A. JOHN SIMMONS

From The Lockean Theory of Rights†

* * *

I do not think Locke saw these secular and religious conceptions of humankind and morality as inconsistent. As a result we find in Locke a variety of styles of argument for moral conclusions, sitting side by side and without any explanation of their differences. Some arguments appeal directly to God's will; others appeal to it indirectly by rule-consequentialist reasoning, * * * still others appeal to it not at all. Of this third (secular) class, some of the arguments are purely conceptual, while others appeal for their moral force to a particular view of the person as free and equal, rational and valuing. The force of these last arguments is best captured in Kantian[1] terms. Locke seems not to want to explicitly explore their potential for a nontheological ethics, emphasizing throughout his work that only God's will can make actions obligatory. But it is precisely this potential that makes intelligible claims to be pursuing a secular, but nonetheless Lockean project in moral and political philosophy. To a certain extent, what Locke is doing is detaching some of his derivations of the specific content of morality from his view of what makes that content obligatory. But seen in another way, Locke is simply working from more than one foundational stance at a time. The result of this is that in his political philosophy we find Locke employing arguments that are designed to appeal both to those who see the secular ends of the state as good in themselves and to those who see them only as means to religious ends. Not only, then, do secular, Kantian enterprises in political philosophy have the machinery to produce the content of Locke's theory. They capture some of its spirit as well.

* * *

The various styles of argument at work in Locke create several problems. At the interpretive level, they allow interpreters to find almost whatever they are looking for in Locke (and to conveniently dismiss the rest as unimportant or confusing), accounting for the astonishingly wide range of interpretations of Locke's "real position" over the years. * * * Locke's arguments suggest that he be-

---

† From *The Lockean Theory of Rights* (Princeton, NJ: Princeton University Press, 1992). Copyright © 1992 Princeton University Press. Reprinted by permission of Princeton University Press.

1. Immanuel Kant (1724–1804), a moral philosopher who based his ethics on the "categorical imperative," the requirement that one act on rational principles that can be applied equally to all mankind. All notes are the editor's unless otherwise specified.

lieved (as we might well) that there are many different kinds of equally good moral reasons all backing one individualist position.

* * *

* * * The natural law theories of Aquinas[2] and Locke stand out as high water marks in the shifting tides of theory, making it interesting to ask this question: What in their respective views of our moral position allows rights to play so much more central a role in Locke than in Aquinas? Any adequate answer, of course, must emphasize the role of God in moral relations, God being at the center of the moral landscape for both philosophers. I want to begin * * * by presenting two pictures of our moral condition in the bluntest possible terms. I suggest neither that these were the respective views of Aquinas and Locke nor that either picture was ever embraced by anyone in so unsophisticated a form. Indeed, the differences between the pictures are largely a matter of emphasis. But this contrast in emphasis is helpful, I think, in understanding the moral fence Locke straddles.

(a) *The First Picture:* God occupies the center of this picture in the fullest possible sense. His creation of the universe and His plan for humankind allow Him to give binding law to us. Our moral duties are owed to God, as creator, moral lawgiver, and sovereign. Importantly, God stands at the center of all moral relations, as a kind of intermediary. Each of us has duties not to harm others, but these duties are owed to God. The benefits others receive as a consequence of our performance of our duties are in part the point of these duties. But other persons exert no direct "ethical pull" on us. Others are to be respected not so much for themselves, but for their status as God's property and parts of His plan. Our moral status is thus largely that of a tool, a cog, a part of some larger enterprise, and the appropriate virtues for such a being are obedience, humility, and industry. Another's property, of course, merits a kind of respect that is rather thin. When I break your shovel (even if it is quite a wonderful shovel), I wrong you, not the shovel. Similarly, breaches of our moral duties to treat others well are in the first instance wrongs done to God, and only derivatively wrongs done to others. This sort of "moral occasionalism" permits me to argue that "to God only have I sinned" even when I have harmed other persons.

Where do rights enter this picture? God has rights of a sort, of course, over His property, although it is in a way demeaning to God to conceive of these as rights, exactly—as if they were mere claims

---

2. St. Thomas Aquinas (1225–1274), medieval theologian who developed an influential theory of natural law, based on the philosophical principles of Aristotle (387–23 B.C.E.).

held against others. The more appropriate emphasis is on our duties of obedience and worship. And we can perhaps also have rights, as third party beneficiaries of duties owed to God (according to certain theories of rights). These rights would, of course, belong to the class of "protected liberties," for the moral freedom to act would be protected by others' duties owed to God. But there is in this picture no room for claim rights of the sort we have discussed, involving pressable (and waivable) claims against those bound by the corresponding duties. Against whom could such claims be pressed? Presumably it would be both unwise and conceptually odd to press claims against the God to whom others' duties are due. For several reasons, then, in this first picture rights-talk is naturally suppressed.

(b) *The Second Picture:* God is still central in this picture, although He is not at the center of all moral relations in the same way. While God is still creator, planner, and lawgiver, the ends promoted by God's law are now seen as "detachable," so that the law is now more *for* us and less *over* us. The law's facilitation of humans' own ends is in this picture as prominent as its facilitation of God's ends. Our fellow persons are not now seen just as God's creatures but as our equals in other ways; their rationality, purposiveness, and manifest similarities to ourselves require that they be taken seriously in themselves. Moral relations hold directly between persons as well as between persons and God, as others exert a "pull" on us. Breaking God's law can involve wronging others directly, so that we have duties that are *owed* to others, not just duties *with respect* to others (the other is not just the "occasion" of the wrong, but the one actually wronged). The deeper equality this signals both requires a different order of respect and makes different virtues appropriate for us. Self-assertion can now be based on a conception of one's independent worth, on the dignity of being "one's own person" (which brings with it, of course, new stances with regard to consent, obligation, obedience, and resistance).

In this second picture, rights naturally move into sharper focus, along with making and pressing claims concerning one's *due*. "Duty," of course, had to do precisely with what was "due" another, typically by virtue of superior status. The claim of status "pulls" duties to it. In the first picture, God's is the relevant moral status to which our duties are pulled, but the "rights" of one who is Omnipotent need no special emphasis. In the second picture, every person enjoys a status that is also the ground of a "due"; but emphasis on our rights is not at all pointless. Duty's primacy in the first picture stems from the gross inequality of the parties concerned (God and humankind). Once the relevant parties are conceived of as equals, rights take a more prominent place.

The two pictures just described, while no better than caricatures of any philosopher's actual views, do capture, I think, a shift in thinking about moral relations that was still taking place when Locke wrote. This shift corresponded, of course, to more obvious changes in economic and social organization and to changes in more inclusive theological and political theories (on which I shall not comment here). My intention in presenting these pictures is only to try to better locate the character of Locke's theory of rights. By contrast with the conceptual scheme for Aquinas' natural law theory, which inclines toward the first picture, Locke's moral-conceptual framework seems to be an attempt to embrace both pictures at once. It is hardly surprising that Locke, who lived "in a 'transitional' society," should employ a conceptual scheme which is also transitional. Locke works with both pictures, or, better, with a kind of synthesis of the two, emphasizing the chief characteristics now of one and now of the other (as his rhetorical, political, and theoretical concerns dictate), trying always to leave room for both. Locke stands near a crossroads. On the one hand, he emphasizes God's rights—His right of creation, His right to our obedience to His law (E, 2.28.8).[3] But Locke also stresses our rights, for reason and its law is what "God hath given to be the rule *betwixt man and man*" (II, 172; my emphasis; see also II, 181).[4] Strong elements of both pictures are thus prominently displayed in Locke's work.

Is it theoretically coherent for Locke to work within both pictures at once? It is easy to see why one might think not, and why this judgment might lead one to dismiss those aspects of Locke's work that emphasize one or the other picture. If we focus on the centrality of rights in Locke, the person-to-person character of moral relations, and the secular arguments he offers, we can plainly see where Hobbesian and libertarian readings of Locke find their support, and whence come their claims for the priority of right. And it is just as easy to focus on those aspects of Locke more amenable to the first picture—the centrality of God, His rights over us, and the theological foundational arguments—and offer as a consequence a reading of Locke that bends too far in its avoidance of his more individualistic moments. Much of the recent history of Locke scholarship revolves around turning a blind eye to one or the other aspect of Locke's thought.

But we save Locke from no very terrible fate when we insist that he work entirely within one picture or the other. For there is no obvious incoherence involved in combining the two views. It is perfectly intelligible for our moral duties to be owed both to God and

3. "E": *Essay Concerning Human Understanding.*
4. "II": *Second Treatise.*

to other people, and for both God and people to be holders of cor-relative moral rights. We owe God obedience to His law because He is our creator and rightly superior lawmaker. We owe duties to others because of our natural equality as rational, purposive beings. There is only a kind of "moral overdetermination" in this view, but no conceptual incoherence. * * *

* * * His emphasis on God's ownership of and interest in hu-mankind as a whole points to the importance of the common good and to the collectivist, communitarian aspects of Locke's thought (the irresistible teleological[5] pull of natural law theory). His em-phasis on the natural equality, freedom, and purposiveness of per-sons points to the sanctity of each person's life and plans and to the individualist, libertarian aspects of his thought. But his Kantian rule-consequentialist arguments constitute a way of pulling the two lines together in what really amounts to a pluralist moral theory. The teleological and deontological[6] aspects of Locke's thought sit coherently together. Locke recognizes both collective and individ-ual goods, acknowledging that rights (and individual goods gener-ally) are not all there is to morality.

* * *

5. Goal-oriented.
6. Inherently valuable.

Locke as Apologist
for Capitalism

In the 1950s and 1960s, liberalism, as represented by the political theory of John Locke, was attacked from both the right and the left. The right was represented by Leo Strauss and his followers, who denounced him for departing from the classical tradition and replacing the idea that there are objective sources of value with the narrow pursuit of hedonism and Hobbesian self-preservation. The textual and interpretative flaws of this approach were pointed out in the preceding section. A second flawed interpretation coming from the left may be found in the writings of a Marxist-oriented Canadian political philosopher, C. B. Macpherson. In journal articles and an influential book (Macpherson, 1962), he also linked Locke to Hobbes, but now the two were seen as fellow apologists for "possessive individualism"—that is, bourgeois capitalism.

In an ingenious analysis of Locke's discussion of property he pointed to a previously unnoticed reference to a property right in "the turfs my servant has cut" (*Second Treatise*, 28) to prove that Locke justified the exploitation of wage labor. He also argued that Locke's description of the results of the invention of money removed the spoilage and sufficiency ("enough and as good for others") limits on property holding. In a less persuasive interpretation of the text he found in Locke the belief that those who did not hold property were not able to know or follow the law of reason and as such were not entitled to political representation. Macpherson concluded that the supposed tension between majority rule and individual property rights in Locke is resolved if we assume, as Locke did, that the majority is composed exclusively of property holders.

In the words of the early critic Alan Ryan, Locke emerges in Macpherson's interpretation as the defender of "the dictatorship of bourgeoisie." Ryan argues that Macpherson does not recognize the broader meaning of property in Locke as "life, liberty, and estate" so that even those without landed property still benefit from the protection of property rights. He outlines Locke's reasons for believing that the invention of money benefits all citizens, by making available, although in differing degrees, "enough and as good for others." He also quotes from Locke to demonstrate that he believed that all free men, not just property holders, are members of society who must give their consent to its basic institutions.

Since the Ryan article was written, the increased awareness of Locke's religious views has further served to undermine the Macpherson thesis, as well as that of Strauss. Locke's belief in the obligations of a divinely sanctioned natural law that requires that property be used for "the preservation of all mankind" places serious limits on the accumulation of property. (See James Tully, p. 328 herein. See also Richard Ashcraft in Harpham 1992, who accuses both Strauss and Macpherson of "monumental obtuseness" in ignoring the "massive evidence" that contradicts their positions [17].)

C. B. MACPHERSON

Locke and Possessive Individualism†

*   *   *

* * * Thus from two postulates, that men have a right to preserve their life, and that a man's labour is his own, Locke justifies individual appropriation of the produce of the earth which was originally given to mankind in common.

Now the individual appropriation justified by this argument has certain limitations; two of them are explicitly and repeatedly stated by Locke, a third has been taken (though wrongly, I shall argue) to have been necessarily implied by the logic of Locke's justification. First, a man may appropriate only as much as leaves 'enough, and as good' for others; this limit, explicitly stated by Locke, is clearly required by the justification, for *each* man has a right to his preservation and hence to appropriating the necessities of his life.

Secondly: 'As much as any one can make use of to any advantage of life before it spoils; so much he may by his labour fix a Property in. Whatever is beyond this, is more than his share, and belongs to others. Nothing was made by God for Man to spoil or destroy' [31].[1] Barter of the surplus purchasable produce of one's labour was permitted within this limit; no injury was done, no portion of the goods that belonged to others was destroyed, so long as nothing perished uselessly in the appropriator's hands [46]. Thirdly, the rightful appropriation appears to be limited to the amount a man can procure with his own labour; this seems necessarily implied in the justification, for it is 'the *Labour* of his Body, and the *Work* of his Hands' which, being mixed with nature's products, makes anything his property.

---

†   From *The Political Theory of Possessive Individualism: Hobbes to Locke* (New York: Oxford University Press, 1962), pp. 201–04, 211–12, 214, 215, 220–21, 245–46, 248–49, 252. Reprinted with the permission of Oxford University Press.
1. Numbers in brackets refer to section numbers of the *Second Treatise*. All notes are the editor's unless otherwise specified.

So far Locke has justified only appropriation of the fruits of the earth.

> But the *chief matter of Property* being now not the Fruits of the Earth, and the Beasts that subsist on it, but the *Earth it self*; . . . I think it is plain, that *Property* in that too is acquired as the former. *As much Land* as Man Tills, Plants, Improves, Cultivates, and can use the Product of, so much is his *Property*. He by his Labour does, as it were, inclose it from the Common [32].

No consent of the others is needed for this appropriation. For God commanded man to labour the earth, and so entitled him to appropriate whatever land he mixed his labour with; and besides, the original appropriation was not 'any prejudice to any other Man, since there was still enough, and as good left' for others [33].

The same limits to the appropriation of land as to the appropriation of its natural produce are implied in this justification. A man is entitled by these arguments to appropriate only as much as leaves 'enough and as good' for others, 'as much as he can use the product of', and as much as he has mixed his labour with.

It is instructive that Locke, speaking here mainly of the appropriation of land 'in the first Ages of the World, when Men were more in danger to be lost, by wandering from their Company, in the then vast Wilderness of the Earth, than to be straitned for want of room to plant in' [36], reads back into primitive society the institution of individual ownership of land, taking it for granted that that was the only way land could then be cultivated. His disregard of communal ownership and labour in primitive society allows him to say that 'the Condition of Humane Life, which requires Labour and Materials to work on, necessarily introduces *private Possesions*' [35].

If Locke had stopped here he would have had a defence of limited individual ownership, though the argument would have had to be stretched pretty far even to cover the property right of the contemporary English yeoman, for it would have to be shown that his appropriation left enough and as good for others. Locke does suggest such a defense in arguing that, 'full as the World seems', a man may still find enough and as good land in 'some in-land, vacant places of *America*' [36]. But he does not base his case on this. When we examine how he does make his case, we shall see that it is a case not for such limited appropriation, but for an unlimited natural right of appropriation, a right transcending the limitations involved in his initial justification.

The Limitations Transcended

The crucial argument has so often been misunderstood that it is necessary to examine it closely. The transition from the limited right to the unlimited right is first stated in sect. 36. After saying by including the vacant lands of America there may still be enough land in the world for everyone to have as much as he could work and use, Locke continues:

> But be this as it will, which I lay no stress on; This I dare boldly affirm, That the same *Rule of Propriety*, (*viz.*) that every Man should have as much as he could make use of, would hold still in the World, without straitning any body, since there is Land enough in the World to suffice double the Inhabitants had not the *Invention of Money*, and the tacit Agreement of Men to put a value on it, introduced (by Consent) larger Possessions, and a Right to them . . . [36].

This is quite explicit. The natural law rule, which by its specific terms limited the amount anyone could appropriate so that everyone could have as much as he could use, does *not* now hold; it 'would hold . . . had not . . . Money . . . introduced (by Consent) larger Possessions, and a Right to them'. The reason the rule does not now hold is not that the land has run out: there is enough in the whole world to suffice double the inhabitants, but only by including those parts of the world where money has never been introduced. There, where the old rule still holds, there are '*great Tracts* . . . which . . . *lie waste*', but 'this can scarce happen amongst that part of Mankind, that have consented to the Use of Money' [45]. Wherever money has been introduced there ceases to be unappropriated land. The introduction of money by tacit consent has removed the previous natural limitations of rightful appropriation, and in so doing has invalidated the natural provision that everyone should have as much as he could make use of. Locke then proceeds to show in more detail how the introduction of money removes the limitations inherent in his initial justification of individual appropriation.

(a) *The spoilage limitation.* Of the two limitations he had explicitly recognized, the second (as much as a man can use, or use the product of, before it spoils) seemed to Locke to be obviously transcended by the introduction of money. Gold and silver do not spoil; a man may therefore rightfully accumulate unlimited amounts of it, 'the *exceeding of the bounds of his* just *Property* not lying in the largeness of his Possession, but the perishing of any thing uselessly in it' [46]. Not only is the limit thus inapplicable to durable movable property; it is inapplicable by the same token to the land itself:

'a man may fairly possess more land than he himself can use the product of, by receiving in exchange for the overplus, Gold and Silver, which may be hoarded up without injury to any one, these metals not spoiling or decaying in the hands of the possessor' [50].

* * *

(b) *The sufficiency limitation.* We may now look at the limit on individual appropriation that Locke mentions first, i.e. that every appropriation must leave enough and as good for others. The limit is less obviously overcome by reference to the introduction of money by consent, yet there is no doubt that Locke took it to be overcome. The initial natural law rule, 'that every Man should have as much as he could make use of', does not hold after the invention of money [36]. In the first editions of the [*Second*] *Treatise* Locke provided no specific arguments on this point. Perhaps he thought it sufficiently evident to need no separate argument. His chain of thought seems to have been that the automatic consequence of the introduction of money is the development of a commercial economy, hence the creation of markets for the produce of land hitherto valueless, hence the appropriation of land not hitherto worth appropriating. And by implication, consent to the use of money is consent to the consequences. Hence an individual is justified in appropriating land even when it does not leave enough and as good for others.

While a case for the removal of the sufficiency limitation can be made out by inference in this way, Locke apparently felt that a more direct argument was needed, for in a revision of the third edition of the *Treatises* he added a new argument following the first sentence of sect. 37.

> To which let me add, that he who appropriates land to himself by his labour, does not lessen but increase the common stack of mankind. For the provisions serving to the support of humane[2] life, produced by one acre of inclosed and cultivated land, are (to speak much within compasse) ten times more, than those, which are yielded by an acre of Land, of equal richnesse, lyeing wast [*sic*] in common. And therefor he, that incloses Land and has a greater plenty of the conveniency of life from ten acres, than he could have from an hundred left to Nature, may be truly said, to give ninety acres to Mankind. For his labour now supplies him with provisions out of ten acres, which were but the product of an hundred lying in common.

Thus, although more land than leaves enough and as good for others may be appropriated, the greater productivity of the appropri-

---

2. Human.

ated land more than makes up for the lack of land available for others. This assumes, of course, that the increase in the whole product will be distributed to the benefit, or at least not to the loss, of those left without enough land. Locke makes this assumption. Even the landless day-labourer gets a bare subsistence. And bare subsistence, at the standard prevailing in a country where all the land is appropriated and fully used, is better than the standard of any member of a society where the land is not appropriated and fully worked: 'a King of a large and fruitful Territory there [among 'several nations of the *Americans*'] feeds, lodges, and is clad worse than a day Labourer in *England*' [41]. Private appropriation, in this way, actually increases the amount left for others. No doubt at some point, there is no longer as much left for others. But if there is not then enough and as good *land* left for others, there is enough as a good (indeed a better) *living* left for others. And the right of all men to a living was the fundamental right from which Locke had in the first place deduced their right to appropriate land. * * *

* * *

(c) *The supposed labour limitation.* The third apparently implied limitation on individual appropriation (only as much as one has mixed one's own labour with) seems the most difficult to transcend or remove, for it seems to be absolutely required by the very labour justification Locke has given for any appropriation. Surely, we may think, the onus is on Locke to show how this limitation, as well as the other two, may be considered to be overcome as a consequence of the introduction of money. But Locke did not think so. He did not need to do so, if all along he was assuming the validity of the wage relationship, by which a man may rightfully acquire a title to the labour of another. * * *

* * *

> Thus the Grass my Horse has bit; the Turfs my Servant has cut; and the Ore I have digg'd in any place where I have a right to them in common with others, become my *Property*, without the assignation or consent of any body. The *labour* that was mine, removing them out of that common state they were in, hath *fixed* my *Property* in them [28].

Had Locke not been taking the wage relationship entirely for granted, his inclusion of 'my servant's' labour in 'the labour that was mine', the labour whose expenditure gave me by natural right a title to the product, would have been a direct contradiction of the case he was making.

* * *

Locke's Achievement

When Locke's assumptions are understood as presented here, his doctrine of property appears in a new light, or, rather, is restored to the meaning it must have had for Locke and his contemporaries. For on this view his insistence that a man's labour was his own—which was the essential novelty of Locke's doctrine of property—has almost the opposite significance from that more generally attributed to it in recent years; it provides a moral foundation for bourgeois appropriation. With the removal of the two initial limitations which Locke had explicitly recognized, the whole theory of property is a justification of the natural right not only to unequal property but to an unlimited individual appropriation. The insistence that a man's labour is his own property is the root of this justification. For to insist that a man's labour is his own, is not only to say that it is his to alienate in a wage contract; it is also to say that his labour, and its productivity, is something for which he owes no debt to civil society. If it is his labour, a man's absolute property, which justifies appropriation and creates value, the individual right of appropriation overrides any moral claims of the society. The traditional view that property and labour were social functions, and that ownership of property involved social obligations, is thereby undermined.

In short, Locke has done what he set out to do. Starting from the traditional assumption that the earth and its fruits had originally been given to mankind for their common use, he has turned the tables on all who derived from this assumption theories which were restrictive of capitalist appropriation. He has erased the moral disability with which unlimited capitalist appropriation had hitherto been handicapped. * * *

* * *

* * * [W]hen man in general is * * * conceived in the image of bourgeois rational man, the natural condition of man is eminently rational and peaceable. This, I suggest, is the first of Locke's two concepts of the state of nature, and it owes as much to his comprehension of bourgeois society as to the tradition of Christian natural law.

Locke's other concept of the state of nature is more directly related to a concept of society which is more markedly bourgeois, namely the concept of human society in which there is an inherent class differential in rationality. The seventeenth-century bourgeois observer could scarcely fail to see a deep-rooted difference between the rationality of the poor and that of the men of some property. The difference was in fact a difference in their ability or willingness to order their own lives according to the bourgeois moral code. But to the bourgeois observer this appeared to be a difference in men's ability to order their lives by moral rules as such. * * * When this class differential in rational morality is read back into the nature of man, it results in a state of nature that is unsafe and insecure. For to say, as Locke did, that the greater part of men are incapable of guiding their lives by the law or reason, without sanctions, is to say that a civil society with legal sanctions (and a church with spiritual sanctions) is needed to keep them in order. Without these sanctions, i.e. in the state of nature, there could be no peace.

* * *

The question whom Locke considered to be members of civil society seems to admit of only one answer. Everyone, whether or not he had property in the ordinary sense, is included, as having an interest in preserving his life and liberty. At the same time only those with 'estate' can be full members for two reasons: only they have a full interest in the preservation of property, and only they are fully capable of that rational life—that voluntary obligation to the law of reason—which is the necessary basis of full participation in civil society. The labouring class, being without estate, are subject to, but not full members of, civil society. If it be objected that this is not one answer but two inconsistent answers, the reply must be that both answers follow from Locke's assumptions, and that neither one alone, but only the two together, accurately represent Locke's thinking.

The ambiguity as to who are members of civil society by virtue of the supposed original contract allows Locke to consider all men as members for purposes of being ruled and only the men of estate as members for the purposes of ruling. The right to rule (more accurately the right to control any government) is given to men of estate only: it is they who are given the decisive voice on taxation, without which no government can subsist. On the other hand, the obligation to be bound by law and subject to lawful government is fixed on all men whether or not they have property in the sense of estate, and indeed whether or not they have made an express compact. When Locke broadens his doctrine of express consent into a doctrine of tacit consent he * * * is explicit that the tacit consent which is assumed to be given by all such men does not make them full members of society: 'Nothing can make any Man so, but his actually entering into it by positive Engagement, and express Promise and Compact' [122]. And the only men who are assumed to incorporate themselves in any commonwealth by express compact are those who have some property, or the expectation of some property, in land [120]. * * *

* * *

Majority Rule v. Property Right

The implicit contradiction in that interpretation of Locke's theory which emphasizes the supremacy of the majority is also cleared. The contradiction, it will be remembered, was between the assertion of majority rule and the insistence on the sanctity of individual property. If the men of no property were to have full political rights, how could the sanctity of existing property institutions be expected to be maintained against the rule of the majority? This was no fanciful problem. When it had been raised during the Civil War all the men of property had seen the impossibility of combining majority rule and property rights. And Locke assumed, correctly, that the propertyless were a majority in England at the time he wrote. But we can now see that there is no confluct between Locke's two assertions, of majority rule and of property right, inasmuch as Locke was assuming that only those with property were full members of society and so of the majority.

* * *

ALAN RYAN

Locke and the Dictatorship of the Bourgeoisie†

* * *

The essence of Macpherson's account is that Locke intends to supply the moral basis of that stage of economic advance which we have called the dictatorship of the bourgeoisie; this is a state of unrestrained capitalism, brutal in its treatment of the labouring classes, ruthless in its destruction of traditional values, of all social ties that impede the advance of the propertied classes. Locke is thus arguing for nothing less than the rightful absolute power of the propertied classes, for a morally justified tyranny of the employers over the employed. Indeed, the labouring and the unemployed classes have their rights so ruthlessly eroded that their status is to be subject to civil society without being full members of it; they are in it but not of it. * * *

I

The twin pivots upon which Macpherson's account turns are the premises he ascribes to Locke of the natural proprietorship of one's

† From *Political Studies*, 13 (1965), 219–30. Reprinted with the permission of Blackwell Publishers.

own labour, and the dependence of freedom and morality, and hence citizenship, upon the possession of rationality. These are, of course, important elements in Locke's political theory; to Macpherson they account for the whole of this theory. They are central, vital, and closely connected. Rationality is evinced by (sometimes it seems that Macpherson is saying it is identified with) the ability to acquire goods and go on acquiring them up to the limits set by the Law of Nature. A rational man is one who obeys the law of Reason, and the law of reason is in turn the Law of Nature, and this is the will of God. Given such a gloss on what it is to be rational, the argument clearly runs that it is morally excellent to accumulate, that success in accumulating is a moral virtue, and hence that the man of property is of greater moral worth than the man without property. In the state of nature before the invention of money the title to property is given by labour, for in the state of nature each man is originally the unconditional owner of his own labour. This doctrine is, on Macpherson's account of it, an important and indeed a decisive break with medieval attitudes to labour and property, which were concerned to emphasize the obligations of a man to society and to his fellows, not his rights against them. So the rational man sets about accumulating property, and because his right to it is derived from his absolute right to his own labour, this right is absolute, too.

*   *   *

* * * In these passages, says Macpherson, 'property' means what we normally mean by the term, and refers particularly to property in fixed capital goods. From this it follows 'the people' to whom Locke entrusts the right of rebellion cannot be the whole population, but must be the propertied classes only. The grounds of revolt are comprised under the heading of the government failing to preserve the property of citizens; since very few people have any property, only this small number have any right to rebel. Labourers without property are in any case not fully rational—as demonstrated by the fact that they have no property—and therefore have no claim to full membership of civil society.

> 'While the labouring class is a necessary part of the nation its members are not in fact full members of the body politic and have no claim to be so . . . Whether by their own fault or not, members of the labouring class did not have, could not be expected to have, and were not entitled to have full membership in political society' [Macpherson, *Possessive Individualism*, 1962:221, 227].

As something less than full members of political society, they are objects of administration rather than citizens. This part of Macpherson's case is a crucial one, and my criticism of Macpherson's interpretation of Locke is largely concerned with this part of his account. An added merit Macpherson claims for his account is that it disposes of such riddles as Locke's basing obligation upon consent. If 'the people' are in fact the propertied classes, then they will readily give their consent to whatever the legislative enacts, since what is enacts will always be in their class-interest, and the interest of the class against the rest of society is more vital to each member of it than is his own interest against other members of his class. The state has thus become a committee for managing the common interests of bourgeoisie. Naturally this also solves the clash between the individualist and collectivist elements in Locke's thought. To behave as an extreme individualist is to behave as a successful capitalist, and this is to achieve moral excellence; it is however a form of moral excellence only possible at the expense of those against whom one competes successfully, and those whose labour one uses to enrich oneself. Hence what is needed by the individualists is a strong government which will hold the ring for their competition. Its strength is no threat to them, since it is a blatant instrument of class-rule. * * *

*   *   *

Confining ourselves to the *Second Treatise*, there is ample room for doubt about Macpherson's account, and some plainly unambiguous statements by Locke that flatly contradict it. On the issue of rationality, for example, it is true that this is Locke's basis for knowledge of the moral law and hence the basis for being able to obey it. But it is quite incredible that Locke intends us to believe it is the property of one class only, or that he thinks it is chiefly displayed in the acquisition of capital goods. It is stated explicitly by Locke that very nearly all men are rational enough to know what the Law of Nature requires of them, though most men are little enough inclined to obey it:

> 'The *State of Nature* has a Law of Nature to govern it, which obliges everyone; and Reason which is that Law teaches all mankind who will but consult it . . . [*Second Treatise*, 6; cf. 12].

The problem is not that some people have not the ability to know what the Law requires of them, but that they will not take the trouble to think that they are morally obliged to do, or if they do take the trouble they will not take the trouble to do what they are morally obliged to. The reason, in general, why the Law of Nature is not enough is human selfishness and not human intelligence. In fact the only qualification Locke places on the general possession of rationality is that of age or mental defect:

'. . . we are born Free, as we are born Rational; not that we have actually the exercise of either; Age that brings one, brings with it the other too.' [*Second Treatise*, 61].

The only persons other than the young who are not qualified by rationality are

'Lunaticks and Ideots'. . . . Madmen [*Second Treatise*, 60]

who hardly seem to be coextensive with the whole class of labouring poor whom Locke is said to have written off as non-rational. Moreover, this statement by Locke comes only one chapter after the account of property rights in which the erosion of the rationality of the propertyless is supposed to have occurred. The total absence of any sign that Locke was sliding into the doctrine which is said to be his considered opinion leaves us with no grounds for supposing that the mere absence of property in the sense of capital goods is sufficient to deny citizenship to persons who, by all normal tests, are sane and rational when they reach years of discretion.

Moreover, there is a good deal of confusion in Macpherson's account of what is supposed by Locke to be the distinctively rational feature about capitalist accumulation. There is initially a good deal of confusion in Locke too, but Macpherson does not so much clear this up as ignore it in favour of a doctrine which he attributes to Locke, apparently for no better cause that that it is the doctrine which a moralizing capitalist ought to have held. The only consistent line for Locke to take is fairly simple, and the elements of it are at least hidden in the account of property rights he does give. The Will of God, which he identifies with the Law of Nature and the demands of Reason, requires all men to be preserved as far as possible. The man who appropriates land, employs his skill upon it, and thus enriches mankind, is thereby obeying the demands of reason, that is, he is being rational. This is Locke's argument in a number of places. He refers initially to the right that each man has of preserving all mankind [*Second Treatise*, 11]—a 'right' which is better termed a duty. He argues that the man who encloses land and works it confers a benefit upon mankind; almost everything required for a civilized existence is due to the skill and effort which men have lavished upon raw materials supplied by nature. * * *

* * *

* * * The only consistent line to be found in Locke is that capitalism is rational—morally—because it is a step to the betterment of society, and that being a capitalist is rational—prudentially—because it enables one to enjoy a greater share of the betterment. A man's share in the general social product is both his incentive and

his reward. But so simple a doctrine as this is far indeed from fulfilling the requirements of Macpherson's theory.

* * *

* * * All discounting made of the ideological overtones which
Macpherson hears in every word of Locke, the force of Macpherson's account challenges one to produce some alternative picture
that fits the text better than his, but which takes notice of what is
most valuable in his account. Let us then agree that the chapter *Of
Property* is intended to justify the achievement of the capitalist, and
the reward he reaps. * * * [T]he simplest argument for this is based
on God's will that all mankind should flourish. Given fair distribution, the greatest social product is the will of God, and the dictate
of reason. Locke never argues explicitly that the distribution is fair,
though the elements of the argument are there. They lie in the insistence that even the worst off in modern society is better off than
he would be outside it, a thesis backed up by the ubiquitous American Indian; these latter it will be remembered:

> '. . . have not one hundredth part of the Conveniences we en-
> joy: And a King of a large and fruitful Territory there feeds,
> lodges and is clad worse than a day Labourer in *England*' [*Sec-
> ond Treatise, 41*].

And they lie too in the suggestion that it is the superior ability and
greater efforts of the capitalist that leads to his greater wealth:

> 'And as different degrees of Industry were apt to give Men Pos-
> sessions in different proportions, so this *Invention of Money*
> gave them the opportunity to continue and enlarge them' [*Sec-
> ond Treatise, 48*].

And perhaps, finally, in the suggestion that even now there is some
surplus land left:

> 'in some inland, vacant places of America' [*Second Treatise,
> 36*].

Thus, the capitalist is worthy of his profit; that he is worthy of all
his profit Locke does not argue: perhaps his *laissez-faire* inclinations were not so strong that he thought it was true; perhaps they
were so strong that he thought it needed no proving. The basic
point, however, is simple enough; since all men have profited by entering a market society, there is no cause for complaint if some men
have done better than others.

* * * In Macpherson's account, Locke now proceeds to pile political oppression on top of inequality of possessions. A more convincing picture is that of Locke moving from the negative point that

the labourer and the capitalist were not at odds to the positive task of showing that they have a shared interest, a common ground of political obligation, and a common right to see to the maintenance of their interests. It is indubitable that both are bound by the law; therefore the law must give something to them both, in return for which they are bound to obey it. And it is this something which Locke calls;

'the Preservation of their Property' [*Second Treatise*, 124]. or else:

> '. . . the mutual *Preservation* of their *Lives, Liberties and Estates* which I call by the general Name, Property' [*Second Treatise*, 123].

*   *   *

* * * In many ways property rights, in the ordinary sense of 'property', are paradigms of the rights that are exchanged and protected by contract. But only a bourgeois mind could fail to see that they are paradigmatic rather with respect to procedure than with respect to the importance of the ethical values involved. * * * In the joint-stock company that is Locke's state, all men are shareholders. Some men hold shares of life, liberty, peace, and quiet alone, while others hold shares of estate as well; these latter may receive more of the benefits and play a greater part in the running of the state, but there is no reason to suppose that in the eyes of God or Nature (or even in the eyes of John Locke) their shares have a peculiar importance. * * *

Equality and Majority Rule in Locke

Locke's political theory, as expressed in *The Second Treatise*, is generally viewed as the classic expression of the argument for political equality and majority rule. Although he was not the first to write on these topics, his arguments and interpretations were different from those of his predecessors. He is the first political theorist to derive from the principle of equality an argument for individual consent by a numerical majority as the basis for and limit on the legitimacy of government.

The selection included here by Paul E. Sigmund (the editor of this volume) attempts to give a clearer definition of Locke's views on these subjects by comparing his theories with earlier writers on equality and majority rule: the late medieval conciliarists; the post-Reformation Calvinist constitutionalists; the Anglican clergyman Richard Hooker, whom Locke cited and quoted often in the *Second Treatise*; the members of the Leveller movement during the English civil wars; and the German natural law theorist Samuel Pufendorf (see p. 251 herein). Sigmund concludes that while his predecessors derived the legitimacy of government from community consent, which in turn was based on original freedom and equality, Locke was the first to base legitimate government on the granting, and possible withdrawal, of *individual* consent (Hobbes and Pufendorf had begun from individual consent but did not use it to argue for the possibility of majority-based revolution) and to make an argument for numerical majorities in the adoption of constitutional decisions. The earlier theories, although often containing references to the "greater part" (*major pars*), nearly always included hierarchical and group-based (corporatist) elements in the theory or the practice of their arguments.

In the *Second Treatise*, Locke seems, at first glance, to argue that equality is self-evident (no. 4) and to base majority rule on a crude physicalism, with majority consent as the default decision mechanism because it has "greater force" (96). However, Jeremy Waldron argues that Locke's theory is more complex. He believes that the basis of equality in Locke lies in the shared moral capacities of human beings, which, he argues, are central to Locke's conception of personhood. In turn, those moral capacities, he maintains, can be justified only by belief in God to whom all men are responsible—a belief that Locke held was accessible by reason. (Waldron thus joins the debate about the

305

place of religion in Locke's thought, which is examined in "Religion and Politics," p. 361 herein.)

Waldron argues that, in Locke's thinking, legislatures and voting requirements that include inegalitarian elements are still justified by the consent of all and that his argument for majority rule is based on moral rather than physical equality. Reflecting a controversial argument that he has often made, Waldron maintains that Locke's concept of limited government does not necessarily lead to the American practice of judicial review of the constitutionality of congressional legislation. In the final section he shows that Locke maintained his commitment to moral equality while accepting and even endorsing economic inequality, but also argued for an enforceable right to subsistence of those who would otherwise die of starvation.

PAUL E. SIGMUND

Equality, Legitimacy, and Majority Rule in Locke: Continuity and Change†

Near the beginning of *The Second Treatise*, John Locke argues that to explain political power we must begin with the "state all men are naturally in" which is one "of perfect freedom . . . within the bounds of the law of nature," as well as "of equality wherein all the power and jurisdiction is reciprocal, no one having more than another" (no. 4). In support of "this equality of men by nature," he quotes *The Laws of Ecclesiastical Polity* by "the judicious Hooker"— the sixteenth-century Anglican clergyman Richard Hooker—linking his own theory with that of a writer whose work is included—correctly—as one of the last great medieval thinkers in the final volume of the Carlyles' six volume *A History of Medieval Political Theory in the West*.

There are important differences between the theories of Locke and Hooker, notably on the character of the consent—whether by the community as a whole, or by the individual—and the role of a numerical majority in legitimizing government. Yet, the fact that Locke could cite Hooker in support of the doctrine of natural equality demonstrates that the idea, if not Locke's conclusions from it, was not new—that its origins go back to the Middle Ages and earlier. Contrary to the views of Leo Strauss and his followers (Strauss, 1953) who link Locke's equalitarianism to that of Hobbes, and contrary, as well, to the argument of C. B. Macpherson that

† From "The Great Chain of Being Was Not the Only Game in Town: The Medieval Roots of Political Equality," paper delivered at the annual meeting of the American Political Science Association, August 31, 1998.

Locke's appeal to natural equality concealed his belief in "an inherent class differential in rationality" (Macpherson, 1962), and to the view of some contemporary liberals who see medieval political thought as uniformly theocratic, heirarchical, and authoritarian (Beer 1986; criticized in Tierney 1987) the doctrine of natural equality which is the basis of his political theory has deep roots in Western political thought. This paper will argue that Locke's theory of equality demonstrates both continuities with past theories, and significant changes in its application.

Despite the hierarchical character of much of medieval society, the idea of natural equality was a commonplace of medieval thought, and occasionally it was cited in ways that had practical consequences. Thus Aquinas argued that slaves have a right to subsistence and family life because "in matters relating to human nature, for example, those relating to bodily sustenance and the procreation of offspring, a man is bound to obey God alone, not another man, because by nature all men are equal" (*Summa Theologiae*, II–II,104, a.5, in Sigmund 1988:76). Aquinas did not refer specifically to natural equality when he argued that there should be a popular element in government because "the people have the right to choose their rulers" (*S.T.* I–II, 105, a.1 in Sigmund 1988:59); but a few decades later, William of Ockham's *A Short Discourse on Tyrannical Governement (Breviloquium)* derived the same claim from the fact that "nature made all men equal" (IV,9 in Ockham 1992:121). In the fourteenth century, when peasant revolts broke out in many parts of western Europe, their leaders also cited the doctrine of original natural equality to support their attack on the feudal system (Cohn 1957:209–17)

The most striking application of the doctrine of natural freedom and equality to medieval political and ecclesiastical structures occurred in the fifteenth-century conciliar treatise by the canon lawyer, and later Cardinal, Nicholas of Cusa, *The Catholic Concordance* (Cusa 1991). Written in 1433 to defend the superiority of the Council of Basel to the pope, it argues for the creation of a system of representative councils to consent to law and government in the church and the empire. Part of the argument is historical and part legal, but the most striking argument that Nicholas makes is from natural freedom and equality. "Since all are by nature free, every governance . . . can only come from agreement and consent. . . . If by nature men are equal in power and equally free, the true properly ordered authority of one common ruler who is their equal in power cannot be naturally established except by the election and consent of the others, and law is also established by consent" (Cusa 1991:98, no. 127). The argument is repeated in words that anticipate more modern theories when he discusses the need for consent to the rule of the German

emperor, arguing that his authority must come from "electoral concordance and free submission," based on "the common equal birth
and the equal natural rights of all men" (Cusa 1991:230, no. 331).

Another modern element is his frequent reference to the role of
"the greater part" (*major pars*), sometimes translated as "the majority." The true church is the greater part of the faithful united to the
see of Peter; the greater part of the priesthood will remain free of
error; the greater part "ordinarily" or "normally" rules in the church
council; the church's coercive power is based on the consent of all
or "of the greater part"; all legislation should by adopted by those
who are bound by it or the greater part of their representatives,
since "what touches all should be approved by all" (Cusa 1991:41,
no. 59; 58, no. 79; 105, no. 137; 201, no. 261, 206, no. 270; 208,
no. 276; 207, no. 278; 211, no. 283).

Cusa also derives the authority of the emperor from the consent
of the people, through electors who were chosen "with the consent
of the nobles and leaders of both estates, the clergy, and the people" (Cusa 1991:229). While allowing for hereditary succession by
consent, he prefers a separate election for each emperor "by all or
the greater part or at least by the nobles who represent all with
their consent" (Cusa 1991:211, no. 283).

The description of the imperial electors—three bishops and four
barons—as representing the greater part indicates how elastic the
term, could be. While many medieval electoral bodies, following the
principles of Roman law on corporate decision making, operated on
the basis of majority rule, canon law provisions requiring decisions
by the "greater (*major*) and sounder (*sanior*)" part allowed considerations other than numbers to be taken into account. Even Marsilius
of Padua, often taken to be a herald of popular sovereignty, required
that decisions be taken by the "weightier (*valentior*)" part "as to
quality and quantity." Nicholas of Cusa himself, after transferring
ellegiance to the pope, complained about the "arithmetic" involved
in the voting procedure of the council which allowed a bishop's servant to vote asking "Does not a pope or prince have greater authority in his vote than a manservant" (Sigmund 1963:264).

The doctrine of conciliar superiority was defeated by the restored
papacy but it continued to be taught at the University of Paris. In
1518, John Mair, a Scottish theologian teaching at Paris, published
a treatise on church government that went beyond the usual claim
to conciliar control of an errant pope to argue that a tyrannical
ruler, whether king or pope, can be deposed because supreme
power rests in the whole people. This action can be taken by the
greater part which, he explains, is represented by the "princes,
prelates, and nobles" (Oakley 1984:IX.19).

Among Mair's students in Paris was George Buchanan whose later work, *De juri regni apud Scotos* (1579) defended the right of the community to depose its ruler—and, more, notoriously that of any individual to kill a tyrant. Buchanan's book is mentioned in Locke's *Second Treatise* (no. 233) and it was publicly censured as "pernicious and damnable" and subjected to a public book burning at Oxford in 1683, shortly before John Locke departed for exile in Holland (text of the condemnation in Wootton 1986:121 ff.). Buchanan begins by arguing from a state of original equality governed by a law of nature which directs men to associate. "Conflicting interests" lead them to "confer their authority on whomever they will" so that "we cannot have a legitimate ruler unless we have elected him with full consent of the people . . . . Since the greater part of the people . . . create the ruler, it may also hold him accountable." Again, however, in practice consent is to be given by "those persons in whom the people or the greater part of the people have vested it"—the orders (*ordines*), i.e. estates or corporate groups, of the kingdom (Oakley 1984:IX.24).

The Oxford condemnation also cited the *Vindiciae contra Tyrannos*, the French Huguenot tract, which also appeared in 1579 under the pseudonym Stephanus Junius Brutus, English translations of which were published three times during the seventeenth century. The *Vindiciae* cites the examples of the Councils of Constance and Basel and derives the right to resist the king from a contract between him and the people who are "free by nature" (Brutus 1994:47, 92). Also included in the 1683 condemnation was Robert Bellarmine, one of numerous sixteenth-century Dominican and Jesuit theorists, writing on constitutionalism and natural law, who argued from original freedom and equality that the source of royal (but not papal) authority was community—but not individual—consent (cf. Hamilton 1963, Skinner 1978:II.155 ff.).

Richard Hooker (1554–1600) in his *Laws of Ecclesiastical Polity* (1593) drew on the tradition of community consent and original equality to defend the legitimacy of the English government and of the Anglican church. In Hooker's (1989:89) view, consent to government had been given by the community "in the times wherein there were no civil societies" by an "order expressly or secretly agreed upon"—although in Hooker's version it might have been given five hundred years earlier. Those who give that consent are aware that they are "equals in nature" sharing a "relation of equality between ourselves and those that are as ourselves" (Hooker 1989:80). Hooker (1989:90) admitted that "some very great and judicious men"—presumably Plato and Aristotle—espoused "a kind of natural right in the noble, wise, and virtuous to govern them which are of servile disposition"; but he argued that the only natu-

ral superiority is that of the father in the family, distinguishing between patriarchal and political authority and deriving the latter
from consent in a way that was cited by Locke in his *Second Treatise*. Since the original consent he is discussing is more like community consensus, he did not discuss electoral procedures and
majorities, although he believed that England has consented to the
rule of parliament (including the king and the House of Lords) as
the supreme legislative body.

A half a century later the tradition of natural equality was also
appealed to by the radicals in the English civil wars. In 1646, the
leader of the Levellers, John Lilburne, wrote that the children of
Adam are "by nature all equal and alike in power, dignity, authority,
and majesty" so that government is exercised "by mutual agreement
and consent" (quoted in Sabine 1961:483) In the Putney debates, a
year later, the Levellers argued against the defenders of the forty-
shilling freehold property requirement for voting by appealing to a
"right of nature" to support an "equal right with another of choosing him that shall govern him," and, famously Colonel Rainbor-
ough stated that because "the poorest he that is in England has a
life to live as the greatest he. . . . every man who is to live under a
government ought first by his own consent put himself under that
government" (Wootton 1986:291).

The first major political theorist to derive the legitimacy of the
ruler from individual consent to obey a numerical majority was
Thomas Hobbes. In his *Leviathan* (1651) he argues that to avoid
"the war of all against all" in the state of nature, men enter a
covenant or contract to form a commonwealth and give absolute
power to a sovereign in order to keep the peace. The covenant is established by "everyone with everyone, that to whatsoever man or assembly of men shall be given by the major part the right to be their
representative, every one—as well he that voted for it as he that
voted against it—shall authorize the actions and judgments of that
man or assembly of men in the same manner as if they were his
own, to the end to live peaceable among themselves, and be protected against other men" (*Leviathan*, chap. 18). Thus in Hobbes's
system there is unanimous—and individual—agreement to act by a
numerical majority to give all power to the sovereign, provided he
effectively protects his subjects.

As the cases of Hooker and Hobbes demonstrate, belief in original freedom and equality need not lead to political democracy. In
his book *On the Duty of Man and the Citizen* (1673) a shortened
version of *On the Law of Nature and of Nations* (1672), (both of
which Locke possessed at the time that he was writing *The Second
Treatise*) Samuel Pufendorf described "the state of nature" as a

"state of natural liberty" in which "every man is held to be equal to every other." It is "antecedent to any agreement" and in that state men "have the light of reason implanted in them to govern their actions." Because of the "disadvantages" of natural liberty, including the lack of an arbiter of disputes, men agree, "every individual with every other one," to act together by majority rule to establish a government. That government can be "by one man, or an assembly of a few, or an assembly of all" and monarchy can be elective or hereditary. In all cases, however, the justification comes from the presumption of consent by the people, even when they are conquered in war (Pufendorf's *On the Duty of Man and the Citizen*, 1991: 117–18, 138, 148). Thus in Pufendorf's theory, original freedom and equality are used to justify authoritarian rule, even that of a foreign conqueror.

In Locke's hands, however, original freedom and equality are used to justify individual consent to be bound by the decisions of a numerical "majority."[1] (He does not use the term, *major part*, as earlier writers including Hobbes had done). "Men, being . . . by nature, all free, equal, and independent, no one can be . . . subjected to the political power of another without his own consent. . . . When any number of men have by the consent of every individual made a community, they have thereby made that community one body, with a power to act as one body, which is only by the will and determination of the majority" (2T, 95–96). As in Hobbes and Pufendorf the legitimacy of government comes from the consent of the majority to the structure of the government which may or may not be democratic (as the English government was not). However unlike Hobbes and Pufendorf, Locke believes that government is always limited to the purposes for which it was established, the protection of the rights of the individual, and it can be overthrown if it subverts those purposes.

Rather than a modern innovation, the doctrine of original freedom and equality was a commonplace of Western political theory. It could be used to justify an authoritarian system as in the case of Pufendorf: it could be utilized in defense of a community's right to take action against an errant ruler as in the *Vindiciae* and Buchanan; it could be made the justification for more or less representative institutions as in the parliamentarism of Hooker; or it could be used to argue for abolition of a property requirement for voting as in the case of the Levellers.[2] Locke uses it in a new way to

---

1. According to the *Oxford English Dictionary*, the word *majority* was first used in the sixteenth century to describe papal power in the Catholic church and the preeminence of charity over the other virtues. Citations of its use in a numerical sense begin only in the late seventeenth century.
2. For Locke's relation to the Levellers, see McNally (1989).

312 PAUL E. SIGMUND

make an argument for political equality, limited government, and individual evaluation of the legitimacy (or illegitimacy) of government, making the *Second Treatise* a founding document of liberalism, constitutionalism, and democracy.

Locke is also the first political theorist to make an explicit argument for constitutional decisions by a numerical majority. As one of his Tory critics pointed out, at least in the adoption of the basic institutions of government Locke's theory implies universal suffrage "without regard to sex or condition" (Ashcraft 1986:236). Consent is given by the individual, not by any corporate group claiming to represent the people, and unlike most earlier theories (e.g., those of Hooker and Grotius), the judgment as to whether the government is violating the rights of its citizens is made by "the body of the people, or any single man" (2T, 168) and "every man is judge for himself" (2T, 241), although the majority should legitimize the overthrow of the government (2T, 209) by supporting the aggrieved individual. Natural equality that earlier had justified community consent and societal resistance to abuse of power now becomes the basis for granting *and withdrawing* individual consent and legitimizing constitutional arrangements by majority rule.

Locke's concept of a state of nature had been implicit in earlier writings—and he could interpolate the words, "i.e. the state of nature," into a quotation from Hooker on the subject (2T, 91)—but now it became more than a mythical state of original equality and freedom. Its law, the law of nature, became the standard to measure the legitimacy of existing governments. As his sixteen quotations from Hooker demonstrate, the materials for his theory were contained in the mainstream of the Western tradition.[3]

The equalitarianism of Locke, marked a break with the political and social structures of the Middle Ages but not with its underlying moral and religious assumptions. He did not need to draw on Hobbes—indeed he repeatedly rejected his teaching—to ground his system. While there are many ways in which men are unequal, there is an "equal right that every man has to his natural freedom without being subjected to the will or authority of any other man" (no. 54), which is "grounded on his having reason which is able to instruct him in that law he is to govern himself by" (no. 63). These are statements that apply to everyone, irrespective of social or economic position.

3. In a forthcoming article, "Corporatism, Individualism, and Consent: Locke and Premodern Thought," Brian Tierney gives examples of individual consent and majority rule in medieval canon law and philosophy. He also provides examples of the derivation of government legitimacy from the (irrevocable) consent of the majority, as well as references to the state of nature in the writings of the sixteenth-century Spanish theologians. See also Tierney's (1987) earlier article on medieval consent.

This book is sent to you with the compliments of W.W. Norton & Company, Inc. Any comment you might care to make on its merits and usefulness for your courses will be gratefully received. For additional examination copies or support materials, please contact your local Norton representative at wwnorton.com/college/sales_rep.htm

BOOK/AUTHOR: _____

Comments:

Name _____ Dept. _____ College _____

City _____ State _____ Zip _____ May we quote you in our advertising? ☐ Yes ☐ No

Email Address _____ Office Hours: M Tu W Th F Times: _____

Men's knowledge of the basic principles of natural law—freedom, equality, and respect for others as products of divine workmanship makes it both necessary and possible to establish government by consent. In practice this consent may be given tacitly and may be used to justify quite undemocratic institutions, but the principle that governments derive their just powers from the consent of a numerical majority of the governed had been established.

The natural equality on which Locke based his political theory is neither hedonist, relativist, nor secular. It is based on a belief in a shared human nature, rationality, and creation by God that had been part of the Western political heritage for centuries. As Quentin Skinner observes at the end of his two-volume work *The Foundations of Modern Political Thought*, "It is an error to think of the development of [the] modern liberal theory of constitutionalism essentially as an achievement of the seventeenth century. . . . The concepts in which Locke and his successors developed their views on popular sovereignty and the right of revolution had already been articulated in legal writings . . . theological treatises . . . as well as in the more famous but derivative writings of the Calvinist revolutionaries" (Skinner 1978:II:348). One of those concepts, drawn from the medieval tradition, but given a more radical and individualistic interpretation, provided the basic building block of Locke's theory—the idea of natural equality.

JEREMY WALDRON

From God, Locke, and Equality†

*   *   *

[*God and Equality*]

* * * Why are we not able to bracket off the theological dimension of Locke's commitment to equality? Why can't we put the religious premises in parentheses—leaving them available for anyone who needs that sort of persuasion, but not presented as an integral part of the package—and still be left with something recognizably egalitarian in its content, which even an atheist could support?

The hope that some trick like this can be pulled off, the belief that some such bracketing must be possible—if not for Locke's

† From *God, Locke, and Equality: Christian Foundations in Locke's Political Thought* (Cambridge: Cambridge University Press, 2002). Reprinted with the permission of Cambridge University Press.

theory, then perhaps for Kant's, or at least for *some* recognizable commitment to equality—this hope is crucial for modern secular liberalism. *Political* liberalism (in Rawls's sense of that phrase)[1] depends absolutely on the success of some such maneuver. Rawls's system definitely requires a premise of equality, a premise strong enough to structure the original position and substantial enough to provide a basis for mutual respect in a well-ordered society; and Rawls's view is that any premise supporting that structure has to stand by itself on the plateau of political values, free of any religious entanglement. Of course, a religious argument for basic equality may be entertained in certain circles in a pluralistic society; but according to the Rawlsian scheme, the very same principle of equality must be conceivable and defensible from a variety of philosophical perspectives, some religious and some not. My approach in the present book indicates that I am doubtful that this Rawlsian strategy will work. What is the basis for these doubts?

* * *

* * * I shall argue in this chapter that, in Locke's account, the shape of *human*, the way in which the extension of the predicate "human" is determined, is not in the end separable from the religious reasons that Locke cites in support of basic equality. * * *

* * *

Let us turn now to the rationality criterion. In the *First Treatise*, Locke said that God made man "in his own Image after his own Likeness . . . an intellectual Creature . . . For wherein soever else the *Image of God* consisted, the intellectual Nature was certainly a apart of it, and belong'd to the whole Species" (1st T: 30). Unfortunately, however, *imago dei*[2] does not solve the following problem. On the one hand, non-human animals have minds, at least to the extent of having and acting on ideas and combinations of ideas (E: 2.11.5–7),[3] Since they are "not bare Machines (as some would have them), we cannot deny them to have some Reason" (E: 2.11.11). On the other hand, those we are accustomed to calling human vary enormously in their intellectual capacities. If the *imago dei* idea is supposed to help us, it has to help us make discriminations along this spectrum—not necessarily now in a way that is guided by some spurious concept of species—but discriminations nevertheless, which will enable us to resist the temptation to treat all beings who are less intellectually able than we are (or than we think we are) as something less than our equals, without giving up some version of the distinction Locke relies on in the *Second Treatise* between ani-

---

1. Rawls, *Political Liberalism*, pp. 19 and 109 * * * [Waldron's note].
2. The image of God. All notes are the editor's unless otherwise specified.
3. "E:" *Essay Concerning Human Understanding*.

mals that are and animals that are not "made for one anothers uses" (2nd T: 6). Taken literally, *imago dei* is not going to help us with this. For even if we (that is, you and I, dear Reader) can confidently think of ourselves as created in the image of God, there is no denying that we are a rather *blurred* image—intellectually as well as spiritually. And the intellectual differences between us would seem to be important in this regard, indicating that some of us are less blurred than others in the image of God that we present. By itself *imago dei* goes no way towards answering our threshold question: how blurred may the image be, exactly, before it ceases to count in the relevant respect?

The difficulty at this stage of the argument is quire general. A principle of basic equality requires a binary distinction—(i) those who are one another's equals, and (ii) those who are not the equals of the members of class (i)—and reason or rationality is not really a binary concept. There are degrees of rationality, both among those we are pre-theoretically inclined to call humans and in a broader class of animals that includes apes and dolphins, dogs and cats, as well as those we call humans. On this gradual scale, who gets the benefit of equality? Or why is it not more sensible to abandon equality and take as the basic premise of moral and political philosophy the idea of a proportionate response to each entity's particular locations on the scale?

* * *

* * * If there is, as Locke says, "a difference of degrees in Men's Understandings . . . to so great a latitude that one may, without doing injury to Mankind, affirm that there is a greater distance between some Men and others in this respect than between some Men and some Beasts" (E: 4.20.5), then how can we work with or justify any notion of basic equality? Against a background of that sort of variation, how are we supposed to set the sharp divides or maintain the thresholds on this scale that the idea of equality appears to presuppose?

* * *

Locke needs to specify a threshold. Here's how I think he does it. In Book II of the *Essay*, he argued that what distinguishes humans from other animals is not the capacity to reason *per se*—for brute animals have some sort of reason—but rather the "power of *Abstracting*," the capacity to reason on the basis of general ideas. Animals have and act on ideas, and therefore have some reason: "but it is only in particular *Ideas*, just as they receiv'd them from their Senses"—they don't have "the faculty to enlarge by any kind of *Abstraction*" (E: 2.11.11). It is "the having of general ideas," a faculty connected of course with the use of language, which puts "a perfect distinction betwixt man and brutes," if not in the sense of biological taxonomy, then at least in the sense required for the moral application of the idea of corporeal rationality. And there is a similar reference to the capacity to entertain general ideas in the passage where Locke inquires about the moral application of his skepticism about species (E: 3.11.16). So, maybe *this* is Locke's equality-threshold. Can we say that he regards possession of the power of abstraction as the basis of a bright line on the rationality scale, for the purposes of his moral definition of humanity and his belief in basic equality?

* * *

* * * Is there anything which can give the Lockean basis of equality—the power of abstraction—its appropriate sense and shape as a range property? Is there anything which can motivate our attention to this as a threshold and our refusal to be distracted by intellectual differences above it?

This, at last, is where the religious argument comes in, on my interpretation. To motivate and explicate the power of abstraction as the relevant equality-threshold, we must consider the moral and theological pragmatics which lie at the back of Locke's account of the human intellect. We must look at what he says about the fundamental *adequacy* of our mental powers and the reasons he has for saying that in the case of all standard-model humans, each of them has *intellect enough*, for some fundamental purpose, whatever the intellectual differences between them. * * * No matter how inadequate the average human intellect is for a "universal, or perfect Comprehension,"

> it yet secures their great Concernments, that they have Light enough to lead them to the Knowledge of their Maker, and the sight of their own Duties . . . It will be no Excuse to an idle and untoward Servant, who would not attend his Business by Candle-light, to plead that he had not broad Sun-shine. The Candle that is set up in us, shines bright enough for all our Purposes.

"[T]hey have Light enough to lead them to the Knowledge of their Maker." The implicit reference here is Locke's argument for the existence of God. The existence of God, Locke believes, is something that can be established by the unaided human intellect, whatever that intellect's other limitations. It is not an idea that is innate in us (E: 1.4.8 ff.) but it is readily attainable. All that is needed is some power of abstraction applied to what we see in the world around us: "For the visible marks of extraordinary Wisdom and Power appear so plainly in all the Works of the Creation, that a rational Creature, who will but seriously reflect on them, cannot miss the discovery of a *Deity*" (E: 1.3.9). Some argue, says Locke, that it is "*suitable to the goodness of God*" (E: 1.4.12) to imprint an idea of His being directly on our minds. But God has used a different strategy. He has conferred on those whom He intends to serve Him the rational power that is required for easy recognition of His existence. Thus we can identify the class of those whom God intends to serve Him by discerning which beings have and which beings do not have these powers.

So Locke's position seems to be this. Anyone with the capacity for abstraction can reason to the existence of God, and he can relate the idea of God to there being a law that applies to him both in his conduct in this world and as to his prospects for the next. The content of that law may not be available to everyone's reason, but anyone above the threshold has the power to relate the idea of such law to what is known by faith and revelation about God's commandments, and is in a position therefore to use such intellect as he has to follow and obey those commandments. Moreover, he can think of himself, abstractly, as a being that endures from moment to moment, and as the same being that may commit a sin today and have to account to the Almighty for it tomorrow: in short he has the minimal capacity to think of himself as a *person*. No doubt there are all sorts of differences in the ways in which people figure all this through—some attempt the precarious path of reason, some wander through the minefield of revelation. (I'll talk more about this in the next chapter.) But the fact that one is dealing with an animal that has the capacity to approach the task one way or another is all-important, and it makes a huge difference to how such a being may be treated in comparison to animals whose capacities are such that this whole business of knowing God and figuring out his commandments is simply out of the question.

The fact that a being can get this far, intellectually, by whatever route, shows that he is a creature with a special *moral* relation to God. As a creature who knows about the existence of God and who is therefore in a position to answer responsibility to His commandments, this is someone whose existence has a special significance. Now, that specialness is a matter of intense interest first and foremost, of course, to the person who has the ability. Knowing that he has been sent into the world by God, "by his order, and about his business," the individual person has an interest in finding out pretty damned quick what he is supposed to do. But Locke believes this also affects fundamentally the way we ought to deal with one another. When I catch a rabbit, I know that I am *not* dealing with a creature that has the capacity to abstract, and so I know that there is no question of this being one of God's special servants, sent into the world about his business. But if I catch a human in full possession of his faculties, I know I should be careful how I deal with him. Because creatures capable of abstraction can be conceived as "all the servants of one Sovereign Master, sent into the World by his order, and about his business," we must treat them as "his Property, whose Workmanship they are, made to last during his, not one anothers Pleasure" and refrain from destroying or harming or exploiting them. *That*, it seems to me, is the interest that is driving and shaping Locke's moral conception of "man," and motivating the interest in the particular range of capacities that forms the basis of Lockean equality.

If all this is accepted then it is pretty clear that the *bracketing* strategy we spoke about at the beginning of this chapter—bracketing off the God stuff from the equality stuff—is simply not going to work. The two parts of the Lockean doctrine are intimately related. Once we see Locke acknowledging that he is not entitled to help himself to any ready-made notion of the human species, then it is clear that he has no choice but to shape his theory of equality on the basis of certain resemblances among created beings. And the significance of those resemblances—their relevance *qua* resemblances at this level of moral theory—can be established only in the light of certain theological truths.

Someone in denial of or indifferent to the existence of God is not going to be able to come up with anything like the sort of basis for equality that Locke came up with. An atheist may pretend to talk about equality of all members of the human species, but his conception of the human species is likely to be as chaotic and indeterminate as Locke's was in Book III of the *Essay*. The atheist may pretend to ground our equality in our rationality, but he will be at a loss to explain why we should ignore the evident differences in people's rationality. He will be at a loss to defend any particular line or threshold, in a non-question-begging way. * * * There is no reason for an atheist to recognize such a threshold, and there is no reason to believe that he could defend it if he did. The atheist has no basis in his philosophy for thinking that beings endowed with the capacity that Locke emphasizes are for that reason to be treated as special and sacred in the way Locke thought.

* * *

[*Majority Rule*]

* * * John Locke is in fact one of very few political philosophers who bother to pay much attention to the defense of majority-decision. Most political philosophers either denigrate it or ignore it. The account Locke gives is not all that substantial; it comprises just a few paragraphs, at the beginning of Chapter 8 of the *Second Treatise*. The key to the argument is this passage:

> That which acts any Community, being only the consent of the individuals of it, and it being necessary to that which is one body to move one way; it is necessary the Body should move that way whither the greater force carries it, *which is the consent of the majority*: or else it is impossible it should act or continue one Body, *one Community*, which the consent of every individual that united into it, agreed that it should; and so every one is bound by that consent to be concluded by the *majority*." (2nd T: 96)

* * *

* * * Though Locke uses the language of force and motion—"it is necessary the Body should move that way whither the greater force carries it" (2nd T: 96)—he does not intend this to be read in a physicalist way. * * * Locke makes it clear that the physics he has in mind is a physics of individual consent, not a physics of individual strength or power. He prefaces the passage I quoted a little while ago by saying that "that which acts any Community"—that which moves it—is nothing but "the consent of the individuals of it" (idem). And it is on that basis that he goes on to say that since it is "necessary to that which is one body to move one way; it is necessary the Body should move that way whither the greater force carries it, which is the *consent of the majority*" (2nd T: 96). Consent does not carry physical force or even pure political force; rather, it carries moral force with regard to the purposes for which consent is required. So Locke is not making a factual claim, that the movement of a political body depends on the force of individuals' participation. The Lockean physics of consent is more in the nature of a normative theory. The claim is that the only thing which *properly* moves a political body is the consent of the individuals who compose it. For the purpose of that normative proposition, consent is a matter of individual authorization. People may vary in their political influence and know-how. But that is not the same as variation in the normative force of individual consent. In that dimension we are equals, and the numerical account is the correct one.

* * *

* * * Locke thinks it important that we establish a place where we do our natural law reasoning together, and come up with determinate (though of course still fallible) results which can stand in the name of us all. Now, if the suggestion that there should be a counter-majoritarian power in the legislature were accepted, then this body too might become one of the places where this collective reasoning takes place. But what we must understand is that the law of nature is not more easily available to such a body than to the majoritarian assembly. It is simply a matter of prudence whether we decide to have an extra layer of this kind.

* * * [I]t is not at all clear whether there is room in Locke's theory for the idea of special expertise in regard to natural rights, which counter-majoritarian institutional proposals often presuppose. (The idea is that we need to have panels of rights-experts as a check on the majoritarian decisions of ordinary inexpert legislators.) * * * Locke rejected the idea of moral experts. He doubted whether there was any expertise to the found in this field, at least any expertise that would not be available more or less as a matter of course to any ordinary person who turned his mind to natural law. * * *

* * *

[Property and Equality]

The argument about property is a challenging case from the point of view of Locke's egalitarianism, because the aim of Chapter 5 of the *Second Treatise* seems patently inegalitarian. Locke is not only arguing for the legitimacy of private property; he is attempting to justify it in the sense that his argument in this chapter would be a failure if inequality were not the outcome; and this makes all the more challenging the interpretive heuristic I am using—that a commitment to equality pervades Locke's work, and that it works throughout the theory as a premise and a constraint.

We should not exaggerate the problem, however. Though Locke's argument aims to explain and justify "disproportionate and unequal possession of the earth" (2nd T: 50), it is certainly not intended as a defense of the seventeenth-century status quo. Richard Ashcraft has drawn our attention to the contrast between Locke's work and that of his friend James Tyrell in this regard. Tyrell was so eager to avoid any imputation of advocating a change in the system of property as it was already established that his argument amounted to a wholesale endorsement of existing property relations, whatever their form, distribution, or utility. Locke was quite critical of contemporary property arrangements, especially in the argument about inheritance and primogeniture in the *First Treatise*—an attack, by the way, which is very clearly grounded on principles of equality, and which was well known in Locke's circle to lead in the direction of smaller estates, more equitably distributed.

* * *

Appropriation, Locke says, is necessary to consummate the usefulness of God's bounty, and labor is the natural mode of appropriation: "God commanded, and [man's] Wants forced him to *labor*" (2nd T: 35). But appropriation by labor is confined within a framework dictated by the overall teleology of Locke's account, and that confinement is represented by the provisos and qualifications with which his account of appropriation is hedged: the spoliation limitation, the so-called sufficiency limitation, and the doctrine of charity. These conditions are the shadows cast by the principle of basic equality on the whole apparatus of property and economy. They are the medium through which the principle of basic equality patrols and disciplines the account.

* * *

* * * [Locke] is at pains to show that they[4] are among the beneficiaries of the sort of unequal money economy that he envisages. The day-laborer may own no property except his wages and the bread and rented housing that he buys with them; but still, compared to a person living as a free man in an undeveloped (and largely egalitarian) economy, he is better off. This is the gist of the famous passage comparing the agricultural economy of England with subsistence economies of the native Americans:

> There cannot be a clearer demonstration of any thing, than several Nations of the *Americans* are of this, who are rich in Land, and poor in all the Comforts of Life; whom Nature having furnished as liberally as any other people, with the materials of Plenty, *i.e.* a fruitful Soil, apt to produce in abundance, what might serve for food, raiment, and delight; yet for want of improving it by labor, have not one hundredth part of the Conveniences we enjoy: and a King of a large and fruitful Territory there, feeds, lodges, and is clad worse than a day Laborer in *England*. (2nd T: 41)

Far from treating the laborer as commodity, this passage seeks to justify the Lockean economy with reference to the laborer's own interest. Notice also that although what is being justified here is an unequal outcome—"disproportionate and unequal Possession" (2nd T: 50) of land in England as opposed to somewhat more equal common right in America—the form of the justification uses a particularly strong version of the egalitarian principle of maximin. Locke actually seeks to show that the poorest participant in the English economy is better off than the *best*-off participant in the native American economy, from which it certainly follows that the poorest participant in the English economy is better off than the worst-off participant in the native American economy. Again, it's a

---

4. i.e., members of the laboring class.

familiar contrast between equal outcomes, on the one hand, and an egalitarian argument, from a deeper premise of equal concern and respect, on the other. * * *

*   *   *

[Locke and the Poor]

* * * Those who want to portray an uncharitable Locke are fond of telling us about the John Locke who was the author of an essay on the Poor Law—a draft of a representation concerning methods of employing the poor. That is not early Locke; it is dated 1697, [far] from the period of our interest. And it certainly seems to be devoid of the sort of compassion that one would associate with a generous spirit of charity. Locke talks about "begging drones" and "superfluous brandy shops," and he suggests that the idle poor should be whipped and mutilated if they go begging, instead of doing the work assigned to them. Even little children should be given two or three hours of labor useful to the parish per day.

There are four things I want to say about this. First, as a matter of personality, we should observe that Locke actually had a reputation for being charitable (though those who mention it also mention its limits):

> He was very charitable to the Poor, except such Persons as were Idle or Prophane, and spent the Sunday in the Alehouses, and went not to Church. But above all he did compassionate those, who after they had labour'd as long as their Strength wou'd hold, were reduced to Poverty. He said it was not enough to keep him from starving, but that such a Provision ought to be made for them, that they might live comfortably.

Secondly, moving now to Locke's political position, we must bear firmly in mind that the paper on the Poor Law *does* assume that the poor have a right to subsistence. Locke insists that "everyone must have meat, drink, clothing, and firing." And he says that "if any person die for want of due relief in any parish in which he ought to be relieved, the said parish [must] be fined according to circumstances of the fact and the heinousness of the crime." Thirdly, we have already seen that Locke is in favor of charity being enforced, but not *radical* charity. Well, now we may think of a *second* form of radical charity that Locke is not prepared to enforce. This would be charity to someone who refuses to work when he *could* work, charity to someone who does not make any efforts to provide for himself or work to subsidize the cost of his provision. And Locke is no more in favor of enforcing this than he is of enforcing the other sense of radical charity—"sell all thou hast and give to the poor."

A final point returns us to the issue of labor. Locke really took seriously the injunction to labor—and a poor man with an offer of gainful employment was not a person who had no means to subsist (within the meaning of 1st T: 42). His view that the "true and proper relief of the poor . . . consists in finding work for them" is not contrary to the egalitarian premise of the doctrine of charity. Quite the reverse: it is what that premise amounts to against the background of what he regards as God's manifest purpose for man, and what reason reveals as the benefit to all of labor.

Locke as Collectivist

In 1980 James Tully published another response to C. B. Macpherson, *A Discourse on Property: John Locke and His Adversaries*. He argued that Locke's ultimate justification of property is not labor, which is only a means of assigning ownership, but its role in promoting God's intention to preserve all mankind. The duty of preservation, however, means that private property is subject to moral limitations. Citing a hitherto largely unnoticed passage from the *First Treatise* (42) on the obligation of charity to contribute from one's surplus to the survival of those in extreme need, Tully maintained that Locke's property right is limited by the enforceable obligation of natural law to provide subsistence to the destitute. Parents too in Locke's theory have an obligation to support their children, an obligation which is the basis of inheritance rights that cannot be restricted by, for example, the English common law principle of primogeniture, the right of the oldest son to inherit the family property. What Tully calls the "familialization" of property rights undermines the dominant patriarchal view and constitutes, he says, a "radical departure from convention."

Tully made another and more controversial claim, originally put forward in 1940 (Kendall) but not generally accepted by Locke scholars, that once consent has been given to the community, the legislature established by the majority has the right to dispose of property in any way that it believes will promote the common good. In a surprising challenge to those who viewed the primary purpose of Locke's social contract as the defense of property, he concluded that "the common ownership of all property" is the logical consequence of the premises of Locke's theory in *The Two Treatises*." He also argued for an individual right of revolution, and more dubiously, that universal suffrage is the only appropriate conclusion from Locke's araguments for equality and consent.

Jeremy Waldron calls Tully's view on the surrender of individual property rights to the legislature "strained and implausible," insisting that Locke allowed for "regulation but not confiscation" of property, since one of the reasons for the establishment of government was the defense of one's property. Thus the legislature can tax property or establish legal regulations for its exercise in the interest of the common good, but it is limited to what is reasonable for the protection of life, liberty, and property. He also notes that regulation of property rights can take place only by consent—that is, by a law adopted by a representative legislature.

Waldron alludes to Locke's acceptance of the right of those who would otherwise die of starvation to what he calls the "surplusage" of property holders. The subsistence right was asserted in many of Locke's predecessors going back to Aquinas and medieval canon law (see Swanson, 1996). Its Lockean version has been given contemporary application in two books in ways that do not go as far as Tully, but involve considerable limits on private property in the interest of the preservation of all mankind. The first, by Gopal Sreenivisan (1995), argues that the application of Locke's principles should lead to major changes in inheritance laws in order to redistribute to the deserving poor (those who cannot work because of ill health, age, child-care responsibilities, or the lack of employment opportunities) whatever is available after the needs of the property owner and his family are ensured. The second book, by Matthew Kramer (1998), calls for a massive worldwide employment program to enable all able-bodied citizens to work. Neither author would claim that Locke himself would have agreed to these radical applications of his theory, although we know from his 1697 suggestions for reform of the Poor Laws that, along with public support for those unable to work, he favored a program to provide jobs for the able-bodied but destitute poor and their children over the age of three.

JAMES TULLY

Property and Obligation in Locke†

Charity and Inheritance

It is sometimes assumed that labour is the only natural title to and justification of individual ownership. Macpherson's interpretation is that 'the whole theory of property is a justification of the natural right . . . to unlimited individual appropriation'. He states that 'the root of that justification' is Locke's 'insistence that a man's labour is his own property'. Consequently, the 'traditional view that property and labour were social functions, and that ownership of property involved social obligations, is thereby undermined'. Aside from the fact that it is Locke's opponents, Grotius and Filmer, who present theories in which property is free of social obligations, Macpherson seems to place the wrong emphasis on labour. Labour justifies neither the accumulation of nor rights over one's goods; it provides * * * a means of identifying something as naturally one's own. Justification of accumulation and use is derived from the prior duty and right to support and comfort God's workmanship. The priority of natural law renders all rights as means to this end, and therefore

---

† From *A Discourse on Property: John Locke and His Adversaries* (Cambridge: Cambridge University Press, 1980). Reprinted by permission of Cambridge University Press.

Locke's account is a limited rights theory. An unlimited theory, like
Grotius', grants priority to exclusive rights.[1] Such a theory employs
natural law to protect exclusive rights, through reducing it to the
natural duty to abstain from another's property. Locke's theory is
constructed in opposition to an unlimited rights theory; precisely
the sort of theory which Marx took to be the typical justification of
private property.

Certainly Locke wishes to emphasise that labour is the most suitable means for a rational animal to perform the first phase of his
duty to preserve mankind. It is not, however, the sole means. In the
same sentence in which he first announces that honest industry
naturally entitles a person to his just products, he also proclaims
two other natural titles: charity and inheritance (1.42).[2] 'Charity
gives every Man a Title to so much out of another's Plenty, as will
keep him from extreme want, where he has no means to subsist
otherwise.' Where no means are available for a man to provide for
himself, the right to the means of subsistence applies directly to another person's goods. 'God the Lord and Father of all, has given no
one of his Children such a Property, in his peculiar Portion of the
things of this World, but that he has given his needy Brother a
Right to the Suplusage of his Goods'. A proprietor who has more
than enough to sustain himself is under a positive duty to sustain
those who do not: 'twould always be a Sin in any man of Estate, to
let his Brother perish for want of affording him Relief out of his
plenty'.

*   *   *

* * * It should be noted as well that the positive duty of charity
is not inconsistent with Locke's definition of property as that which
cannot be taken without the proprietor's consent. The inclusive
rights of each refer to the goods of a given society, and these are
held individually because this serves the function of preserving
mankind. If a case of need arises then, *ipso facto*, one man's individual right is overridden by another's claim, and the goods become
his property. By failing to hand over the goods, the proprietor invades the share now belonging to the needy and is liable to punishment (2.37).[3] The necessary goods 'cannot justly be denied him'
(I.42). Individual ownership provides the means by which a moral
agent may exercise his choice in performing his duties to others.

*   *   *

* * * Locke's account of inheritance unfolds another dimension
of the social nature of man. Men's duties to God and 'the Duties

1. See Grotius (p. 238 herein). All notes are editor's unless otherwise specified.
2. "1": *First Treatise.*
3. "2": *Second Treatise.*

they owe one another' (2.5) constitute the community of mankind (2.128). Since man cannot exist without society, the performance of these duties is existentially necessary. In addition to this community man is also born into, and dependent upon, conjugal society, which is sustained by a set of familial duties (2.52–86). The individual commoner in the state of nature is twice removed from the isolated and presocial individual, who is often thought to underlie late eighteenth-century economic and political thought. * * *

Locke acknowledges that there is almost universal consent to the institution of inheritance and infers, 'where the Practice is Universal, 'tis reasonable to think the Cause is Natural' (1.88). Parents have a natural and positive duty to provide support and comfort for their children, and the children have 'a Right in the Goods they [the Parents] are possessed of' (1.88). It follows that any family man's property is not his property at all; it is the common property of the whole family. 'Men are not Proprietors of what they have merely for themselves, their Children have a Title to part of it, and have their Kind of Right joyn'd with their Parents.'

The standard form of a right of property is not an individual right for Locke; it is a common right enjoyed by all the family and, if necessary, by the whole kinship unit (1.90). The reason for this unique familialisation of property is to preserve mankind by preserving its basic unit: the family (1.88, 89). Locke destroys the very foundation of individual rights: the unquestioned assumption that a proprietor is the patriarchal head of a family. * * * The family remains the basic sociological category but, instead of a hierarchy, it becomes a communal organisation with common property, 'Community of Goods and the Power over them, mutual Assistance, and Maintenance . . . [are] things belonging to *Conjugal Society*' (2.83). Just as Filmer uses his patriarchal family as a model for society, so Locke uses his radically restructured communal family as a model for society. A father has no more dominion over the property of his children than Adam and his descendants have over man's property. Children, like God's children, do not require their father's consent to individuate their common property (2.29).

Inheritance is not justified in terms of a father's right to dispose of his property as he pleases, since it is not wholly his property. Inheritance marks the fact that the parents have ceased to use that which belongs to the family in common. A possession 'comes to be wholly theirs [the children's] when death having put an end to their Parents use of it, hath taken them from their Possessions, and this we call Inheritance' (1.88; cf. 99). It now belongs to them for 'maintenance, support, and comfort . . . and nothing else" (1.93). The whole institution of primogeniture is unceremoniously dismembered, and all the children share in the inheritance (1.93). If

there is no heir, the goods revert to the community; that is, they become common in the state of nature or pass into the hands of government in political society (1.90).

* * *

Property in Political Society

* * * When society's power is in each man's hands in the state of
nature, it has as its end the preservation of mankind. It has the
same end, therefore, when it becomes political power in the hands
of the legislative: 'the *end and measure of this Power*, when in every
Man's hands in the state of Nature, being the preservation of all of
his Society, that is, all Mankind in general, it can have no other
end or measure, when in the hands of the Magistrate, but to preserve the Members of that Society' (2.171). This natural end is
thus the aim of legislative power, 'a *Power to make Laws*, and annex
such *Penalties* to them, as may tend to the preservation of the
whole'. * * *

Locke redescribes the natural end of political society as the public good: 'Their Power in the utmost Bounds of it, is *limited to the
publick good* of the Society. It is a power, that hath no other end
but preservation' (2.135). Common good, good of society or community and good of the public are various synonyms he uses to describe the purpose for which a commonwealth is instituted. * * *

* * *

* * * Although a man enters into a polity to preserve his liberty,
as a condition of membership he abjures to the community his
natural liberty—the power of doing whatsoever he thinks fit for
the support and comfort of himself and others. This is necessary
because he is not now an independent individual but, rather, an in-
terdependent member of an unified whole, orchestrated by government. * * * He is now immediately under civil rather than natural
law; his new, conventional liberty is formally identical yet materially
different from natural liberty.

It follows, *a fortiori*, from his liberty or natural power to dispose
and order his person, action and possessions being yielded to, and
under the direction of, the community, that his possessions also belong to the community. For what he relinquishes is his power to
come to have and to possess these goods. 'To understand this the
better', Locke explains, 'it is fit to consider, that every Man, when
he, at first, incorporates himself into any Commonwealth, he, by
his uniting himself thereunto, annexed also, and submits to the
Community those Possessions, which he has, or shall acquire, that
do not already belong to any other Government' (2.120). All the
possessions a man has in the state of nature, or shall acquire in his

commonwealth, become the possessions of the community. As with
liberty, men preserve their possessions by exchanging natural possessions for conventionally defined ones. * * *

* * * The crucial point * * * is that community ownership of all
possessions is the logical consequence of the premises of Locke's
theory in the *Two Treatises*. Natural acquisition and possession are
legitimate in the state of nature as long as the 'enough and as good
for others' proviso is satisfied. With the introduction of money, land
becomes scarce and men's claim rights conflict; then the theory of
natural appropriation and use has no application. The basic premises that God gave the earth to all men in common for all time, and
at any particular time, necessarily invalidates all exclusive rights
once the proviso is no longer met. Therefore, * * * when the vital
proviso is no longer satisfied, goods once legitimately acquired can
no longer be retained in exclusive possession, but revert to common
ownership.

*   *   *

The crucial point for Locke in any distribution of property is
twofold: that everyone has the means necessary for comfortable
subsistence; and that everyone is able to labour in, and enjoy the
fruits of, his calling in a manner appropriate to man, and analogous
to God's activity as a maker. These are the explicit premises of the
argument and the normative framework in terms of which a system
of property relations is assessed. The validity of any distribution is
conditional upon the fulfillment of these two social functions. * * *

*   *   *

* * * It is remarkable that Locke has been depicted as a defender
of unconditional private property in land. Any distribution which
conduces to the performance of the form of activity he saw as a
duty to God; which ensures the means of preservation for each,
and which protects each man in the enjoyment of the fruits of his
labour, is a just arrangement. * * * It is a system in which private
and common ownership are not mutually exclusive but mutually related: private ownership is the means of individuating the community's common property and is limited by the claims of all other
members. What particular legal form this might take in a given
commonwealth is not a problem of theory but of prudence.

Property and Revolution

*   *   *

* * * [Locke] places the right to resist the illegal acts of the
Crown in the hands of each citizen. His audience could hardly fail
to understand the practical implication of his theoretical redescrip-
tion of the traditional negative duty in terms of an individual and

active natural property or right to exercise sovereignty over their civil rights. It is an unequivocal incitement to revolution: 'whenever the *Legislators endeavour to take away and destroy the Property of the people*, . . . [they] are thereupon absolved from any farther Obedience, and are left to the common Refuge, which God hath provided for all Men, against Force and Violence' (2.222).

It is essential to see that Locke is protecting individual civil rights from arbitrary interference of the Crown by giving the ultimate right to enforce the law to the citizenry. A kind of historical foreshortening is required to impute to Locke, as Macpherson does, the attempt to preserve capitalist property against the proletariat. * * *

*   *   *

* * * The conventional criterion for the right to vote in the seventeenth century was the possession of property. Filmer's theory systematically denies property, and therefore suffrage, to all but independent landholders. In demonstrating that every man has property in his life, liberty, person, action, and some possessions, Locke extends the franchise to every adult male. He does not explicitly state the criterion in the *Two Treatises;* he simply assumes it as the basis for his discussion of various forms of representation: 'whenever the People shall chuse their *Representatives upon* just and undeniably *equal measures* suitable to the original Frame of Government, it cannot be doubted to be the will and act of the Society' (2.158). The equal measures suitable to the original constitution cannot but be the natural equality of all men. (2.5). * * *[4]

JEREMY WALDRON

Locke's Discussion of Property†

* * * Locke takes great pains to distinguish the regulation of property from its confiscation or redistribution:

> But Government into whatsoever hand it is put, being as I have before shew'd, intrusted with this condition, and for this end, that Men might have and secure their Properties, the Prince or Senate, however it may have power to make Laws for the regulating of Property between the Subjects one amongst another, yet can never have a power to take themselves the

---

4. For the argument that the original constitution need not require universal suffrage, see Geraint Parry (p. 349 herein).
† From "Locke, Tully, and the Regulation of Property," *Political Studies*, 32 (1984), pp. 98, 104, 105–06. Reprinted by permission of Blackwell Publishers.

whole or any part of the Subjects Property, without their own consent. For it would in effect be to leave them no property at all (II, 139).[1]

To support otherwise, Locke suggests, would be to embroil oneself in the contradiction that men 'must be suppos'd to lose that by entering into Society, which was the end for which they entered into it' (II, 138).

It is important to see that Locke's contrast here is between regulation of property by the legislature and its confiscation again *by the legislature*. The former is a proper discharge of legislative power; the latter, Locke suggests, can never be legitimate. This makes nonsense of Tully's suggested interpretation of these passages. He reads them as follows: when a man enters society he surrenders the property he has acquired to the community; the community then, by legislative processes, redistributes these resources on the basis of the general good; and then, in respect of these redistributed holdings, falls under an obligation of natural law not subsequently to disturb them. This interpretation is strained and implausible. It seems to indicate that the Lockian legislature is under *fewer* constraints of natural law with respect to its dealings with *natural* entitlements than it is with respect to its dealings with *conventional* entitlements. Natural entitlements, according to Tully, may be redistributed as the legislature sees fit; whereas conventional entitlements acquire all the protection of natural law. If this sort of contrivance is the cost of Tully's reading, clearly the traditional reading is preferable.

* * *

Bearing all this in mind, we can see what Locke means when he suggests * * * that anyone joining a political society must 'submit' his possessions to the community. Tully's interpretation of the passage is as follows: 'All the possessions a man has in the state of nature, or shall acquire in his commonwealth, become the possessions of the community.' But there is nothing in Locke to support that reading. The correct interpretation is stated by Locke a few sentences later:

> By the same act therefore, whereby any one unites in Person, which was before free, to any Commonwealth; by the same he unites his Possessions, which were before free to it also; and they become both of them, Person and Possession, subject to the Government and the Dominion of that Commonwealth. . . . (II, 120).

Unless Tully wants to suggest that the citizen's own *person* also becomes 'the possession of the community', his interpretation is

1. "II": *Second Treatise*. All notes are the editor's unless otherwise specified.

hopeless, since Locke is suggesting here that person and property are subject to the community only to the same extent. The extent of that subjection is made perfectly clear elsewhere in the *Treatise*: both in his own actions and in the use and enjoyment of his property the citizen is to be governed by the legitimate laws of the community. And one of the *conditions* of the legitimacy of those laws is that the legislature 'cannot take from any Man any part of his property without his own consent' (II, 138–40).

* * *

One final point. To maintain that Locke believed that natural entitlements survive the transition to civil society is not to suggest that he regarded private property in civil society as 'absolute' or 'unlimited'. Locke's position on the fundamental limitation of property entitlements is by now well known: all entitlements, whether they are natural or conventional, are subject at all times to the requirement of charity and the demands of abject need. On Locke's view, a person simply has no right, natural or otherwise, to retain control over resources which are superfluous to his own needs if they could be used to keep another 'from extream want. where he has no means to subsist otherwise' (I, 42). But there is no need to make property rights conventional in order to bring this limitation into play. Since it applies already to natural entitlements, it is therefore one of the natural duties that civil authorities legitimately may enforce in the discharge of their function of preserving existing property rights. * * *

Lockean Individualism: Atomistic or Social?

Following the examples of Thomas Jefferson and the Founding Fathers, Americans have always seen Locke as the great defender of the rights of the individual. As the preceding selections on Locke as collectivist illustrates, this view has been criticized by James Tully and, earlier, by Willmoore Kendall (1940).

Charles Taylor emphasizes Locke's individualism. He sees Locke as representative of a new "atomistic" worldview that breaks with the hierarchical and communitarian thinking of ancient and medieval thought and transforms previous doctrines of community consent into an assertion of individual autonomy that makes politics the creation of the "sovereign individual." He also equates, incorrectly, Locke's rejection of innate moral ideas with the rejection of any source of moral obligation outside what he calls "the punctual self." Himself committed to a more communitarian view, Taylor contrasts what he describes as the instrumentalism and atomism of modern liberalism that begins in Locke with more "holistic" views, such as republicanism and civic humanism, which can, in his view, provide "the matrix within which the noble ends of life devoted to the public good are first conceivable."

Ruth Grant criticizes those like Taylor who turn Locke's political individualism—his belief in original freedom, political equality, and government by consent—into a broader philosophy that sees human beings only as "rational maximizers of utility." Locke, she argues, was fully aware of moral, social, and community bonds but was concerned to limit the domain of politics to "the protection of individual rights and the pursuit of the public good understood in terms of peace and prosperity." Advocates of a more communitarian politics, she says, must make a case for the coercive imposition of broader community norms, and limits on individual freedom by government.

Locke did favor "the corpuscularian hypothesis" to explain "the qualities of bodies" (*Essay*, IV.3.16) but this did not carry over into his view of the relation of the individual to society. Despite Taylor's claims to the contrary he did not reject divine purposes evident in God.s creation ("teleology") as a source of morality. (See for example, *Second Treatise* 77, which argues that man is driven into society by "strong obligations of necessity, convenience, and inclination.") He believed in limited government and individual consent to the establishment by the majority of a government whose powers are limited, both by natural law and by the knowledge that "a long train of abuses" (*Second Treatise*, 225) may lead the people, which he usually defines as the majority or even "any single man" (*Second Treatise*, 168) to "appeal to heaven"—that is, to overthrow the government.

CHARLES TAYLOR

The "Punctual" Self: Locke and Atomistic Instrumentalism†

* * *

The subject of disengagement and rational control has become a familiar modern figure. One might almost say it has become one way of construing ourselves, which we find it hard to shake off. It is one aspect of our inescapable contemporary sense of inwardness. As it develops to its full form through Locke and the Enlightenment thinkers he influenced, it becomes what I want to call the 'punctual' self.

The key to this figure is that it gains control through disengagement. Disengagement is always correlative of an 'objectification', if I may introduce this as another term of art. Objectifying a given domain involves depriving it of its normative force for us. If we take a domain of being in which hitherto the way things are has set norms or standards for us, and take a new stance to it as neutral, I will speak of our objectifying it.

The great mechanization of the scientific world picture of the seventeenth century, which Descartes helped to carry out, was an objectification in this sense. On the previously dominant view, the cosmic order was seen as the embodiment of the Ideas. The physical world around us takes the shape it does in order to body forth an order of Ideas. This can be taken itself as an ultimate in explanation, as it is in Plato, as ordered for the Good; or it can be integrated into Christian theology, and the Ideas understood as the thoughts of God. But in either case, the order is seen to be what it is because it exhibits Reason, Goodness; in the theological variant, the Wisdom of God. * * * On the Platonic-influenced conception which had been handed down through neo-Platonism and the pseudo-Dionysius,[1] and which was dominant in medieval and early

---

† From *Sources of the Self: The Making of the Modern Identity* (Cambridge, MA: Harvard University Press, 1989), pp. 160–61, 164–65, 192–94, 195–96, 197. Copyright © 1989 by Charles Taylor. Reprinted by permission of the publisher.
1. (6th century Pseudo-Dionysius), monk who pretended to be "Dionysius the Areopagite" mentioned in the New Testament (Acts 17:34) as an Athenian, converted by St. Paul. His works, *The Ecclesiastical Hierarchy* and *The Celestial Hierarchy* had a quasi-

modern Europe * * * [t]hings are as they are in order to conform to a pattern to rational self-manifestation, in which the One turns into the Many, in which all possible niches are occupied (Lovejoy's "principle of plentitude")[2] and the like. An order conceived after this fashion I want to call a 'meaningful' order, or one involving an 'ontic logos'.[3]

It is plain that an order of this kind sets the paradigm purposes of the beings within it. As humans we are to conform to our Idea, and this in turn must play its part in the whole, which among other things involves our being 'rational', i.e., capable of seeing the self-manifesting order. No one can understand this order while being indifferent to it or failing to recognize its normative force. Indifference is a sign that one has not understood, that one is in error, as Epicureans and other atomists were widely condemned as being by the premodern mainstream.

The move to mechanism neutralizes this whole domain. It no longer sets norms for us—or at least it does not set norms in the traditional way. Nor was this simply a side effect of a move prompted by purely epistemological[4] considerations. On the contrary, part of the impetus for the new science came from an anti-teleological[5] morality. The source of this was theological: the nominalist revolt against Aristotelian realism, by figures like William of Occam,[6] who was motivated by a sense that propounding an ethic founded on the supposed bent of nature was attempting to set limits to the sovereignty of God. God must preserve the fullest freedom to establish good and bad by fiat. The further developments of this Occamist line of thought played an important role in the scientific revolution of this century, as has often been remarked. In the end, a mechanistic universe was the only one compatible with a God whose sovereignty was defined in terms of the endless freedom of fiat.

*   *   *

The modern figure I call the punctual self has pushed this disengagement much further, and has been induced to do so by the same mix of motivations: the search for control intertwined with a certain conception of knowledge. * * *

*   *   *

---

scriptural authority in the Middle Ages and were cited as justifications for hierarchies in the Church, the state, and among the angels. All notes are the editor's unless otherwise specified.

2. Arthur O. Lovejoy, *The Great Chain of Being* (Harvard University Press, 1936).
3. An internal rational principle of being.
4. Based on theories of knowledge.
5. Opposed to the derivation, by Aristotle and St. Thomas Aquinas, of norms from goals (Gr. *tele*) inherent in nature.
6. William of Ockham (14th century), English theologian who argued that ideas do not represent anything "real" but only names (Latin *nomina*) given to common qualities in individual things.

Locke took the really uncompromising stance, the one which set the terms in which the punctual self was to be defined through the Enlightenment and beyond. * * *

* * * In rejecting innateness, Locke is also giving vent to his profoundly anti-teleological view of human nature, of both knowledge and morality. The motives for this are complex and have much to do with the winning of a certain kind of control.

In respect of knowledge, Locke aligns himself against any view which sees us as naturally tending to or attuned to the truth, whether it be of the ancient variety, that we are qua rational beings, constitutionally disposed to recognize the rational order of things; or of the modern variety, that we have innate ideas, or an innate tendency to unfold our thought towards the truth. * * *

* * *

Both disengagement and this understanding of the nature of things as within them helped to generate a new notion of individual independence. The disengaged subject is an independent being, in the sense that his or her paradigm purposes are to be found within, and not dictated by the larger order of which he or she is a part. One of the fruits of this is the new political atomism which arises in the seventeenth century, most notably with the theories of social contract of Grotius, Pufendorf, Locke, and others. Contract theory as such wasn't new in this century, of course. There is a rich background to it in the tradition. It had its roots in Stoic philosophy and mediaeval theories of rights. Moreover, there had been an important development of theories of consent in the late Middle Ages, most notably around the conciliar[7] movement in the church. And the sixteenth century saw the contract theories of the great Jesuit writers like Suarez.[8]

Nevertheless, there was something importantly new in the seventeenth-century theories. Previously the issue of consent had been put in terms of a people establishing government by contract. The existence of the community was something taken for granted in all earlier versions. * * * For a post-seventeenth-century reader, an obvious question arises: How does the community get started? Where does it get its authority to determine the nature of political authority over its constituent individuals? Before the seventeenth century this issue is not raised. The big innovation of contract theorists from Grotius on is that they do address it; it now begins to appears self-evident that it has to be addressed.

---

7. The theories associated with the Councils of Constance (1414–18) and Basel (1431–46), which held that the councils, representing the consent of the Church, had the power to define doctrine and to depose and control the pope.
8. Francisco Suarez (1612), Spanish Jesuit who wrote *On the Laws and God, the Lawgiver*, which argued, against the divine right of kings, that political authority was based on the consent of the community.

The new theories add to the traditional contract founding government a second one, which precedes it: a contract of association. This is a universal agreement which founds a political community and confers on it the power to determine a form of government. The shift between these two kinds of contract theory reflects a shift in the understanding of the human moral predicament. Previously that people were members of a community went without saying. It didn't need to be justified relative to a more basic situation. But now the theory starts from the individual on his own. Membership of a community with common power of decision is now something which needs to be explained by the individual's prior consent. Of course, each may be seen as a social being in another sense. Locke's picture of the state of nature seems to involve a lot of interchange between people. But what cannot now be taken for granted anymore is a community with decisional powers over its members. People start off as political atoms.

Underlying this atomist contract theory, we can see two facets of the new individualism. Disengagement from cosmic order meant that the human agent was no longer to be understood as an element in a larger, meaningful order. His paradigm purposes are to be discovered within. He is on his own. What goes for the larger cosmic order will eventually be applied also to political society. And this yields a picture of the sovereign individual, who is 'by nature' not bound to any authority. The condition of being under authority is something which has to be *created*.

* * *

We inherit atomism from the seventeenth century. Not that we still espouse contract theories (although various transposed versions are still popular). But we still find it easy to think of political society as created by will or to think of it instrumentally. In the latter case, even though we no longer understand the origins of society as reposing in agreement, we nevertheless both understand and evaluate its workings as an instrument to attain ends we impute to individuals or constituent groups.

And we inherit from this century our theories of rights, the modern tendency to frame the immunities accorded people by law in terms of subjective rights. This * * * is a conception which puts the autonomous individual at the centre of our system of law. From Locke comes an influential gloss on this, what Brough Macpherson has called 'possessive individualism',[9] a conception of the most basic immunities we enjoy—life, liberty—on the model of the ownership of property. This construction reflects the extreme stance of

---

9. C. B. MacPherson, *The Political Theory of Possessive Individualism* (Oxford: Oxford University Press, 1962).

disengagement towards one's own being of the Lockean punctual self. The continuing force of the individualism is a sign of the enduring attraction of the self-understanding.

The atomism/instrumentalism complex belongs to those ideas I spoke about above which are somehow easier for us, in that they benefit from the onus of argument, or at least explanation. This is not to say that we are imprisoned within it. Quite the contrary: there are a number of influential doctrines in the modern world which have tried to recapture a more holistic view of society, to understand it as a matrix for individuals rather than as an instrument. And some of these have been important for our political practice. But they have remained burdened with the onus of explanation. Atomist views always seem nearer to common sense, more immediately available. Even though they don't stand up very well in argument (at least, so I believe), even though a modicum of explanation is enough to show their inadequacy, nevertheless this explanation is continually necessary. It's as though without a special effort of reflection on this issue, we tend to fall back into an atomist/instrumental way of seeing. This seems to dominate our unreflecting experience of society, or at least to emerge more easily when we try to formulate what we know from this experience. It's a naturally favoured idea, benefiting from a built-in ever-renewed initial plausibility.

This occurs in spite of the fact that modern political life has generated powerful counter-ideas. In particular, there is the understanding of society which has been described as 'civic humanist.'[1] This draws on the ancient republic or polis for its model. It came to the fore briefly in fifteenth-century Italy, played some role in the troubles which led to the English Civil War, and then was central to the great revolutions of the eighteenth century in America and France which have helped to shape modern politics.

The notion of citizen virtue, as we see it defined in Montesquieu and Rousseau,[2] can't be combined with an atomist understanding of society. It assumes that the political way of life, in devotion to which Montesquieu's 'virtue' consists, is in an important sense prior to the individuals. It establishes their identity, provides the matrix within which they can be the kinds of human beings they are, within which the noble ends of a life devoted to the public good are first conceivable. The political structures can't be seen simply as instruments, means to ends which could be framed without them.

* * * In this tension, the natural favour the first idea enjoys has

---

1. See discussion of the republican or civic humanist tradition by Steven Dworetz (p. 388 herein).
2. Jean-Jacques. Rousseau, *The Social Contract* (1762). Charles-Louis de Montesquieu, *The Spirit of the Laws* (1748).

played some role. But the citizen understanding, however recessive and distorted and relegated to the background it may be, still is needed to capture an essential part of our practice as citizen republics.

* * *

RUTH GRANT

Locke's Political Anthropology and Lockean Individualism†

* * *

* * * [T]he opinion persists, despite general agreement among contemporary Locke scholars to the contrary, that Locke's individualism is "atomistic" individualism: that Locke envisioned a state of nature peopled by dissociated individuals, for example; or that the Lockean individual resembles the model economic man, guiding his actions by calculations of his own personal advantage based on his private estimation of his interests. By looking at Locke's historical and anthropological descriptions, I hope to assist in dispelling such notions.

* * * [C]ontemporary communitarian critics of liberalism [also] * * * fault liberal thinkers, Locke included, for their inadequate understanding of the self, and in particular for their failure to recognize the simple fact that every individual is embedded in social relationships. Liberalism is said to depend upon an individualistic premise which cannot be supported by the facts. Liberal individualism is "bad sociology."

My purpose is to show that at least one classical liberal recognized fully the extent to which human beings are social beings, but did not believe that that fact dictated any particular political conclusions. Locke's disagreement with contemporary critics would be not so much about the facts as about their import. He recognized the social character of human life and the extent to which individuals develop beliefs, ideas and interests in a social context. The question is what that recognition ought to mean for politics. The premise of Locke's political argument—that men are born free—is not a sociological claim, but a moral one. And to understand that is central to appreciating what could properly be meant by Lockean "individualism."

† From "Locke's Political Anthropology and Lockean Individualism," *The Journal of Politics* 50. 1 (February 1988), pp. 42, 43, 50–51, 60–61. Reprinted with the permission of Blackwell Publishers.

* * *

Locke begins with the thought that every man has an equal right
to govern his actions as he sees fit. Men are equal in the sense that
they are by nature free; there is no natural political authority. It
follows then that political authority must be a created condition.
Political authority and obligation are man-made, conventional, created by agreement. If political authority is created, there must be a
condition without it. That condition is called the "state of nature."
The state of nature and political society are mutually exclusive categories, something like the categories "married" and "single." Men
are either part of the same political community or they are not, and
if they are not, they are in the state of nature with respect to each
other. The phrase means nothing more than the relation among any
men at any time who have between them no legitimate superiority
or subjection, no political authority, who remain in their natural relation as free and equal to one another. The state of nature is a necessary logical inference from the premise of natural freedom, and it
also exists in fact whenever and wherever there are men who do not
belong to the same political community.

Locke scholars have sometimes proceeded as if the question
were whether the state of nature is peaceful or warlike; that is, as if
the question were whether Locke's premise is natural sociality or
natural selfishness, isolation and hostility. If it were either of these,
the anthropological evidence would have a direct bearing on the argument. But it is not; his premise is natural freedom. And the
record of life in early communities, peaceful or not, cannot show
that there is a natural right to rule. Man's natural sociality and family structure do not imply political authority, and this is the whole
point of Locke's discussion of the historical origins of political life.
He means to show, contra Filmer, that obedience to fathers is not
the same as a natural monarchic right to rule and the fact that men
are born into preexisting social and political groups does not mean
that they have a preexisting duty to obey the authorities within
those groups. * * *

We are now in a better position to see what Locke's individualism
is. Locke's individualism is a political individualism at the level of
normative theory. The term could be used to characterize his response to the question of the origins of legitimate political authority, the central question of the *Second Treatise*. Legitimate political
authority arises from individual consent. "Individualism" is not, of
course, Locke's term, and it is an unfortunate term in his case. In
contemporary discussions, we expect that the opposite of "individualism" would be something like "communitarianism"; the implication of the term is that it is somehow in tension with community or
society. The opposite of Locke's political individualism, however, is

not community, but hierarchy. He is opposing the equality and freedom of men to the idea that there is a natural or divinely ordained
hierarchy among them. Lockean individualism therefore is not incompatible with the recognition of the importance of communal
ties, family associations, and social norms, though it is a critique of
authoritarian political communities.

* * *

* * * Lockean individualism is not what it is often thought to be.
First, it is not social atomism: Locke makes no claim that men ever
lived in isolation from their fellows. Man's natural condition is to
be embedded in a series of social relations throughout life. Second,
men are not rational maximizers of utility; Locke does not describe
men according to the model economic man of contemporary theory. By and large, their conduct in life is not governed by the independent calculation of how best to satisfy their individual interests.
On the contrary, their conduct is most likely to be governed by
common opinions and beliefs as to what constitutes a happy and
respectable life. And men are often led to quite unreasonable
things on the basis of these powerful social norms.

In both political and the epistemological discussions, Locke gives
full recognition to the importance of the social. And in both cases,
what he does is try to alter radically its relation to politics. Social
bonds are natural and strong, but they do not imply political obligations. Political relations can only be created by consent in accordance with the premise of natural freedom. Similarly, Locke
acknowledges that a concern for the good opinion of others is a
powerful motivating force and that men's beliefs and their conduct
are strongly influenced by what we would call "socialization." But
his response to this is to treat education as the responsibility of the
private institutions of family and church, to teach toleration and
the authority of reason, to isolate controversial religious opinion
from the sphere of politics, and to limit that sphere to the protection of individual rights and the pursuit of the public good understood in terms of peace and prosperity. Custom and traditional
opinion are to lose much of their political importance. Locke de-
politicizes the social.

In one sense, then, Locke is not so "individualistic" after all. His
political doctrine is perfectly compatible with community in many
forms and with strong communal institutions. In another sense,
Locke seems to make men more "individualistic"; more osuspicious
of authority, less likely to take anything on faith. Locke's individualism is to be found in his assertion of individual natural rights and
in his encouragement of independent individual thought. His object in both cases is to combat authoritarianism, to combat the subjection of any man to the will of another politically or intellectually,

and particularly when intellectual oppression is a tool of political oppression. Locke means to make men independent judges of the truth and watchful guardians of their rights.

A convincing attack on liberal individualism of this Lockean sort would have to do at least one of the following. It would have to attack the true individualistic premise of Locke's thought, which is the normative proposition that men are by nature free and equal. It might go on to demonstrate how political obligations can be grounded in involuntary social relationships. Lastly, the heart of the argument would be a case for choosing a politics based on communal attachments and traditions over a politics that emphasizes voluntary political action based on reflection and choice. This is an argument concerning a moral choice. The two sides face off not over the question of whether or not men are social, but over the question of the place their social attachments ought to have in their adult lives. The challenge to the liberal individualists is to show either that individualism is not identical to egoism or loneliness (that there are liberal forms of community) or that, if it is, political freedom is worth the price. The challenge to the communitarians is to show either that a communitarianism that attacks liberal individualism can nonetheless produce nonauthoritarian communities, or that, if it can't, community is worth the price. A repetition of the facts of human sociality comes nowhere near to settling this argument.

Consent and Representation: Genuine or Fictitious?

Echoing Locke, Thomas Jefferson in the Declaration of Independence asserted that "governments derive their just powers from the consent of the governed." What do we mean by "government by consent"? How can the governed give their consent? If it is through their representatives, how can they claim to speak for those who elected them? Locke thought he could answer these questions, but his answers have provoked a large and often contradictory literature.

The selections in this section attempt to determine how Locke's theories of consent and representation are to be understood. A. John Simmons (1993, 1992) seems to agree with what he calls the standard criticism of Locke's theory of tacit consent, that it can be used to legitimate any de facto government—a view first articulated by Filmer in his *Patriarcha* (p. 000 herein). He criticizes those (e.g., Pitkin, 1965) who have interpreted Locke as requiring only that the government be one to which a rational person would consent (hypothetical consent), rejects Locke's tacit consent argument as meaningless, and insists that we must understand Locke's theory as requiring individual personal consent. That consent is necessary, but not sufficient, because it may be given only to a government whose functions are limited to "the ends whose promotion by government would make it rational for people to subject themselves to government." Observing that few citizens in the modern world have an opportunity to give express consent, he concludes that nevertheless we should work to establish "genuinely voluntary political societies" that "would help to secure the natural right of self-government to which each of us is born."

Geraint Parry, writing on Locke's views on representation, rejects both the view of James Tully that Locke was really calling for universal manhood suffrage (see p. 349 herein) and that of C. B. Macpherson (p. 292 herein) who believes that Locke wished to restrict the vote to property holders. In Parry's view, Locke believed that the specific institutions of government, such as the extent of the right to vote, were to be decided by majority rule. In the English case, the majority had consented to a limited government by the king in Parliament, one branch of which (the House of Commons) should be chosen in ways that were roughly proportionate to population and to economic contribution. He thus concludes that Locke draws "conservative conclusions from radical premises." (On the radicalism of Locke's theory of numerical majorities compared to earlier group-oriented doctrines of majority rule, see Paul E. Sigmund, p. 306 herein.)

A. JOHN SIMMONS

The Meaning of Consent in Locke†

[*The Critique of Lockean Consent Theory*]

* * * There is simply not much evidence in actual states of ordinary citizens doing things that look very much like giving morally interesting consent to political authorities. The problem * * * is not one of intuitive *force*, but rather one of *realism*. And this problem was, of course, Locke's problem as well. * * * [H]ordes of active consenters were no more in evidence in Locke's England than in twentieth-century England. Locke's solution to the problem was to offer * * * his famous theory of tacit consent. * * *

Because that theory of tacit consent allows Locke to portray residents, landowners, travelers on the highways, and lodgers in the inns—in short all who enjoy the state's territories—as consenters, he has no problem appearing to show that actual states can be legitimate. But his solution also seems to face a series of devastating objections, which have collectively become the (dismissive) *standard critique* of Lockean consent theory.

* * *

Locke's theory of tacit consent (or his applications of that theory) undermines the whole point of consent theory. For Locke allows that tacit consent can be given by mere residence, for instance, apparently without conscious choice; such a consent theory (or application of consent theory) can in no way be consistent with Locke's affirmation of our natural freedom to choose where our allegiance will lie.

Locke's theory justifies precisely what Locke (along with all consent theorists) wishes to oppose. Tacit consent is so wide a notion for Locke (or is applied by him so widely), that it justifies virtual subjection by birth, since all residents can be taken as obligated consenters. And it seems to justify as well subjection even to oppressive regimes or conquerors, since obedience is virtually equivalent to consent.

* * *

† From *On the Edge of Anarchy: Locke, Consent, and the Limits of Society* (Princeton, NJ: Princeton University Press, 1993), pp. 199–200, 202, 204, 205, 206–7, 208–9, 266–68. Copyright © 1993, 1995 Princeton University Press. Reprinted by permission of Princeton University Press.

* * * Locke at least often seems to confuse two quite different sources of political obligation in his discussion of consent: deliberate, intentional undertakings of obligation, on the one hand, and the willing receipt or acceptance of benefits provided by the government, on the other ("the enjoyment of any part of the dominion of any government" stressed by Locke). While only the former is properly called "consent" (despite Locke's broader use of the term), the latter seems another reasonably plausible suggestion concerning the source of people's political obligations.

* * *

Just government, for Locke, operates within certain bounds (II, 142)[1] and aims to promote certain ends (those ends whose promotion by government would make it rational for people to subject themselves to government [II, 137]). More specifically, just government aims at the preservation of its subjects' property (II, 124, 134), that is their "lives, liberties and fortunes (II, 137; see also II, 123); it has as its end "the securing of mens' rights" (II, 219). The promotion of this end seems to be meant by Locke to be equivalent to the promotion of the "common good" (e.g., II, 131, 134, 135, 142). And just governments must promote these ends nonpaternalistically (i.e., in accordance with the people's own assessment of what counts as promoting them). When governments have these qualities (and only then), it is rational for all of us to live under them, since they then facilitate the advancement of both our civil and religious interests. But is this not just a way of saying that governments with these qualities are *legitimate* with respect to all persons? Governments that best solve the problem of social interaction are legitimate and hence owed obedience (a la Hobbes), this line of argument suggests.

But now it seems easy to see consent dropping out of Locke's true account of political authority and political obligation. If it is the quality and structure of government that make it legitimate why should Locke be concerned with the origin of government's authority or with their subjects' personal consent. What really matters to Locke is that government is of such a quality that a rational person *would* consent to it authority. * * * All of the consent talk in Locke is just his (misleading) way of emphasizing a hypothetical (rational) consent standard. This interpretation of Locke's consent theory is (roughly) the one offered by Hannah Pitkin[2] (and others), and if adequate it would clearly save Locke from much of the force of the standard critique. For on Pitkin's reading, Locke cannot be accused

1. "II": *Second Treatise*. All notes are the editor's unless otherwise specified.
2. Hannah Pitkin, "Obligation and Consent," *American Political Science Review* (1965), 69.

of resting his case on a weak, virtually "automatic" kind of actual consent, which would bind us to even unjust governments. He is not centrally concerned with *actual* consent at all, and his hypothetical consent standard would clearly rule out obligations to unjust regimes (although on this reading Locke would still face the problem of relying on a nonvoluntary ground of obligation and authority).

But the hypothetical contractarian reading of Locke * * * simply cannot be rendered consistent with the many passages in Locke in which he stresses his interest in the *actual, personal* consent of each individual subject—not the consent of the subject's parents, the majority of subjects, the people as a whole, some ancient historical consent, the hypothetical consent of a rational person, or the subject's disposition to consent. The consent that makes persons subjects is the consent "*of every individual*" (II, 96, 106), it is "his [or their] *own* consent[s]" (II, 15, 95, 119, 138, 139, 189), given *separately* in their turns" (II, 117) by "*actually* entering into" a promise or compact (II, 122; my emphasis throughout).

* * *

* * * Governments are "legitimate" with respect to individuals *only* by virtue of the actual, personal consent of those individuals. Governments may be good or desirable in many other ways; they may be the sort to which a rational chooser would give his consent. But without his actual consent, they cannot have legitimate authority (political power) over him. Similarly, it is "*by consenting*" that one "puts himself under an obligation" to society (II, 121; my emphasis). The political obligation anyone is under binds him "*by virtue of*" his performance of consensual acts (II, 121; my emphasis). Actual, personal consent is the ground of both political obligation and political power (authority, legitimacy); they are logical correlates, obligations and rights both generated in accordance with the natural law precept that voluntary undertakings must be respected.

But if consent occupies this central role in Locke's theory of obligation and authority, what role remains for Locke's quire obvious interest in the quality of government independent of the origins of its rights over individuals? * * *

Considerations of the quality of government serve as a crucial limit on consent—that is, a limit on what we may create consensual obligations to do. A political society's being good (and its having good government) cannot make it legitimate with respect to independent persons or ground their obligations to obey it. But it does bring that society into the class to which we may give binding consent; its goodness makes it possible for our consent to be morally effectual. Locke's position is that consent is *necessary* for political obligation and authority but not *sufficient* for either. * * *

* * *

[Consent, Obligation, and Anarchy]

* * * Those of us who live under good governments (to whose authority we never consented) are not * * * members of an originally legitimate community who are now being wronged by the society's breach of its legitimating contract or by the government's breach of its trust. We never contracted with those around us or entrusted any government with our rights. Neither, however, are we * * * in a state of war with our governments. For while our governments have used against us "force without right," * * * such a wrong is not in fact sufficient to originate a state of war (Locke's own claims to the contrary notwithstanding). Most of our governments (or at least most of those whose legitimacy might seriously have been maintained) have not conspired or acted to deprive us of our lives or freedom, and so have not made war upon us. * * * Rather, most of us in the "free world" are in Lockean terms just persons in the state of nature (simpliciter), subjected by our governments to a variety of (usually) relatively minor, but frighteningly regular, wrongful acts and policies. Illegitimate governments need not be warmakers. They can be quite benign, even progressive or responsive. They can govern the sorts of societies to which residence *would* give consent, if only residents were offered a clear choice situation. They can also, of course, be the sorts of governments we are entitled (or even obligated) to oppose, with all means at our disposal. Most often in the "free world," however, they are merely bumbling and inefficient, sometimes well-intentioned, sometimes moved by personal or partisan concerns, occasionally oppressive or tyrannical, and still somehow able to do a reasonable amount of good.

Should those of us living under such governments, then, just obey our moderately good laws and support our moderately good polities? Or should we pursue some alternative course? Here we do well to attend to the Lockean position on justified *individual* resistance, even though that position was framed primarily for those who began in a consensual political relationship (as we did not). For while "the majority" has no moral standing in the state of nature (there being no "people" there on whose behalf they may decide), individuals (such as ourselves) whose rights are violated by de facto governments or societies are in much the same moral situation as individuals who are *returned* to the state of nature by a previously legitimate government's or society's violation of their rights (with this exception: that a contract is breached in the latter case, but not in the former). * * * Individuals have the right to resist and repair violations of their rights and to recruit others who are entitled to assist them in this, regardless of whether the individuals live within or without political society. And in the state of nature (but not in political society) they may resist, repair, and punish even nonsystematic, nondeliberate violations. In thus enforcing our rights, we are limited only by the requirements that we avoid infringing the more pressing rights of others and avoid causing dramatic social harm (or preventing the accomplishment of dramatic social good).

When we confront a moderately good (but still illegitimate) legal system and government, then, we must weigh the importance of the rights it violates against the consequences of our various possible strategies. If the government is a good one, its violations of our rights would need to be very serious indeed (which will be unusual under a good government) for us to be justified in doing anything that will cause it to be unable to function effectively. For it will likely be doing significant good and preventing significant harm. And while we have no contractual duty to resist wrongs done to others (as we would toward fellow members of a legitimate polity * * *), we have a natural duty to aid those in need, as far at least as we comfortably can (and perhaps farther). This duty may require us in certain ways to support the efforts of governments (if only by refraining from disabling them) when they assist those in need. Finally, of course unless the government's violation of our rights is very serious, the acts we will be morally entitled to perform (in order to justly resist, punish, and repair those wrongs) will anyway be unlikely to be violant or destructive enough to cause serious disruption of a government's functions. For we are not at war with such governments as I am considering here. These moral facts, plus considerations of simple prudence (i.e., our interest in avoiding legal punishment), seem to dictate that moderately good governments which violate our rights only in the ways such governments typically do, ought not to be resisted in ways that threaten to destroy them or to replace them with distinctly inferior alternatives. Lockean anarchism acknowledges that there can be strong moral reasons for supporting, or at least not actively resisting, even (certain) illegitimate governments. In this regard, again, Lockean anarchism is not dramatically counterintuitive in its implications. It is only philosophically, not practically anarchic.

* * *

What we certainly have good reason to do is to press by legal means for those changes in our political arrangements that will permit the establishment of genuinely voluntary political societies. Thus, changes that would clarify the resident's choice situation, expand membership options, reduce the cost of membership, facilitate internal or external emigration, and so on, would all go far toward making the choice between membership and its alternatives adequately informed and fully voluntary. Such changes would help to secure the natural right of self-government to which each of us is born, a right that includes the privilege of genuine freedom in the choice of political (or nonpolitical) forms of life. Although Locke may have been wrong in claiming that life in the state of nature is always precarious and unstable (our lives in *this* state of nature are not, for instance, as he described them), he was surely right at least in maintaining that life in a free, consensual polity is *morally* preferable to life in even a stable, structured society built on force and acquiescence.

* * *

GERAINT PARRY

Locke on Representation in Politics†

* * *

Certain passages in the *Second Treatise* might suggest that Locke too saw representation as authorisation. He argues (II, 88) that the individual has granted a right to the Commonwealth to employ his power to ensure peace, and that he must accept the Commonwealth's judgements as his own since they were made by his representative. Locke could not however grant such a representative the plenitude of power of Hobbes's sovereign. The representative is limited by the law of nature to a more real extent than is Hobbes's sovereign. As Locke insists, the legislative has only a fiduciary power. It is entrusted to defend the civil interests—the property— of the subjects within a framework of law. The subjects are moral agents presumed to be the ultimate judges of how to control their property in lives, liberty and estates. It would be an absurdity for them to surrender this moral agency blindly to a government (II, 93). * * * [H]e sees representation as a means of ensuring some correspondence between government, the community, and the individual and through them to the law of nature.

Locke's argument does not necessarily imply radical democracy. Initially, indeed, Locke accepts that the first governments were

† From "Locke on Representation in Politics," *History of European Political Ideas* 3.4 (1982), pp. 409–11, 412, 413–14. Reprinted with permission from Elsevier.

likely to have been patriarchal monarchies. These were however instituted by some act of trust and would on Lockean terms have represented the people and be political societies. Peoples in relatively
simple societies, little experienced in government, would under-
standably have chosen those whom they knew and trusted. Further
experience, however, usually revealed that later monarchs could
not be trusted not to abuse power. The history of civil governments
thus displays successive attempts by the people to reconstitute political authority in order to make it correspond to the popular will
as representing the law of nature (II, 110–11). Locke explicitly argues that the culmination of this process occurs with the institution of representative forms of government. People concluded that
their properties were not secure. They were not genuinely in civil
society

> till the Legislature was placed in collective Bodies of Men, call
> them Senate, Parliament, or what you please (II, 94).

Civility of government therefore seems to imply that the government is made to represent more adequately * * * the people who
create it.

Mixed forms of government, on the English model, are clearly
also capable of representing the people adequately, providing the
people is vigilant. The legislative function represents the will of the
community. The executive * * * also represents the commonwealth
since it is acted on by, and reproduces, the will of the legislative.
But the English executive also had a part in the legislative. The
monarch's assent was required for legislation. The executive had
the power to call and to dissolve the legislature and even in extreme
circumstances to employ prerogative against the law. The 'double
trust' placed in such a system is not the sole and independent representative of the community. It cannot act alone in determining
the dissolution of government, which is a right possessed only by
the people.

The legislative function is, however, the prime representative
body. Who is included in the representative process? This is a highly
controversial matter. C. B. Macpherson's celebrated argument is
that only those with a property in estates are full citizens with the
right to vote. More recently, James Tully has attributed to Locke the
extremely radical position of a full adult male franchise.[1] * * *

*   *   *

The form of government is established by a constitutive act of
trust by the people or, strictly, by a majority of the people. It may

---

1. See Macpherson, p. 292 herein, and Tully, p. 325 herein. All notes are the editor's unless otherwise specified.

decide to place the legislative power where it thinks fit. If this power abuses the trust placed in it the people retains the constituent right to re-order the constitution. The people may therefore establish such a representative system and such a franchise as it believes appropriate (II, 149–58). Does it follow that there is a form of representation uniquely appropriate to a modern civil government? A radical democratic interpretation of Locke would argue that the principle of natural equality must imply that every adult male must have the vote. Locke does indeed state that the best guarantee that the will of the legislative is he will of the society occurs where the people is able to choose 'Representatives upon just and undeniably *equal measures* suitable to the original Frame of Government . . .' (II, 158).

Manhood suffrage would seem to go beyond the broad franchise which one would expect Locke to support as a member of Shaftesbury's party. The basis of the franchise in boroughs was subject to both variation and interpretation. The Whigs constantly sought to interpret the franchise as widely as possible and where the Commons had to rule on the issue it consistently favoured a wide electorate. In some cases the franchise was extended to all free men. This would not extend to dependent persons, such as servants, as would appear to be required by a determinedly egalitarian view of Locke. * * *

* * * Locke argues for just and equal measures 'according to the original Frame of the Government' rather than in an absolute sense. He argues very powerfully against the distribution of the franchise in England but not for its extension. A franchise which would originally have corresponded to the distribution of wealth and population in the country has with economic and social change ceased to do so. Instead, 'Representation becomes very *unequal* and disproportionate to the reasons it was first establish'd upon' (II, 157). It is clearly anomalous that a deserted tract of land with a few sheep should send representatives to the assembly simply because it is the site of a once great town, whilst an area which has recently grown in people, riches, trade and power should have no representatives. This requires a remedy. If the original system of representation was based on criteria of wealth and power, as well as persons, then 'a fair and equal Representative' (II, 158) would be one which reinstated this correspondence, not a system based on 'one man one vote'. The people, however much they may be incorporated as members of the body politic, have only a right to be represented 'in proportion to the assistance it affords to the publick'.

* * * If a property in life and liberty is not essentially different from a property in estates the defense of property would be a defence of it in all its forms. It might then be reasonable for those

with the greatest experience in controlling property to act as representatives on behalf of all property owners. Such a restriction on the franchise might be defended on principle or on pragmatic grounds. In the *Second Treatise* Locke does not state in full the grounds on which a people might establish its system of representation. An egalitarian suffrage might appear the obvious conclusion for rational individuals to select but Locke was often able to draw more conservative conclusions from radical premises.

* * *

* * * The duty of the Lockean representative is the duty of the Lockean individuals. It is to ensure that in social and political transactions men observe the duties laid down by God and in the law of nature. Representation reinforces this obligation by promoting the identity of understanding, the continuity of consciousness of the duty, between representative and represented. It does not deny moral agency to either representative or represented. Both have the combination of liberty and understanding necessary to making right judgements. Without representation the subject is in fact a slave under the will of a lord. With representation the subject has a political status as a partner, and ultimately, the senior partner, in a common endeavour to ensure that the law of nature prevails, which is 'the end and use of our liberty'.

Locke as Revolutionary?

Until the mid-twentieth century, it was generally accepted that Locke's *Second Treatise* was written in 1689 in order to defend the Glorious Revolution of 1688 which had removed James II from the throne because of the birth of a Catholic heir, and replaced him with the Dutch prince, William of Orange, and his wife, Mary, James's Protestant daughter. The most widely used text of the time, George H. Sabine's *History of Political Theory*, described Locke's work as a conservative document, the effect of which is to justify the powers of the Parliament, the king, and the aristocracy while giving lip service to the principles of freedom and consent. "Only in the remote event that society itself is dissolved, a contingency which Locke never seriously contemplated," may individuals resort to revolution. Society, the legislature, even the king were all treated as having a kind of vested right, or permanent authority, only to be forfeited for cause" (Sabine 1961; 538). Sabine recognized that "Locke's defense of resistance in the name of inalienable rights of personal liberty, consent, and freedom to acquire and enjoy property" became important in the American and French Revolutions at the end of the next century but argues that "all these conceptions were in germ much older than Locke" and describes him as "a force in propagating the ideals of liberal but not violent revolution" (1961: 539–40)

In the 1980 article, reprinted in part here, as well as in the book that followed (1986) Richard Ashcraft suggests that Locke in the *Two Treatises* was not a conservative defender of property but rather a proponent of radical revolution. As early as 1960, Peter Laslett had argued convincingly that the *Two Treatises*, although first published in 1689, were composed, nearly in their entirety, almost a decade earlier. Ashcraft argues that the *Two Treatises* were part of a larger effort by the Whig Party to exclude Charles II's Catholic brother, James, the duke of York, from the throne by parliamentary action (the Exclusion Crisis) and, later, after Charles II's dissolution of Parliament in March 1681, by revolution. Locke's unwillingness to admit authorship of the *Treatises* until shortly before his death in 1704, was thus related to the radical circumstances of their composition. His flight to Holland in 1683, when the plot was discovered, is seen as an effort to avoid arrest and possible execution as a traitor. The link between the political circumstances of the early 1680s and the composition of the *Two Treatises* is now generally accepted, although there is disagreement about the exact dates of their composition (see p. xvi herein); and more recent scholarship has questioned the degree of direct involvement of Locke in the plotting, particularly the historical evidence cited by Ashcraft (Milton 2000).

The evidence on both sides is examined by Mark Goldie, who concludes that although Locke believed that "every private citizen, acting alone or collectively" had the right to revolt, he was "about as conservative as a revolutionary could be" about putting it into practice. On the other hand, Goldie argues, Locke puts many limitations on private property while it is his opponent, Filmer, who defends absolute property rights, so that Locke appears to be closer to the position of modern social democrats than to the libertarians who claim his legacy.

RICHARD ASHCRAFT

Radicalism and Lockean Political Theory†

* * *

* * * If space permitted, I would attempt to demonstrate that the argument of [the First Treatise] belongs to the political debate of 1680–1681, when the central question was that of determining succession. In the immediate sense, this is, of course, the political problem of the Exclusion Crisis. In its more general form, the argument in the *First Treatise* poses the choice between the view that power flows from the will of one man, leading towards tyranny, and the view that power arises from the people and is expressed through consent and elections [*First Treatise*, 148]. As a political tract, the *First Treatise* was intended to form part of Shaftesbury's[1] electoral and Parliamentary campaign to win support for the passage of the exclusion bill[2] during the elections and Parliamentary sessions of 1680–1681, and to achieve this objective, in part through attacking and countering the clergy's electoral influence over the gentry. Finally, if the issue of succession is not resolved in a manner that reaffirms "the old way" of instituting government through "the consent of men making use of their reason to unite together into society," Locke warns, the consequences of an insistence on the divine right approach to the problem of succession will certainly be "endless contention and disorder," i.e., civil war [*First Treatise*, 6, 166]. This not-so-veiled threat was frequently

---

† From "Revolutionary Politics and Locke's *Two Treatises of Government*," *Political Theory* 8.4 (November 1980), pp. 448, 449, 450, 468, 474. Reprinted by permission of Sage Publications.

1. Anthony Ashley Cooper, Lord Shaftesbury, the founder of the Whig Party, with whom Locke worked from 1667 until his fall from power, imprisonment, exile, and death in the early 1680s. All notes are the editor's unless otherwise specified.

2. The unsuccessful effort of the Whig parliamentary opposition to pass a law preventing the future James II, a convert to Catholicism, from succeeding to the throne.

made by the Whigs in the Parliamentary debates and in their pamphlets in 1680, and it was intended to give force to the Whig argument that Parliamentary passage of the exclusion bill was the only *alternative* to a civil war. Without a sitting Parliament, obviously, this entire political argument, and the political strategy which informed it, collapsed. Therefore, when the King dissolved the third elected Parliament in two years, and moved in the direction of ruling without one, a new political strategy, and with it, a new political argument, was required for those who, like Shaftesbury, were determined not to give up in their opposition to [James], the Duke of York's succession to the Crown.

* * * [T]he primary target of Locke's attack [in the *Second Treatise*] is not Filmer, but Charles II. * * * The perils to Locke in advancing arguments in support of resistance to Charles II were tremendous—as the fate of Sidney[3] demonstrates. * * *

* * * [T]he *Second Treatise* * * * seeks to provide a justification for the political activity of those who have *decided* to resist, on the grounds of self-defense (of their "lives, liberty, property and religion"), the actions of a tyrant, i.e., one who exercises "force without lawful authority." They are placed in this situation because "the executive power" has employed "the force of the Commonwealth" to "hinder the *meeting* and *acting* of the Legislative" power, contrary to both "the original Constitution" and to "the public exigencies" which "require" such a legislative body to be in session. For Locke, this is a paradigmatic instance of "exercising force without authority." * * *

This political problem arose in its most acute form when the King peremptorily dissolved the Oxford Parliament in March, 1681. Some Whigs—especially Shaftesbury—were now convinced that Charles II intended to rule without calling a Parliament into session, as, indeed, he did. If this were true, it raised "the old question" of who shall judge when a ruler is making improper use of his power, i.e., exercising it "without authority." To this question, Locke replied:

> I answer: between an Executive power in being, with such a prerogative ["calling Parliaments in England, as to precise time, place, and duration" par. 167—RA] and a Legislative that depends upon his will for their convening, there can be no

---

3. Algennon Sidney (1623–1683), English aristocrat who was deeply committed to republicanism and an opponent of the Stuart monarchy. Exiled from the time of the Restoration of the monarchy in 1660 until 1677, he returned to England to become involved in the Whig opposition to the succession of the future James II. In 1683 he was convicted of involvement in a plot to kill the king and was executed. His *Discourses Concerning Government*, a treatise against Filmer, written around the same time as Locke's *Two Treatises*, was published posthumously in 1698. The American revolutionaries regarded him as a martyr to the republican cause.

judge on earth. . . . The people have no other remedy in this, as in all other cases where they have no judge on earth, but to appeal to Heaven [*Second Treatise*, 155].

In short, the King's actions in preventing Parliament from meeting to redress the grievances of the people through its passage of the exclusion bill was a violation of the "original Constitution." The result was that the government was now "dissolved," and the people free to "constitute themselves as *new Legislative*, as they think best, being in full liberty to resist the force of those, who without authority would impose anything upon them."

*   *   *

* * * From some of the conspirators we learn that "my Lord Shaftesbury was preparing a Declaration to be published" in conjunction with their revolution, and West was asked to submit a proposal. "For, says he, I would have several people draw it, to pick one good out of all. And he told me he had made collections toward it, and showed me a paper" which described the various "attempts to introduce arbitrary government and popery" under the present government. The paper, according to West, then went on to maintain "that government was dissolved, and they were free to settle another government. These I perceived, were the topics my Lord Shaftesbury laid weight upon."[4]

Since all of the radical intellectuals were busily engaged in drafting papers, discourses, proposals, and declarations on behalf of the radical movement, I find it difficult to imagine that Locke was the only unemployed intellectual in the group, when he, after all, was the only adviser to the leader of the movement who was actively commissioning such draft proposals from others.[5] * * *

*   *   *

Locke's position is that it is the possibility of "invasion of others" which makes the individual's enjoyment of life, liberty, or property "very uncertain" in a state of nature [*Second Treatise*, 123]. Therefore, anyone who "unjustly invades another man's right" becomes an aggressor, robber, or thief who may be resisted or killed. Moreover, "the injury and the crime is equal, whether committed by the wearer of a crown, or some petty villain" [*Second Treatise*, 176]. Thus, whenever magistrates "invade" the liberties and properties of the people "contrary to the trust put in them," the people "are ab-

---

4. From James Ferguson, *Robert Ferguson the Plotter* (Edinburgh, 1887), append. 1 (a manuscript account of the revolutionary movement).
5. Philip Milton (Milton 2000), citing Locke's *Journals* and other evidence, argues that Locke was careful to avoid direct involvement in the plotting. ("It looks as though Locke was keeping his head down," p. 657). He also challenges much of the historical evidence cited by Ashcraft and argues that in the early 1680s he was not an "adviser" to Shaftesbury.

solved from obedience" and may resist [*Second Treatise*, 228]. * * *
Locke argues that with respect to foreign "invasions" the legitimacy
of this remedy "is agreed on all hands. But magistrates doing the
same thing may be resisted hath of late been denied" [*Second Treatise*, 231]. It is just this distinction Locke attempts to undermine,
and, in the course of doing so, he advances the argument that there
is no essential difference between a foreign or a domestic invasion
of the people's rights and liberties [*Second Treatise*, 239]. In short,
the *Second Treatise* defends revolutionary action. * * *

*   *   *

MARK GOLDIE

Conservative Revolutionary or Social Democrat?†

*   *   *

* * * [S]ome commentators stress Locke's radicalism. Ashcraft
(1986) shows him engaged in a career of conspiracy and under surveillance by government spies. He argues that Locke's radicalism
extended to a social critique, that he appealed to the trading and artisanal class, and to the minor gentry, against the idle rich, and that
he had affinities with the Levellers of the 1640s. Much of this case
is persuasive, for in two ways Locke's argument was strikingly radical. First, the right of revolution lies with every private citizen
acting alone or collectively. There is no theory of the 'lesser
magistrates', of nobles or parliament, as the agents of revolution.
Most earlier radicals had cautiously avoided placing revolutionary
violence in the hands of the lower orders. Second, Locke's theory of
dissolution was too radical for most contemporaries. At the beginning of 1689 the Convention parliament hurried to install William
of Orange as king with a minimum of disruption to the existing constitution. A minority, however, argued that the entire constitution
was now in the melting pot, and Locke seems to share this view. His
is not a theory about parliament's redressing a constitutional balance unhinged by a wayward king. He argues that in a revolution,
power reverts to the community as a whole, which may establish
whatever form of government it pleases. * * * His fellow Whig, Atwood, the only person who mentioned Locke's book in the debate
on allegiance during 1689–93, criticized him for unnecessarily dissolving government into the hands of the 'confused multitude'.

† From Introduction to *John Locke: Two Treatises of Government* (London, Everyman,
1993), pp. xxxv–xxxvii, xxxix–xli. Reprinted with the permission of JM Dent, a division of
The Orion Publishing Group.

Nonetheless, we should be cautious about seeing Locke as a revolutionary in too expansive or heroic a way. First, he is anxious to
deny that his theory encourages anarchy and rebelliousness. Not
every injury by a prince should be redressed, for 'a long train of acting' must be visible; not a mere caucus of malcontents, but the
whole body of the people, must judge of the oppression; and a people must first exhaust all possibility of legal redress (168, 203–10,
223–5, 230).[1] Second, the social bearing of Locke's philosophy is
consonant with the hierarchies of his day. He served a great aristocrat and wrote for landed gentlemen. * * *

* * * Third, despite being at the intellectual extreme of the Revolution debate in 1689, Locke became complacent about post-
Revolutionary governments. It is true that he sponsored the ending
of press censorship (1695), yet he sat on the Board of Trade when
other Whigs were renewing a polemic against the Court, and his
new patron was Lord Somers, a leader of the establishment 'Junto'
Whigs, whom radicals saw as betraying Whig principles for the sake
of power. When William Molyneux used Locke's book in 1698 to
deny that Ireland had consented to English conquest, Locke dis-
tanced himself from the argument. One explanation for Locke's
compliance was his acute sense of the paramountcy of King
William's war to defend Protestantism against French Catholic absolutism. Fourth, Locke kept faith with the traditional Ancient
Constitution, with its executive monarchy and hereditary nobility
(213, 223). Despite the theoretical right to erect a new form of government, in practice he did not want this to happen. In 1689 he
told a friend that the Convention should be 'restoring our ancient
government, the best possibly that ever was'. In short, Locke was
about as conservative as a revolutionary could be (Marshall, 1994).

*   *   *

Locke upholds the grossly unequal property relations of his time
(46, 48, 50). In the aftermath of the Civil War he had strong motives for detaching his political radicalism from suspicion that he
was a harbinger of social levelling. His message is that a gentleman
could support an uprising against the king without fearing for his
property. The *Fundamental Constitutions of Carolina*, which he
helped Shaftesbury to draft, constructed a hierarchic society of
carefully graded landholdings, including an hereditary aristocracy.

*   *   *

However there are significant elements in Locke's text which
tend the other way. * * *

1. By 'property' Locke does not mean simply material goods. He
speaks of having property in one's person, life, liberty and religion,

1. All references are to the Second Treatise unless otherwise specified [editor's note].

as well as estates (27, 123, 173, 209). To have a right of property is to exact from others the duty of recognizing our personhood. Labour is a creative act by which we impress our conscious will on the brute things of the earth, and it is labour that puts the value on things (40). Labour is necessary to our being, not just because we must eat, but because we must make of ourselves a distinctive moral character. Property rights must be framed around the rights of personality, to which every rational being is entitled. Later radical readers of Locke took him to be insisting upon a universal right to work.

2. Locke emphasizes that we are God's property. God laboured to create us and therein lies His property right. We are an expression of God's divine being, of God's 'workmanship', and God is the sole true proprietor of the world (6: I, 39). Consequently we are not free to act as we please, with our lives or goods. For example, it is sinful to commit suicide, for we do not fully own ourselves (6). Among the obligations we bear, as property owners, is to respect the needs of others, who are God's workmanship.

3. Locke is clear that the right of subsistence remains: the impoverished must be fed (25, 70, 183). There are important passages in the First Treatise about our duty to a 'needy brother' (I, 41–3). The holding of property, like the exercise of government, is a trust, a stewardship: we are permitted private property only so that the earth may fructify for the common good.

4. Locke exhibits a doctrine of communal rights which have been called 'use rights' or 'claim rights'. The original common ownership in *Genesis* I:28 was such that everybody had a right of access to use God's gifts. In Locke's society, and ours, this notion persisted in 'commons': public, unenclosed land, which anybody could use (28). An instance of 'use rights' today is public rights of way: the farmer owns the land, but not absolutely, for he cannot exclude members of the community from walking across it. Locke holds that in modern times such commons were secured by 'compact' and law, so that no enclosure could occur without the community's consent (35). Historians have documented the long struggle of the early-modern English to maintain their communal rights against enclosures.

5. Locke perhaps takes one further step, arguing that once we enter political society, the legislature legitimately intervenes. The sovereign is bound to arrange property rights in such a way that they do not hinder productive labour and so that subsistence will be available for all. Locke argues that, in his society, unlike in ancient times, there is a land shortage (except in America) and so the sufficiency principle is breached; governments may therefore redress the balance. Positive law thus enforces natural law entitle-

ments, and he speaks of governments 'regulating' property (3, 30, 45, 50, 120).

If these propositions about community rights can be sustained from Locke's text, there is an ironic outcome. It is Filmer, the Royalist absolutist, with his emphasis on Adam's absolute proprietorship, who is closer than Locke, the supposed modern liberal, to the modern capitalist doctrine of indefeasible property rights. Locke, by contrast, would turn out to be what we would now call a social democrat.

*   *   *

Religion and Politics

Until the late 1980s, with a few exceptions (Dunn 1969b; Ashcraft 1969a) students of Locke's political theory gave little attention to Locke's religious beliefs. W. M. Spellman, whose 1988 book, *John Locke and the Problem of Depravity* was an early example of the new interest in Locke's religious views, argues that Locke's denial of innate ideas and of inherited guilt because of Adam's sin does not mean, as some commentators have argued, that he believed in the perfectibility of man through educational and environmental influences. He places Locke (via Hooker) in the Thomistic tradition of the *via media* (middle way) that is neither as pessimistic about the possibilities of knowing and doing the good as St. Augustine and his successors nor as optimistic as the contemporary Deists who believed man could achieve virtue under the guidance of reason, without the help of revelation. As Locke argued in the *Reasonableness of Christianity* (p. 207 herein) because of the Fall it is difficult, although not impossible, for man to know the good and even more difficult to do it. Human weakness can be remedied only by faith in Jesus as the Messiah and repentance for sin.

Locke's *Letter Concerning Toleration*, which argues that the magistrate (civil authority) does not have the right or the capability to determine the religion of its citizens ranks with the *Second Treatise* as one of the classic texts of liberalism. Early in his life Locke published English and Latin tracts defending the right of the magistrate to regulate religion in "things indifferent," (Locke 1967), but a few years later because of his association with Anthony Ashley Coopler (who in April 1672 became the first Earl of Shaftesbury) and his own experience in European travel his views changed. In 1667 he wrote a short essay advocating religious toleration, largely for political and economic rather than religious reasons. In 1685–86 while in exile in Holland he wrote the *Letter Concerning Toleration*, defending religious toleration as a necessary conclusion from the different characteristics of the spheres of religion and politics, with religion as a matter of the individual conscience and relation to God, and politics as concerned with public order and security. Written in Latin for a European audience in reaction to Louis XIV's revocation of the Edict of Nantes, which had granted toleration to the Huguenots, it was translated by William Popple, a leading English Unitarian, and published in 1689 after Locke's return to England.

The arguments of the *Letter* have produced a large critical literature.

David Wootton criticizes a well-known article by Jeremy Waldron that argued against Locke's claim that persecution cannot change beliefs. Wootton points out that Locke's more important arguments were not based on a judgment of the effectiveness of persecution but on the nature of Christianity as a religion of love and freedom and on the lack of competence of political authorities to make religious decisions for their citizen (which he places in a more modern framework by linking it to modern decision theory). Wootton also highlights the implicit distinction in the *Letter* between public and private matters as an anticipation of the arguments of John Stuart Mill in *On Liberty* (1859).

John Dunn discusses the cases in which the magistrate's legitimate concern for the common good and the individual citizen's religious beliefs come in conflict, concluding that for Locke the goal of eternal life must take precedence over civil concerns and that in some instances there is no appeal but to God—that is, revolution. He cites Locke's unwillingness to tolerate atheists as an example of the central position of religion in his thought and argues that Locke defined more broadly than we do today the moral issues that could be regulated by the magistrate in the interest of the common good.

In his first book on Locke, John Dunn (1969a) wrote that Locke's religious beliefs are so central ("His thinking in its entirety was dominated by a picture of the early setting of human life as an order designed and controlled . . . by the God of the Christians") as to make his political theory inapplicable in a more secular world. More recently he has modified this view, admitting that, even if some of Locke's arguments depend on Christian beliefs, the most important elements of his political theory—human rights, property, contract, and religious freedom—"can in large measure stand free" of their religious setting as a "theory of human agency and identity, a vision of the nature of human society as the unintended product of an immense variety of human contrivances, and a view of the natural and historical basis of any acceptable and lasting form of human social cooperation as the genesis and reproduction of human trust" (Dunn 1990).

As I argued in the introduction to the selections from *The Reasonableness of Christianity* (p. 207 herein), Locke was a Christian, an independent-minded Anglican who, despite his criticisms of some central Christian beliefs, such as inherited original sin ("imputation"), believed both in the possibility of man knowing the good and the likelihood that he would not in fact do so without the assistance of biblical revelation. Locke thought that all human beings could know enough about human nature to provide the moral and psychological foundations for the social contract and that uncoerced Christianity would provide clearer knowledge of and greater motivation for moral conduct. Current debates about the relation of religiously based moral beliefs to public policy in pluralistic modern democracies continue to reflect the tensions in Locke's thought.

W. M. SPELLMAN

Locke and Original Sin†

The long-established view that Locke repudiated original sin and considered children to be born without a fixed nature is based chiefly on statements made in his most important and best-known writings. In the opening paragraphs of the *Reasonableness of Christianity*, for example, Locke appeared to question the Pauline[1] interpretation of the Paradise story by observing that "If by death, threatened to Adam, were meant the corruption of human nature in his posterity, it is strange that the New Testament should not any where take notice of it". Earlier in the *Essay Concerning Human Understanding* he described, in language now familiar to most of us, how the mind at birth resembled "white Paper, void of all Characters, without any Ideas" and implied in the *Two Treatises of Government* that children were not to be held responsible for their actions since "no Body can be under Law which is not promulgated to him; and this Law being promulgated or made known by Reason only, he that is not come to the Use of his Reason, cannot be said to be under this Law". Finally, in *Some Thoughts Concerning Education*, Locke purportedly gave license to all subsequent eighteenth-century champions of environmentalism by insisting that "all the Men we meet with, Nine Parts of Ten are what they are, Good or Evil, useful or not, by their Education". According to most readings of such statements, what Locke aimed at was the final demolition of the Christian doctrine of total depravity which had for centuries frustrated the work of educational reformers. John Passmore's recent claim that Locke "laid the foundation of what was to be one of the most influential forms of eighteenth and nineteenth-century perfectibilism, according to which men can be morally improved to an unlimited degree by education and other forms of social action,"[2] is today widely accepted, and Locke has been placed at the forefront of an important movement that was committed to undermining one of the central beliefs of the historic Christian faith.

* * *

† From "Locke and the Latitudinarian Perspective on Original Sin," in *Revue Internationale de Philosophie*, (1988); rpnt. in Vere Chappell, ed., *John Locke: Theory of Knowledge*. (New York: Garland Publishing, 1992), pp. 215–16, 221, 223–24, 225, 228. Reprinted with the permission of the author and publishers *Revue Internationale de Philosophie*.
1. Romans 5:12. All notes are the editor's unless otherwise specified.
2. John Passmore, *The Perfectibility of Man*, London: Duckworth, 1970, p. 153 [Spellman's note].

* * * [I]n the *Two Treatises* [Locke] had observed how "Adam was created a perfect Man, his Body and Mind in full possession of their Strength and Reason"; thereby enabling him to "govern his Actions according to the Dictates of the Law of Reason which God had implanted in him". But through the disobedience of Adam and Eve, Locke went on to argue in the *Reasonableness*,[3] men have lost both the state of immortality and perfect obedience or righteousness. Their continuing failure to obey God's law for them, the law of nature or reason; "that rule which was suitable to his nature" as a rational being, only served to further magnify the serious repercussions of the first sin. Subject to the many errors and passions which accompanied mortality, each man "under the difficulties of his nature, beset with temptations and hedged in with prevailing custom", and forever "apt to run into corruption and misery", all depended entirely for their salvation on the work of God's only son, who came to "reform the corrupt state of degenerate man" and would account their belief in him for the righteousness of which they were no longer capable because of the pride of the archetypal man. * * *

*   *   *

* * * Locke was adopting some important elements of the Thomist view of original sin in the *Reasonableness*. For despite Aquinas's conviction that the first sin was transmitted to Adam's descendants directly, St. Thomas could not believe that man's nature was as hopelessly corrupt as Augustine had suggested. The Bishop of Hippo's claim that fallen man could not even will the good, that in fact by the evil use of his free will man had destroyed both it and himself, seemed to strike at the very base of moral accountability. "The first sin may have diminished our natural inclination to virtue", Aquinas wrote, but it "cannot entirely take away from man the fact that he is a rational being" created in God's image. Man's natural end—the vision and knowledge of God—was for Aquinas both the product of diminished reason and an unmerited supernatural gift. Richard Hooker agreed entirely. The Law of Reason, he believed, included all those things which men by the light of their natural understanding may know to be good or evil for them to do, but he insisted that in an iniquitous world outside of Paradise "there is no kind of faculty or power in man or any other creature which can rightly perform the functions allotted to it, without perpetual aid and concurrence of that Supreme Cause of all things".[4] * * * In continuing this tradition, Locke wanted men to realize that

---

3. *The Reasonableness of Christianity.* (p. 207 herein)
4. St. Thomas Aquinas, *Summa Theologiae*, II, qu. 85, a.2, 3. Richard Hooker, *Of the Laws of Ecclesiastical Polity*, I.8.10, I.8.11 [Spellmen's note].

although they had been created capable of fulfilling the law of works by virtue of their God-given status as rational beings, Adam's violation of his one probationary law in Paradise had destroyed their chances of ever meriting salvation as a debt discharged. It was only the new law of faith, proposed by the Almighty to "sinful and lost man" which justified, but while faith in Christ as Messiah was the single article necessary to be believed before one qualified as a true Christian, Locke also insisted that repentance is as absolute a condition of the new covenant as faith, the natural corollary of true belief. * * *

＊　＊　＊

* * * Locke was making a case for the universality of human sinfulness with his book on Christianity, premeditated sinfulness, the deliberate repudiation of God's eternal law. "To disobey God", said Locke, "in any part of his commands (and it is he that commands what reason does) is direct rebellion; which, if dispensed with in any point, government and order are at an end; and there can be no bounds set to the lawless exorbitancy of unconfined man". Here was the pride of Adam, rebellion against God, made an essential part of man's temperament, affecting his entire being by virtue of the Fall. It would take more than good works to remedy this disturbing situation; for if they truly were born without any fallen nature, then they would have no real need for a Redeemer in the person of Christ. They would be free both to choose the good and to obey the law of their own nature in its entirely. Christ's life and death would not matter, Scriptural revelation would become a supernumerary support because of the sufficiency of the law of nature. This was the position of the Deists * * *—a position which was emphatically rejected by Locke. * * *

＊　＊　＊

* * * Locke was no adventurous innovator in theology when it came to his understanding of man's place in the divine scheme of things. He may have challenged innate ideas—most importantly innate moral ideas—but he never questioned innate dispositions, especially dispositions opposite the good which was, for him, God's love. He doubtless indicated new opportunities for the improvement of man's moral life with his book on education, but he never suggested that proper pedagogy might someday vitiate the significance of Christ's life and death. * * * [H]e identified true faith in Christ not with a mastery of Scripture, but with repentance for sins past and a resolution to conform all future actions to the law of God. * * *

JOHN DUNN

The Claim to Freedom of Conscience: Freedom of Speech, Freedom of Thought, Freedom of Worship†

* * *

The single most important feature of Locke's understanding of the principles and practice of toleration was the far greater trenchancy and determinacy of his conception of freedom of conscience as freedom of worship than as freedom of speech or freedom of thought. In one crucial respect Locke always continued to see toleration in the last instance, as he had done in his earliest extended writings, from an essentially *politique* point of view: as a practical issue of statecraft which no holder of state power could be freed from the responsibility of judging for himself. But by the time he wrote the *Epistola*[1] he had come to combine this consistently (and very perceptively) political perspective with an unyielding conviction of the priority of individual religious duty over terrestrial public right. Because individual religious duty, in his view, must always dominate over any purely human exigencies, the responsibility of individual human agents to assess for themselves and to enact the forms of worship that God required of them always has rational priority over any possible coercive interventions by other human beings. At least from the Christian revelation onwards, the political space of collective public life in any society at any time was a space of potential confrontation between two ineluctably present *loci*[2] of judgement, the individual believer, interpreting the requirement for saving his own soul, and the political ruler, interpreting the demands of the public good. Neither could escape the responsibility for making this judgement; and each, of course, might very easily prove to be wrong in the judgements at which he arrived. What there could not be in the last instance, in Locke's view, was any coherent human mediation between the authority of these two judgements, if and where they came into serious conflict. What, Locke asks, if the magistrate believes that what he commands lies within the scope of his power and is useful to the commonwealth, but his subjects believe the contrary? Who shall be judge between them? 'Respondeo: Solus Deus, quia inter legislatorem et populum nullus interris est judex.'[3]

---

† From *From Persecution to Toleration: The Glorious Revolution and Religion in England*, Ole Peter Grell, Jonathan I. Israel, Nicholas Tyacke, eds. (Oxford: Clarendon Press, 1991), pp. 174–75, 178–79, 182, 186, 187. Reprinted by permission of Oxford University Press.
1. *Letter*. All notes are the editor's unless otherwise specified.
2. Locations.
3. "I answer: God alone, because there is no earthly judge between the legislator and the people."

*   *   *

* * * It is to God that human beings owe their primary obedience, and only secondarily and derivatively to the laws of the political community to which they happen at the time to belong. The right of freedom of conscience in Locke's eyes is fundamentally a right to worship God in the way one judges that God requires: a right which follows from, and is barely intelligible without the duty to do just that. Its priority over all other possible demands for a human agent likewise follows rigorously from the priority of the goal of attaining eternal life over all other human goals. It is a grotesque impertinence for any human authority to intrude its inept and irrelevant pretensions into this overwhelmingly important individual preoccupation.

*   *   *

* * * But any opinion which has definite practical implications outside the restricted purlieus[4] of private worship is perfectly capable of encroaching upon the interests and rights of others; and the magistrate must judge which opinions do posses such practical implications and when and where they are likely to encroach upon the public good. Having made this judgement, he must also do his best to prevent such encroachments in practice. He must do so, not because he is gifted with greater natural sagacity than his subjects possess, but because it is his responsibility to protect the rights of all his subjects and to exercise his judgement as best he can to provide this protection.

Locke's second reason for repudiating any general entitlement to freedom of thought (let alone freedom of expression) is that at least some beliefs are an inherent menace to every other human being. The belief which he especially singles out, notoriously, is the belief that there *is* no God to worship: atheism. This is hardly an exclusion that any Western society today would regard as furnishing a very handsome allowance of freedom of thought—even if it might still evoke some applause in Tehran. As an exclusion, moreover, it is certainly incompatible with at least one of the arguments that Locke himself regularly advances in favor of toleration—that human belief is not a voluntary affair: that no one can simply choose his beliefs or promptly alter them at the behest of another human being. It is important to register that this incompatibility does not represent a mere oversight on Locke's part but instead provides a clear index of the extremely restricted scope that he was prepared to allow to the argument that belief is not a discretionary matter.

*   *   *

4. Bounds.

* * * The reasons why Locke himself regarded atheists as such a practical menace lie at the very foundation of his thinking over almost half a century and rest ultimately upon his despondent and disabused views about the structure of human motivation and about the conflicts between the interests of human beings seen simply as mortal creatures within a natural world. It is possible that these views are excessively pessimistic, though no one has yet given very cogent reasons for supposing them to be so; and no one, quite certainly, has in any sense subsequently *demonstrated* that they are so. Where Locke does strain the credulity of most readers today, by contrast, is in his remarkable optimism about the rectificatory services offered by the world to come.

His own estimate of the practical menace of atheism is best captured in Popple's ringing translation: 'Promises, Covenants, Oaths, which are the Bonds of Humane Society, can have no hold upon an Atheist. The taking away of God, though but even in thought, dissolves all.'[5] Believing this, Locke would certainly have been justified, on his own theoretical premises, had he ever had to exercise political authority in the matter himself, in refusing toleration to those who denied the existence of a God. But it is important to note that his reason for doing so was simply a personal opinion about a matter of fact. Personal opinions about matters of fact obviously cannot be eliminated from the exercise of governmental authority. But they are distressingly fallible; and the only privilege which they enjoy derives from the prudential preconditions for human beings to live with one another in reasonable peace and security.

* * *

* * * [I]t is notorious that in his own later service on the Board of Trade Locke himself was prepared to advocate the most draconic interference with the rights of at least some of his fellow citizens to be poor in their own way. The concern of the commonwealth with industry is plainly not to be taken lightly.

It should certainly be set beside the recurrent indications throughout the *Epistola* that there were other forms of conduct, and more particularly sexual conduct, which Locke was quite unprepared to tolerate, even where they were undertaken under supposedly religious inspiration. 'Plunging into promiscuity' (*in promiscua stupra ruere*) is not lawful at home or in civil life, and is therefore no more lawful on religious pretexts or in an ecclesiastical setting. Anything harmful to the commonwealth can and should be forbidden in common life by public laws enacted for the com-

5. William Popple translated Locke's *Letter on Toleration* from Latin to English. For the differences between Locke's Latin text and Popple's translation, see edited text on *The Letter on Toleration* herein (pp. 125 ff.).

mon good by the magistrate. It is his responsibility to ensure that the commonwealth is protected from harm. Purely speculative beliefs cannot entrench on the civil rights or property of others; and they cannot and will not be altered by the threat of force. But to be confident of Locke's immunity from the magistrate's attentions the members of Locke's society must be at pains to avoid not merely sedition, murder, theft, and slander, but also for example, adultery. Furthermore (since adultery is presumably an example of a civil wrong as well as a sin), they should be at pains to exhibit '*mores casti et inculpati*'.[6] * * *

I have tried to show how strong the case which Locke developed for religious toleration in Europe of the 1680s really was, and how weak, by contrast, the protection which that case would have offered for many eagerly proclaimed contemporary instances of freedom of personal choice, freedom of expression, and in the last instance even freedom of thought.

DAVID WOOTTON

An Evaluation of Locke's Argument against Persecution†

* * *

* * * We need first to note that the *Letter Concerning Toleration* is partly a work about what Christians should believe. Locke insists that toleration is the mark of a true Church; that the clergy should preach peace and love; and that the true Church should not require that its members believe more than is specified in the Gospel as necessary for salvation. He implies that the ceremonies of the Church should be closely based on biblical precedents. He is apparently reluctant in conceding that authority in a Church is properly exercised by bishops or presbyters, and is unhappy at the thought that a convention of clergymen can claim to represent the church as a whole. He suggests that there may well be more than one 'true' Church, that those issues on which the Churches are in conflict are of secondary importance or 'indifferent'. He insists that the Mosaic law against idolatry no longer applies (although one may wonder whether, on his arguments, it can ever have been just, even if ordained by God). And he claims that there is no commis-

---

6. Chaste and blameless morals.
† From *Political Writings of John Locke* (New York: Mentor Books, 1993), pp. 97–99, 100, 102, 103, 104–6. Reprinted by permission of Hackett Publishers Company, Inc. All rights reserved.

sion in the Gospel for persecution (ignoring the parable in which
Christ says that his guests should be compelled to come in to the
feast). The *Letter* is thus partly a religious tract, and the religion it
upholds is very much that which we have come to expect from
Locke. Again and again his arguments are at odds with the practices and claims of the Anglican Church. For example, he claims
that the only punishment Churches should be able to impose is
that of excommunication, and this should have no secular consequences. In England, Church courts had traditionally had extensive
jurisdiction in cases involving, for example, adultery, and had been
able to impose fines and other punishments.

*   *   *

* * * In Waldron's view [1993] Locke's key argument is not
Christian at all: it is the claim that the state can shape only behaviour, not belief, through punishments. Punishments do not serve to
change beliefs because we cannot change what we think merely because we are told to, not even if we want to. Consequently it is irrational to punish people for what they believe. And therefore the
state has no business interfering with beliefs. Having isolated this
as Locke's best argument, * * * Waldron then claims that the argument is defective. * * * [S]ocial pressures do affect what people
think. Government intervention to punish dissent is not irrational
or necessarily ineffectual. Censorship, for example, can significantly affect the information we have access to, and the beliefs we
consequently come to hold. Locke is wrong to claim that persecution will not work. * * * His argument is concerned with what is
rational behaviour on the part of the government, not with what is
right for citizens, with what is effective, not with what is legitimate.
As such it is fundamentally misconceived. Locke should have argued * * * that it is the particular attribute of the state to lay claim
to a monopoly of force, but from what we might think of as properly liberal premise, that of the rights of citizens, Locke's argument,
in short, is insufficiently Lockean.

If Locke's argument was really open to this attack it would be a
poor thing indeed. * * *

The first argument is not about what is rational for rulers, but
about what is rational for subjects. It is not rational for subjects to
hand over to their rulers responsibility for deciding what they
should believe. And this because they would be placing an obligation on themselves that they could not be confident of fulfilling.
The ruler may tell me to be a Hindu, but he cannot make me believe. And I cannot agree that he is doing me any good if he makes
me act contrary to my beliefs. Consequently I ought to regard my
right to think for myself as inalienable. In no rational original contract will I cede control over this belief to the magistrate. * * *

* * *

His third argument is that it is not rational for a subject to let the magistrate decide for him, even if it is the case that magistrates can make people believe whatever they want. Rulers are not impartial: they, and the clergy who support them, have corrupt interests in furthering their own power and wealth. They are not necessarily learned. Of all the possible ways I might adopt for determining which religion I should hold, that of holding the religion of my ruler is not the most likely to lead to the correct choice. Indeed, there are many rulers in the world, and they uphold many different religions. Consequently, if there is only one true religion the odds are that my ruler upholds a false one. I am betting against the odds, and once again the price of losing is too high; I am not just gambling with my worldly wealth (for loss of which the ruler could in any case compensate me) but with my eternal happiness. * * *

* * *

* * * It is sensible for me to let the state decide conflicts over property for me, because my own decisions in a state of nature would be partial and unenforceable. Moreover it is not too difficult to construct a state that has an interest in getting such decisions right: the state can be made not only more powerful, but also impartial. And such decisions can be enforced: property can be forcibly transferred from one party to another, while beliefs cannot be forcibly imposed. There are no comparable arguments, Locke believes, for thinking that I will benefit from giving up my independent right of judgement in matters of religion.

Locke recognizes that it is often sensible to allow others to make decisions for us. If a mathematician tells me I have got my sums wrong, I should try to learn from him, not argue with him. But religious beliefs are not about deductive certainties but, in the end, about reliability of testimony of matters of fact. Did Christ rise from the dead? What is involved here is a judgement of probability, but one of a particular sort. I can entrust my money to an investment company who think the market is going to rise when I happen to think it will fall. If they are right I will profit, and if they are wrong I will lose. But in the case of religion I cannot in this way hand the decision over to someone who I suspect is better informed than I. For in the case of religion, only sincere believers can hope to be rewarded: this was the standard objection of the Protestants to the 'blind faith' they believed was required by Catholicism. * * *

Locke's * * * arguments are thus explorations of problems in decision-making theory, problems concerning making decisions on the basis of probabilities, and making decisions that not only have to be correct, but must also be reached in the right way. * * *

* * *

Suppose that the core argument of the *Letter* is a good one, what of the other objection often levelled against it, that the concessions Locke makes to persecutors go so far as to make the text intolerant by modern standards? Locke, after all, intends to be intolerant towards the intolerant, and also towards Catholics and atheists. Although he thinks that there should be freedom of thought where what he terms speculative opinions are concerned, he insists that it is right to discriminate against ideas that have anti-social consequences. It is not that the government has a right to step in wherever the practical opinions are concerned; it can only do so where public interests (with which alone it is properly concerned) are at stake. Locke's distinction within the sphere of practical opinions thus depends on his being able to draw a line between public concerns and private matters: a line corresponding to his earlier distinction between the realm that is the legitimate concern of the state and that which is properly to be left to the voluntary actions of individuals. Slander should be punished, but not laziness or greed. My laziness or greed do not necessarily injure society or my neighbour; nor is it easy for society to be sure that I am really greedy (as opposed to industrious cautious, foresightful). * * *

Locke's argument thus depends on a distinction between what Mill was later to term self-regarding and other-regarding actions, and it obviously runs into the severe problems that bedevil Mill's own version of the argument. It simply is not true that nobody's interest but my own are at stake if (to use Locke's horrifying example) I make my daughter marry someone unsuitable. The solution to this problem is not to have the state step in, but to let my daughter choose for herself. Locke's problem is that he has taken the family as a paradigm of what is private, rather than acknowledging that family life involves conflicts of interests between individuals, other-regarding as much as self-regarding behaviour.

Locke's argument, for all the occasional inconsistencies with which he formulates it, was to become that of classical liberalism. Underlying it, one can surely see the values of a market society. Locke assumes that consumers should have the right to make choices. They may make bad choices or good ones: there is at least no reason to think that they will make worse ones than the state would make on their behalf, and where there is a variety of choices on the market (for example, a variety of medical therapies on offer), there is a prospect for progress. * * *

*   *   *

Women and Slavery: Liberal or Conservative?

The basic premise upon which Locke builds his political theory, original freedom and equality, was in contradiction with two significant social institutions of his time: slavery and the patriarchal family. This section critically examines the relationship of Locke's discussions of women and slavery to his arguments for freedom and equality, demonstrating the tensions and inconsistencies among them.

James Farr outlines Locke's argument against the morality of slavery, except for those directly involved on the unjust side in a just war. Even in that case, he argues, their wives and children cannot be enslaved. Farr then examines the historical evidence that Locke was aware that Negro slavery was employed by companies with which he was financially involved and that it was in opposition to his theory. He knew that Africans were captured by slave traders and sent to places like Barbados and the Bahama Islands, where Locke had made investments. He also knew that their families were also enslaved and that their subsequent offspring continued as slaves, although they had incurred no guilt. Thus there was a contradiction between his theoretical liberalism and his practical acceptance of contemporary institutions that were not in accordance with it. Farr also concludes that Locke was not a racist— that is, did not believe that racial differences were significant—and links Locke's views on slavery with his polemic against Filmer.

Melissa Butler describes a similar tension between Locke's criticisms of patriarchalism, not only in government but also in the family, and his contradictory argument for a basis in nature for a (limited) paternal power because the father is "abler and stronger." Butler believes, however, that Locke's discussion of the contractual basis of marriage and the property rights of the wife were a significant contribution to the feminist cause. (For more critical comments on Locke's views on women see Clark 1977, Okun 1978, Pateman 1985, Sample, 2000. For a reply to Sample arguing that final authority of the husband was a "default position" in the absence of different arrangements expressly consented to by both parties, see Simmons 2001.)

The two articles note that Locke's theories on both subjects were strongly influenced by his polemical purpose, opposition to royal absolutism. Thus his relatively advanced views on female equality were conclusions that were linked to a general effort to refute Filmer's patriarchal defense of divine right monarchy, and subjection to oppressive government was described by Locke as a form of slavery. His starting points for those efforts, original freedom and equality, are basic doctrines of liberalism, but it has taken many centuries to work out their liberating implications.

JAMES FARR

"So Vile and Miserable an Estate": The Problem of Slavery in Locke's Political Thought†

* * * The preeminent theorist of natural rights and human freedom was himself a merchant adventurer in the African slave trade and an instrument of English colonial policy who proposed legislation to ensure that "every freeman of Carolina shall have absolute power and authority over his negro slaves." * * * How could Locke's passionate advocacy of universal natural rights be squared with an institution that annihilated those rights altogether?

* * * Some writers claim that Locke's theory is inconsistent with his views on natural rights.[1] Others assert that, in spite of its flaws, the theory satisfied Locke as an explanation and justification of Afro-American slavery.[2] Still others hold that Locke was a racist who believed that blacks deserved slavery because they were not fully human and so had no rights.[3]

In this essay I propose to challenge these three interpretations, and to show that Locke's just-war theory of slavery *is* consistent with his account of natural rights. But more important, I hope to show that this theory is woefully inadequate as an account of Afro-American slavery and, further, that *Locke knew this.* * * * I suggest that Locke articulated his just-war theory with more local objectives in mind: namely, to refute the theorists of royal absolutism, and Filmer in particular. Locke was accusing them of rationalizing the "enslavement" of Englishmen "under arbitrary power" (2.222), and his own theory justified rebellion, if need be, against "so vile

---

† From *Political Theory* 14.2 (May 1986), pp. 263, 264, 270–71, 272–73, 274, 275, 276, 277, 280–82. Copyright © 1986. Reprinted by permission of Sage Publications.

1. Peter Laslett argues such in his edition of the *Two Treatises of Government* (New York: Cambridge University Press, 1963), 325n (paperback edition). All notes are Farr's unless otherwise specified.
2. Laslett argues this case as well, *Two Treatises*, 326n. So does David Brion Davis, *The Problem of Slavery in Western Culture* (Ithaca: Cornell University Press, 1966), 118; and Martin Seliger, *The Liberal Politics of John Locke* (London: Allen and Unwin, 1968), 116.
3. Seliger suggests this in *The Liberal Politics of John Locke* [London, Allen and Unwin, 1968] 199n. The case is more systematically argued by both H. M. Bracken, "Essence, Accident and Race," *Hermathena* (Winter 1973), 81–96; and Richard H. Popkin, "The Philosophical Bases of Modern Racism, "*Philosophy and the Civilizing Arts*" ed. by Craig Walton and John P. Anton (Athens:, Ohio: Ohio University Press, 1974), 126–165.

and miserable an estate" (1.1).[4] Although this clarifies Locke's intentions, it unfortunately does nothing to lessen the principal contradiction between his theory and his and his age's practice. Locke's silence about the Afro-American slave practices that he helped forward remains profoundly unsettling and poses one of the greatest problems for understanding Locke as a theorist and political actor.

* * *

Locke begins the *Second Treatise* by bidding his readers to "consider what State all Men are naturally in, and that is, a state of perfect Freedom, to order their actions, and dispose of their Possessions and Persons, as they think fit." It is "a state also of Equality" (2.4). By nature, then, "men" (to follow Locke's usage) are born free and equal with a full complement of natural rights to ensure the facts of their nature. In at least three different ways, however, natural rights and freedoms are not absolute. First, according to the law of nature, one's rights and freedoms do not extend to the violation of others' rights and freedoms. Second, in order to have civil society at all, men must surrender certain natural rights, particularly the right to judge and punish those who transgress against the law of nature. Third, a man does not have the right or the freedom to undermine the very conditions of his rights or freedoms. Thus, a man "has not Liberty to destroy himself" (2.6); nor can a man "by Compact or his own consent *enslave himself* to anyone" (2.23). Indeed, suicide and slavery not only are not rights, they are positively unnatural, for they make a man not a man.

Slavery exists, however, as a matter of *fact*, whenever a conqueror subdues his enemies and forces them to exist under absolute bondage. Mercy, not right, is the condition of their existence. Such was the fare of countless peoples in ancient and medieval times, to whom Locke's theory of natural rights would doubtless have seemed a tract of abolition and liberation. But even Locke allows for—and justifies—slavery as a matter of *right, if* the slaves were "Captives taken in a just War" (2.85). A just war is one waged against unjust aggressors by an innocent people defending its rights and its property. And when "victory favors the right side," then, subsequently, "the perfect condition of Slavery . . . is Conqueror, and a captive" (2.85, 24). The captive is wholly to blame because he had "quitted reason" by violating the rights of the innocents and so rendered himself "liable to be destroyed by the injur'd person and the rest of mankind that will joyn with him in the execution of Justice, as any other wild beast or noxious brute" (2.172). In the face of the demands of justice, enslavement of such a beast is no injustice. * * *

4. "1": *First Treatise.* "2": *Second Treatise* [Editor's note].

Slavery, then, is not in all cases categorically unjust. Indeed, there must be justly held slaves insofar as there are unjust aggressors and just conquerors. * * *

The emphasis on unjust *action* serves to distinguish Locke from many other theorists of slavery. Before and after Locke's time, slavery was justified by nature, by original sin, by pagan belief, or by contract. We may suppose that Locke intended to refute (or was aware he was refuting) versions of the theories of Aristotle, St. Augustine, the Christian Crusaders, and Hobbes, among others. * * *

                              *   *   *

* * * Locke stipulates what he admits is a "strange Doctrine"— namely, that the lawful conqueror has no right to the possessions of the conquered people, except insofar as to "make reparation for the damages received, . . . and the Charges of War" (2.180, 182). And depending upon the economic plenty or penury of the enslaved people, Locke even states that no seizure of possession is just if wives and children have more "pressing and preferable Title" (2.183). The seizure of land itself is explicitly excluded by this constraint, for land is by right the inheritable property of future innocent generations, especially "in any part of the world, where all the Land is possessed, and none lies waste" (2.184).

* * * [T]he lawful conqueror has slave rights only over those who "actually assisted, concurred, or consented to that unjust force" (2.179). Principally, this means combatants and government officials. "All the rest are innocent"—noncombatants, wives, and children. Certainly a whole population cannot be enslaved, "the people have given to their Governors no Power to do an unjust thing, such as to make an unjust war (for they never had such a Power in themselves)" (2.129).

An important corollary of this is that slavery cannot extend to future generations. Children born of slaves cannot themselves be retained as slaves, for slavery "reaches no further than the Persons" of those who acted unjustly, and thus it "dies with them" (2.189). Slaves' children have committed no injustice, no act deserving of death. Hereditary slavery—that is, any *institution* of slavery—is positively unjust and falls well beyond the limits of Locke's theory.

Locke's theory stands out by combining severe constraints on what may be regarded as just slavery, with an absolute and "purely despotical" power for the masters once those constraints are met (2.178). No act of the lawful master can violate the rights of a slave, who, through an earlier act of his own, has no rights. The master may dispose of his slave's labor, or otherwise "make use of him to his own Service" (2.23). Of course, he may even kill his slave since the slave deserves death. However, if the constraints are not met, then the slavery is unjust, and the master ranks on a par with the unlawful conquerors of history. Such a conqueror has "no Title to the Subjection and Obedience of the Conquered" (2.176). He deserves what he will probably receive: the rebellion of an oppressed people (2.196). If vanquished, the master is himself deserving of death or slavery, that vile and miserable estate.

* * *

Whatever else might be said of Locke's just-war theory of slavery this much is clear: *It neither explains nor justifies the practice of seventeenth-century slavery.* The African slave trade and the institution of chattel slavery in the Americas flagrantly violated the theoretical constraints he so painstakingly set. Surely Locke knew this, not only as the principal theorist of his age, but as a counselor and secretary on colonial boards setting slave policy, as a merchant adventurer and profiteer in the Royal African Company, as a friend and correspondent of both slave owners and abolitionists, and a Christian advocate for the baptism of African slaves. In brief, three facts of Afro-American slavery, facts of which he was abundantly aware, violate Locke's just-war theory of slavery: (1) the methods of capture, (2) the demography of enslavement, and (3) the institution of hereditary bondage. The first two occurred in Africa, the third in America.

Take Africa first. The methods used to obtain slaves varied considerably.[5] Among these methods were slave raids by Europeans themselves, and there could be no pretense that such raids were just wars. * * *

* * * But more frequently, slaves were obtained from African chiefs who had originally taken them either by intertribal wars, or by raids, or because of debt or other crimes. Whatever the justness of intertribal wars (and one rather doubts that Locke could have believed them just), slavery-by-debt was not a proper candidate for Locke's theory. And slave raids by Africans were no more just than were those by Europeans—especially when the African raids were the direct consequence of the European demand for slaves. * * *

* * *

Locke's just-war theory also comes a cropper on a second score. Women and children were captured and traded in Africa. In his various administrative posts, Locke had access to innumerable shipboard manifests reporting on slave cargoes. Invariably these included demographic reports on the purchase and sale, health or death of countless women, boys, and girls bound for America. * * *

Some of these slave boys and girls attested to the third and most flagrant violation of Locke's theory: the institution of hereditary

5. See James A. Rawley, *The Transatlantic Slave Trade* (New York, Norton, 1981), esp. 272, 432.

slavery. Children of adult slaves were born into slavery, even though they had themselves committed no "act which deserved death." Here too the information available to Locke was, to say the least, abundant. It lay about his desk at the Council of Trade, filled many a letter from an American friend, and was neatly shelved in his voluminous library.

*   *   *

But, was Locke a racist? * * * Nowhere does Locke say that the black race was degenerate (for example, in terms of color or rationality); nor does he in any other way commit himself to the theories usually advanced to account for degeneracy (for example, the climatic theory). Still less did he hold that black Africans morally deserved slavery because of their race, or that they were to be counted among "the inferior ranks of Creatures," placed by God under (white) man's dominion (2.6). Indeed, the opposite conclusion could conceivably be drawn from his *Letter Concerning Toleration*. There Locke denounced the arbitrariness of religious intolerance as being analogous to the arbitrariness of "distinctions made between men and men upon account of their different complexions, shapes, and features, so that those who have black hair (say) or grey eyes should not enjoy the privileges as citizens" [54]. Of course, Locke was not making a cryptic case for abolition, much less for the enfranchisement of blacks. But his reasoning on these matters provided him no grounds whatever for justifying slavery by race, nor is there any evidence that he though that they did. For these reasons, I conclude that Locke, *qua* theorist at least, was no racist.

*   *   *

What was Locke doing, then, when he thundered against that "vile and miserable estate? * * *

I suggest that Locke was mobilizing his just-war theory of slavery in order to attack theories of royal absolutism. In this way his theory contributed directly to the general arguments of the *Two Treatises*, arguments that were patently irrelevant to Afro-American slavery. The *Two Treatises* waged war against a panoply of absolutist arguments: divine right monarchy, patriarchalism, sovereignty by conquest, and passive obedience. These shared common elements, in particular that the king's power was absolute, his will law, and the liberties of Englishmen his grants and privileges. For Locke the notions unbridled government and made the people "*Slaves* under the Absolute Dominion of a Monarch" (1.146). This was but "slavery under arbitrary power" (2.222). "Slavery" had numerous meanings in English political discourse, and Locke here employed the term as a code word for absolute monarchy. * * *

Locke was engaged in more than mere propagandist metaphor, of

course. He was mobilizing his political theory for practical purposes. According to his general theory, men were born free, were
bound to obey only those governments to which they gave their
consent, and could not be brought under absolute authority—that
is, made slaves—unless by some act that deserves death. By establishing such strict constraints on what would count as just conquest and enslavement Locke neutralized royalist arguments for
absolute sovereignty by conquest. * * *

* * *

MELISSA BUTLER

Early Liberal Roots of Feminism: John Locke and the Attack on Patriarchy†

* * *

In early seventeenth-century England, patriarchalism was a dominant paradigm, a world view, a weltanschauung. For many Englishmen, it represented the truth of their time and all time. It was a
fully articulated theory which expressly accounted for all social relations—king-subject, father-children, master-servant, etc.—in patriarchal terms. Sir Robert Filmer and other patriarchal writes
insisted that the king ruled absolutely, the divinely ordained father
of his people. No one was born free; everyone was born in subjection to some patriarchal superior. Each individual human being
could find his or her proper place by consulting patriarchal theory.
Places were not matters of individual choice but were assigned according to a divinely ordained pattern set down at the Creation.

By the end of the seventeenth century, the patriarchal world view
had crumbled. It was replaced by a new understanding of human
nature and of social and political organization. Whigs such as Sidney, Tyrrell and Locke grounded political power in acts of consent
made by free-born individuals. Contract and individual choice sup-
planted birth and divine designation as crucial factors in social and
political analysis. These changes raised problems concerning the
status of women in the new order. At first, liberal theorists resisted
the suggestion that the old assigned position of women might have
to be abandoned. The champions of consent theory saw no need to
secure the consent of women. Yet their critics insisted that excluding women violated the very theory of human nature on which liberalism was based. Eventually, liberals would be forced to bring

† From *American Political Science Review* 72.1 (March 1978), pp. 135–36, 142, 144,
145, 147, 148, 149, 150. Reprinted with the permission of Cambridge University Press.

their views on women into line with their theory of human nature. This changing image of women certainly played a part in that shift in consciousness which paved the way for the sexual revolution.

*   *   *

Locke's Attack on Patriarchy

While other Whig writers simply declared that their theories necessitated no new roles for women, John Locke treated the problem somewhat differently. He was among the first to sense the inherent contradiction in a "liberalism" based on the natural freedom of mankind, which accorded women no greater freedom than allowed by patriarchalism. New places had to be opened to women. This is not to claim that John Locke planned or even foresaw the feminist movement. It does seem true, however, that Locke took his individualist principles very seriously, even when they entailed an admission that women, too, might have to be considered "individuals."

Clearly Locke was not interested in creating a world in which all were equal; in his view, there would always be differences among individuals. The key question here concerns the extent to which a Lockean society would discriminate on the basis of sex. Would the fact that some are more equal than others be determined by traditionally-assigned sex roles?

In the first of his *Two Treatises of Government*, Locke showed little interest in the constitutional or classical arguments offered by Filmer. Doubtless he believed that these arguments were simply not at the heart of Filmer's theory. Instead, Locke charged that the scripture-based arguments were unproved, not because he doubted the truth of the Bible, but because he realized Filmer had distorted that truth. Locke's attack stemmed from no impious disregard for Filmer's evidence, but from a different method of construing that evidence. * * *

Since Filmer's patriarchal theory included a particular view of the status of women, based on biblical arguments, Locke's refutation also had to deal with that view. Concerning the benediction of Genesis 1:28, Locke noted that it was bestowed on "more than one, for it was spoken in the Plural Number, God blessed *them* and said unto *them*, Have Dominion. * * *" [*First Treatise*, 29]. This argument introduced the possibility that Adam's dominion was not exclusive but was shared with Eve. Further, Eve's subjection to Adam need not have prevented her from exercising dominion over the things of the Earth. Eve, too, might have property rights.

In the fifth chapter of the *First Treatise*, Locke argued against "Adam's title to Sovereignty by the Subjection of Eve." There, Locke had much more to say about the patriarchal conception of women. He took issue with Filmer's use of Genesis 3:16 ("And thy desire shall be to thy Husband and he shall rule over thee"). Those words, Locke objected, were a "punishment laid upon Eve." Furthermore, these words were not even spoken to Adam. The moment after the great transgression, Locke noted, "was not a time when Adam could expect any Favours, any grant of Privileges from his offended Maker." At most the curse would "concern the Female Sex only," through Eve, its representative [*First Treatise*, 45–47].

*   *   *

Social Relations in the Second Treatise

For Filmer and his sympathizers there was only one type of power: paternal power. Filmer's simplistic uncluttered view of power fit in perfectly with his view of social relations. Filmer admitted only one kind of social relationship: the paternal relationship. Each member of society was defined by his or her relation to the patriarchs of the family and of the nation.

Locke, however, maintained that there were many kinds of power and many types of social relations. He analyzed several nonpolitical relationship including those of master-servant, master-slave, parent-child, and husband-wife. Each of these forms of association was carefully distinguished from the political relationship of ruler-subject. Two of the nonpolitical relationships, namely the parental and the conjugal, reveal a great deal about the status of women in Lockean theory.

From the very outset of the discussion of the parent-child relation, Locke rejected the terminology of patriarchy, claiming that "[paternal power] seems so to place the Power of Parents over their Children wholly in the Father, as if the Mother had no share in it, whereas if we consult Reason or Revelation, we shall find she has an equal Title. . . . For whatever obligation Nature and the right of Generation lays on Children, it must certainly bind them equal to both the concurrent Causes of it" [*Second Treatise*, 52].

The basic argument at the root of his terminological objection was one familiar from the *First Treatise*. Patriarchal theory could not stand if power were shared by husband and wife. As Locke argued in the *Second Treatise*, "it will but very ill serve the turn of those Men who contend so much for the Absolute Power and Authority of the *Fatherhood*, as they call it, that the *Mother* should have any share in it" [*Second Treatise*, 53]. Nevertheless, Locke was not consistent in his own use of the term he introduced. He reverted to the use of "paternal" to describe the relationship he defined as "parental." Yet it is clear from this discussion as well as from the analysis of the fifth commandment[1] that Locke was willing to elevate women's status if he could overthrow the patriarchal monarch.

Locke's examination of the conjugal relationship demanded a more extensive analysis of the roles and status of women in society. He described conjugal society as follows:

> *Conjugal Society* is made by a voluntary Compact between Man and Woman: tho' it consists chiefly in such a Communion and Right in one anothers Bodies, as is necessary to its chief End, Procreation; yet it draws with it mutual Support and Assistance, and a Communion of Interest too, as necessary not only to unite their Care, and Affection, but also necessary to their common Off-spring, who have a Right to be nourished and maintained by them, till they are able to provide for themselves [*Second Treatise*, 78].

Conjugal society existed among human beings as a persistent social relationship because of the long term of dependency of the off-spring and further because of the dependency of the woman who "is capable of conceiving, and *de facto* is commonly with Child again, and Brings forth too a new Birth long before the former is out of a dependency" [*Second Treatise*, 80]. Thus the father is obliged to care for his children and is also "under an Obligation to continue in Conjugal Society with the same Woman longer than other creatures" [*Second Treatise*, 80].

Though the conjugal relationship began for the sake of procreation, it continued for the sake of property. After praising God's wisdom for combining in man an acquisitive nature and a slow maturing process, Locke noted that a departure from monogamy would complicate the simply natural economics of the conjugal system [*Second Treatise*, 80]. Though conjugal society among human beings would be more persistent than among other species, this did not mean that marriage would be indissoluble. Indeed, Locke wondered "why this *Compact*, where Procreation and Education are secured, and inheritance taken care for, may not be made determinable, either by consent, or at a certain time, or upon certain Conditions, as well as any other voluntary Compacts, there being no necessity in the nature of the thing, not to the ends of it, that it shall always be for life" [*Second Treatise*, 81]. * * * Nevertheless, Locke described what he took to be the normal distribution of power in marital relationships:

> The Husband and Wife, though they have but one common Concern, yet having different understandings will unavoidably

---

1. The fifth of the Ten Commandments: "Honour thy father and thy mother (Exodus 19:12; King James version). All notes are the editor's unless otherwise specified.

sometimes have different wills, too; it therefore being necessary, that the last Determination, i.e. the rule, should be
placed somewhere, it naturally falls to the Man's share, as the
abler and the stronger [*Second Treatise*, 82].

Clearly all forms of patriarchalism did not die with Filmer and his
fellows. Here, the subjection of women is not based on Genesis,
but on natural qualifications. Nature had shown man to be the
"abler and stronger." Even James Tyrrell,[2] while denying any need
to obtain women's consent in the formation of civil society, thought
it possible that, in some cases, women might actually be more fit to
act as household heads and final decision makers. Unlike Tyrrell,
Locke did not equivocate on this point. Rule must be placed somewhere, so he placed it in the husband. Locke's patriarchy was limited, though. The husband's power of decision extended only to
those interests and properties held in common by husband and
wife. Locke spelled out the limits on the husband's power:

[His power] leaves the Wife in the full and free possession of
what by Contract is her Peculiar Right, and gives the Husband
no more power over her Life, than she has over his. The *Power
of the Husband* being so far from that of an absolute monarch
that the *Wife* has, in many cases, a Liberty to *separate* from
him; where natural Right or their Contract allows it, whether
that Contract be made by themselves in the state of Nature or
by the Customs or Laws of the Country they live in; and the
Children upon such Separation fall to the Father or Mother's
lot, as such contract does determine [*Second Treatise*, 82].

In addition, Locke distinguished between the property rights of
husband and wife. All property in conjugal society was not auto-
matically the husband's. A wife could have property rights not subject to her husband's control. Locke indicated this in a passage on
conquest: "For as to the Wife's share, whether her own Labour or
Compact gave her a Title to it, 'tis plain, her Husband could not
forfeit what was hers" [*Second Treatise*, 183].

* * *

Though Locke gave the husband ultimate authority within conjugal society, this authority was limited and non-political. Yet when
Locke's account of the husband's conjugal authority was combined
with his account of the historical development of political society,
several questions occur which were never adequately resolved in
Locke's moral theory. Did not the award of final decision-making
power to the father and husband (in conjugal society) result in a

---

2. A contemporary of Locke, author of another treatise against Filmer, *Patriarcha, non
Monarcha* (1881).

transformation of "parental power" into "paternal power"? Was the subsequent development of political power based on paternal power a result of that transformation? What was woman's role in the establishment of the first political society? Since her husband was to be permitted final decisions in matters of their common interest and property, and since political society, obviously, was a matter of common interest, would her voice simply be "concluded" in that of her husband? If so, then Filmer's question recurs—what became of her rights as a free individual? Did she lose her political potential because she was deemed not as "able and strong" as her husband? If this were the case, Locke would have had to introduce new qualifications for political life.

* * *

* * * While decision-making power over the common interests of a conjugal unit belonged to the husband, Locke admitted that the wife might have interests apart from their shared interests. Women could own separate property not subject to their husband's control. If a husband forfeited his life or property as a result of conquest, his conquerors acquired no title to his wife's life or property.

Did these capacities entitle women to a political role? Locke never directly confronted the question; nevertheless, it is possible to compare Locke's qualifications for political life with his views of women. Locke used the Genesis account to show that women possessed the same natural freedom and quality as men. Whatever limitations had been placed on women after the Fall could conceivably be overcome through individual effort or scientific advance. Furthermore, women were capable of earning through their own labor, of owning property and of making contracts.

Locke and the Rational Women

* * *

* * * Locke believed that women shared the basic freedom and quality characteristic of all members of the species. Women were capable of rational thought; in addition, they could make contracts and acquire property. Thus it appeared that women were capable of satisfying Locke's requirements for political life. Yet Locke was never explicit about women's role in the formation of civil society. * * *

* * * In 1696 Locke, together with King William, attended a service led by a Quaker preacher, Rebecca Collier. He praised her work and encouraged her to continue in it, writing, "Women, indeed, had the honour first to publish the resurrection of the Lord of Love; why not again the resurrection of the Spirit of Love?"[3] It is

---

3. Locke to Rebecca Collier, Nov. 21, 1696, reprinted in [H. R.] Fox Bourne, 1876, p. 453 [Butler's note].

interesting to compare Locke's attitude here with the famous re-
mark made by Samuel Johnson on the same subject in the next
century: "Sir, a woman's preaching is like a dog's walking on his
hindlegs. It is not done well; but you are surprized to find it done at
all."

Perhaps a similar conclusion might be reached about the roots of
feminism in Lockean liberalism. In a world where political anti-
patriarchalism was still somewhat revolutionary, explicit statements
of more far-reaching forms of anti-patriarchalism were almost un-
thinkable. Indeed, they would have been considered absurdities.
* * * Though his feminist sympathies certainly did not approach
the feminism of Mill writing nearly two centuries later,[4] in view
of the intense patriarchalism of seventeenth-century England, it
should be surprising to find such views expressed at all.

4. John Stuart Mill, *On the Subjection* of Women (1869).

Locke in America

The English colonies in North America were significant in Locke's life and thought. In turn his political philosophy had an important influence on American thinking on government. The content and value of that influence has been a subject of intense debate.

Locke was involved in shaping and influencing English policy toward its colonies through his association with Anthony Ashley Cooper, after 1672 the first Earl of Shaftesbury. In 1669 he had a major role in preparing for Ashley a draft of *The Fundamental Constitutions of Carolina*. While it accepted Negro slavery and recommended institutions that were not democratic it also forbade enslavement of American Indians and provided for freedom of worship, permitting any seven colonists to form a church (see Locke 1993:210). (For the continuing influence of the Carolina example on Locke, see Armitage 2004.) In 1673 Locke became secretary of the Council of Trade, and in the same year he invested in the Bahama Islands, selling his investment at a profit in the following year (Cranston 1957:115)

Toward the end of his life, beginning in 1696, he was secretary of the Board of Trade, which regulated economic policies of the colonies. In 1697 he submitted to the board a proposal for the reform of the government of Virginia that reflected his views in the *Second Treatise* in calling for a strong legislature and an independent judiciary. It also endorsed freedom of conscience and recommended that missionaries be sent to convert the Indians to Christianity (Ashcraft 1969b)

The influence of the American example is clear in the *Second Treatise*, where there are repeated references to the American Indians and to the "empty places" in America. It has also been argued that his rejection of occupation or conquest as titles to ownership were influenced by the need to justify English—but not Spanish or Portuguese—expansion in America and that his justirication of property from labor could be, and was, used to argue that the Indians were entitled to only those lands that they actively cultivated, so that their lands that were not being used for agriculture could be taken over and developed by the colonists (Arneil, 1996).

The principal debates about Locke's influence on America have centered around his defense of property. In some ways this is odd because the most obvious example of Locke's influence is the beginning of the Declaration of Independence, which is a defense of government by consent and the right of revolution. Its enumeration of the inalienable rights, the violation of which can justify revolution—life, liberty, and the pursuit of happiness—does not include property, an omission that Vernon Parrington (1974:344), a "progressive historian" of the first part of the twentieth century described as "a revolutionary shift." Historians also cite the fact that Jefferson later advised Lafayette not to include property in his draft of the French Declaration of the Rights of Man. However, in other writings, Jefferson spoke of a natural right to subsistence while recognizing that society could alter the definition and extent of that right, a position similar to that of Locke. One well-known authority on Jefferson maintains that the reasons for his choice of the more felicitous "life, liberty, and the pursuit of happiness" were primarily stylistic (Koch 1960:78–80) In any case the Fifth Amendment to the U.S. Constitution made use of the Lockean trilogy of life, liberty, and property.

In the 1950s the hegemony of Lockean liberalism over American thinking was celebrated by Lewis Hartz and others. In the 1960s, when the liberal consensus began to fray, a debate ensued over the extent and nature of Locke's influence. The English Locke scholar John Dunn, after examining the catalogs of American libraries, argued that the *Second Treatise* was not known in America until the 1760s, although later critics, citing the sermon literature as well as the wide knowledge of writers influenced by Locke such as Emerich de Vattel, maintained that his political ideas were pervasive in the American colonies throughout the century.

Also in the 1960s, respected scholars such as Bernard Bailyn, Gordon Wood, and John Pocock began to focus on an alternative American tradition of classically based "civic republicanism" that was more altruistic and socially committed than the supposed egoistic individualism of Locke. In the American bicentennial year, George Lodge (1976), a professor at the Harvard Business School, even called for the abandonment of Lockean individualism by American corporations in favor of a more communitarian "New American ideology." Two years later Gary Wills published *Inventing America*, which argued that Thomas Jefferson was not influenced by Locke—indeed had not even read him—but rather was familiar with the more socially oriented writers of the eighteenth-century Scottish Enlightenment, especially Francis Hutcheson. Specialists on Jefferson ignored Lodge, and a devastating review of the evidence on Jefferson's knowledge of Locke and his complete ignorance of Hutcheson destroyed the Wills thesis (Hamowy, 1979). However, the broader liberalism-civic republicanism debate produced a large literature from which finally emerged a consensus that the Founding Fathers were *both* Lockean liberals and civic republicans and that Locke was not as egoistic or materialistic as his detractors maintained. ("It is time then to discard the essentially misleading Lockean/republican dichotomy"; Huyler 1999:39).

Steven M. Dworetz reviews the debate on Locke's influence in America. He dismisses the Wills interpration, and argues that the evidence for the predominance of civic republicanism over Lockeanism is not persuasive. He concludes that what he calls the "revisionist position" of

Locke as a conservative defender of unlimited appropriation is "historically flawed," partly because there is strong historical evidence against it but mainly because it accepts unquestioningly the misleading interpretations of Locke by Leo Strauss (p. 274 herein) and C. B. Macpherson (p. 292 herein) and ignores, as they do, the central position in Locke's thought of man's duty to God to preserve himself and all mankind. Like a number of writers in the 1990s Dworetz emphasizes the religious assumptions that underlie the rationalism of his political theory.

STEVEN M. DWORETZ

Locke, Liberalism, and the American Revolution†

* * *

In American historiography there has indeed been a fundamental reinterpretation of the founding doctrine—specifically, of the ideology and political thought of the American Revolution—and this scholarly achievement has some serious political implications. Inadvertently, it seems, scholars have cut the historical grounds of legitimacy out from under the defense of constitutional politics by denying that liberalism was an essential ideological component of the founding doctrine; and they have escalated the danger by reinterpreting Revolutionary thought primarily, or even exclusively, in terms of that republican tradition (which is referred to in the literature as classical republicanism, civic republicanism, civic humanism, "country" ideology, the libertarian creed, the commonwealth tradition, etc.).[1] Consider briefly how this historiographic revolution in the study of American Revolutionary thought has transformed our understanding of that chapter of the founding doctrine.

Liberalism once was deemed by scholarly consensus to have held undisputed sway over the political thought of the American Revolution, and historians proclaimed "the Great Mr. Locke, America's Philosopher," as the Revolution's "guide and prophet." From this

† From *The Unvarnished Doctrine: Locke, Liberalism, and the American Revolution* (Durham, NC: Duke University Press, 1990), pp. 5–6, 8, 9, 13–19, 22–23, 25, 30–31, 70–71, 118, 131–132. Copyright © 1994 Duke University Press. All rights reserved. Used by permission of the publisher.

1. See for example, Bernard Bailyn, *The Ideological Origins of the American Revolution* (Cambridge, MA: Harvard University Press, 1967); Gordon Wood, *The Creation of the American Republic* (Durham: University of North Carolina Press, 1969); J. G. Pocock, *The Machiavellian Moment* (Princeton, NJ: Princeton University Press, 1975); John Patrick Diggins, *The Lost Soul of American Politics: Virtue, Self-Interest, and the Foundations of Liberalism* (New York: Basic Books, 1987). All notes are the editor's unless otherwise specified.

perspective John Locke's *Two Treatises of Government* looked like "the textbook of the American Revolution" and the source "from which Americans drew the 'principles of 1776.' " Locke's political thought had thoroughly "dominated the political philosophy of the American Revolution," the totality of which could therefore be summarized simply as "an exegesis upon Locke."[2] A few years later Louis Hartz, in his classic study, *The Liberal Tradition in America*, extended Lockean intellectual dominion beyond the Revolutionary period, to the whole of American political thought and behavior. With Hartz (and to Hartz's apparent dismay) the triumph of "Lockean liberalism" was complete.

By the late 1960s, however, a new consensus had begun to emerge. Scholars now criticized the interpretation of Revolutionary thought that comprehended *Locke et praeterea nihil*.[3] They initiated an "essential historical shift away from Locke" and began to develop a new interpretive paradigm to replace what I shall call the Locke model of interpretation.

* * *

The stakes are high, for both citizens and scholars. The historiographic revolution has changed America's historical self-understanding and thus deeply affects the republic as a whole and all of its citizens. On another level it represents a major revision in the history of political thought and thus falls within the jurisdiction of the ivory tower. But as a historical account of Revolutionary doctrine, and with regard to the interpretation of Lockean and republican political theory, revisionist historiography is seriously flawed.

On the one hand, the revision either denies the historical significance of Locke's liberalism or casts it in an anti-Revolutionary light, while proclaiming the decisive importance of republican sources in the formation of American Revolutionary thought. But * * * in relation to the most crucial issues in the Anglo-American dispute (for instance, representation, taxation, consent, religious liberty, the limits of civil authority per se, the right and duty of revolution, and the ultimate sovereignty of the people), the Revolutionists' writings do not support either of these claims. The historical-textual evidence testifies consistently and often explicitly in the language of "Locke on Government." On the other hand, the republican revision rests on specific, unexamined interpretations both of Lockean thought and of the political thought that, the revisionists say, inspired and shaped the development of American re-

2. Vernon L, Parrington, *Main Currents in American Thought* (Harvest Books, 1927) v. 1, p. 193; John C. Miller, *Origens of the American Revolution* (Stanford University Press, 1966) p. 170 [Dworetz's note].
3. Locke and nothing else.

publicanism. Yet these interpretations either fail the test of close textual analysis or are historically inappropriate for the period under investigation.

This point about the interpretation of political theory is extremely important. What the republican revision lacks in its most important formative works is, if you will, the interpretative discipline of political theory, born of an intimate acquaintance with the classic texts. * * * The contemporary scholars of early American history appear to know these texts only casually, or on the basis of secondhand reports. If the goal is to estimate the relative significance of different theoretical traditions in a specific historical context, and to determine the nature of the impact within that context, then a clear, and clearly defined, understanding of those traditions, and of their parent texts, is absolutely essential. It should be obvious that this kind of historical research therefore requires the consistent application of some rigorous standards of interpretation.

For example, the search for Locke in American Revolutionary thought should be informed by an understanding of Lockean thought that satisfies *two criteria of interpretation*. First, the interpretation must be textually sound, or available in Locke's texts; that is, it should be an interpretation that can be legitimately carved out of the Lockean corpus. Second, in developing or choosing a textually sound interpretation of Lockean thought (for there could be more than one textually available Locke), we should try to be sensitive to how Lockean thought most likely would have been interpreted by the contemporaries of the period under investigation. The interpretation, then, must also be appropriate for the Revolution's historical context; that is, it should be an interpretation that most likely *would* have been carved out of Locke's texts by eighteenth-century American readers.

So far, the study of American Revolutionary thought has not satisfied both of these criteria of interpretation with respect to Lockean thought. * * *

* * *

* * * Since it was Louis Hartz who most cogently and comprehensively argued the case for a Lockean America, his *Liberal Tradition in America* is for us, as it was for the revisionists, the place to begin. Hartz became famous for putting the whole of American political and intellectual history into the framework of "Lockean liberalism," although he spelled it differently, viewed it critically, and took pains to distinguish it from the teaching of the "actual historic" Locke—an interesting point which Hartz's critics apparently failed to appreciate. Deemphasizing Locke in, not to mention excluding him from, the ideological foundations of the Revolution

thus presupposed the refutation of Hartz's thesis or the development of a more persuasive one.

According to Hartz, American political society is, always has been, and presumably would continue to be, under the intellectual, ideological and psychological domination of Lockean liberalism— by which he meant, among other things, an ethos of individualism, economic self-interest, and materialist values. In thus maximizing the significance of Lockean liberalism, however, Hartz was not concerned so much with an explicit phenomenon in the history of ideas as with the "Lockean" mode of thought and behavior that seems always to prevail in America at both the individual and the collective-cultural levels. It was in this sense that "Locke has been so basic that we have not recognized his significance."

Only in America has the sway of Lockean liberalism been so ubiquitous, unchallenged, and absolute. And its stranglehold on American intellectual and political life, according to Hartz, can be explained only through a comparative analysis of eighteenth-century social structures in America and in Europe, and analysis which reveals the crucial absence of the "feudal factor" in America's past."[4]

Europeans, in Hartz's account, entered modernity mired in Filmer's feudal patriarchalism and moved, convulsively, to the liberalism of Locke, apparently en route to the socialism of Marx. America, however, was essentially unaffected by the historical dynamics of Western Europe; for these were generated in the feudal system, which America did not share and consequently did not have to overthrow. The original immigrants left this feudal baggage, as it were, on the pier; they did not transport the sociopolitical structures and hierarchies of the Old World to the new. As a result, their descendants, as Tocqueville[5] observed, were "born equal," in a place which Locke himself had cited as an empirical instance of the state of nature. Unlike the Europeans, they did not have to destroy a social system in order to achieve that equality. And this fact, for Hartz (and Tocqueville), explained the singular achievements of the American Revolution—its relatively low level of internal violence and the lack of a Thermidorean reaction[6]—as well as America's enduring, "Lockean" political personality.

4. Lewis Hartz, *The Liberal Tradition in America* (Harcourt Brace and World, 1955) [Dworetz's note].
5. Alexis de Tocqueville, a French aristocrat who, after an extended visit to the United States, wrote *Democracy in America* (1835), which emphasized the equalitarian aspects of the American character.
6. The conservative reaction to the excesses of the French revolution, especially the Reign of Terror. It took place in 1793, in the month of Thermidor, according to the new revolutionary calendar.

In Hartz's view Lockean liberalism in America did not depend upon knowledge of Locke—an argument not without significant methodological implications. Hartz, indeed, explicitly declined to portray the colonists as "splendid citizens" reading Locke and then acting out the revolutionary scenario of the *Second Treatise*. Locke had merely provided the modern social scientist with categories to describe a mode of behavior which subsequently became virtually universal under specific socio-structural conditions. Those conditions prevailed in the New World, where Lockean liberalism consequently had no "natural enemies" to keep it in check. The social structure did not provide an effective foothold for the force of Filmer or of Marx. The unique social conditions in colonial America thus allowed America to begin with Locke, to stay with Locke, and to develop an "absolute and irrational attachment" for him. As a result, "Locke dominates American political thought, as no thinker anywhere dominates the political thought of a nation. He is a massive national cliché."[7]

Carl Becker was another major proponent of the Locke model of interpretation. More than Hartz, Becker specifically addressed and maximized the influence of Locke upon the American Revolution.[8] * * * Becker * * * singled out "Locke's natural law and natural rights philosophy" as the decisive, radical element in the political theory of the Revolution.

Despite these differences between them, however, Becker and Hartz, and the Locke model of interpretation in general, came under the revisionists' fire for the same reasons—methodological and substantive. Both scholars, according to their critics, failed to provide, indeed were not concerned to provide, an adequate textual basis for their arguments; neither draw conclusions chiefly from the political writings of the Revolutionary period; thus, neither took into account what the Revolutionists actually said, the political language they spoke, and whom they quoted in their pamphlets, sermons, and newspaper essays. Becker, in particular, paid dearly for invoking a methodologically problematic "intellectual osmosis" of ideas that were "in the air," and not in available books, to account for the allegedly decisive significance of Locke's ideas.

The methodological critique of the "Locke model" of interpretation was accompanied by vigorous denials of its substantive claims about the predominance of Lockean-liberal ideas in American Revolutionary thought. The revisionists rejected the unverifiable "climate of opinion" as a basis for intellectual history and turned their attention to the actual political writings of the Revolutionary

---

7. Hartx, *Liberal Tradition*, p. 140 [Dworetz's note].
8. Carl Becker, *The Declaration of Independence* (Vintage Books, 1958) [Dworetz's note].

period. There they found very little that could be designated "Lockean." What did emerge from that literature seemed to them very different indeed from the political theory of "Lockean liberalism."

One historiographic alternative to the Locke model, which did not fall within the republican paradigm but should nevertheless be mentioned here, emerged from the research—some would say from the imagination—of Garry Wills. Wills sought to replace Lockean liberalism with the philosophy of the Scottish Enlightenment at the intellectual center of the Revolution. He claimed that Revolutionary thought bore the stamp of a "massive Scottish presence," as exemplified in the writings of Thomas Jefferson. Wills banished Locke to make way for a host of Scottish philosophers, including Adam Smith, David Hume, Thomas Reid, Adam Ferguson, Lord Kames, and, above all, Francis Hutcheson. And according to Wills, the men "stood at a conscious and deliberate distance from Locke's political principles." Wills thus portrayed Jefferson as some kind of communitarian, steeped in the moral philosophy and worldview of the Scottish Enlightenment—the absolute antithesis, it seems, of a Lockean.[9]

The "blatant errors of fact" and the lack of "scholarly substance" in Wills's major book have already been well documented.[1] They account for his failure to change the way we think about the American Revolution. For this reason, Will's reinterpretation of Revolutionary political thought should not detain us much longer. We need only pause to note that Wills simply took for granted (and with evident distaste) the bourgeois Locke and to consider how his dependence upon a hostile interpretation of Lockean thought might have influenced his entire project.

The Locke whom Wills enthusiastically dissociated from the Declaration of Independence is casually assumed to be a hedonist in the spirit of Thomas Hobbes. As defined by Wills, "Lockean man" is spurred to action only by the prospect of "immediate gratification," not by any long-range hopes for the "hereafter." Wills's Locke, moreover, is concerned above all with private property. Property is "*the* fundamental right" and "the basis for all other rights in Locke." Finally, Wills did not take seriously Locke's actual definition of property as life, liberty, and estate [*Second Treatise*, 97, 123]. Instead, he extrapolated an understanding of Lockean liberalism exclusively from the last item in that formulation. Wills's Locke

---

9. Gary Wills, *Inventing America: Jefferson's Declaration of Independence* (Vintage Books, 1979) pp. 183, 201, 206, 217, 238, 315, 368 [Dworetz's note].

1. Ronald Hamowy, "Jefferson and the Scottish Enlightenment: a Critique of Gary Wills' *Inventing America, William and Mary Quarterly*, 36 (1979) [Dworetz's note]. Hamowy cites ten examples of documentary evidence that Jefferson knew Lockes works, adding that there is no evidence that Locke knew the writings of Hutcheson [Editor's note].

thus seems close indeed, in his essential concerns, to the Locke of Macpherson and (especially) Strauss.[2] And it is easy to see why Wills wanted to rid the founding doctrine of his grasping, hedonistic presence, even if the purge required "blatant errors of fact."

The republican alternative proved much more effective in transforming historical understanding—and banishing Locke—than Wills's attempt to recast the founding ideology in terms of the philosophy of the Scottish Enlightenment. We can now examine these more important and influential contributions to that successful historiographical revolution.

Bernard Bailyn's *Ideological Origins of the American Revolution* presented the revisionist hypothesis in its seminal and most elegant form. * * * Bailyn argued that the politics and political thought of the American Revolution had been decisively conditioned and constrained by an essentially non-Lockean ideological tradition.

According to Bailyn, this tradition had originated in the antiauthoritarian writings of Milton, Harrington, and other republicans or "commonwealthmen" who were active during the tumultuous years of the English Civil War and the interregnum. It was later developed (though never systematized) and utilized by "opposition" theorists, "radical whigs," and "country" politicians and publicists, such as Trenchard and Gordon, Molesworth, and Hoadly (on the "left") and Bolingbroke (on the "right"), in their losing struggle against Robert Walpole and the "court." In eighteenth-century colonial America this tradition brought together and harmonized various discordant intellectual themes, only one of which was Lockean. It thereby constituted a comprehensive worldview and an effective revolutionary ideology.

* * * Transplanted into the sociopolitical context of colonial America, this relatively incopsequential tradition of political thought quickly acquired explanatory salience and explosive ideological power. Through quotation, citation, and plagiarism, the political ideals of this republican ideology, particularly those of Trenchard and Gordon, were incorporated "wholesale" into the Revolutionary writings and thereby came to exercise a decisive-indeed, a determinative—influence on the minds of Americans.

It is ironic that here Bailyn offered what was in form, but not in content, a Hartzian argument: America served as a unique context—"an altered condition of life"—in which a particular outlook in politics and society assumed ubiquitous and decisive power. For Hartz that outlook was Lockean; for Bailyn, however, it was the commonwealth, or republican, tradition. Indeed, there is even an echo of Carl Becker at this point in Bailyn's analysis. Like Becker,

2. See p. 279 and p. 281 herein.

Bailyn attributed a specific ideology's extraordinary influence in America to the uncanny way in which it reflected the experience of colonial politics. * * *

* * *

* * * [J. G. A.] Pocock's work is the more provocative; by itself it is rich and intricate enough to warrant a book-length treatment by a political theorist. The historiography of the American Revolution constitutes only one chapter in the larger history of political thought that unfolds in a series of essays and in *The Machiavellian Moment*. In these works, Pocock aims at nothing less than a complete revision of late seventeenth- and eighteenth-century Anglo-American political thought in its entirety.

The revision stressed a non-Lockean—indeed an anti-Lockean—civic humanist or classical republican tradition: "Machiavelli at the expense of Locke." This tradition provided the ideology which, in Pocock's view, Bailyn had correctly perceived as having held an "absolute," "conditioning," and "imprisoning" grip upon the American colonial mind, acting as a "restricting and compulsive force in the approaches to the Revolution." Pocock thus endorsed Bailyn's interpretation of Revolutionary political thought, declaring that it "altogether replaces" the interpretative model based on Locke and associated with Louis Hartz. * * *

* * *

Here, as with Bailyn, we can note the ironic reproduction of a distinctively Hartzian characteristic in the republican paradigm: the tendency to make the chosen ideological perspective ubiquitous and inescapable by situating it in a context where all opposing perspectives are objectively suppressed. Hartz cited the absence of a feudal sociological inheritance for having left Locke with no "natural enemies" in America. Pocock substituted civic republicanism for "Lockean liberalism" and asserted that the colonists had no perspective from which to view, explain, and respond to the events leading to 1776 other than the one that was supplied by the republican tradition. " 'Country' ideology ran riot in America" because there was no "court" tradition to hold it in check, "no alternative" to the "neo-classical" tradition in which to be schooled.

In short, Pocock beat Hartz at his own game. He proposed a historical alternative to Lockean liberalism that would tolerate no historical alternatives. He liberated the American Revolutionists from the Hartzian prison of Lockean liberalism only to reincarcerate them within the paradigmatic walls of republican ideology. And with the Revolutionists objectively committed to virtue, historiographic redemption became a real possibility.

* * *

[Theism and Lockean Liberalism]

Locke is a sincere theist whose political theory cannot be detached from his "religious preoccupations" without unhistorically secularizing, and thus distorting, its character. Locke's overriding concern is for the "*eternal* estate," not real estate. His political thought flows from the premise of, and depends fundamentally upon, belief in, a benevolent, rational (that is, not arbitrary) God who makes nothing in vain, whose "workmanship" men are, and whose law of nature lays down social and political obligations that are binding upon all individuals, "*legislators* as well as others." Human political arrangements are legitimate only insofar as they accommodate the general purposes of God (for instance, civil government cannot be arbitrary and must always serve the public good). To cite Dunn, "the axiomatic centrality of the purposes of God dominates the entire intellectual construction."[3]

This Locke, moreover, is a political radical, and his radicalism flows directly from his theistic philosophy. To summarize the position that is fully set forth in the book: The justification for revolution, which is the theme of Locke's *Second Treatise*, involves the emphatic assertion of the people's inalienable right, duty, and competence to judge the conduct of their government and to reassume, when *they* deem it appropriate, the sovereign constituent power. This justification originates simultaneously—and divinely, so to speak—in the suicide taboo and the inseparable moral connection between individual judgment and salvation. With the obligations of the law of nature—which is God's law—incorporated and operationalized in the establishment of civil government, the exercise of individual *political* judgment, culminating in the fateful decision whether to obey or to resist political authority, becomes an essential requisite for salvation.

This is not the place for a detailed account of Lockean thought or a critique of opposing interpretations. But this view of Locke's liberalism can be summarized in Locke's own words, drawn from the *Letter on Toleration*, and, according to Locke, relevant in *every* sphere of human life and association: "The taking away of God, even only in thought, dissolves all." * * * Displacing the notational principal—"the taking away of God"—in Lockean thought converts the "theistic Locke" into the bourgeois Locke, the bane of the republican revision. What the revisionists call Lockean liberalism, however, might be described more accurately as liberalism without Locke's unifying theistic assumption or, if you will, as post-Lockean, secularized liberalism. Their perspective on Lockean lib-

3. Dunn, *The Political Thought of John Locke*, 87, 93, 12 [Dworetz's note].

eralism was framed, not by Locke himself, but by three hundred years of post-Lockean history.

* * *

* * * It should be noted that in establishing the Lockean-liberal defense of liberty and property, the Revolutionists drew not at all from chapter 5 ("Of Property") of the *Second Treatise*, but primarily from chapter 11 ("Of the Extent of the Legislative Power"). The issue in dispute was not the right of the subject to appropriate from nature, but the right of the government to expropriate the subject. Accordingly, the Revolutionists did not call upon the "bourgeois Locke" to justify unlimited appropriation; they used Locke's political theory to do what it does best, that is, to define the inherent and moral limits of civil authority with respect to liberty (civil as well as religious) and property and to justify resistance and revolution when government exceeds, or threatens to exceed, those limits. The formal Lockean connection, then, was not an ideological rationalization for unlimited capital accumulation; it was, instead, a demand for constitutional political and limited government; and when England failed to honor that demand, it became a justification for armed resistance and revolution.

* * *

It is a strange kind of secular rationalism that regards belief in God as a precondition for ethics and social existence, but this is indeed Locke's view. Civil society presupposes that all its members recognize their mutual obligations and respect the sanctions behind them, and this requires belief in God; for "what duty is cannot be understood without a law, nor a law be known without a lawmaker, or without reward and punishment." God is the lawmaker; the law of nature is "the decree of the divine will discernible by the light of nature," that is by reason (while Scripture, we shall see, is the same divine law made known through revelation); and it is the belief in the pleasures of heaven and pains of hell that encourages us to fulfill our obligations.[4] * * *

* * *

Locke's theism inspires the secularization of politics in his political theory. Since the law of nature, which we know by reason, is indeed an expression of divine will, God remains essentially, although not explicitly, within the Lockean polity; for, as Locke says, "the obligations of the Law of Nature cease not in society but only in many cases are drawn closer, and have by human laws known penalties annexed to them to enforce their observation"; and "the municipal laws of countries . . . are only so far right as they are founded on

---

4. Locke, *Essay Concerning Human Understanding*, bk. 1, ch. 3, para. 12; Locke, *Essays on the Law of Nature*, (von Leyden, ed.) first essay, p. 111 [Dworetz's note].

the Law of Nature, by which they are to be regulated and interpreted" [*Second Treatise,* 135]. All "social intercourse and union" among men depend upon the law of nature, which "God hath given to be the rule betwixt man and man, and the common bond" of "fellowship" and social existence. Moreover, "the law of nature stands as an eternal rule to all men, legislators as well as others." God's law thus defines the "extent of the legislative power," just as God ultimately judges the moral status of resistance in particular cases.

Resistance to the exercise of arbitrary power is itself rooted in a theistic context: our duty to the Creator, whose "workmanship" and "property" we are, to preserve ourselves. * * * Arbitrary power must be resisted because, as it negates freedom, which is the "fence" to preservation, it is life-threatening and therefore illegitimate by definition. The divine prohibition of suicide thus has revolutionary political implications. And as for the fateful decision whether or not to make a revolution in a specific situation, Locke's argument, which again flows from his "theological commitments," is more radical still; for God assigns to "the people"—and, indeed, to "any single man"—the responsibility for judging whether or not government follows the "law antecedent and paramount to all positive laws," and for obeying or resisting that government accordingly; and this is a "judgment they cannot part with." The exercise of sound, socially responsible political judgment is a requisite for salvation [*Second Treatise*, 240, 168, 176].

* * *

So how did Lockean liberalism become the "Lockean liberalism" which revisionist historians, political theorists, and critics of modernity love to hate? Perhaps Locke's theistically inspired secularization of politics has somehow interacted historically with social, economic, and technological changes to produce the more radical secularization, personal and political, which characterizes modern Western life. The dynamics remain unclear. But we do know that the theistic foundation of Lockean individualism—indeed, of Lockean liberalism—has evaporated; and as Locke himself warns, "the taking away of God, even only in thought, dissolves all." The duties which arise from each individual's relationship to a common creator no longer carry much weight in Western political theory. Twentieth-century observers may applaud or regret this development; but in either case they should stop trying to attribute it to Locke. * * *

Selected Bibliography

• indicates items included or excerpted in this Norton Critical Edition.

Armitage, David. "Locke and the Carolinas." *Political Theory* 32, no. 5 (October 2004), 602–37.

Arneil, Barbara. *John Locke and America: The Defence of English Colonialism*. Oxford: Clarendon Press, 1966.

Ashcraft, Richard. "Faith and Knowledge in Locke's Philosophy." In *John Locke: Problems and Perspectives*, ed. John Yolton, 194–223. Cambridge: Cambridge University Press, 1969b.

Ashcraft, Richard. "Political Theory and Political Reform: John Locke's Essay on Virginia." *Western Political Quarterly* 22, no. 4 (December 1969a), 742–58.

Ashcraft, Richard. *Revolutionary Politics and Locke's Two Treatises of Government*. Princeton, NJ: Princeton University Press, 1986.

Bailyn, Bernard. *The Ideological Origins of the American Revolution*. Cambridge, MA: Harvard University Press, 1967.

Barger, Bill. *Locke on Substance*. Manhattan Beach, CA: Sheffield Press, 1976.

Barzun, Jacques. *From Dawn to Decadence: 500 Years of Western Cultural Life*. New York: HarperCollins, 2000.

Becker, Carl L. *The Declaration of Independence, A Study in the History of Political Ideas*. New York, Harcourt Brace, 1922.

Beer, Samuel H. "The Role of the Wise and Holy: Hierarchy in the Thomistic System." *Political Theory* 14, no. 3 (August 1986), 391–422.

Berns, Walter. *Making Patriots*. Chicago: University of Chicago Press, 2001.

Bill, E. G. W. *Education at Christ Church Oxford (1660–1680)*. Oxford: Clarendon Press, 1988.

Bluhm, William T., Neil Winfield, and Stuart H. Teger. "Locke's Idea of God: Rational Truth or Political Myth?" *Journal of Politics* 42, no. 2 (May 1980), 414–38.

Bourne, H. R. Fox. *The Life of John Locke*. Aalen, Germany: Scientia-Verlag, 1969.

Brutus, Stephanus Junius. *Vindiciae contra Tyrannos*, ed. and trans. George Garnett. Cambridge: Cambridge University Press, 1994.

• Butler, Melissa. "Early Liberal Roots of Feminism: John Locke and the Attack on Patriarchy." *American Political Science Review* 72, no. 1 (March 1978), 135–50.

Clark, Lorenne M. G. "Women and Locke: Who Owns the Apples in the Garden of Eden?" In *The Sexism of Social and Political Theory: Women and Reproduction from Plato to Nietzsche*, ed. L. M. G. Clark and L. Lange, 16–40. Toronto: University of Toronto Press.

Coby, Patrick. "The Law of Nature in Locke's Second Treatise: Is Locke a Hobbesian?" *Review of Politics* 49 (winter 1987), 3–28.

Cohn, Norman. *The Pursuit of the Millennium*. London: Secker & Warburg, 1957.

Colman, John. *John Locke's Moral Philosophy*. Edinburgh: Edinburgh University Press, 1983.

Cranston, Maurice William. *John Locke, A Biography*. London: Longmans, 1957.

Cusa, Nicholas of. *The Catholic Concordance*, ed. and trans. Paul E. Sigmund. Cambridge: Cambridge University Press, 1991.

• Dunn, John. "The Claim to Freedom of Conscience: Freedom of Speech, Freedom of Thought, Freedom of Worship?" In *From Persecution to Toleration: The Glorious Revolution and Religion in England*, ed. O. P. Grell, J. I. Israel, and N. Tyacke, 171–94. Oxford: Clarendon Press, 1991.

Dunn, John. *Interpreting Political Responsibility: Essays 1981–1989*. Princeton, NJ: Princeton University Press, 1990.

Dunn, John. "Measuring Locke's Shadow." In John Locke, *Two Treatises of Government and a Letter Concerning Toleration*, ed. Ian Shapiro, 257–85. New Haven, CT: Yale University Press, 2003.

Dunn, John. "The Politics of Locke in England and America in the Eighteenth Century." In *John Locke, Problems and Perspectives*, ed. John Yolton, 45–80. Cambridge: Cambridge University Press, 1969b.

Dunn, John. *The Political Thought of John Locke: An Historical Account of the Argument of the 'Two Treatises of Government.'* London: Cambridge University Press, 1969a.

• Dworetz, Steven M. *The Unvarnished Doctrine: Locke, Liberalism, and the American Revolution*. Durham, NC: Duke University Press, 1990.

Eisenach, Eldon. "Religion and Locke's *Two Treatises of Government*." In John Locke, *Two Treatises of Government: New Interpretations*, ed. Edward J. Harpham, 50–81. Lawrence, KA: 1992.

Filmer, Robert. *Patriarcha and Other Writings*, ed. J. P. Sommerville. Cambridge Texts in the History of Political Thought. Cambridge: Cambridge University Press, 1991.

Forde, Steven. "Natural Law, Theology, and Morality in Locke." *American Journal of Political Science* 45, no. 2 (April 2002), 396–409.

Glendon, Mary Ann. *Rights Talk: The Impoverishment of Political Discourse*. New York: Free Press, 1991.

Goldie, Mark, ed. *The Reception of Locke's Politics*, 6 vols. London: Pickering & Chatto, 1999.

Grant, Ruth W. *John Locke's Liberalism*. Chicago: University of Chicago Press, 1987.

Hamilton, Bernice. *Political Thought in the Sixteenth Century*. Oxford: Clarendon Press, 1963.

Hamowy, Ronald. "Jefferson and the Scottish Enlightenment: A Critique of Garry Wills's *Inventing American: Jefferson's Declaration of Independence*." *William and Mary Quarterly* 3rd ser., no. 4 (October 1979), 503–23.

Harpham, Edward J. *John Locke's Two Treatises of Government: New Interpretations*. Lawrence: University Press of Kansas, 1992.

Harrison, John R. and Peter Laslett, eds. *The Library of John Locke*, 2nd ed. Oxford: Clarendon Press, 1971.

Hartz, Louis. *The Liberal Tradition in America: An Interpretation of American Political Thought since the Revolution*. New York: Harcourt Brace, 1955.

Hooker, Richard. *Of the Laws of Ecclesiastical Polity, Preface, Book I, Book VII*, ed. Arthur Stephen McGrade. Cambridge: Cambridge University Press, 1989.

Hunt, Gaillard. "The Virginia Declaration of Rights and Cardinal Bellarmine." *Catholic Historical Review* 3 (1917), 276–89.

Hutchinson, Ross. *Locke in France, 1688–1734*. Oxford: Voltaire Foundation, 1991.

Huyler, Jerome. *Locke in America: The Moral Philosophy of the Founding Era*. *American Political Thought*. Lawrence: University Press of Kansas, 1995.

Jaffa, Harry V. *American Conservatism and the American Founding*. Durham, NC: Carolina Academic Press, 1984.

Josephson, Peter. *The Great Art of Government: Locke's Use of Consent*. Lawrence: University Press of Kansas, 2002.

Kendall, Willmoore. *John Locke and the Doctrine of Majority Rule*. Urbana: University of Illinois Press, 1940.

Kirk, Russell. *The Conservative Mind, from Burke to Santayana*. Chicago: Regnery, 1953.

Koch, Adrienne. *Jefferson and Madison: The Great Collaboration*. New York: Knopf, 1950.

Kramer, Matthew H. *John Locke and the Origins of Private Property: Philosophical Explorations of Individualism, Community, and Equality*. Cambridge: Cambridge University Press, 1997.

Kraynak, Robert. "John Locke, from Absolutism to Toleration." *American Political Science Review* 74, no. 1 (March 1980), 53–69.

Locke, John. *The Correspondence of John Locke*, 8 vols., ed. E. S. De Beer. Oxford: Clarendon Press, 1976–89.

Locke, John. *Essays on the Law of Nature, The Latin Text, with a Translation, Introduction, and Notes, Together with Transcripts of Locke's Shorthand in His Journal for 1676*, ed. W. von Leyden. Oxford: Clarendon Press, 1954.

Locke, John. *Locke: Political Essays*, ed. Mark Goldie. Cambridge: Cambridge University Press, 1997.

Locke, John. *Political Writings*, ed. David Wootton. New York: Mentor Books, 1993.

Locke, John. *A Paraphrase and Notes on the Epistles of St. Paul to the Galatians, 1 and 2 Corinthians, Romans, Ephesians*, 2 vols., ed. Arthur William Wainwright. Oxford Clarendon Press, 1987.

Locke, John. *Questions Concerning the Law of Nature*, ed. R. H. Horwitz, Jenny Strauss Clay, and Diskin Clay. Ithaca, NY: Cornell University Press, 1990.

Locke, John. *The Reasonableness of Christianity*, ed. John C. Higgins-Biddle. Oxford: Clarendon Press, 1999.

Locke, John. *The Reasonableness of Christianity with a Discourse of Miracles and Part of a Third Letter on Toleration*, ed. L. T. Ramsey. Stanford, CA: Stanford University Press, 1958.

Locke, John. *Some Thoughts Concerning Education; and, Of the Conduct of the Understanding*, ed. Ruth W. Grant and Nathan Tarcov. Indianapolis, IN: Hackett, 1996.

Locke, John. *Two Tracts on Government*, ed. Philip Abrams. London: Cambridge University Press, 1967.

Locke, John. *Two Treatises of Government*, ed. Peter Laslett. Cambridge: Cambridge University Press, 1988.

Locke, John. *The Works of John Locke*, 10 vols. Aalen, Germany: Scientia-Verlag, 1963.

Locke, John. *Writings on Religion*, ed. Victor Nuovo. Oxford: Clarendon Press, 2002.

Lodge, George C. *The New American Ideology: How the Ideological Basis of Legitimate Authority in American Is Being Radically Transformed, the Profound Implications for Our Society in General and the Great Corporations in Particular*. New York: Knopf, 1975.

Lough, John, ed. *Locke's Travels in France, 1675–1679, as Related in His Journals, Correspondence, and Other Papers*. Cambridge: Cambridge University Press, 1953.

Lutz, Donald S. *The Origins of American Constitutionalism*. Baton Rouge: Louisiana State University, 1988.

• Macpherson, C. B. *The Political Theory of Possessive Individualism: Hobbes to Locke*. Oxford: Clarendon Press, 1962.

Marshall, John. *John Locke: Resistance, Religion and Responsibility*. Cambridge: Cambridge University Press, 1994.

Marshall, John. "Locke, Socinianism, 'Socinianism', and Unitarianism." In *English Philosophy in the Age of Locke*, ed. M. A. Stewart, 111–82. Oxford: Clarendon Press, 2000.

McClure, Kirstie M. *Judging Rights: Lockean Politics and the Limits of Consent*. Ithaca, NY: Cornell University Press, 1996.

McNally, David. "Locke, Levellers and Liberty: Property and Democracy in the Thought of the First Whigs." *History of Political Thought* 10 (1989), 17–40.

Meyers, R. G. "Was Locke an Empiricist?" *Locke Studies* 1 (2001), 63–85.

Milton, J. R. "Dating Locke's Second Treatise." *History of Political Thought* 16, no. 3 (autumn 1995), 356–90.

Milton, Philip. "John Locke and the Rye House Plot." *Historical Journal* 43, no. 3 (2000), 647–58.

Muñoz, Vincent Phillip. "James Madison's Principle of Religious Liberty." *American Political Science Review* 97, no. 1 (February 2002), 17–32.

Murray, John Courtney. *We Hold These Truths*. New York: Sheed and Ward, 1960.

Myers, Peter C. *Our Only Star and Compass*. Lanham, MD: Rowman and Littlefield, 1998.

Nozick, Robert. *Anarchy, State, and Utopia*. New York: Basic Books, 1974.

Oakley, Francis. *Natural Law, Conciliarism, and Consent in the Late Middle Ages*. London: Variorum Reprints, 1984.

Ockham, William of. *A Short Discourse on Tyrannical Government*, ed. Arthur Stephen McGrade. Cambridge: Cambridge University Press, 1992.

Okin, Susan. *Women in Western Political Thought*. Princeton, NJ: Princeton University Press, 1979.

Parker, Kim Ian. *The Biblical Politics of John Locke*. Waterloo, ON, Canada: Wilfred Laurier University Press, 2004.

Parrington, Vernon Louis. *Main Currents in American Thought: An Interpretation of American Literature form Beginnings to 1920*, 3 vols. New York: Harcourt Brace, 1927.

Parry, Geraint. *John Locke*. London: Allen & Unwin, 1978.

Pateman, Carole. *The Problem of Political Obligation: A Critique of Liberal Theory*. Berkeley: University of California Press, 1985.

Pitkin, Hanna. "Obligation and Consent." *American Political Science Review* 59, no. 4 (December 1965), 39–52.

Pocock, J. G. A. *The Machiavellian Moment: Florentine Political Thought and the Atlantic Republican Tradition*. Princeton, NJ: Princeton University Press, 1975.

Pufendorf, Samuel. *On the Duty of Man and Citizen According to Natural Law*, ed. James Tully. Cambridge: Cambridge University Press, 1991.

Rabieh, Michael. "The Reasonableness of Locke, or the Questionableness of Christianity." *Journal of Politics* 53 (November 1991), 933–57.

Rager, John C. "Blessed Cardinal Bellarmine's Defense of Popular Government in the Sixteenth Century." *Catholic Historical Review* 6 new ser. (1925), 504–14.

Rahe, Paul. *Republics Ancient and Modern: Classical Republicanism and the American Revolution*. Chapel Hill: University of North Carolina Press, 1994.

Rawls, John. *A Theory of Justice*. Cambridge, MA: Harvard University Press, 1971.

Robbins, Caroline. "Absolute Liberty: The Life and Thought of William Popple, 1638–1708." *William and Mary Quarterly* 3rd ser., 24, no. 2 (April 1967), 190–223.

• Ryan, Alan. "Locke and the Dictatorship of the Bourgeoisie." *Political Studies* 13, no. 2 (1965), 219–30.

Sabine, George H. *A History of Political Theory*. 3rd ed. New York: Holt, Rinehart & Winston, 1961.

Sample, Ruth. "Locke on Political Authority and Conjugal Authority." *The Locke Newsletter* 31 (2000), 115–46.

Sandel, Michael. *Liberalism and the Limits of Justice*. Cambridge: University of Cambridge Press, 1982.

Sandler, S. Gerald. "Lockean Ideas in Thomas Jefferson's *Bill for Establishing Religious Freedom*." *Journal of the History of Ideas* 21, no. 1 (1960), 110–16.

Schiff, David C. *The Bellarmine-Jefferson Legend and the Declaration of Independence*. New York: Knickerbocker Press, 1927.

• Sigmund, Paul E. "The Great Chain of Being Was Not the Only Game in Town: The Medieval Roots of Political Equality." Paper delivered at the annual meeting of the American Political Science Association, August 31, 1998.

Sigmund Paul E. "The Influence of Cicero ('Tully') on John Locke." Paper presented at the annual meeting of the American Political Science Association, August 1997.

Sigmund, Paul E. *Natural Law in Political Thought.* Cambridge, MA: Winthrop, 1971.

Sigmund, Paul E. (ed. and trans.). *St. Thomas Aquinas on Politics and Ethics.* New York: Norton, 1988.

Simmons, A. John. "The Conjugal and the Political in Locke." *Locke Studies* 1 (2001), 173–90.

• Simmons, A. John. *The Lockean Theory of Rights.* Princeton, NJ: Princeton University Press, 1992.

• Simmons, A. John. *On the Edge of Anarchy: Locke, Consent, and the Limits of Society.* Princeton, NJ: Princeton University Press, 1993.

Skinner, Quentin. *The Foundations of Modern Political Thought,* 2 vols. Cambridge: Cambridge University Press, 1978.

Spellman, W. M. *John Locke and the Problem of Depravity.* Oxford: Clarendon Press, 1988.

Sreenivasan, Gopal. *The Limits of Lockean Rights in Property.* New York: Oxford University Press, 1995.

Stevens, Jacqueline. "The Reasonableness of John Locke's Majority." *Political Theory* 24 (1996), 423–63.

Stewart, M. A. "Review of Horwitz, Robert, et al. (eds.), 'John Locke, Questions Concerning the Law of Nature.' " *The Locke Newsletter* 23 (1992), 155–16.

Strauss, Leo. "Locke's Doctrine of Natural Law." *American Political Science Review* 52, no. 2 (January 1958), 490–501.

• Strauss, Leo. *Natural Right and History.* Chicago: University of Chicago Press, 1953.

Strauss, Leo. *Persecution and the Art of Writing.* Glencoe, IL: Free Press, 1952.

Swanson, S. G. "The Medieval Foundations of John Locke's Political Thought." *History of Political Thought* 28 (1997), 399–459.

• Taylor, Charles. *Sources of the Self: The Making of the Modern Identity.* Cambridge, MA: Harvard University Press, 1989.

Thompson, Dennis. "The Education of a Founding Father." *Political Theory* 4, no. 4 (1976), 523–29.

Tierney, Brian. "Hierarchy, Consent, and the 'Western Tradition.' " *Political Theory* 15, no. 4 (November 1987), 646–52.

Trenchard, John, and Thomas Gordon. *Cato's Letters,* 4 vols., ed. Ronald Hamowy. Indianapolis, IN: Liberty Fund.

Tuck, Richard. *The Rights of War and Peace: Political Thought and the International Order from Grotius to Kant.* New York: Oxford University Press, 1999.

Tuckness, Alex. "The Coherence of a Mind: John Locke and the Law of Nature." *Journal of the History of Philosophy* 37, no. 1 (January 1999), 73–90.

• Tully, James. *A Discourse on Property: John Locke and His Adversaries.* Cambridge: Cambridge University Press, 1980.

• Waldron, Jeremy. *God, Locke, and Equality: Christian Foundations of John Locke's Political Thought.* Cambridge: Cambridge University Press, 2002.

Waldron, Jeremy. "Locke, Toleration, and the Rationality of Persecution." In *Liberal Rights,* 88–114. Cambridge: Cambridge University Press, 1993.

Wills, Garry. *Inventing America: Jefferson's Declaration of Independence.* Garden City, NY: Doubleday, 1978.

Wood, Gordon S. *The Creation of the American Republic, 1776–1787.* Chapel Hill: University of North Carolina Press, 1969.

Wood, Neal. *John Locke and Agrarian Capitalism.* Berkeley: University of California Press, 1986.

Wootton, David, ed. *Divine Right and Democracy.* New York: Viking Penguin, 1986.

Yolton, John W. *John Locke: Problems and Perspectives: A Collection of New Essays.* London: Cambridge University Press, 1969.

Yolton, John. *The Two Intellectual Works of John Locke: Man, Person, and Spirits in the "Essay."* Ithaca, NY: Cornell University Press, 2004.

Zinaich, S. "Locke's Moral Revolution: From Natural Law to Moral Relativism." *The Locke Newsletter* 31 (2000), 79–114.

Zuckert, Michael P. *Launching Liberalism: On Lockean Political Philosophy.* Lawrence: University Press of Kansas, 2002.

Zuckert, Michael P. *Natural Rights and the New Republicanism.* Princeton, NJ: Princeton University Press, 1994.